Marriage &

Life

Choices

The Catholic Experience

Teacher's Manual

David Thomas, Ph.D.
Student Text

Mike Amodei, M.A.
Teacher's Wraparound Edition

Benziger Publishing Company
Mission Hills, California

Send all inquiries to:
BENZIGER PUBLISHING COMPANY
15319 Chatsworth Street
P. O. Box 9609
Mission Hills, California 91346-9609

ISBN 0-02-655911-0 (Student's Edition)
ISBN 0-02-655912-9 (Teacher's Wraparound Edition)

Printed in the United States of America

1 2 3 4 5 6 7 RRW 99 98 97 96 95 94 93

About the Authors and Consultant

David Thomas, the author of the student text, is the Director of Graduate Studies in Christian Community Leadership, Regis University, Denver, Colorado. Dr. Thomas holds a Ph.D. in Historical and Systematic Theology from the University of Notre Dame with an emphasis in the Theology of Sexuality and Marriage, along with post-doctoral training in family studies and family therapy. He served as a *peritus* for the Bishops of the United States at the 1980 World Synod on Family Life, and as a theological consultant to the Bishop's Committee on Youth and the Family. He has lectured internationally, and has authored numerous books and over 100 articles. He serves as General Editor of Benziger's Family Life Program.

Mike Amodei, the author of the Teacher's Wraparound Edition and Teacher's Resource Book, holds a Master of Arts Degree in Religious Education from Loyola Marymount University. He is an experienced high school religion teacher and is currently active in parish youth and adult ministry. Amodei has collaborated on many projects for Benziger, including the *In Christ Jesus* and *Come, Follow Me* religion series.

Charles M. Shelton, S.J., consultant for the student text, has a Master of Divinity from the Jesuit School of Theology, Berkeley, and a Ph.D. in clinical psychology from Loyola University, Chicago. He has taught at the high school, college, and graduate level and is currently on the faculty of Regis University, Denver. He is the author of *Morality of the Heart: A Psychology for the Christian Moral Life; Adolescent Spirituality: Pastoral Ministry for High School and College Youth;* and *Morality and the Adolescent: A Pastoral Psychology Approach.*

Introduction

Marriage and Life Choices is a book that helps high school students make decisions for now and for the future based on Jesus' call to truth. As Jesus told Pontius Pilate: "Everyone who belongs to the truth listens to My voice" *(John 18:37).*

Adolescents are often engulfed in a tide of half-truths and falsehoods. The general society (through the public media) encourages people to work in high-paying, but otherwise dissatisfying careers without regard for personal satisfaction or vocational choice. Relationships are situations where personal satisfaction comes first. Values filtered down from soap operas and song lyrics often form the basis of how teenagers make decisions.

Marriage and Life Choices reintroduces high school students to Christian values, and encourages them to make vocational and career decisions in light of these values. *Marriage and Life Choices* asks high school students to make decisions in a world where God is obviously present, not seemingly absent.

This is a need that often must be reawakened. In a reply to the questions asked of him by teenagers, Pope John Paul II said:

> "God is present, but it is true that *we can be absent.* It is not God who fails to turn up at the rendezvous: the risk is that we fail to meet Him. . . Many of our contemporaries too live in *religious indifference,* forgetful of God, organizing their lives without Him; they try all the paths to happiness, without daring to believe that Christ is the Truth, the Way, the Life" *(Youth and the Future of the Church).*

In just this type of bewilderment, Pontius Pilate asked: "What is truth?" *(John 18:38).* Put simply, living in truth means living in reality. *Marriage and Life Choices* is a book that calls teens to explore the reality of their own lives: "What talents do I have?" "What am I interested in doing?" And, "How can I translate my talents and interests into a meaningful career and vocation?"

Marriage and Life Choices looks at the total spectrum of developing careers and vocations. The text suggests relevant issues, questions, and steps to assist teens in moving from one stage of life to the next, remaining ever-mindful of the personal gifts and freedom possessed by each individual. *Marriage and Life Choices* challenges each teen to offer his or her own interpretation of the call to Christian living.

In some ways, the future is unimaginable. A forty-year old man often can't conceive of himself at sixty. In other ways, the future may seem very real and possible: A high school calculus student easily imagines herself as an engineer in the space program. A single man imagines himself as a husband and a father. Envisioning one's desired future is a necessary step in making it come true.

Marriage and Life Choices introduces issues that can help a person reach his or her dreams at each stage of life. These include the requirements and preparation for religious life; the transitional stages of marriage; and career related moral dilemmas. Dreaming lofty dreams is one of the great benefits of being a student. *Marriage and Life Choices* encourages them to dream and suggests a plan to turn their dreams into Christian careers and vocations.

Components

Marriage and Life Choices consists of the following components:

- Student Text;
- Teacher's Wraparound Edition;
- Teacher's Resource Book.

The Student Text

Marriage and Life Choices is divided into four units. Each parallels the development of a person's career and vocation.

- **Unit One** *The Freedom to Be You,* examines the importance of developing self-worth and provides a set of skills necessary to make good choices.

- **Unit Two** *At the Crossroads,* looks at how the personal choices made by high school students in friendships, dating, sexuality, and career planning can have an effect on who they become.

- **Unit Three** *For A Lifetime,* defines love, commitment, and trust as foundations for all life callings.

- **Unit Four,** *Always Evolving,* incorporates the daily conversions that are a part of all careers and vocations to a life focused on God's kingdom.

For Christians, the common thread running through all careers and vocations is the baptismal call to discipleship. Jesus said: "Whoever wishes to come after Me must deny Himself, take up His cross, and follow Me" *(Mark 8:34).* Pope John Paul told teens: "Do not compromise on truth, on goodness, on respect for human dignity" *(Youth and the Future of the Church).*

Marriage and Life Choices provides a companion to the freedom, decisions, celebrations, struggles, and conversions that will be faced by a person who seeks to live life as a disciple of Jesus Christ.

Marriage and Life Choices Unit and Chapter Titles

Unit One *The Freedom to Be You*
- **Chapter 1**—Looking Into the Future
- **Chapter 2**—Discovering Your Richness
- **Chapter 3**—Choices for Life

Unit Two *At the Crossroads*
- **Chapter 4**—Friendship and Communication
- **Chapter 5**—Dating
- **Chapter 6**—Love, Sexuality, and Your Life
- **Chapter 7**—Fullness of Life

Unit Three *For A Lifetime*
- **Chapter 8**—Callings and Commitments
- **Chapter 9**—Answering A Call
- **Chapter 10**—Preparing for Marriage
- **Chapter 11**—The Marriage Covenant
- **Chapter 12**—The First Years of Married Life

Unit Four *Always Evolving*
- **Chapter 13**—Responding to Life's Challenges
- **Chapter 14**—Preparation for Life

Student Text Structure

Each unit contains the following elements:

Unit Opener: A personal account of someone who is living out one of the vocations discussed in the text.

Unit Review

- Questions that review the main content of the unit.
- A project idea called "Making It Real" that suggests ways for the students to practically apply what they have learned in the unit.
- A way to combine traditional prayer with relevant action.

Chapter Organization

Each chapter contains the following elements:

Chapter Opener

- An introductory photo suggesting the theme and content of the chapter.
- A significant quotation related to the chapter theme.
- Learning objectives for the chapter.

Within The Chapter

- Each chapter is divided into two sections. Each section begins with a short introduction.
- Discussion and application questions are appropriately labeled and placed throughout the chapter.
- Each chapter includes regular features that have built-in questions or suggestions for student application. Each chapter also contains the following features:

1. *To Your Health:* suggests practical ways of maintaining and improving physical, mental, emotional, or spiritual health.
2. *Media Watch:* encourages students to be critical and analytical participants in the communication process, using all forms of media, including newspapers, television, movies, and the music industry.
3. *Well-Being:* profiles ways that groups and individuals promote and maintain overall health.
4. *Prayer In Action:* tells how saints and Christian heroes have combined prayer with action and suggests ways for the students to do the same.
5. *Family Living:* explores the dynamics of being a part of a family and offers tips to help students improve their family relationships.
6. *Sharpening Your Skills:* provides ideas for students to practice to assist their growth into Christian adulthood.
7. *In Focus:* adds further detail to a theme or idea presented in an accompanying lesson.

- Pertinent random features within the text. These features relate particularly to the material covered in the lesson.

- An activity. Within each chapter is a full page activity with practical ways to apply or extend what is learned. Most of the activities require the students to do additional research and learn skills that they can use in life.

- Photos and their captions used throughout the text will stir reflection, serve as discussion starters, and illustrate the text material.

Chapter Summary and Review

Each chapter features a chapter summary which includes:

- A point-by-point review of the most important information presented in the chapter.

- Questions that help the students recall what they have learned.

- Application project ideas for individual or small group use.

- A list of words introduced in the chapter.

- An exercise to help the students put the vocabulary words to use.

The Teacher's Wraparound Edition

The Teacher's Wraparound Edition (TWE) provides directions for teaching the material. The TWE follows the same design as the student text; lesson ideas are listed for most of the student text headings.

The TWE offers the teacher several ways to present the material.

1. In the outside margins, the TWE lists aims and suggestions for beginning each section.

2. Sections are divided into lesson formats according to major learning objectives.

3. The TWE provides an overview for each of these lessons.

4. A bulleted list of ideas for each heading offers many ways to present, apply, and extend the text material.

The outside margins include these components for lesson planning:

- *Focus On: Chapter* this material introduces the main themes and directions of the chapter and provides an overview of the material to be covered.

- *Aims:* introduces the teaching objectives of the lesson.

- *Begin the Section:* these are suggestions that recall previous material and establish the atmosphere for the coming lessons.

- *Lesson Overviews* presents general approaches for communicating the main ideas presented under a particular heading. *New Words,* definitions and explanations of italicized vocabulary words found in the chapter, is provided for the teacher as part of the Lesson Overview.

- *Teaching Approaches:* offers ways to explore the text and relate the material in a practical way to the students' lives.

There are suggestions to *Reteach* and *Extend the Lesson* as part of each Approaches section.

1. **Reteach** makes connections between current and past lessons and with material that may have been learned in other classes. It also serves as a reminder and offers material to help the teacher review previous lessons.

2. **Extend the Lesson** overcomes the constraints a classroom applies to the application of a lesson by suggesting alternative ways to teach, apply, or develop an idea or concept.

The bottom-of-the-page annotations include many other suggestions to help the teacher prepare the text material for presentation.

1. **Background**—A "for-your-information" panel provides supportive material for the teacher on people, Scripture citations, and new ideas presented in the student text.

2. **Journal Assignment**—These story-starter ideas relate to the lesson. The students are often asked to finish a given sentence or apply a lesson theme to their own lives.

3. **Resources**—This panel refers the teacher to ancillary material, including blackline masters from the Teacher's Resource Book and media suggestions.

The *Marriage and Life Choices* TWE presumes that teachers will develop their own lessons plans for each class. The TWE does not intrude on the teachers' freedom in this regard. The lesson ideas and resource suggestions presented in the TWE may be followed in their entirety, or the teacher may pick and choose as needed. There is no one *best* way to teach any lesson; the best way is the one that will best reach your students.

Catechism of the Catholic Church

Marriage and Life Choices was developed in faithfulness to the full teaching of the Catholic Church. To help teachers identify and access this teaching, the *Marriage and Life Choices* TWE provides ongoing references to the *Catechism of the Catholic Church*. These references can be found in the **Background** section of the TWE where appropriate. References to the Catechism are cited by paragraph number.

Teacher's Resource Book

The Teacher's Resource Book provides materials for use with the students, correlated to the Teacher's Wraparound Edition. Each blackline master (which can be used to create student handouts or an overhead) mentioned in **Resources** in the TWE will appear in the TRB. Also included in the TRB are:

- Abridged lesson plans
- Chapter tests
- Feature profiles
- One student retreat experience per unit

The teaching plan for *Marriage and Life Choices* fits comfortably into many different time frames and catechetical settings. There is much freedom to incorporate the lessons in a variety of ways within any of the time frames. The most common settings are listed below; however, you are encouraged to adapt the material in any way that best meets the needs of your students.

The most familiar model is based on a 14 week semester course. Models are also provided for using *Marriage and Life Choices* three times a week, once a week, in a workshop series, over the course of a two or three weekends in a retreat setting, or even for five days a week for twenty-eight weeks.

Model 1: 5 Day per Week Semester Course

This model will be used most commonly in a one semester course in a Catholic high school setting. One chapter per week will be covered during a 14-week session. The model:

- **Day 1:** Introduce the chapter; begin first section.
- **Day 2:** Conclude first section.
- **Day 3:** Begin second section.
- **Day 4:** Conclude second section.
- **Day 5:** Review chapter, share student activities, and take test.

Note: Teachers using this model may also want to use the abridged lesson included in the TRB to develop their lessons.

Model 2: 1 Day per Week Course

This model will be used most commonly in a parish youth ministry or high school Confirmation or religious education setting. The material from one chapter can form the framework for a one night session. Topics for sessions might include:

- Building self-esteem
- Friendships
- Dating
- Love and sexuality
- Religious vocations
- Preparing for marriage
- Parenthood
- Life transitions

With this model, the youth minister or catechist must cover the material relevant to the topic in one session.

Note: Teaching the material may be facilitated by assigning pre-reading prior to the session, by following the abridged lesson plan included in the TRB, by highlighting certain material, discussion questions, and projects, and by assigning some reading, activities, and projects as review.

Model 3: Mini-Workshop or 2-3 Day Retreat

Use the abridged lesson plans in the TRB to cover all the chapters of a unit. The focus of a retreat or workshop may focus on:

- The importance of self-esteem (Unit 1)
- Friendship, dating, sexuality, or discipleship (Unit 2)
- Committed marriage or religious vocations (Unit 3)
- Life transitions (Unit 4)

Model 4: 5 Day per Week Year Course

This model will be used in some Catholic high school settings. Typically, the focus of the class will be on marriage, religious vocations, careers, and applications of moral choices. One chapter per two weeks will be covered over a 28 week period. The model:

Week 1
- **Day 1:** Introduce the chapter; establish aims and themes.
- **Day 2:** Begin first section.
- **Day 3:** Talk It Over discussion, journal writing, assign and begin projects or activities.
- **Day 4:** Conclude first section.
- **Day 5:** Talk It Over discussion, share completed projects.

Week 2
- **Day 1:** Review first section; begin second section.
- **Day 2:** Talk It Over discussion, journal writing, assign and begin projects or activities.
- **Day 3:** Conclude second section.
- **Day 4:** Talk It Over discussion, share completed projects.
- **Day 5:** Review chapter using Chapter Summary material.

The following teaching suggestions are strongly recommended for use to enhance *Marriage and Life Choices* in a course of study.

Teaching Students with Special Needs

Students with special needs are most always included in regular religion classes or parish ministry programs. These students are learning the same information and skills, competing for the same grades, and thinking of future jobs, careers, and vocations just as other students are. Because students with special needs are often slower to respond to questions, it is tempting to skip their responses when trying to meet class objectives. This deprives special needs students of equal opportunities.

In some cases you'll need to alter your teaching methods when working with these students. The important thing is that if an activity requires students to write on the board or share a journal entry, these students should be required to do so also—as long as they are physically and mentally capable. Students in wheelchairs may require a lowered writing board or the use of an overhead transparency. For the visually impaired, an oral response is appropriate. Hearing impaired students may need the assistance of an interpreter to help with journal sharing or in other class discussions.

The following suggestions can help your classroom or adapt your teaching methods to create a positive learning environment for all your students.

The Physically Challenged

- Adjust the room arrangement to fit students' needs.
- Encourage verbal activities and small group participation.
- Encourage these students to participate in physical activities within their capabilities.

The Learning Disabled

- Focus on the positive; point out students' strengths.
- Avoid assigning these students to seats around distracting students.
- Encourage small group participation.
- Encourage students to express themselves verbally.
- Be very clear in the directions you provide.
- Adapt lessons to fit the needs of these students; for example, you may need to provide them with a greater amount of time for an assignment.
- Provide and organized environment in which expectations are clear—and realistic.
- Provide positive feedback whenever possible.

The Visually Impaired

- Seat the students in good light near the area where the main presentation will be given.
- Whenever possible, provide hands-on experiences.
- Assign another student to assist the visually impaired student.
- Allow students to record assignments or complete them verbally.
- Tape-record each chapter of the textbook.
- Encourage verbal participation.
- Administer tests and quizzes orally.
- Allow students to move about freely so they can get close to charts or displays.

The Hearing Impaired

- Seat students near the area where the main presentation will be given.
- Use the board to highlight key terms and phrases.
- Guide students to the appropriate text page during discussions.
- Ask a good student to make copies of his or her notes for the hearing impaired students.
- Provide written copies of tests, assignments, and discussion questions.
- Look directly at hearing impaired students when speaking. Talk normally.
- Learn sign language or provide an interpreter who knows sign language.
- Write directions for activities on the chalkboard.
- Encourage as much verbal interaction as possible.

Teaching Students from Various Cultural and Ethnic Backgrounds

Choices about careers and vocations are areas that are influenced by culture, ethnicity, and socioeconomic background. It is important that teachers be sensitive to these differences in students.

Parents, grandparents, and other relatives may have passed on long-standing beliefs about careers and vocations deemed appropriate for males and females, or members of a particular cultural, ethnic, or socioeconomic group. While in practice, some of these beliefs ultimately may be part of a person's experience, the opportunity to dream openly and freely about the future should never be lost.

If students are willing to share practices and beliefs unique to their culture, it may help other students better understand the culture and the cultural influence on one's career and vocational planning.

Teaching Students with Limited English Proficiency

Students with limited English proficiency may not have trouble mastering the content. Their difficulty may be only with the language. With these students it is important to remember that requiring tasks before a student is ready for them can slow down the learning process. The following guidelines can help you pace and reinforce the instructions for these students:

1. *Allow time for students to become familiar with the structure of English.* Some students may know many English words but have difficulty with word order. For example, adjectives often precede the nouns they modify in English: "That is a yellow pencil." But in Spanish, the usual order would be "That is a pencil yellow." By accepting mistakes and praising students' efforts, you will provide an atmosphere in which students can experiment with English.

2. *Remember that students can often understand more than they can express.* Students may be able to use simple, direct English sentences but have trouble with figures of speech, idioms, and words with multiple meanings. Further development of their oral language, along with written English forms, can help these students develop more sophisticated English language skills.

3. *As students begin to develop writing skills, they may mix English with their native language. Accept these language mixtures.* At this stage, confidence and enjoyment of writing are the most important goals. Students who feel comfortable with English will be more motivated to write in English.

4. *Provide peer learning by grouping English proficient students with students with a limited proficiency.* Encourage students working in pairs or small heterogeneous groups to teach one another skills.

Helping students think should be a primary goal of all education. Learning only easily testable facts is inadequate preparation for living in the twenty-first century.

Definitions of Thinking

Critical thinking can be defined as the process of reasonably or logically deciding what to do or believe. It is a process that is made up of many considerations. The learner needs to:

1. understand his or her own and other's meanings and views;
2. look for relationships, causes, inferences, theories, patterns;
3. look for alternatives; and
4. make judgments, choices, or decisions based on the information.

Creative thinking requires the ability to identify and formulate problems, as well as the ability to generate alternative solutions. Fluency (quantity of ideas), flexibility (variety of ideas), originality (unusual or unique ideas), and elaboration (details for the implementation of ideas) are necessary components of creative thinking.

Assumptions for Teaching Thinking

These assumptions underlie the teaching of thinking:

- All students are capable of higher level thinking.
- Thinking skills can be taught and learned.
- Thinking can be effectively taught within any content area.
- Appropriate expectations for logical thinking are based on physiological maturation, social experiences, and the knowledge level of the students.
- Learners can be taught to transfer thinking skills from a specific content area to an internalized process applicable to a variety of new learnings.

Actions for Teaching Thinking

How then do we teach thinking? Doesn't all learning require thinking? What is meant by higher level thinking? These questions and questions like them require teachers to reflect upon the instructional strategies used in daily lessons and to include opportunities for students to reason and think about what is being learned.

All learning does require thinking. Benjamin Bloom's *Taxonomy of the Cognitive Domain* is probably the most widely recognized schema for levels of thinking. Questions, statements, and activities can be designed based on the taxonomy that will elicit the complexity of thinking congruent with the lesson's objective(s). Here are some examples:

- **Knowledge:** define, recognize, recall, identify, label, understand, examine, show, collect.
- **Comprehension:** translate, interpret, explain, describe, summarize, extrapolate.
- **Application:** apply, solve, experiment, show, predict.
- **Analysis:** connect, relate, differentiate, classify, arrange, check, group, distinguish, organize, categorize, detect, compare, infer.
- **Synthesis:** produce, propose, design, plan, combine, formulate, compose, hypothesize, construct.
- **Evaluation:** appraise, judge, criticize, decide.

Certain misunderstandings need to be cleared away if Bloom's *Taxonomy* is to be used successfully:

- The levels of taxonomy build, one on the other. Students cannot be expected to operate at a higher level of thinking without necessary foundation. For example, a student cannot plan and participate in a pro-life campaign without understanding the entire spectrum of life issues affecting all those from the unborn to the aged.
- The level of complexity (from knowledge to evaluation) is not equal to the level of difficulty. For example, listing the prerequisites for various jobs and careers is a difficult task, but it remains a task at the lowest level of the taxonomy, knowledge.
- All students at any age and any ability level can experience thinking at each of the levels of taxonomy. For example, even very young students can be asked to evaluate which careers best suit the talents of various individuals.

Questions and Activities

Examples of questions that promote thinking at various levels are shown below.

Knowledge—the identification and recall of information:
- Who, what, when, where, how . . .?
- Describe . . .

Comprehension—the organization and selection of facts and ideas:
- Retell in your own words . . .
- What is the main idea of . . .?

Application—the use of facts, rules, principles:
- How is . . . an example of . . .?
- How is . . . related to . . .?

Analysis—the separation of a whole into component parts:
- What are the parts or features of . . .?
- Classify . . . according to . . .
- How does . . . compare/contrast with . . .?

Synthesis—the combination of ideas to form a new whole:
- What would you predict/infer from . . .?
- What might happen if you combined . . . with . . .?

Evaluation—the development of opinions, judgments, or decisions:
- What do you think about . . .?
- Prioritize . . .

Not all questions or interactions need to move from teacher to student. Dialogue among peers is an effective technique to use when teaching thinking. When students discuss, explain, debate, decide, or solve problems together they increase their thinking and learning. Asking students to generate their own questions and activities is another strategy that encourages student thinking.

Responses

Responses to student interaction can be crucial. Dialogue and thinking can be readily turned off by criticism or praise. It is easy to recognize that such responses as "Wrong," "Who has the right answer?" or "Oh no!" are obvious turn-offs. But so are responses that praise: "That's right!" "Exactly," or "What a great answer." After hearing responses like these, students will consider the dialogue closed and be reluctant to add alternative ideas or contribute new thoughts.

By using silence (wait time) you demonstrate to students that you expect answers and have faith in the students' ability to provide those answers. Given sufficient time, students will respond with more complete thoughts, show evidence of more creative thinking and exhibit an increased speculation in their thinking.

Your accepting responses can provide a psychologically safe climate in which students can take risks and time to explore their own thinking. When using passive types of responses, you simply receive the student's input with such phrases as "I see," "That's one idea," or "Um hmm." More active kinds of responses allow you to rephrase, translate, or summarize the input: "You say that . . .," "Your point then is that . . ." Emphatic acceptance lets you show feeling as well as understanding: "I can see why you would violently disagree . . .," "That would certainly make us all feel safer . . ."

Use clarifying strategies when you need more information so that the student's point of view can be understood. It requires the student to give more information and to talk about his or her thinking.

Classroom Climate and Structure

The classroom climate and structure or meeting format provide further opportunities to foster thinking among students. If thinking is the objective, students need to interact and be in decision-making roles. They need to feel responsible for their learning.

Recognize Special Issues and Needs

Resource and media aids need to be ordered in advance. Materials needed for projects and activities also need to be at hand. If guest speakers or panelists are to come to class, they need to be invited and the time arranged well in advance. Speakers and panelists should always be pre-screened to see what they plan to say. Plan ahead!

The Importance of Stories

Marriage and Life Choices features many real-life stories of people who faced the issues presented in the text. The value of such stories should not be diminished. It is through the telling and retelling of stories that the aims of the lesson become a part of the students' own lives. The stories may be presented in a variety of ways; the students may read them individually, or with a partner or small group. Allow time for the students to comment on the situation presented and share their own similar experiences. In some cases, you may have the students role-play the story that is presented in the text, an extension to the story, or a similar story from their own experience.

Working with a Partner or in a Small Group

Questioning, discussing, and sharing comments on any lesson is important. An easy and immediate way to accomplish this is to have the students work through all or part of a lesson with a partner or in a small group of five or six students. This concept also encourages the students to learn as much as they can from the lesson, and then present their ideas to their classmates for discussion.

The **Talk It Over** ideas at the end of each lesson are discussion starters. Also, certain journal entries may be shared. Projects may be completed with a partner or with several others in a small group. The more familiar everyone is with a topic, the more lively and focused the discussion can be. It is often helpful to choose one person to moderate the discussion in small group settings. It is the moderator's responsibility to make sure that everyone has a chance to be heard.

Projects and Activities

Marriage and Life Choices works best in a hands-on environment. Class time should be made available for the students to be introduced to, plan for, and, in some cases, work on projects and activities. In most cases, it is best to allow the students to choose their own projects. The **Application** section of the **Chapter Review** lists several ideas related to the material. Also, refer to the **Extend the Lesson** suggestions in the TWE. In addition, there is one in-text activity per chapter in the student text. Give the students the freedom to use these projects as starting points and to develop them in creative new directions.

Role Plays

For role plays, it is wise to set the specific scene and explain the characters before assigning roles. If the students have developed their own role play idea, ask them to at least follow this common format. Leave time for the students to prepare their roles (at least part of a class period). Allow the scenes to go no longer than four to five minutes. Always include a follow-up discussion for comments and questions. Several groups can act the same scene and the class can discuss the differences.

Debate

Present the students with a strongly sided issue. For example, you may use this format: "Do you agree or disagree with the proposition that . . ." The aim is to provide students with direct experience in taking positions on issues and defending them. After the class receives the statement or the case, groups can be formed to discuss reasons for one position or the other.

Brainstorming

Many suggestions in the TWE call for the students to "brainstorm" answers or ideas. Brainstorming is a form of free association. There are no right or wrong answers. You will want to establish rules for brainstorming sessions, such as:

1. No commenting on anyone else's suggestion.
2. Raise your hand and wait to be called.
3. If your idea is on the board, please don't repeat it; think of a new idea instead.

Allow the students time to offer their ideas. Record their ideas, as they are mentioned, someplace where all can see. After the brainstorming session, examine the ideas more closely. Ask the students to look for commonalities and differences in what they have suggested. Evaluate the ideas and narrow the choices to those acceptable to the whole class. Use the ideas throughout the lesson.

Journal Writing

Each student should have his or her own personal journal. Journal writing entries should remain private, unless specified. The TWE provides regular opportunities for journaling. Allow the students frequent opportunities to write in their journals. Journal writing may be used to:

1. clarify ideas and feelings;
2. trace growth in prayer life;
3. voice opinions privately.

Media

Augment your lessons with various forms of media: videos, music, and magazine and newspaper articles help to keep the lessons relevant and breaks up the usual format. The TRB provides an up-to-date list of media resources for your convenience. In each chapter, students are taught to be critical media consumers. Incorporate these critical thinking skills into your lessons by having students critique the media you use.

Scripture/Church Tradition

What makes *Marriage and Life Choices* different from all other career and vocation texts is its firm foundation in the Judeo/Christian Scriptures and Catholic Tradition. The teachings of Jesus Christ and the Church form the basis for material covered in the text. When possible, expand the cited in-text Scriptures. Have the students read the entire surrounding Scripture chapter directly from the Bible. To extend, have them look up and research other Scripture citations applicable to the theme of the lesson. Saints and other Church heroes have faced many of the decisions that are faced by people today. Sometimes they did not make the right choices. Hearing their stories illustrates God's mercy and compassion and helps students recognize that they have the same chance to learn from their mistakes and move ahead. Have the students read more of the lives of saints, research and write interesting stories of their lives, and share them with the class.

Prayer

Prayer—communication with God—should be a primary activity of the class. Communication and relationship issues form a main part of the course's content. Recognizing that God is present in the class dynamic is crucial. Begin and end class meetings with a prayer. Look for ways to help the students pray, and live out their prayer, in new ways (see **Prayer In Action** in each chapter). The TRB also provides prayer services to accompany each chapter.

Scope and Sequence

The scope and sequence for *Marriage and Life Choices* is divided into 4 major topic areas, and each topic, in turn, is divided into subtopics. A total of 16 subtopics are given.

Those chapters in brackets indicate the major treatment of the subject matter.

	Unit 1	Unit 2	Unit 3	Unit 4
Growth and Development				
Self-esteem	1, [2]	[4], 5, 6		
Decision-making	1, 2, [3]	8, 9, 10	[14]	
Career planning	1, 2,	[7]	8	13, 14
Discipleship		[7]	8, 9	13, 14
Relationships				
Communication	[2], 3,	[4], 5, 6	10, 11, 12	
Friendship		[4], 5, 7	9, 12	13
Dating	1	[5]	10	
God	[1], 2	7	8, [9], 10	13, [14]
Sexuality				
Chastity		[6]	8, 9, 10, 12	
Procreation		[6]	[12]	
Love and Intimacy		[6, 7]	[10, 11, 12]	
Abuse and Misuse		[5, 6]	12	
Vocation				
Single Life	1		[8, 9]	
Religious Life/Priesthood	1		[8, 9]	[13]
Marriage	1		[8, 9, 10, 11]	[13]
Baptismal Call to Love	1, 3	6, 7,	[8, 9]	

Benziger Publishing Company
Mission Hills, California

Marriage & Life Choices

The Catholic Experience

David Thomas, Ph.D.

Benziger Publishing Company
Mission Hills, California

Scripture passages are taken from *The New American Bible with Revised New Testament,* copyright © 1988 by the Confraternity of Christian Doctrine, Washington, D.C. All rights reserved.

Excerpts from *Vatican Council II, The Conciliar and Post Conciliar Documents,* Austin Flannery, O.P., ed., reprinted with permission of Costello Publishing Co., Inc., Northport, NY 11768.

Excerpts from the English translation of the *Roman Missal* © 1973, ICEL. All rights reserved.

The excerpt from the "The Road Not Taken" is from *The Poetry of Robert Frost* edited by Edward Connery Lathem Copyright 1916, © 1969 by Holt, Rinehart and Winston. Copyright © 1944 by Robert Frost. Henry Holt and Company, Inc., Publisher.

The excerpt from *Parent Effectiveness Training* by Dr. Thomas Gordon. Copyright © 1970 by Dr. Thomas Gordon. Reprinted by permission of David McKay Co., a division of Random House, Inc.

The excerpt from *The Seven Storey Mountain* by Thomas Merton. Copyright © 1978. Published by Octagon Books, A Division of Hippocrene Books, Inc. Used with permission.

"QUE SERA SERA" Words and Music by Ray Evans and Jay Livingston Music. © Copyright 1956 by St. Angelo Music and Jay Livingston Music. Rights of St. Angelo Music administered by MCA Music Publishing, a Division of MCA Inc., New York, NY 10019. Copyright renewed. Used by Permission. All Rights Reserved.

Consultant for Adolescent Development
The Reverend Charles M. Shelton, S.J., Ph.D.

Nihil Obstat
The Reverend C. A. Soleta, CSC
Censor Deputatus

Imprimatur
The Very Reverend Donald F. Dunn
Vicar General for the Diocese of Colorado Springs
Given at Colorado Springs, Colorado on October 15,1992

The nihil obstat and imprimatur are official declarations that a book or pamphlet is free of doctrinal or moral error. No implication is contained therein that those who have granted the nihil obstat and imprimatur agree with the contents, opinions, or statements expressed.

Send all inquiries to:
BENZIGER PUBLISHING COMPANY
15319 Chatsworth Street
P. O. Box 9609
Mission Hills, California 91346-9609

ISBN 0-02-655911-0 (Student's Edition)
ISBN 0-02-655912-9 (Teacher's Wraparound Edition)

Printed in the United States of America

1 2 3 4 5 6 7 AGK 99 98 97 96 95 94 93

Table of Contents

Unit 1

The Freedom to Be You

Life, like a complicated maze, has many paths and roadblocks. These opportunities and obstacles, however, need not interfere with our journey. Ultimately, discovering the right direction means finding God's will for our lives. When that happens, we are truly ourselves, and truly free.

Unit 1, "The Freedom to Be You," looks at the students' experiences, shows how these experiences have shaped the present, and how they open up a wide range of possibilities for the future.

The students:

- Are called to recognize their personal goodness and develop a healthy self-concept in preparation for the coming challenges.
- Will consider the importance of using good communication skills in building relationships.
- Will learn that honest communication with themselves and others is essential for positive human relations.
- Will practice the skills necessary for them to make good choices throughout life.
- Will examine how their consciences operate when they make choices.
- Will be introduced to a process of discernment.

Teaching Objectives

- To introduce students to the different ways that people live a Christian vocation.
- To help students understand how bringing God's love to others is part of the Christian vocation.
- To challenge students to learn techniques for improving their self-esteem.
- To help students recognize the importance of honest communication.
- To encourage students to examine the decision-making process.

Chapter 1: **Looking into the Future**

Chapter 2: **Discovering Your Richness**

Chapter 3: **Choices for Life**

The Freedom to Be You

I am single, rather than "not married" or "not a religious sister." I have chosen to remain single and feel very positive about living this vocation. I feel that God is a God of abundance, not denial, who wants me to be happy. For me, the single vocation is not a punishment; I am not a martyr. I enjoy life.

The single vocation offers me the gift of availability. There are other advantages, but having time is most important for me. I am challenged to find a balance between hoarding that time for myself or using it for the sake of others. It is an ongoing struggle. In my job, I help parishes and church groups use their computers and phone systems more efficiently. I feel that I am a part of their ministry. I also volunteer a lot of my time using my talents any way that I can. Some people ask: "Why would anyone choose to be single?" I can't fully answer that question. Calls from God do not always come with absolute certainty or clarity. However, I do not feel called to marriage. I see several men socially, but they are intimate friends, not potential husbands. We are not afraid to share hugs and kisses. Intimacy is important for single people, too: it is simply channeled and expressed in other ways.

I cannot picture my life as a wife and mother or as a religious. I feel comfortable as a single person. I can imagine my future is this vocation. For now, this is how I choose to respond to God's call. It is how I am most at peace.

Background

Eileen E. O'Brien is a communication specialist with the Archdiocese of Los Angeles. She is responsible for the telephone and computer network systems in diocesan offices and between parishes. She attended Catholic schools from first grade through graduate school. She holds a Masters in Business Administration from the University of Notre Dame, and is presently working on a Master of Arts in Religious Studies from Mount Saint Mary's College. Eileen spent three years of

NAME:	Eileen O'Brien
CAREER:	Communication Specialist
VOCATION:	Single Life

her life as a Claretian Volunteer working in parishes in St. Louis, Missouri. She continues to use her time generously in volunteer efforts in the Los Angeles area.

Unit 1 Overview
Chapter 1 Looking into the Future
Connecting one's personal life plan to a Christian vocation.
Chapter 2 Discovering Your Richness
A positive self-image is the first step in making wholesome life choices.
Chapter 3 Choices for Life
Our values and our consciences help us make good decisions.

Scope and Sequence
As baptized Christians, we are called to choose God's will for our lives.

"Therefore, let there be no false opposition between professional and social activities on the one part, and religious life on the other. The Christian who neglects his temporal duties neglects his duties toward his neighbor and even God, and jeopardizes his eternal salvation. Christians should rather rejoice that they can follow the example of Christ, who worked as an artisan. In the exercise of all their earthly activities, they can thereby gather their humane, domestic, professional, social, and technical enterprises into one vital synthesis with religious values, under whose supreme direction all things are harmonized unto God's glory" (The Church Today).

Begin the Unit
1. Ask the students to share their interpretations of the unit title, "The Freedom to Be You." Discuss how a person's freedom is limited.
2. Read and discuss the unit objectives.
3. Say: "What one word describes the person you want to be in the future?" Write the students' words on a poster or on the board. You may wish to have the students write a brief explanation of the words they choose for themselves.
4. Read and share comments on the "Single Life" feature.
5. Ask the students to formulate one or two questions about the vocation to the single life. Refer to these at an appropriate time during the course of the unit study.
6. Ask the students to respond in writing to Eileen O'Brien's question, "Why would anyone choose to be single?"

Focus on: Chapter 1

God has gifted us with the freedom to develop a unique life based on our personal gifts and talents. This life becomes connected with Christian vocation when a person puts God in touch with his or her dreams and visions. Chapter 1 introduces students to some of the individual and social dynamics that are a part of their developing Christian vocations.

The power to share God's love is not restricted to any special age or state in life; it is, rather, a part of every Christian's primary vocation received at Baptism. Have students reflect on the topic of vocation and baptism.

God has a role in all of our "life plans." Help the students begin to understand the reality of this. How can Jesus help them discover and implement their own personal plans for life?

Plan Ahead

- Incorporate formal and/or spontaneous prayer into each lesson. A participatory prayer service is provided in the Teacher's Resource Book (TRB).
- Note the **Resources** suggestions in the TRB. These suggestions can be used to teach or extend the lessons of the chapter.
- Preview the **Application** project ideas from the Chapter Review. Refer to **Teaching Approaches** for suggestions on when to assign these projects. The projects may also be used as part of a lesson, section, or chapter review.
- Decide how you will group students for projects and discussions.

CHAPTER I

Looking Into the Future

We can say that youth is the time for discerning talents. It is also the time when one starts out on the many paths along which all human activity, work, and creativity have developed and continue to do so.

Pope John Paul II

This chapter will help you to:

- Recognize work and career as parts of your vocation.
- Understand that single life, marriage, and religious life are ways of living a vocation.
- Realize that the primary Christian vocation is to bring God's love to others.

Media Suggestions (Optional)

- *Called by Name* (Franciscan Communication) 12 minutes. A montage of interwoven stories and symbols of Baptism. What does it mean to live a baptismal commitment?
- *To Everything There Is a Season* (Oblate Media) 30 minutes. A musical meditation on the four seasons combines natural scenery with music. Best used in parts as a piece of a prayer experience.

Aims

1. To help students understand that each person is called to a unique vocation.
2. To help students discover ways to combine talents and interests with vocational life choices.

Begin the Section

1. Divide the class into groups of five or six students. Give each group a piece of butcher paper with a timeline marked from zero to twenty-one years. Give each student a different color marker or crayon. Say: "Draw symbols to represent key experiences in your life at the appropriate places on the timeline from infancy to the present." The students should work on this part of the assignment in silence. When all have finished, a group member may point to a symbol and ask the person who drew it to explain its meaning. The person may be specific or not, as he or she wishes. Allow a few minutes for the process to repeat.
2. Introduce the section by summarizing or assigning for reading the first three paragraphs.
3. Ask the students to comment on the timeline activity based on one of these statements: (a) The past, present, and future are all related; (b) How you were raised contributes to who you are now; (c) Making life choices requires active participation in one's own life.

I. Life Plans

This book is about you and your life choices. It is rooted in the belief that God created you for a reason. As you learn to live with the challenges of adolescence and move into adulthood, it is also important to ask, "How do I fit into God's plan?" How you answer that question will shape the course of the rest of your life.

The person you are today has been greatly influenced by your past (ethnic background, family traditions, childhood experiences, decisions you've made or those made for you). Equally important is the influence of your future (your dreams, ambitions, and life goals). Somewhere in between these two, in a state of constant change and development, is the "you" that is in the process of developing.

You will explore life choices in this book. It will help you to see how your personal *life plan* is intimately tied to a Christian lifestyle or vocation. It will help you to understand how your personal vocation is God's plan for you, and how your life vocation is a Christian vocation. Learning to make life choices requires your active participation.

7

Resources

Resource 1A from the Teacher's Resource Book is a blackline master of a timeline. The students may use it to record their own symbols and as a reference for use during future lessons.

Do You Have a Life Plan?

Lesson Overview

The lesson is focused on the premise that each person is able to form a plan for his or her own life. Illustrating this idea is a story about a group of high school friends who reunite ten years after graduation at a class reunion.

New Words

Vocation literally means "calling"; the call from God to live out our Christian commitment—to grow in holiness and to serve others—in a particular way.

Teaching Approaches

- As an introduction to the lesson, assign either **Application** Project 1 or Project 7.
- **Reteach**—Allow time for the students to share their stories or prayers.
- **Extend the Lesson**—Have the students return to their small group areas. Using their timelines, continue the activity. Mark symbols for what they imagine will be important events in their lives between now and the time they are twenty-five. Allow time for them to explain the symbols in their groups.

Decision-making is a process. How can you do it better? In the coming chapters, you will think about the experiences of others and how they relate to you. You will practice making decisions by imagining yourself in a variety of situations and by considering many possible life choices. You will also work at determining what God has in mind for your life.

Do You Have a Life Plan?

Imagine what your ten-year high school reunion will be like. How will you look? What kind of career will you have? Will you be married? Will you be a parent? Where will you live? What will be your relationship with God?

In truth, most everyone has dreams of the future. You may have a life plan already established for yourself. It may include college, travel, and ro-

Have you considered your life plan? How do your dreams for the future shape your life today?

mance. Later you might consider religious life, marriage, or a successful business career. This plan becomes connected with "vocation" when you make God a part of the equation. As Pope John Paul II said, "One's life plan and vocation are related when a person asks God: 'What must I do? What is Your plan for my life? What is Your will? I wish to do it.'"

Reunion

"Patty, there's got to be a fire exit we can slink through, or something," Melissa begged as she and her best friend of over 20 years walked arm-in-arm down the long corridor of the Hacienda Country Club.

"Would you relax?" Patty answered. This reunion stuff was tough enough without Melissa's anxiety. Besides, Patty was here with a purpose. Ten years after high school graduation, Patty felt that this would be her last chance to meet up with Charlie Gard.

Patty didn't want to be distracted from her search for Charlie. Wouldn't you know that she would keep a crush on a guy who would turn out to be the class's mystery man? No one had heard from him in years. Janice Murphy, the reunion chairperson, told Patty she had not received a reply from him of any kind.

Patty had dated Charlie during the summer after graduation. To be honest, Patty didn't remember any real magic, but he was a friend. When Charlie told her he was going to college in the east, she hadn't been heartbroken. But as the years passed, and meeting nice guys became a rare experience, Patty began to remember Charlie fondly. When she heard about the ten-year reunion, she began to dream.

It had been a long night and Melissa was tired. "Time to go," she said, pulling Patty by the arm. Patty yawned her consent as they walked slowly to the parking lot. As Melissa put the car into reverse, Patty rubbed her eyes just in time to see Charlie Gard pull into the next space. "Wait!" Patty screamed.

Background

Pope John Paul II addressed the youth of the world in an apostolic letter in 1985. The pope asked the youth to consider the vocations to the priesthood and the religious life, but also noted the expanding idea of vocation: "Every human life vocation is a Christian vocation, and corresponds to the evangelical call."

What will your life be like in 10 years? What do you expect to happen at your 10 year reunion?

She rolled down her window. "Charlie?" she said. Charlie looked pretty sleepy himself. "Hi, Patty," said Charlie. "Pretty dumb of me to be six hours late, but my plane was delayed. Is anyone still inside?"

The women coaxed Charlie to the all-night coffee house. Patty couldn't believe her luck! Charlie all to herself (Melissa didn't count).

"So, do you girls still live in town?" Charlie wanted to know. Melissa told Charlie about her job with Parks and Recreation. "I remember you as a rec leader in high school," he said. Patty explained a little about her private business as a seamstress. "Patty makes beautiful wedding dresses," Melissa chimed in, sounding all too obvious. Charlie laughed.

"Charlie, where have you been all these years? Don't you know it's impossible to meet nice guys like you anymore?" Patty told him. Charlie took a sip of his coffee and looked right at Patty. "I live in New York City, near Madison Square Garden actually. I work at a shelter for the homeless. I'm a Catholic priest."

After seconds of silence, Melissa spoke up. "I remember when you organized that trip to the soup kitchen downtown. I guess I always knew you had a vocation," she said.

That's when Patty spilled her coffee.

Journal Assignment

Say: "At high school reunions, some awards like, 'Married the Longest' or 'Most College Degrees' are sometimes given. Write about the award you expect to receive at your ten-year reunion."

Reunion

Teaching Approaches

- Discuss: "How will your relationships with high school classmates change following graduation?"
- Say: "How have your relationships changed during the last five years?" or "Tell us about your longest-lasting relationships."
- After the students have read the story, ask: "Why did Melissa immediately connect the word, 'vocation' with priesthood?"
- **Reteach**—For homework, students are to interview a parent or another adult who has attended a high school reunion. What expectations did the person have for the occasion and how well were those expectations met?
- **Extend the Lesson**—Assign several students to research agencies that specialize in organizing class reunions. How many former students attend their reunion? Are there any general tendencies about the kind of people who do or do not attend reunions?

Planning for Tomorrow

Look ahead! Do one or more of these future-related activities on your own, with some friends, or with the entire group:

Résumé—You're ready to enter the work force. Use the sample format to write a résumé. Follow these steps:

1. Write a career objective. This means more than just what you want out of a particular job. An objective is a statement that expresses how your talents and skills can contribute to your chosen field.
2. List your experience. Plot what experience you will need after finishing school to reach the career objective that you are seeking.
3. List your references. Write three or four names of people who can vouch for your skills and character.
4. Write a cover letter. This needs to be straightforward, yet catchy at the same time. Convince an employer that you are the right person for this particular opportunity.

Time Capsule—Your class is putting together a collection of items to be buried in a time capsule that will be opened at your ten-year reunion. Make a list of the items that you would want to include in the capsule that would capture what

life means to you now. Write a brief description of what you expect life to be like in the year 20??. How will things change? How will life remain the same?

Parent's Dreams—It's the first day of kindergarten, and you are a parent. Write a letter to your child telling her (or him) about the real meaning of school, and your dreams for her (or his) school years.

10

Resources

Resource 1B from the Teacher's Resource Book is a sample résumé the students may use as a reference while completing Project 1.

I Knew You Had a Vocation!

Charlie laughed again. "Melissa, I always knew you had a vocation, too! Watching you with those little boys and girls at Live Oak Park, I knew working with children was your life. It doesn't surprise me one bit that you're working in youth recreation."

This was all too much for Patty. Just a few minutes ago she was dreaming about Charlie: romance, marriage, kids. Now, not only is he a priest, but he's telling her best friend that she has a vocation as well. "Hey, what is this, Sister Kathleen's third period religion class?" Patty said halting the conversation for a moment. "It's 2:45 in the morning and we're talking about vocations!"

Charlie was right. Priests, sisters, and brothers aren't the only ones who have vocations. God has a plan for everyone, including you. In fact, you are living out a part of your vocation now as a student, friend, and someone's daughter or son. The process of understanding your vocation is not so much a matter of figuring out what you are to be or what you will do with your life. Rather, it's understanding that who you are now and who you will become is all part of God's gift, God's plan for you and your life.

The mention of God might distract you. What does God have to do with your future anyway? Doesn't God only pay attention to holy people? Actually, God is very interested in you and your future. You have been created by God and may even experience a "hunger" for God. According to Saint Augustine: "Our hearts were made for God and will not rest until they rest in God."

The desires for unconditional happiness, deep love and togetherness, and truth were all placed within you by God. When you combine these searchings with your work, you have truly found a vocation. How so? You have been discovering your talents for some time. What do you do well? What do you like to do? Do any careers combine your likes and skills? How can you prepare for such a career? How would a career in this field help you satisfy your desire to love and serve God? These questions will be explored throughout this book.

✚ To Your Health
My Talents

What is your own special field of competence: sports, drama, calculus? Are you a good listener, a considerate friend, a loving son or daughter? For a few minutes, be boastful. Tell someone or write down at least ten things that you are good at and why. This is a way to identify your strengths and feel good about yourself at the same time. By improving your attitude you're helping your mental health. You might want to begin your statements with "I am the best because..." or "My special talent is..." Remember to be honest in your boasting!

Talk It Over

1. Who do you expect to be your companions at your high school's ten-year reunion?
2. What will you have accomplished ten years after high school?
3. What emotions might be part of your ten-year reunion: joy, sadness, jealousy, revenge, peace? What might lead to these emotions instead of others?
4. What is your immediate reaction to the concept that everyone has a vocation? How are Charlie's and Melissa's vocations similar or different?

I Knew You Had a Vocation!

Teaching Approaches

- Ask: "When have your dreams not turned out as you planned? What interfered with your plans?"
- **Reteach**—Review Augustine's comments about our hearts hungering for God. How do students understand this concept?
- **Extend the Lesson**—Assign **Application** Project 2.

✚ To Your Health

Teaching Approaches

- Assign this as homework or do as a class activity. Tell the students not to write their names on their lists of talent statements.
- Collect the lists and read part or all of them to the class. Have the students guess the person who the talents describe.
- Have students compile similar lists for their friends. How do students feel when they receive praise from friends?

Talk It Over

Have students discuss Question 2 in terms of individual as well as relational accomplishments. For Question 3, have the students suggest how the emotions of joy, sadness, jealousy, revenge, and peace were part of Patty's night at the ten-year reunion.

Journal Assignment

Say: "Dream about your future. How will your life's work bring you happiness, love, and closeness with God?"

People with a Purpose

Lesson Overview

Saint Paul's message is that our weaknesses become strengths through God. This lesson encourages students to recognize their personal goodness and provides suggestions on how they can build up their self-confidence.

New Words

Each gene consists of a part of a *DNA molecule.* The DNA molecule is about 1 ten-millionth of an inch in diameter. It resembles a twisted ladder, the rungs of which are made up of a chemical compound called "bases." There are four kinds of bases that can be paired only in certain combinations according to their size, much like a jigsaw puzzle. There are more than ten thousand genes in every cell, and they all contain the same four bases. The variation among genes is a result of the arrangement of these bases along the DNA molecule. Since several hundred pairs of bases are in each gene, a countless number of arrangements are possible.

✠ In Focus

Teaching Approaches

- Tell the students to think of positive messages to counteract any of the negative messages they might give themselves.
- Encourage students to make a habit of repeating these affirmation messages to themselves as an exercise along with their morning prayer at the beginning of each day.
- Have students write short stories about themselves that affirm their talents and abilities.

Teaching Approaches

- Assign either **Application** Project 3 or Project 6 as a lead-in to the material.
- **Reteach**—Have students write about the following topic: "Imagine that you are God drawing up the original blueprints for creating you. Describe in detail some of the good ingredients that God decided to include."

People with a Purpose

As you know from biology class, *heredity* is extremely complicated. A special chemical compound called *deoxyribonucleic acid,* or *DNA,* contributes to a seemingly unlimited number of possible arrangements of genes in a human being. For that reason, every person is biologically different from every other person. Even identical twins are not truly identical.

God did not create the unique you without reason. From literally countless other possibilities, God selected you as an unique individual. God's care and concern for you lasts much longer than just the thought that began your life. God's love for you is eternally relentless. It will be with you forever.

You may have trouble accepting this, especially during times when you feel like a failure or unloved, but there is a prominent and divinely chosen role for each person. One of the reasons for so much diversity in the universe is that each living thing has a role to play. The key is to learn what God's plan is for you and then to follow through with it.

Unfortunately, before you can find out what God's unique mission is for you, you have to discover time and again that you are indeed special. When you have difficulty liking yourself, it's nearly impossible to believe that you are loved by God. Yet, a fundamental Christian belief is that when we are weak, God's strength is most present to us. As Saint Paul says:

> "If I must boast, I will boast of the things that show my weakness. …I will rather boast most gladly of my weaknesses, in order that the power of Christ may dwell with me. Therefore, I am content with weakness, insults, hardships, persecutions, and constraints, for the sake of Christ; for when I am weak, then I am strong"
> *(2 Corinthians 11:30, 12:10).*

Paul's comments are not meant to belittle your strengths or deny the good that you do. They are meant to help you realize that God is with you, even when you may not be at your best. For too many people, this message is lost. All they see is their *failure,* never their goodness. Have you noticed this attitude among classmates and friends?

This is a hyper-critical attitude that, at one time or another, seems to affect everyone, but it can be easily overcome.

The solution starts when you take time to examine the goodness that you possess. Listen for positive messages. Imagine the applause of a large stadium crowd after you finish studying for a big test, or as you burn off calories during a workout. The cheers come for you. They come from God all for you.

✠ In Focus
Affirmations

Affirmations are positive statements made about yourself or others. Affirmation statements build up your confidence. For example, the statement, "I am a competent person," is an affirmation you might use when you have studied for an exam but are still nervous about taking it. Try using affirmative statements as a daily discipline.

Here's a list of positive attributes that you can make a part of your regular internal conversation. Add your own to the list:

1. I'm prepared. I know I will do well.
2. I can if I think I can.
3. I believe I can, so anything is possible.
4. I know that I am loved.
5. I am a winner.
6. I am a friend to others and to myself.
7. I am the best I can be right now.
8. I will make this the best day possible.

Background

Paul's boasting in the Second Letter to the Corinthians comes in two parts. In the first, he focuses on his labor and afflictions, in which true service of Christ exists. In this, his second boast, Paul writes that personal weakness is also an occasion to boast.

Talk It Over

1. What are some factors involved in recognizing one's own goodness?
2. What is one practical thing that you can do every day to improve the way you feel about yourself?
3. Describe a time when you didn't feel good about yourself and what happened to make you feel better.

Work and Careers

Lately, you may have noticed how your concerns for the future have intensified. As a young child, you did not think of the future in the same way. To a child, the future seems very much like the present: same school, same home, and same friends. For you, the pattern doesn't hold anymore. In the next few years, you may be working at a full-time job, living in a new place, going to college, or beginning your own family. What does the future hold for you?

A president of a university recently commented that he wished undergraduate students would choose majors based on what subjects or fields they enjoyed, rather than majors they thought would benefit their future careers. "Our greatest contributions to society are usually made doing something we love," he said.

Pope John Paul II has written: "Work is a good thing for us—a good thing for our humanity—because through work we not only transform nature, but we also achieve fulfillment as human beings and, indeed, in a sense become more human" *(To the Youth of the World).*

Not all work is as fulfilling as the pope suggests. Some people work at jobs they dislike because it is their only means of support. Others are fortunate enough to make a living at something they love. Most people's work falls somewhere in between. Whether we enjoy it or not, work is a natural part of being human. The challenge is to find work that is appropriate to our likes, abilities, and values.

You began work appropriate for your age when you started school. School is the work of the young. It has helped to unlock your talents and

Some people work at jobs they dislike, while others love what they do. Why might someone work as a secretary or a fire fighter?

- **Extend the Lesson**—Assign the students to research the work of Gregor Mendel, a nineteenth century Austrian monk who, through plant breeding experiments, discovered how dominant and recessive genes influence the inheritance of physical characteristics.

Talk It Over
Encourage the students to think of factors related to each stage of development, from infancy to the teenage years.

Work and Careers

Lesson Overview
This lesson differentiates between the meanings of job, career, and vocation. Each has value for the Christian, but vocation is intimately linked to a person's deep, inner callings. In this lesson, the students will explore a variety of ways this calling is lived out.

Teaching Approaches
- Ask: "What do you find exciting about the future? What do you find scary about the future?"
- Ask the students if they think society holds to the belief that some career choices are better or more acceptable than others.
- Read or summarize the section.
- Have students define in their own words the meaning of "vocation," "career," and "job." Discuss why it is important to make these distinctions.
- **Reteach**—Remind the students of Pope John Paul's respect for the uniqueness of each person's vocation. The pope called young people to practice living their vocations on a daily basis—beginning with the decisions they make in their lives right now.
- **Extend the Lesson**—Have students develop a list of jobs that they would not want to do for any amount of money. What is it about these jobs that they don't like? What would they feel if they were forced to take one of these jobs? What do they think people should do to avoid such traps?

Resources

Resource 1C provides more information on DNA.

Resource 1D provides a biographical sketch on Gregor Mendel and information about his research.

Journal Assignment

Have the students write about how they envision themselves contributing to society doing something that they love. This assignment may be combined with **Application** Project 4.

Teaching Approaches

- Ask the students to make a list of the benefits that they would seek in their future career. Then, have them prioritize these benefits in order of importance.

- Have the students discuss the text questions with a partner.

- Arrange a debate on the two sides of the issue: working for more pay versus working for more satisfaction.

- Assign **Application** Project 2, if you have not already done so.

interests, and has prepared you for adult work. Work is always one part of vocation. What kind of work do you like to do? How can you make a living doing this kind of work?

Vocation literally means "calling." All people are called to holiness. But holiness is not reflected only by people who spend their lives at prayer in church. You may know many holy people: Mike, the boy in the leather jacket and weird haircut, who looks after his mentally retarded sister; or Enid, the girl who does her disabled neighbor's weekly shopping. A holy person can like loud music or football. Someone might even describe you as holy! Holiness, then, is a general vocation we all share. Individually, we believe that God calls each of us to use our talents and gifts to make life better for all. This is the way every person is called to vocation; we are called to holiness.

Most dictionaries define the word "vocation" as an occupation or profession. Vocations are definitely connected with one's life work, but there's more to vocation than work. Vocations also express how a person chooses to live one's life. Consider a few examples:

◊ Greg works at the local sub shop making sandwiches. He earns a little more than minimum wage, likes his boss, and is looking forward to the day when he can do some-

thing more compatible with his talents. He knows that this has been a good job for him: the flexible hours have fit into his school and drama schedules nicely, he's learned a lot about the retail food business, and he has developed confidence in his ability to work with the public. But Greg recognizes that his future is not as the next submarine sandwich king. This has been a good job, but it's not his life's work.

◊ Sally is thrilled to be working in the mayor's office as a part-time clerk. Her boss is often rude, and her hours are inflexible, but Sally can't wait to start work each day. She's learning so much about how government works and the political process. Sally wants a career in public service and this job is the first step. She has no doubt that she can make a difference in people's lives.

◊ Craig sells fire insurance. As an English major in college, he hoped to write novels and award-winning articles. But, to Craig, his wife and three children come first. He still writes when he has the chance and still dreams of publishing his novel. Selling insurance pays the bills better than prose, however. Craig's love for his family has given importance and meaning to his work.

◖ **Well Being**
Working for Less?

Imagine that you are working at a job that pays you $25,000 a year. Your salary allows you to live in your own apartment, make car payments, and dress the way you like. However, during your six months on the job you've not received one minute of enjoyment or satisfaction from your labor. Someone has offered you a job that you know you would love. At the end of each workday you would feel good about yourself because you would have accomplished something worthwhile. It's perfect, except that you would have to take a $5,000 cut in pay. What's your decision—do you keep the job you hate or take the one you love? Would the benefits of working at what you love be worth the financial sacrifice you'd have to make? What would you consider before making such a decision?

Background

The Encyclopedic Dictionary of Religion defines Vocation as "one's calling or profession in life; in a restricted ecclesiastical sense, a special call to serve God in the priestly or the religious state." People called to priestly or religious life vocations should possess the qualities needed for these lifestyles and the will to dedicate self to God's service. Religious vocations not only require a call from God; they also require an invitation from the bishop or a community.

Vocations are different than careers, and careers are different than jobs. How so?

Can you see the difference in these three examples? Greg is clearly working at a job. There is no hint as to his career or vocation. We only know that he works to make money around his schedule. Sally seems to be on a vocational track. Her work environment is not the best, yet she's willing to persevere because of her commitment to public service. Craig has made both a career choice and a vocational choice. Vocationally, he is dedicated to family life, while his career is selling. He's invested a lot of time and effort into becoming good at his work and would not leave it willingly, but it's not his life.

Any career you choose can help you in your quest to love and serve God.

A job is different from a *career*. Jobs are merely ways to earn a living and often do not express anything about the talents or interests of the worker. They can be changed frequently for a better salary or working conditions. People also change their careers, but a lot less frequently than they change jobs. A career does express a person's talents and interests. Careers build upon what we like to do and our aptitude for a certain kind of work.

How are *vocations* similar to or different from jobs and careers? Vocations are our responses to what we love to do. Because they are in response to our natural talents and gifts, vocations call us to what makes us happy. A true vocation is generally personally satisfying. It promotes personal growth.

No career or vocation is necessarily better than another, although people can choose vocations that are not right for them. Melissa's choice to work with young people after working as a recreation leader in high school seems more appropriate for her than a solitary job, like being a truck driver. Charlie's care for the homeless as a priest in the inner city arises out of a deep concern for them. Both of these vocational choices are great

Journal Assignment

Say, "Define vocation in your own words. Explain how a vocation differs from a career or a job."

Sharpening Your Skills

Teaching Approaches

- Have students develop a list of long-term goals as suggested in "Sharpening Your Skills."
- Discuss the importance of setting goals and have students volunteer techniques for implementing goals.
- Have students identify a goal that they have recently reached. What has reaching the goal meant for them?
- Have the students work in pairs or small groups to role play some possible scenarios that might force them to change their goals, such as an unexpected pregnancy or a parent's loss of a job.

Talk It Over

Have the students discuss the questions in small groups. Assign one student in each group to record each person's responses to the questions. Choose other students as leaders. The leaders are to summarize their group's responses for the entire class.

Sharpening Your Skills
Setting Goals

What do you hope to accomplish during the next week? The next six weeks? The next ten years? Many people find it helpful to set goals according to what they hope to accomplish in a set amount of time. To do this for yourself, list the following on a separate sheet of paper.

- 1 week
- 2 weeks
- 1 month
- 3 months
- 6 months
- 1 year
- 5 years
- 10 years
- 20 years
- 40 years

Next to each, write what you hope to have accomplished by that time. What steps do you need to take to make these hoped-for accomplishments a reality?

Not everything you list needs to be an important life goal. Be creative; remember, no one is stopping you from dreaming.

---

gifts. "What an enormous range of possible directions, capacities, and interests there are!" said Pope John Paul II.

The list goes on. Some people are adept at manual labor like carpentry, mechanics, or farming, and are skillful enough at the trade to prosper financially. Patty, for example, chose to be a seamstress. These creative fields are a way for people to live out their vocations as well. Pope John Paul adds, "It is always a question of the effort that is creative."

But for every optimistic statement made, a disclaimer must be added. In a free market economic system, people are, ironically, not always free to make a living doing what they love to do. The money runs out before you can finish college; there are too many computer programmers and too few jobs; you can't pass the test to qualify for medical school; and so on. Your vocational plans will need adjusting and adapting to the forces you experience in society.

Talk It Over

1. What special talents do you possess? How do you expect to use these talents in your career? What criteria do you use to judge one talent as being more special than another?
2. How can work be a response to God's call? How can the career you choose be a vocation statement?

How can the work of this carpenter be an act of vocation?

Journal Assignment

Goals are different than wishful thinking. Goals express possible realities. Students are to explain why their goals are possible, and how they expect to reach these goals.

Resources

See **Resource 1E** from the Teacher's Resource Book for role play and character suggestions mentioned in "Sharpening Your Skills."

II. VOCATIONAL CHOICES

So far, the word "vocation" has been used in two ways:

1. As a way to express how every Christian is called to live out God's life.
2. As a specific response to implement God's call through work.

Vocation is also used to identify a person's lifestyle or way of life. As with work and career, this life-giving vocation may take many different paths. The opportunities for creativity in forming your own vocation are endless and the preparation can take a long time.

Traditionally when Catholics spoke of a vocation they meant only one thing: life as a vowed brother, sister, or priest. Today, while religious vocations are still honored and admired, the single and married life vocations are also recognized as valid ways of living and of responding to God.

Christian Marriage

Most people eventually marry. Marriage is the most common way people live out their vocations. The duality between man and woman is a critical theme in Scriptures. In the beginning, God created male and female to love one another and to live as one. This call was the beginning of the human family. This call is the beginning of the Christian family today.

People marry for many different reasons. Some people marry because of social pressure. They figure that, if everyone else is getting married, they should too. Some people marry because of problems at home, or because of pregnancy. Others marry because they are in love, although they have not considered exactly what that means; romantic love and physical attraction are only parts of being in love.

Marriage is a vocation when it is based on the joint decision of a man and a woman to form an intimate partnership with one another. This bond reflects the bond between Jesus and the Church. It is an irrevocable, never-ending bond that should not be entered into frivolously. Marriage should lead to a deep sense of joy and excitement. Setting up a new household, learning to share deeply with another, and taking on the role of parent are all parts of the process of marriage. Each part demands preparation. The unfortunate couple who enters marriage without considering these and other ramifications of married life faces a very difficult challenge.

There are many things that you do right now that prepare you for Christian marriage. The respect and honor with which you treat friends of both sexes forms the foundation for how you will treat a spouse and children. The ways in which you live through the ups and downs of friendship now will help you meet and grow with similar experiences later in marriage.

Through dating, you learn many of the skills you will need for marriage, especially how to interact with people of the opposite sex. By meeting and spending time with a variety of people, you learn what types of people you like and get along with best.

Pope John Paul II said: "To set out on the path of the married vocation means to learn married love day by day, year by year: love according to soul and body. It is precisely this love that you young people need if your married future is to 'pass the test' of the whole of life."

II. VOCATIONAL CHOICES

Aims
1. To become familiar with different kinds of Christian vocations.
2. To understand that a Christian's primary vocation is to bring God's love to others.

Begin the Section
1. Ask the students to brainstorm ways people may live out their vocations. List these suggestions on the board.
2. Point out the variety of vocations. Mention to the students that their personal "plan of life" will always involve other people. A Christian vocation will always involve witnessing God's love to others.
3. Read the introductory paragraph and ask for comments or questions.

Christian Marriage

Lesson Overview
This lesson explores Christian marriage, the most common vocational choice. Marriage is a vocation only when it is based on the joint decision of a man and woman to form an intimate partnership with one another. When this bond reflects the love that Jesus has for the Church, it begins to take on sacramental overtones. This issue will be explored in more detail in later chapters of the text.

Teaching Approaches
- Ask the students how they can practice today some of the positive qualities they have witnessed in married life.
- Have the males and the females in the class make separate lists of reasons for getting married. (If the school is not coed, have the students interview members of the opposite sex for their answers to the question.) Compare the two lists. How are they similar? How are they different? Discuss with the class.

Background
"Married love is an eminently human love because it is an affection between two persons rooted in the will and it embraces the good of the whole person; it can enrich the sentiments of the spirit and their physical expression with a unique dignity and ennoble them as the special elements and signs of the friendship proper to marriage" (*Pastoral Constitution on the Church in the Modern World,* #49).

▲ Family Living

Teaching Approaches

- Allow the students the opportunity to comment and ask questions on the points raised in the feature.
- After students have had an opportunity to reflect on the feature questions in their journals, begin a general discussion on the questions. (Do not ask students to tell you what they wrote in their journals.)
- Discuss the benefits and problems associated with each type of family.
- Have students gather statistics from an almanac on the number of families in their community that fall into the various categories. A local librarian can help them find this information.

Christian Marriage

Teaching Approaches (continued)

- Assign **Application** Project 5 at this time.
- **Reteach**—Remind the students of their timelines. Ask: "If you were to write one symbol of God's love in your life, what would it be?" Call on volunteers to share their ideas with the class.
- **Extend the Lesson**—Point out the unifying nature of the creation stories and the origins of married love from Scripture (*Genesis 1—3:24*). Share with the students some of these other Scripture readings that are used at the celebration of the sacrament of Marriage: Genesis 24:48-51, 58-67; Tobit 7:9-10, 11-15, 8:5-10; Song of Songs 2: 8-10, 14, 16a; 8:6-7a; Jeremiah 31-32a, 33-34a; Romans 8:31b-35, 37-39; Romans 12:1-2, 9-18; 1 Corinthians 6:13c-15a, 17-20; 1 Corinthians 12:31; 13:8a; Ephesians 5:2a, 21-33; Colossians 3:12-17; 1 Peter 3:1-9; 1 John 3:18-24, 4: 7-12; Revelation 19:1, 5-9a; Matthew 5: 1-12, 13-16; Matthew 7:21, 24-29; Matthew 19:3-6; Matthew 22:35-40; Mark 10:6-9; John 2:1-11; John 15:9-16; and John 17:20-26.

How can your present friendships help you prepare for the vocation of marriage?

▲ Family Living
Nuclear Families: Still Possible?

American families are often *nuclear* or *extended* families. The nuclear family refers to a mother, father, and children living under the same roof, with the father being the primary wage earner. Extended families also include grown children and other relatives living with the nuclear family in the same home. Is one of these the family model you imagine for yourself?

Today, only about nine percent of all families in North America have a traditional structure where the mother does not work outside the home. Twenty-five percent of all families seem to fit the nuclear model, although in many of these families both parents now work. Approximately twenty-five percent of all families are *single-parent families*. Divorce is the major reason for single-parent families, although teenage pregnancy contributes significantly to the statistic. Most single-parent households are headed by women. *Blended* families are created when two single or divorced parents marry and bring their children together.

How do you plan to combine career with family life? Do you think traditional family models are still possible? How would your goals and expectations change if you found yourself living in a single-parent or blended family? These are some of the many family life questions you might consider.

Resources

Resource 1F from the Teacher's Resource Book provides a blackline master for the survey assignment suggested in "Christian Marriage."

Journal Assignment

Assign the questions in "Family Living" to the students for comment. Tell students that these questions will also be discussed in class, and this exercise is meant to help them clarify their thoughts on the matter.

Talk It Over

1. What is your vision of married life?
2. What are some of the reasons that people marry? What do you think people hope to gain from marriage?
3. What does it mean to say that a person marries for love? How does society shape our understanding of love in marriage?
4. What does being in love mean to you?

Other Choices

Right now, you are a single person. Usually, most people spend a part of their adult lives single, neither married nor committed to religious vows. For many people, being single is a way station, a place to wait before marriage, between marriages, or after the death of a spouse. Yet, a growing number of people today choose a vocation to the single life as their committed, lifelong response to God.

A vocation to the single life may sound like a lonely way to live. For people who choose the single vocation, this is usually far from the truth. The single vocation is a special, people-oriented call that allows a person to respond freely to God. The choice of the single life, like any other vocation decision, is arrived at in dialogue with friends, family, and with God.

There are many stories of people who lead rewarding single lives. A teacher who spends years devoted to his students; a daughter who cares for her ill mother; or a scientist who diligently searches for a cure for cancer. While these special calls can be answered within the context of Christian marriage, many people find that the single lifestyle affords them a better opportunity to dedicate their lives to the single-mindedness of their call.

For many of the same reasons that some people choose to be single, other people choose a vocation to religious life. Father George Maloney, a professor at Fordham University, once likened such people to "skydivers or other

People who choose to live as religious provide a living witness to an alternative way of life. They offer an example to us all.

such daredevils." Those who take the risk of commitment to the life of a religious man or woman are people who are taken to living on the edge, of providing a living witness to the alternative; a life lived in love and service of all of God's family in preparation for the coming fullness of God's kingdom.

Talk It Over

1. Can you foresee a commitment that could lead you to choose a vocation to the single life?
2. What does it mean to say that those with a religious vocation can be likened to "skydivers or other such daredevils"? How would the same be true for the married or single vocation?

Background

Jesus not only never married, but He chose not to become a priestly member of any of the religious communities of His day. There were Jewish priests associated with Temple worship and a religious community called the Essenes who lived near the Dead Sea. But Jesus remained a "lay person."

Talk It Over

Use both Questions 1 and 2 to introduce the section. For Question 1, you may want to have the students write in their journals prior to the discussion a brief statement of their vision of married life. For Question 2, have the students list specific stories to illustrate their example. You may wish to have the students answer Questions 3 or 4 in their journals.

Other Choices

Lesson Overview

This lesson introduces the vocations of single life and religious life. Both callings require single-minded devotion to serving God through caring for the needs of others.

Teaching Approaches

- Ask: "What would you find attractive about living the single life? What would you find most difficult about living the single life?"
- Briefly clarify the difference between members of religious communities and ordained ministers (priests and deacons are ordained, religious aren't; every member of a religious community takes the vows of poverty, chastity and obedience, even the priests and deacons; diocesan priests do not take these vows and are not members of religious community). Explain that religious brothers and sisters remain lay people, just like the students themselves.
- **Reteach**—Have the students identify various priests, religious, and single people that they know. How do these people live their vocations differently than married people?
- **Extend the Lesson**—Have students write a brief essay explaining the advantages and disadvantages of being single or being a member of a religious community.

Talk It Over

For Question 1, help the students to see the advantages of the single vocation in carrying out some of their chosen commitments. For Question 2, ask the students to give examples of other people who "live on the edge" and to tell how their lives are positive examples to others.

♣ Prayer in Action

Teaching Approaches

- When do students pray? why? for what? How comfortable are they with formal prayer? with personal prayer in private? prayer with the community?

- Ask students to comment on Terry Anderson's experience. Why do people turn to prayer when times are tough?

- Have a volunteer(s) present a report on Terry Anderson's ordeal as a captive in Lebanon.

- Ask the students to make notes during the course of one day, listing all the opportunities they have for prayer. Then, have them share examples of these with the rest of the class.

One Vocation

Lesson Overview

The primary Christian vocation is given at Baptism: to bring God's love to others. This vocation must be accomplished in relationship with Jesus Christ. One of the main objectives of this course is to encourage the students to dream all their dreams and do all their life work in concert with Jesus. This lesson introduces the story of the young man who asked Jesus how to attain perfection. Jesus' answer remains a challenging one for us today.

Teaching Approaches

- Ask the students to recall the relationship they had with Jesus as a primary grade student, perhaps near the time of their First Communion. Ask: "How has your image of Jesus changed from then to now?"

- Read or have the students read Matthew 19:16-30. Explain that for this man, being perfect meant selling all of his possessions. Ask the students to think of what changes Jesus would ask of them if they were to seek perfection.

- If **Application** Project 7 has not been assigned, you may wish to do so now.

♣ Prayer in Action
Times of Prayer

Prayer for many people is only for quiet times. However, nothing prevents you from praying during other times of the day as well. Have you ever said a prayer of thanks while running the last few yards of a race? or a prayer of blessing before eating a meal with your friends? a prayer for strength before taking a big exam? a prayer for courage before giving an oral report?

Terry Anderson, an American held hostage in Lebanon for nearly seven years, considered that everything of value had been taken from him—his family, his property, his freedom. After thinking about it for a while, he realized that no one could take away his prayer. He could pray anytime or anyplace. On his release from captivity, he commented that he survived because of his faith and because of prayer.

Terry Anderson

One Vocation

Developing a mature relationship with Jesus may be difficult for you to accomplish at this particular time. When you were younger, this relationship was easier; Jesus was so powerful. You really needed Him and made sure that He was a part of your life.

How is that relationship different for you now? How has your life changed in the past few years? Do you have more freedom about where you go and at what time you must return home? Do you feel in charge of your life? If so, you may not feel the same urgent need to talk with Jesus.

Regardless of your present relationship with Jesus, this is a critical time for self-reflection. Whatever career or lifestyle you choose to lead, as a baptized person of growing faith your life is rooted in Jesus Christ. Without Jesus, you may very well attain all your goals and dreams—great job, wonderful husband or wife, loving and respectful children—and still not be satisfied.

Consider the story of the young man who asked Jesus how to attain perfection. Jesus told him "to sell what you have and give to the poor, and you will have treasure in heaven. Then, come follow Me" *(Matthew 19:23)*. The young man went away sad. What is the challenge offered to us by Jesus' request to the young man? What would be your reply to Jesus? How does this story apply to your life now?

At Baptism, you were given your primary Christian vocation to bring God's love to others. You were washed and anointed into the death of Jesus with the promise of eternal life. This is the vocation of every Christian, a vocation that is capable of changing a world full of greed, lust, jealousy, and violence into a world that is a preview of God's kingdom.

Journal Assignment

Ask the students to write about the meaning of the "vocation of perfection" for their own lives.

Resources

Resource 1G is the profession of faith used at the celebration of Baptism. You may wish to give a copy to each of your students.

✴ Media Watch
How Much Influence?

Young children watch Saturday morning cartoons and want to grow up to be the latest superhero. Such role–playing and imagination probably seems funny to you now. Yet, the media—magazines, radio, and especially television—may continue to influence who you are now and who you want to be.

Researchers tell us that not many things are as pervasive as television. By the time you graduate from high school, you will have spent 15,000 hours watching TV as compared to 12,000 hours in school. Ask yourself: Where will I have learned more, in front of the television or in school?

The media gives us countless images of what it means to be a man or a woman. Some images are true and some are not. Looking carefully at those images, comparing them to people you know, and being aware of how you react to these images can help you understand how men and women relate to one another in life.

The first step in becoming *media aware* is to review your media viewing habits. Keep a *media diary* over the next month. Write down what you see, read, and listen to and how much time you spend doing each. At the end of each week see how much time you've spent on these activities. Evaluate what you saw or heard. How much was for entertainment? How much was to waste time?

The challenge is to become a discriminating listener, viewer, or reader where *you* make the choice based upon preference and taste, not because of peer pressure or out of boredom.

Talk It Over

1. How might your primary vocation of being a Christian fit in with any other life vocation that you choose?

2. If God said to you, "I have a special plan for you and only you," what would your reaction be? Then what would God say, and how would you respond to it?

Chapter Summary

- Everyone has a vocation, not just priests and religious. God has a plan for everyone.
- Vocation means calling.
- Work is part of every vocation.
- Married life is the most common vocation. The vocation of Christian marriage is based on the joint decision of a man and woman to form an intimate partnership with each other.
- Vocations to the single life and religious life are also life-giving.
- The primary Christian vocation is given at Baptism.

Resources

Resource 1H is an activity to accompany "Media Watch."

- **Reteach**—Note that at Baptism, a person is anointed in the Spirit. Ask the students to talk about ways that they can live out their roles as witnesses of Christ through the Holy Spirit.
- **Extend the Lesson**—Share the words of the profession of faith and renunciation of sin spoken at Baptisms with the students. Allow time for the students to comment on or question the meaning of any of the questions.

Talk It Over

Request that responses to each of the questions be specific.

✴ Media Watch

Teaching Approaches

- Family relationships on television are often not portrayed accurately. Have the students compare a family on television with their own families. Points of comparison could include how children get along, how brothers and sisters treat one another, how conflicts are handled, and what are the causes of disagreement.
- Why do students watch TV? What do they get from the experience? How do they think they are affected by what they see and hear.
- Explain how to keep a media diary.

Chapter Summary

- Before assigning the review exercises, ask the students if they have any questions or comments on Chapter 1.
- Have the students read each statement. Or, you may wish to have the students read and discuss these statements in small groups before reporting back to the entire class.

Chapter 1 Review

What Have You Learned?

Listed below are suggested answers. For many of the questions, the answers will vary.

1. Everyone has a vocation because God has a plan for everyone. A vocation involves understanding what you are now and what you will become.

2. God creates unique and special people through the process of heredity and from literally countless possibilities. This explains the diversity in the world.

3. Augustine's words recognize that we have been created with a "hunger" for God. The desire for unconditional happiness, deep love and togetherness, and for truth have all been placed within us by God. These longings can only be satisfied when we rest with God.

4. Science points out that the special compound called DNA makes for a seemingly unlimited number of possible arrangements of genes in a human being.

5. Answers will vary. Check to see whether student answers include a variety of both good and questionable reasons for marriage.

6. Respecting and honoring people of both sexes are ways to prepare for Christian marriage. Dating also affords an opportunity to learn about people of the opposite sex.

7. These special calls to single and religious life afford people the chance to share God's love with more people than imagined. The people they serve become members of their larger, shared family of faith.

8. A Christian's primary vocation, given at Baptism, is to bring God's love to others.

9. In a media diary, a person would record program watched, time of day, and special information about the program.

10. The four steps for preparing a résumé are (1) write a career objective, (2) list experience, (3) list references, and (4) write a cover letter.

11. Affirmation statements can help build a person's confidence.

12. "Vocation" may be used to describe (1) how a Christian is called to live God's life, (2) a specific response to implement God's call through work, and (3) a way to identify a person's lifestyle or way of life.

REVIEW

What Have You Learned?

1. Explain how everyone has a vocation.
2. What is one reason why there is so much diversity in the world?
3. What is the meaning of Saint Augustine's words: "Our hearts were made for God and will not rest until they rest in God"?
4. How does science explain each person's uniqueness?
5. What are some reasons that people get married?
6. What are ways that you can prepare for Christian marriage right now?
7. How are the special calls of single and religious life life-giving?
8. What does your primary Christian vocation entail?
9. What does it mean to keep a "media diary"?
10. What are the four steps in preparing a résumé?
11. How can affirmation statements help you?
12. Discuss three uses of the word "vocation."

Application

1. Write a story about what your life will be like ten years from now. Include details about your Christian vocation as it relates to your work and family life.
2. Make a list of five of your talents. Show your list to a partner. Ask your partner to suggest one or two careers for you based on the list.
3. Research your past. Ask a parent or other family member what special skills or aptitudes you had as an infant and young child. What were your family's expectations for you when you were younger? How do you continue to use these skills?
4. Choose one field of work that you might consider as a career. Make a list of positive aspects about that career in one column and negative aspects in another. Write a paragraph about your lists.
5. Interview a married couple other than your parents. Ask them to tell you about the decision-making, preparations, joys, and difficulties leading up to their wedding day.
6. Write a magazine-style ad marketing yourself as a good person. Keep the ad in a place where you can refer to it when you are in the need of affirmation.
7. Compose a prayer to Jesus asking Him to be with you as you decide on a life plan.
8. Attend a Baptism preparation class. Learn more about the promises made in your name at your own Christian Baptism.

REVIEW

Chapter Vocabulary

- vocation
- affirmation
- life plan
- heredity
- DNA
- religious life
- marriage
- single life
- self-reflection
- God's kingdom
- career
- Baptism
- nuclear families
- extended families
- single-parent families
- blended families

Life must be understood backwards, but . . . it must be lived forwards.

Søren Kierkegaard

Putting Vocabulary to Use

Supply the missing word or phrase from the chapter vocabulary list.

1. At _____, your primary Christian vocation was given to you.
2. Though you may not feel the same urgent need to talk with Jesus today as you once did, now is the time to tell Jesus about the important things going on in your life. In reality, this is an important time for _____.
3. Families with a traditional structure are called _____ or _____. Most _____ are headed by women. _____ are created when single or divorced parents marry.
4. _____ is the most common way people live out their vocation.
5. _____ literally means "calling."
6. An _____ is a positive statement that can be used to build up a person's confidence.
7. A special compound called _____ is involved in the intricate process of _____.
8. Before you can discover the unique _____ God has for you, you have to discover and rediscover that you are one of a kind.
9. People who choose to live a _____ _____ are usually people-oriented.
10. Some people choose a vocation to the _____ live in love and service of all of God's family in preparation for the coming fullness of _____.

Application

Have the students read the directions for each project. You may assign a particular project, or allow the students to choose a project they prefer. Allow some class time for the students to share their work.

Putting Vocabulary to Use

1. Baptism
2. self-reflection
3. nuclear or extended families, single-parent families, blended families
4. marriage
5. vocation
6. affirmation
7. DNA, heredity
8. life plan
9. single life
10. religious life, God's kingdom.

Final Thought

Background

Søren Kierkegaard, a Danish philosopher and theologian, lived from 1813 to 1855.

Focus on: Chapter 2

Though a person's self-image is largely formed early in life, maintaining and developing a positive self-concept is important at every stage of life. By the time they reach high school age, many people will concede that how they thought of themselves as children affected their experiences. These same people may not recognize the benefits of having a healthy self-image now.

In this chapter, the students will study how important having a positive self-concept is to their future success. Chapter 2 explores steps the students can take to improve their self-esteem. The students will discover ways to diffuse the negative messages they receive about themselves from many sources, including from their own critical "self-talk." They will also learn techniques to recognize themselves as the special and unique creations of a loving God.

Although the concepts present in this chapter may be familiar to the students, it is very important that you review them fully. One's vocational choices will be affected by a person's self-esteem.

Plan Ahead

- Incorporate formal and/or spontaneous prayer into each lesson. A participatory prayer service is provided in the Teacher's Resource Book.

- Note **Resources** suggestions which can be applied to, or extend, the lessons of this chapter.

- Preview the **Application** project ideas from the Chapter Review. Refer to **Teaching Approaches** for suggestions on when to assign the projects. Or, the projects may be used as part of lesson, section, or chapter reviews.

- Decide on a method for grouping students for projects and discussion.

Discovering Your Richness

I am the gate. Whoever enters through Me will be saved, and will come in and go out and find pasture. A thief comes only to steal and slaughter and destroy; I came so that they might have life and have it more abundantly.

John 10:9-10

This chapter will help you to:

- Recognize the importance of self-esteem.
- See the role other people play in forming one's self-concept.
- Understand that honest communication with yourself and others is essential to positive human relations.
- Discover ways to control the negative messages that you communicate to yourself.

24

Media Suggestions (Optional)

- *Free to Be Me* (Argus Communications) Nine 20-minute segments by John Powell designed to help youth and adults develop positive attitudes about themselves, others, the world, and God.

- *Classroom of the Heart* (Focus on the Family) 40 minutes. Guy Dowd inspires and challenges students with this simple truth: You begin to discover your own worth after you recognize the worth of others.

Aims

1. To help students see the importance of having a healthy self-concept.
2. To help students come to a realization that God loves all people for who they are, not for what they do.

Begin the Section

1. Write the term *self-concept* on the chalkboard. Develop with the students a definition to which most of them can agree. Discuss how self-concept and positive self-image are developed.
2. Ask the students to imagine themselves walking in a shopping mall at three different times: (1) by themselves; (2) with a best friend; and (3) with a parent. Ask volunteers to describe how they would act and feel in each of those situations. You may want to have students act out each of these situations to show how their behavior is shaped by whom they are with. Why do the students act as they do? Have students identify and discuss the various attitudes expressed in these situations.
3. Have students make two columns on a sheet of paper. In the first column, students are to write some of their personal gifts and talents. In the second column, they are to write how those gifts and talents can be of value in a career.
4. Read or summarize the opening paragraphs of the section.

1. DEVELOPING A POSITIVE SELF-IMAGE

Choices about one's career and vocation are often based on a person's special gifts and talents. People adept at mathematics often find satisfaction in careers that involve working with numbers: accounting, statistics, engineering, or physics. Those blessed with quick reflexes and remarkable dexterity make brilliant surgeons, pilots, and artisans. For men and women called to service professions, there are many caring positions.

Career and vocation choices affect the kind of work you will do as an adult and how you will choose to accomplish it. No matter how you choose to use your gifts and talents, you will act out your choices in society. Are you prepared to enter this world? What do you think about yourself? How do you feel about the person you are becoming? When you look in the mirror is the person you see the real you?

Resources

   Resource 2A from the Teacher's Resource Book provides a form to use with "Begin the Section" Activity 3.

Recognizing Your Gifts

Lesson Overview

A positive self-concept and healthy self-esteem are vitally important qualities for a person making career and vocation choices. Without liking oneself, a person cannot even consider many possible dreams. Help the students to see how a sense of worth can lead to personal success. This material reviews and builds upon the lessons covered in Chapter 1.

New Words

Self-concept can be described as "the sum total of how a person views himself or herself."

Esteem means "to value" or "to praise." Praising oneself is an important tool in building self-esteem. While one's self-esteem can be high or low, healthy or poor, one cannot have negative esteem.

Teaching Approaches

- Divide the class into two groups. Have one group develop a list of negative comments a person might hear while growing up that might damage one's self-concept. Have the other group develop a list of positive comments that would enhance a person's self-concept. Compare the lists. Discuss the impact of positive and negative comments on a person's self-worth. You may wish to incorporate the suggestion from **Application** Project 2 into this opening activity.

- Compare the class's definition of self-concept with the definition and examples listed in the text.

- **Reteach**—Affirmation exercise: Have the students write anonymous letters of praise to three individuals in the classroom. During the course of the next week, the students should secretly give the letters to the appropriate people. At the end of the week, have students share how they felt when they received their letters of affirmation.

- **Extend the Lesson**—Have the students make a list of common adolescent behaviors—both positive and negative. How do these different adolescent behaviors relate to one's own self-concept?

The first step in making positive decisions concerning your life is to develop a positive image of yourself. Everything else, including the choices you will make, flows from that image. In this chapter, you will investigate how this image develops, the importance of having a positive image, and a few simple steps that you can take to improve your *self-esteem*.

Recognizing Your Gifts

You have probably had the experience of being rejected. You were not invited to a big party, or did not make the final cut in the school play. You may have been embarrassed in front of friends or classmates. What was the result of these feelings and events?

Every experience of rejection affects what you think about yourself. For many people, these experiences of rejection date back to early childhood. These memories can remain painful for years, leaving lasting scars on a person's "self-worth."

Amanda was laughed at in the second grade when she read aloud because she stumbled over the words. As a senior, she still dislikes reading aloud in public. Her friends think she would be perfect for a part in the class play, but she doesn't want to be laughed at again.

People who are criticized or told that they are no good at something will often take these opinions as if they were God's truth. They may hesitate risking that specific activity again for fear of being criticized. After all, why should they try when their failure has already been predicted?

People with a positive sense of their worth expect success. They can't wait to participate in a new or challenging activity. A high school chess team with a winning tradition expects to win, even against a superior opponent. A team with a losing tradition often expects to lose, even to weaker opponents. Attitude and a person's, or team's, *self-concept* have a powerful influence on how well gifts and talents are used.

Self-concept refers to what you think about yourself. It is concerned with what you believe to be the truth about who you are and the gifts and talents you have. Your self-concept determines whether or not you like what you see when you look in the mirror. When you like who you are, you have self-esteem.

Self-esteem is vital if you are to be successful at your career or vocation. If you feel good about yourself, life is a big adventure. New experiences are challenging and stimulating. Meeting new people is enjoyable. However, if you have a poor image of yourself, every day can seem never-ending and filled with dangers; each new experience another opportunity to fail.

For people who feel good about themselves, life is a big adventure.

Journal Assignment

Ask: "What are six things you like about yourself and six things you like about a friend? Which list is more difficult to write?"

Rating Your Self-Esteem

You can find out how much you value yourself by taking a closer look at your behavior. Thoughts and words are important, but the best way for you to analyze your self-esteem is to look at your actions. Read the lists below. Ask yourself if these characteristics describe how you feel most of the time.

Feeling Comfortable about Myself
- I can express personal thoughts and feelings to others.
- I can express my emotions in an appropriate fashion and am not overcome or immobilized by them.
- I can cope with both disappointment and success.
- I am growing in my ability to recognize personal shortcomings.
- I can usually laugh at myself.
- I am often optimistic.
- I am generally cheerful and active.
- I know my limits as well as my abilities.
- I try to live by a set of standards and know what is important to me.
- I usually like who I am.

Feeling Right about Other People
- I occasionally enjoy spending time alone.
- I usually get along well with others.
- I can interact with people and work with a group.
- I continue to participate when I do not get my way.
- I try not to dominate conversations.
- I can accept differences in other people.
- I like being part of a group.
- I am interested in and enjoy being with others.
- I have several satisfying personal relationships.

Meeting the Demands of Life
- I attempt to face my problems rather than avoid them.
- I can ask for help when I need it.
- I usually do not make excuses for my actions.
- I try to set realistic personal goals and have a plan for working toward them.
- I try to give my best effort in whatever I do.
- I can usually cope with change.
- I generally see challenges and experiences as opportunities for growth.

Think more about the statements that *do not* describe your behavior. Can you come up with a plan to help you improve in these particular areas?

Who Do You Think You Are?

Lesson Overview

Many people and things influence our sense of self-worth. These influences begin from the time we are born. Through nonverbal and verbal communication, an infant receives the foundation of his or her developing self-image. Encourage the students to think of the many influences that have shaped their lives in both positive and negative ways.

Teaching Approaches

- Ask: "Were you ever compared unfavorably to a brother, sister, or friend? How did the comparison make you feel? How did it affect your performance?"

- Discuss this statement: "The more affirmation people receive, the greater will be their self-esteem."

- Ask: "What is one personal experience that has caused you to think negatively about yourself? What is one personal experience that has caused you to think positively about yourself?"

- **Reteach**—Discuss how belief in one's self can become a self-fulfilling prophecy. (It's easier to fail when I don't think I can succeed; i.e., the story of "The Little Engine That Could"—"I think I can, I think I can.")

- **Extend the Lesson**—Assign **Application** Project 1 as an individual in-class assignment or for homework.

Who Do You Think You Are?

Have you ever been compared unfavorably to a brother or sister? Or have you ever been asked why you don't do as well in school as some of your friends? That is a common experience. People are often compared to relatives and peers. Sometimes these comparisons are positive ("You're as fine an actor as any student I've ever had!"), but far too often the comparison serves as a put-down.

In the television program, "Beverly Hills 90210," the character of David was originally portrayed as a ninth grader who was in everyone's way. David is actually a talented D.J. and in a later episode gets his chance on the school's radio station. He is a big hit. As his peers compliment him, David's confidence grows. Before long David believes in himself enough to ask a popular girl, Donna, for a date. Before our eyes, David has grown in stature and confidence. He is a different person than he was at the beginning of the series.

In Beverly Hills 90210, as David's confidence grew, so did his self-esteem.

Well Being
Zero to One

Did you know that you have already lived the most important year of your life? It's true. Child development studies show that the most important year of life starts at birth. From birth, infants process information and are formed through that process. Acceptance and love are things that can't be put on hold. They must begin right away or the infant will suffer.

Newborns experience acceptance through four primary actions.

1. Their basic bodily needs must be satisfied. They are fed when hungry, changed when wet, and sleep when tired (up to 18 hours a day).

2. Babies need contact with people to establish the ability to relate to others. This is very important as they form friendships.

3. Babies need to experience motion. Seeing and feeling movement helps babies to know that they are alive.

4. Babies must be held and touched gently. This helps to build a sense of trust, and it helps babies know that they are loved.

It has been shown that children who are not well-fed, nurtured, cuddled, rocked, or hugged have stunted growth and more frequent illness. They also have a harder time making friends and developing a sense of intimacy. That is why the first year is so important—it lays the foundation for all that follows.

Journal Assignment

Have the students write about a situation similar to David's in *Beverly Hills 90210:* How can a person's developing confidence lead to an improved self-esteem?

☾ **Well-Being**

Teaching Approaches
- Encourage the students to share any experiences they have of caring for a baby in its first year of life. Ask: "What patterns of growth and development did you observe?"
- Have a parent of an infant come to class and describe the care an infant requires. Students, with the parent's permission, might help to care for the child.
- Have students care for a baby doll for a week to get the feel of caring for an infant. The baby is to be carried constantly, fed every four hours, and rocked whenever possible.

Your self-concept will affect how well your gifts and talents are used.

What you think and feel about yourself is greatly influenced by what others say about you and how others treat you. This process of formation begins in infancy. When a baby seeks comfort and affirmation (when it cries and wants to be held), it is nonverbally asking the questions: "Am I accepted here? Will you care for my needs? Do you love me?" If the infant's needs are met with acceptance, love, and care, self-esteem begins to develop. Infants can also receive the message that they are not loved.

As the infant grows to the toddler stage, a new question is added, "What do you think of me?" From the parent's response (verbal and nonverbal), the child will learn: "You are a good boy or you are a bad boy. You are a naughty girl or you are a nice girl." Whether intentional or not, these messages are continuously sent by adults and older children, and continuously heard and processed by the child.

While these questions are being received and processed throughout life, the building blocks (or foundation) for one's self-image are laid early. And although a person's self-image changes and matures throughout life, this early foundation

will always remain. Generally speaking, the more affirmation people receive, the greater will be their self-esteem.

Ongoing negative experiences can permanently damage a person's sense of personal value. A person who hears repeatedly that he or she is stupid or worthless will begin to conform to those comments. The person forms a negative cycle of thinking that is difficult to break.

We have a strong need to know that our gifts and talents are recognized and that we are considered good and valuable. Every human being needs to feel worthwhile, that he or she can make important contributions to the world. We need positive reinforcement that we can do something well if we are to grow. Affirmation helps build self-esteem.

Experiences shape who we are, as well as influence how we react to and interpret other experiences. Experiences showcase our talents and help us achieve personal goals. They help to distinguish us as individuals from the group. While positive experiences can increase our self-esteem, negative experiences can leave us wounded or doubting ourselves, and produce low self-esteem.

Background

Parents can stimulate a child's senses at a very young age so that the child becomes more keenly aware of the surrounding environment. Bright colors stimulate eye development, soft music encourages talking and singing, and interesting noises stimulate curiosity. Objects with a variety of textures help a child develop a sense of touch. Being held and cuddled communicates love and acceptance.

Talk It Over

For Question 1, the students may choose to share something they have written in their journals about a positive or negative experience. For Question 2, ask the students how the reactions of others to their special skills influenced how they feel about themselves. You may wish to suggest that they role play a debate between two students who are deciding whether or not to study abroad. Have the other students comment on the characterizations of each person's role.

The Benefits of a Positive Self-Concept

Lesson Overview

How can having a positive self-concept benefit a person during adolescence? A focus of the lesson is to point out the importance of continuing to develop one's self-concept.

Teaching Approaches

- Begin with the debate proposed in **Application** Project 3: "One's self-concept improves with age."
- **Reteach**—Ask: "Why do you think the most successful adults are the ones with the highest self-concept?"
- **Extend the Lesson**—Ask the students to finish this sentence: "If I had more or better self-esteem, one new thing I would like to try is . . ."

> ### ⚠ Sharpening Your Skills
>
> **Teaching Approaches**
> - Have students complete the exercise.
> - Students may develop posters of their mottoes to display around the classroom or throughout the school.

Talk It Over

1. Tell about an experience that has changed your self-concept for better or worse.
2. What is a special skill you possess that makes a positive difference in how you think about yourself?
3. What are some additional comments that can either build up or tear down a person's self-esteem?

Do you have a personal motto that affirms your life?

The Benefits of a Positive Self-Concept

You might be willing to concede that your self-concept has been affected by both good and bad experiences. But what does it matter? You've made it this far. What difference will it make now if you develop a more positive self-concept?

In fact, developing a positive self-concept (or self-esteem) is very important at any stage in your life. People with high self-esteem compete to get into the best colleges or work at the best companies. People who believe in their own goodness seek friendships and dates with people who also value themselves. People with self-esteem continue to grow and to accept new challenges in their relationships with others with each new experience.

Loving Yourself

Randy, an old man from the retirement home, came to daily Mass but never received communion. One day, in passing, Father Bob asked Randy why he never received the Eucharist.

"I haven't been to confession in 35 years," Randy said.

"Well let's take care of that right now," Father Bob said, leading Randy into the Reconciliation room.

> ### ◆ Sharpening Your Skills
> **Personal Mottoes**
>
>
>
> Avis, the car rental company, uses the slogan, "We try harder." This phrase is a commercial device used to convince customers that they will get better service at Avis than at any other car rental company. But it's also the motto of the company. Employees are expected to go out of their way to satisfy customers. The motto reminds them of what they hope to accomplish and encourages them to meet their goals.
>
> Write one or two positive and affirming "mottoes" for your life. Here are two well-known life mottoes:
> 1. Winners never quit and quitters never win.
> 2. I never met a person I didn't like.
>
> If you wish, share your life motto with a friend or family member. Explain why this motto is important to you.

Background

Self-concept is probably the single most important factor influencing what a person does and how he or she does it. Self-concept is directly related to people's general level of wellness. How people feel physically, as well as how they take care of themselves, are both affected by their self-concept.

A week passed and while Randy was again present at Mass daily, he still did not receive the Eucharist. Father Bob cornered Randy one day: "Randy, what's keeping you from the Lord's Table? You have received absolution. Your sins are forgiven."

Randy spoke matter-of-factly. "I know God has forgiven my sins. I believe that with all my heart. But I cannot believe that God has forgotten what I did. I cannot believe that God likes me for who I was, and who I am."

Father Bob looked thoughtfully at Randy, collected himself for a minute, then responded, "Randy, you give yourself too much credit! Do you think God's love for you is based on anything you did or did not do? Do you think you can do anything at all to win God's approval?"

A Difficult Challenge

Loving oneself can be a difficult challenge. There are so many critics out there! A teacher writes a big, red "C" on a journal entry where you've expressed your most personal feelings. You might as well sew it to the front of your sweatshirt (like in *The Scarlet Letter*)! Your father cringes when you tell him you called the automobile service to change a flat tire on the car. What he says is, "You mean you couldn't do something as simple as that yourself?" What you hear is, "My incompetent child, the failure!" Your best friend meets you on the way to school and immediately comments on your new hairstyle. "Why did you change it? I liked your hair the way it was." Even from your closest friends you experience rejection.

Unfortunately, as the story of Randy reminds us, no matter how critical someone else is about us, they are never as harsh as we can be on ourselves. We are our own worst critics. There seems to be a belittling voice inside of everyone that picks up on the littlest and silliest things and turns

them into major flaws. You may be convinced by the voice that everyone you meet looks only at the pimple on your chin, or, that you can't possibly be good at basketball because you don't have the right brand of shoes.

As difficult as it may be to believe, God loves you as you are, flaws and all. As you grow in your understanding of God's kingdom, you may be increasingly surprised about how much God really does care and love you.

Talk It Over

1. What is one "unattainable" goal you have that would be more attainable with an improved image of yourself?
2. In what ways are you your own worst critic?
3. Have you ever felt it was necessary for you to "please God"? Explain.

Rejection of your best work is always hard to take. How do you respond to rejection?

❋ Media Watch

Teaching Approaches

- Read or summarize the information presented in the panel.
- Assign **Application** Project 7. If possible, arrange for a panel of younger students to come to the class to answer your students' queries.
- As an assignment, have the students watch a dramatic television program and identify the problem or conflict presented in the opening segment. While watching the program, have the students write down the problem. They should speculate on the solution as well. At the end of the program, have them compare their guessed solution with the one actually presented.

II. IMPROVING YOUR SELF-ESTEEM

Aims

1. To help students practice ways to improve their self-esteem.
2. To help students appreciate the part that God plays in their lives.

Begin the Section

1. Have the students brainstorm what they would like to change about school. Then, ask: "Which things do you have control over? Which things do you not control? Why would it be wise to pay foremost attention to those things that you are able to control?"
2. Ask: "Why would a person not want to take the necessary steps to feel better about him or herself?"
3. Summarize by reading the introductory paragraphs.

❋ Media Watch
The Role of Television

How big a role does television play in your life? Are you able to control how much TV you watch? What would your life be like without TV?

Television is watched regularly by 90 million households in the United States, double the number from 1960! In 1989, average households watched *seven hours* of television a day. Even if you watch little television, the images presented on entertainment programs can have a great influence on you. Most of the styles, words, and behaviors that are popular today have their origins in television.

One message television promotes is that every conflict or problem can be resolved neatly by the end of a half-hour or hour program. Is that realistic? Can you solve your problems so quickly? For most people, life is a little more complex than that.

Family relationships on television are seldom portrayed accurately. Brothers and sisters seem to get along perfectly, even when they criticize and ridicule each other. Characters don't hold grudges or get angry when a kid brother or sister ruins a favorite sweater or breaks a prized CD player. Conflict between siblings or parents is resolved quickly, without any lasting consequences. How would you expect realistic problems to be resolved? What long-range consequences would you expect from a family conflict?

Realistic family arguments cannot be presented, or resolved simplistically. Complex issues cannot be adequately addressed in only 24 minutes! No wonder family relationships seem so lacking by comparison.

Violence—including ridicule and verbal abuse—is prevalent on television.

During prime time (usually between 8 and 11 pm, Monday through Friday), an average of five to six acts of violence happen during an hour. On Saturday morning cartoons, that number rises to 26.4 per hour! Do you think that TV violence leads people to violent acts or makes them insensitive to personal or social violence? shapes and molds people's personal values? Researcher Nancy Signorielli of the University of Delaware believes that it does: "Television's mean and dangerous world cultivates a sense of insecurity, vulnerability and mistrust—despite its supposedly 'entertaining' nature" *(Media and Values, Number 52-53).*

As you watch television during the next week, note in your media diary each act of violence you see. Make special note of the show and the time of day. List also how families behave toward each other and the way they resolve conflict. Consider how TV families differ from your family.

Journal Assignment

Have the students decide what they would do with their time if they did not watch television. Ask the students to write a schedule for each night of the week of what they would do instead of watching T.V.

Resources

Resource 2C accompanies the "Media Watch" feature.

II. IMPROVING YOUR SELF-ESTEEM

You might think that the desire to improve oneself would be universal. Who wouldn't want to feel better about himself or herself? In fact, those most in need of improving a poor self-concept are those least likely to try. For people with little self-esteem, any new experience or change is very threatening; any challenge has the potential for renewed failure.

Feeling poorly about oneself does not have to be permanent, however. There are things that you can do to improve your self-esteem.

Everybody is good at something. Sharing a hobby with a friend can help build your self-esteem.

Steps in the Process

You can begin to improve your self-esteem by paying attention to a few simple matters.

1. Recognize that there are some things you can control and some things you can't. Work on those areas over which you exercise some control: your habits, personal behavior, schoolwork, and a positive attitude.

2. Try to ignore those things outside of your control: other people's comments and your past mistakes are two examples. Also, keep track of changes you are making in a chart or journal.

3. Praise yourself when you have done things well. Identify concrete ways to improve when possible.

4. Every few weeks review your progress. Reflect on how these simple steps help you to improve your self-esteem.

5. Look for people to support your efforts with positive reinforcement. Share your love for a particular hobby with someone who thinks what you do is important. Look for positive reinforcement from people you trust.

Learn from your successes and gradually build upon them. Things you do well are opportunities for success. Do you like to sew or knit? Then take on a challenging project that you can accomplish.

Steps in the Process

Lesson Overview

What are some practical steps a person can take in improving his or her self-concept? This lesson provides some suggested answers to this question, including ways to improve one's relationships with others. Encourage the students to add some of their own ideas for building self-concept.

Teaching Approaches

- Have students identify one thing that they would like to improve about themselves.

- Write what they would like to accomplish during the first week of their improvement schedule. For example, a person who would like to begin exercising might make it his or her goal to run one lap around the football field after one week.

- **Reteach**—Have students record daily entries on a chart or in their journals on how they went about working to attain their goal.

- **Extend the Lesson**—After a week, have the students share their impressions of the activity. Ask: "When did you find it most difficult to ignore other people's comments about your goal? Who supported you in your efforts? How did you feel when you were successful? How did you feel when you had a setback? In what direction do you see yourself going in this area in the future?"

Journal Assignment

Have the students comment on one piece of advice offered in this section. For example, "Praise yourself when you have done well." Or, "Look for positive reinforcement from people you trust." Ask the students to write why they do or do not agree with that advice.

In Focus

Teaching Approaches

- For Project 2, have the students record their findings in a scientific data format.
- Project 3 may be completed in class. Assign students to groups of five or six. Remind them to make their letters positive and specific and to sign their names to each. Tell students that you will investigate any letters that do not meet these criteria.
- Reserve class time for the students to share the results of their projects.

Relationship with Parents

Teaching Approaches

- Ask the students if they have ever felt that they were becoming just like one of their parents.
- Encourage volunteers to share ways that they have successfully improved their relationship with their parents.
- **Reteach**—Discuss the following tips for improving family communications: (1) **Communicate often.** Take the time to share thoughts, feelings, hopes, and fears with family members, and listen to them as well; (2) **Communicate with respect.** Don't use sarcastic replies; (3) **Back up your words with actions.** If you promise to honor a later curfew, then make sure that you do.
- **Extend the Lesson**—Relationships between parents and children are constantly changing. Have the students write or share what they thought of their parents five years ago, what they think about them now, and how they expect to think about them in five years.

In Focus
Building Relationships

Here are three activities that may provide insight and help as you work to improve your self-esteem:

1. **Start a journal.** Try faithfully to schedule time each day for writing. Write for yourself and not for others. Keep in mind that this journal does not have to be read by anyone else. Write how your experiences and the people you meet each day touch your life. Note the high and low points of your day. Examine why you react to situations the way you do. You may write chronologically—that is, from the time you wake up until the time you go to bed at night—or you may wish to write according to themes. Write about parents, siblings, friends, teachers, and "enemies," too! Keeping a journal is a safe way to express anger or love. It's a means to sort things out so that they make more sense.

2. **Do research.** With a partner, plan to say "hi" during the course of a day to five people with whom you never talk. Also, don't greet or say "hi" to five people with whom you usually do talk. Note the reactions of both groups of people. Compare your findings with those of your partner. Write a conclusion to this experiment.

3. **Form a support group.** Join with a group of five or six of your classmates. Write a letter to each person in your group praising their positive characteristics and telling them what you admire about them. Remember to be specific. After you check to make sure that everyone has completed one letter for every person, exchange them and read them in private. Be ready for a boost in your self-esteem!

When you finish, you will have something to show for your efforts that says, "Look what I can do!" If you like to tinker with mechanical things there are many projects that you can build to show your prowess. If you are unsure of your abilities, check out ready-to-make kits, available for many hobbies, that walk you to a successful conclusion.

Expect the results of these changes to be slow; learn to be patient. Establish simple goals and rejoice in the small, noticeable steps of improvement you see. It takes perseverance in order to change.

Relationship with Parents

Your relationship with the person who raised you—usually a mother or father—is directly related to how you feel about yourself. At this time in your life, parents may seem to be the source of never-ending tensions and conflicts. You know you love your mom and dad. You appreciate the care they provide, yet you wonder why you seem to be so often at each other's throats. Sometimes you might even fear that you are becoming just like one of your parents.

◊ Tom, a high school senior, favored a local candidate for Congress who spoke out strongly on protecting the environment, an issue that was very important to Tom. Tom's mom supported an opposing candidate in the election. Tom and his mom argued their points for weeks. Then one day Tom found himself in an election debate in his Government class at school. After both sides were presented, Tom began to cite point after point that he had heard from his mother. "Yikes," Tom thought. "I'm becoming just like her."

Resources

Resource 2D from the Teacher's Resource Book provides a list of suggestions to assist the students with journal writing.

Background

While parents have an obligation to care for their children, children, in turn, contribute to their parents' growth in holiness. (See *Catechism of the Catholic Church*, 2224-2228.)

Tom recognized just how much influence his mother had on his life, regardless of their differing politics.

Do you ever find yourself acting or sounding like your parents? Is that a problem for you? To some degree, we are all shaped by the thoughts and actions of our parents or the people who raised us. For some people that is a cause of concern. Their relationships with their parents are not very positive. They may have been mistreated or simply feel that "mom and dad don't understand me." Many children are well into adulthood before they achieve a good and comfortable relationship with their parents.

Gaining an improved sense of self will help you in your relationship with your parents. You will be more open to learn from them and recognize their comments as evidence of their concern for you. Instead of rejecting everything your parents say just because they said it, you will be able to choose wisely from their teaching. Being comfortable about who you are in relationship to your mom or dad is a big help in being more comfortable about yourself.

▲ Family Living
They Always Remember

Do you ever feel that your parents don't understand you? Do you feel like your family still treats you as if you were in grammar school? Well, if you do, you're not alone. Many adults have similar feelings.

One teacher, a family therapist, confessed that he hated to attend family reunions. When pressed on the subject he explained: "I'm 45, with a doctorate in psychology. I'm married and my children are almost grown. Yet, as soon as I get together with other family members, all of that is forgotten. I consider myself a competent adult, yet it seems they think of me as if I were still 15! I'm very comfortable with who I am now, but they haven't shared my experiences. All they have to go on is the kid who fell in the lake trying to board a canoe 30 years ago. I tell myself I won't let that bother me, but it always does. So I just don't go anymore. I refuse to take the abuse!"

Does it surprise you that other people have this feeling? Why do you think this happens? What can you do to change your family's attitudes? What can you do to cope with their images of you?

▲ Family Living

Teaching Approaches
- Read the feature aloud. Have students answer the questions and discuss the merits of the family therapist's comments.
- Discuss with students how they would respond to the situation presented in the feature.

Background

Men and women between the ages of thirty-five and forty-five have reached a unique position; they are the authorities to those people younger and older than themselves. At the same time, they often feel for the first time the limits of their life and that they may not accomplish all that they had first dreamed of accomplishing. This period of life is at once very powerful and very precarious.

The Need for Support

Teaching Approaches

- Ask for volunteers to role play two scenes from this story: (1) Marcia interacting with her junior varsity teammates, and (2) Marcia being shunned by her varsity teammates.

- Ask: "How have supportive groups helped your self-image to flourish? How have other groups contributed to limiting your self-image?"

- **Reteach**—Read and discuss the text of Jesus' rejection at Nazareth from Matthew 13:54-58. Have students ever experienced rejection similar to that of Jesus?

- **Extend the Lesson**—Complete **Application** Project 5. Then, have the students compare Marcia from the story with their descriptions of people who have and those who lack self-esteem.

✠ To Your Health

Teaching Approaches

- Ask the students to offer specific examples to illustrate the meaning of the old saying, "I am not what I think I am; I am not what you think I am; I am what I think you think I am."

- Have students develop a new statement that expresses a more positive concept.

The Need for Support

Marcia was a sophomore sensation on the junior varsity basketball team. Her specialty was shooting three-pointers. When the game was on the line, her teammates made sure she had her hands on the ball. They believed in Marcia. She believed in herself. Marcia always came through. The team was a winner.

Midway through the season, Marcia was called up to play on the varsity team. Marcia was a shy person who didn't particularly enjoy new experiences. She wanted to stay on the junior varsity with her friends. Nevertheless, she went along with the coach's wishes.

Marcia's game suffered on the varsity. She didn't feel accepted by the older girls and so she didn't feel very comfortable. She played poorly. Before the end of the season, the coach sent her back to the junior varsity.

✠ To Your Health
I Am, I Think

There is an old saying that goes: "I am not what I think I am; I am not what you think I am; I am what I think you think I am." What does this mean? Do you agree? disagree? How would this saying affect how you feel about yourself?

This story points to the human need to belong. People need encouragement from others. We need to feel like we belong and are a valued member of a group. People are social; we need to love and be loved by others. We need to know that people believe in us and the things that we can do.

One solution to this need is to join and be a part of groups that support us. Marcia played better basketball around teammates who encouraged her and believed in her abilities. You may have a well-developed talent or skill. You may like to dress in a certain style of clothing or like a particular kind of music. If you are with people who like you and treat you well, your self-image is more likely to flourish.

The Gospel recounts an experience Jesus had when he was not accepted. Jesus had traveled throughout Galilee preaching and healing those who were sick. When He returned to His hometown of Nazareth, He began to teach. While Jesus had been welcomed all over by friendly crowds, in Nazareth people took offense: "Isn't this the carpenter, the son of Mary?" they said. "Who does he think he is?"

Jesus was amazed by their lack of faith and was not able to perform any mighty deeds there *(see Matthew 13:54-58)*. Why do you think Jesus was treated so poorly in His own town? Why do you think He couldn't perform any mighty deeds in Nazareth?

Jesus was not respected by the people who *thought* they knew Him. They were not open to this older Jesus. All they could see was the child who grew up with their children.

Respect is essential in relationships if self-esteem is to develop. When you treat people with respect you are saying that they are of great value. When you show lack of respect you are saying that people are worth little.

A frequent cause of parent-teen confrontations is the failure of both parties to show respect to the other, each taking the other for granted. Parents may fail to notice the person their child has become, just as teens may fail to understand the loving motives behind a parent's actions. Because of this, the other person's unique identity is lost: "She's just mom," or "She's just my daughter, I don't have to treat *her* special."

One way to overcome this difficulty is to treat everyone you meet with the dignity and respect you would show if he or she were the messenger of God. Not only will your behavior positively affect the other's self-esteem, but also you will see improvements in yourself, too.

Background

Jesus compared the people's lack of faith in Nazareth to previous Hebrew prophets who the people rejected. This rejection by His townspeople foreshadowed the eventual rejection of Jesus by the Jewish nation. In Mark's Gospel account, Jesus' power could not take effect without the cooperation of a person's faith.

Talk It Over

1. How are you like your parents? What are you presently doing to establish an identity separate from theirs?
2. How do you act differently with someone you're trying to impress than with someone with whom you're very familiar?
3. What effect do non-supportive groups have on your attitude or self-esteem?

Internal Messages

Each day you give yourself thousands of messages. This "self-talk" is like a 24-hour radio station constantly blasting news, conversation, commentary, and other information your way. During the day, this steady stream of information influences your activities. At night, these conversations are transformed into dreams.

Research has indicated that these internal messages are formed from personal experiences. All of the information you have ever received—good and bad—is replayed over and over again, frequently with editorial comments added! That is, what is remembered is not what actually happened, but what we believe happened or what we feel should have happened. Sometimes these internal conversations can be friendly and supportive, while at other times they can be destructive.

Negative internal conversations can take many forms. While admiring an attractive guy or girl you hear: "She's too popular for you" or "You'd never stand a chance with him." Prior to class registration you hear, "Don't even think about taking pre-calculus. You had trouble with geometry. You'll fail in a minute."

In moderation, *negative self-talk* can serve as a reality check for us. Doubting whether you can beat a railroad train at a crossing is a survival mechanism, not a voice intent on destroying your self-esteem. It causes you to consider the wisdom

It's one thing to doubt the wisdom of a dangerous decision and quite another to doubt your basic goodness and ability.

Talk It Over

Discuss all three questions in small groups. Encourage the students to give specific examples to support each of their answers. Call on volunteers to share with the entire class general comments based on their small group discussions.

Internal Messages

Lesson Overview

There is no doubt that the person with the greatest influence on who we are, and who we are to become, is ourselves. This lesson looks at the positive and negative implications of "self-talk," the internal messages that we shower ourselves with day and night, and ways to use self-talk to our greatest advantage. This section further develops some ideas presented in Chapter 1.

New Words

Internal messages refer to communication between our unconscious and conscious minds.

Teaching Approaches

- Ask the students to compare these two kinds of internal messages: (1) "I won't ask her to the dance because she will say no;" (2) "I didn't get an 'A' on the report, but I know I tried my best."
- Read or summarize the entire section.
- Ask: "What kind of messages do you give yourself? Are your internal messages generally positive or negative?"
- Have the students suggest several negative self-talk messages. Then, have them restate them in a positive way.
- **Reteach**—Assign **Application** Project 6. Have the students report on their results.
- **Extend the Lesson**—Have the students research and report on the effect sleep and dreams have on creating a positive self-image.

Background

The mind operates on many levels. Every detail is recorded in a person's unconscious mind. The unconscious mind provides a source bank for internal messages and dreams.

Resources

Resource 2E provides more information on dreams and their effect on people's lives.

🙵 Prayer in Action

Teaching Approaches

- Explain to students that Jesus' Good Shepherd discourse is a follow-up to the story of the man born blind *(John 9).* The hired hands are the Pharisees who show no compassion for the cured blind man. In contrast, Jesus, the Good Shepherd, will lay down His life for His people.
- Discuss how we are all blind at times to God's gifts.
- Have the students write their response to the reflection question found in "Prayer in Action."

Talk It Over

Assign the questions for small group discussion. Have group leaders summarize and share some of the group's techniques to use internal messages (Question 2).

🙵 Prayer in Action
Live More Abundantly

Jesus' declaration, "I came so that they might have life and have it more abundantly," is a part of the Good Shepherd text in John 10:1-21. Read the entire section from Scripture. Then, reflect on this question: How do I feel when I give of myself to others like the Good Shepherd?

of an act before you do it. We need some negative feedback to keep us honest, otherwise we go to the opposite extreme: *narcissism,* an exaggerated love of oneself where there is not room for anything or anyone else.

People who have a reputation as being too "big headed" or "stuck up" may have an over-inflated self-concept. They are unwilling to accept criticism or to see the need for personal growth or change. They have created a "personal fable" or a web of deceit around themselves. These people need to learn how to accept the truth, both from themselves and others.

Learning how to distinguish negative self-talk from necessary reality checks is the first step in benefiting from internal messages. Pause, and consider the message that just crossed your mind. Is it a message that will keep you out of trouble or is it a put-down? Make an effort to restate the message in a positive way. For example, "Yes, I had trouble with geometry. But I know I can do better. I don't have an after-school job now, so I'll have more time to study." Giving yourself positive messages will improve your self-esteem.

Talk It Over

1. Make a list of the negative self-talk you hear, or negative comments from your friends. Note which of the statements can be considered reality checks. Discuss your findings.
2. What makes self-talk healthy or unhealthy? What personal techniques do you have for addressing internal messages?
3. What is meant by the term "personal fable"? How common are personal fables among young adults?

How do you hide your treasures?

Background

Saint Paul highlighted God's neverending love for creation: "If God is for us, who is against us? For I am certain that neither death, nor life, nor angels, nor principalities, nor things present, nor things to come, nor powers, nor height, nor depth, nor anything else in all creation will be able to separate us from the love of God in Christ Jesus our Lord" *(Romans 8:31, 38-39).*

Hidden Treasure

An old beggar woman wandered through the town each evening after dusk. Clink. The man on the park bench would drop a coin on the weathered plate. Clink. The woman from the large apartment house would stop to drop another coin. Sometimes the men playing basketball would go through the pockets of their sweatsuits to give her money: Clink. Clink. It was a difficult life.

The days and nights finally got to the beggar. She became ill and was taken to the county hospital where she died of pneumonia. Her body was buried, and her belongings were to be thrown away when the county worker in charge of estate auctions began to rub on the filthy plate that the woman had used for begging. It wasn't long before the worker knew what he held in his hand: this plate was made of gold worth thousands of dollars. The poor lady, the worker thought. Her life could have been so different.

The beggar woman didn't realize the value of what she had. She couldn't see the gold for all of the grime. Some people have the same problem; they can't recognize their worth because of the "grime" of a bad attitude, bad complexion, or low self-esteem.

You were made in the image of the Creator of the Universe, more precious than the most expensive gold. Yet, how many layers of junk and crud do you have piled on top of your self-concept?

You carry within yourself the truth of your goodness. You may occasionally doubt that you are lovable, wonder about your self-esteem, and even develop a negative self-concept. This certainly isn't the life God intended for you.

What can you do to strip away the layers of doubt, shame, guilt, lack of confidence, and other emotional baggage that prevent you from being the person that God intended?

First, continue working on the positive self-concept techniques that have been presented in this chapter. Until you like yourself for who you are, your life will hardly be life-giving and productive.

Second, try to incorporate Christ into your daily life. This may sound too pious or even impossible, but actually living as Jesus did is the best way that you, as a baptized Christian, can live. When you need a friend, look for Jesus in the Scriptures, in prayer, at Eucharist, and in people you trust. Be in tune to the ways that Jesus speaks to you. Take notice and give thanks for the graces that Jesus brings to your life.

Living is the best of gifts. Your very being cries out for each sustaining breath. It is a gift that will carry you into the eternity of God's kingdom where all joy will be yours, and your joy will be complete!

Talk It Over

1. In what ways can you incorporate Christ into your daily life?
2. How would you compare the way the beggar used her hidden treasure with the way you use your talents and gifts?

Chapter Summary

- A healthy self-concept is vital to successful, productive living.
- Self-esteem forms from the earliest years of life.
- Experiences, positive or negative, will alter self-esteem.
- Encouragement from others helps to build a positive self-concept.
- Loving oneself is an important, yet difficult, challenge.
- Self-talk—both positive and negative—influences self-esteem.

Journal Assignment

Say: "Write about one of your gifts that has been present from the beginning, and one that has recently developed."

Hidden Treasure

Lesson Overview

Convincing someone else of their preciousness in the eyes of God is a difficult task. The story in this lesson illustrates that people tend to pile on layers of negativity that can cause them to forget their true goodness. The lesson reminds students of the importance of continuing to work at the positive self-concept techniques presented in this chapter.

Teaching Approaches

- Ask the students to comment on the meaning of this statement: "When you love yourself, you are most real." Have them give specific examples to back up their comments.
- Help the students make the connection between the beggar's hidden gift and the hidden gifts that they mentioned for themselves.
- **Reteach**—Have volunteers share ways they have found a friend in Jesus in the Scriptures, in prayer, at Eucharist, and in people they trust.
- **Extend the Lesson**—Have the students write down five of their own "unique characteristics." Then, ask them to share the lists with a partner. Say: "Cross out any characteristics that are common on both lists." Have the students repeat the process with a number of partners using the same list. At the end of the exercise, the students may have truly discovered one or two unique characteristics.

Talk It Over

For Question 1, have the class brainstorm ideas. For Question 2, ask the students to consider similarities and differences between themselves and the beggar.

Chapter Summary

- This section lists the main points of summary of this chapter. To use as a review, you might have the students list examples from the text to illustrate each point, rewrite each point in their own words, or find creative ways to teach each point.
- Have the students share their review techniques with a partner.

Chapter 2 Review

What Have You Learned?

Listed below are suggested answers. For many of the questions, the answers will vary.

1. One's self-concept is formed in a number of ways. For example, a young child is affirmed both verbally and nonverbally by parents and care-givers. These affirmations result in the forming of a positive self-concept.

2. Recognizing an individual's special talents and gifts is one way to improve a person's self-concept once he or she has reached school age.

3. People with positive self-concepts seek the best for their lives. They continue to accept new challenges in their relationships with each new experience.

4. People have control over areas like personal habits and behavior, school work, and maintaining a positive attitude. They do not have control over things like other people's comments and their own past mistakes.

5. Relationships with one's parents are based on how the person feels about him or herself. If a person lacks self-esteem, the parental relationship may be the source of conflict.

6. As with Jesus in Nazareth, people are often not able to reach their full potential until they experience the love and acceptance of others.

7. Self-talk is the stream of messages that people give to themselves during all hours of the day and night. Negative self-talk can be beneficial when serving as a reality check. It can keep us from becoming narcissistic. At the other extreme, negative self-talk can constantly criticize everything a person does or tries to achieve.

8. Jesus means that we have been chosen to live the life of Children of God. We are meant to love ourselves for the great gift of life that God has bestowed upon us.

9. For example, the violence portrayed on television may lead people to commit violent acts or make them insensitive to personal or social violence.

10. The first year of life lays the foundation for all that is to come. Acceptance and love experienced in the first year allow

a person to develop a sense of intimacy that will be necessary and beneficial in forming relationships later. Fortunately, if one's first year lacks essential love, it can be added in the years that follow.

11. Negative messages, either from others or

REVIEW

What Have You Learned?

1. What are some of the ways one's self-concept is formed?
2. What are some ways to improve one's self-concept?
3. Why is having a positive self-concept important?
4. What are some things people can control to improve their self-esteem? What is something over which they have little or no control?
5. What is a cause of many problems between parents and youth?
6. What does the story of Jesus' return to his hometown of Nazareth say about the need for the love and acceptance of others?
7. What is self-talk? Explain the problems and benefits of negative self-talk.
8. What did Jesus mean when he said, "I have come so that you might have life and have it more abundantly" *(John 10:10)*?
9. How does TV influence popular culture?
10. Why is the first year of life so important?
11. How can negative comments affect one's self-esteem?
12. What can you do to improve your self-esteem?

Application

1. You have many good qualities. But are you aware of them? Knowing your good qualities increases the healthy love for yourself that you need. Make a list of your good qualities. Keep it in your wallet or purse. Read it whenever you need a reminder.
2. Make a list or role-play with a partner a series of general criticisms and put-downs that are common among people your age. The longer the list, the more silly they should sound.
3. Debate this statement with a friend or in a small group: "One's self-concept improves with age."
4. Develop an advertising campaign to combat low self-esteem. Write public service announcements, ads, or television and radio commercials directed at teens with negative self-concepts.
5. In small groups design a person with positive self-esteem. What attributes would this person have? How would he or she look, act, perform? Describe this person's relationship with teachers and parents. What would this person do to maintain his or her self-esteem? Explain whether this person would be someone that people would want as a friend? Answer the same questions for a person who lacks self-esteem.
6. Keep a notepad with you. Record both positive and negative insights or self-talk for one week.
7. Identify the influence that TV has over younger children. Talk to at least five children under the age of six. What are their favorite shows? How often do they watch them? What attracts them to these programs? Present your findings to the class.

from oneself, can destroy a person's confidence and adversely affect a person's self-esteem.

12. One's self-esteem can be improved by positive self-talk and by succeeding in small projects.

REVIEW

Chapter Vocabulary

- self-concept
- self-esteem
- critic
- experiences
- acceptance
- internal messages
- respect
- narcissism

Putting Vocabulary to Use

Identify the characteristics below with the most appropriate word or term from the Chapter Vocabulary list.

_____ **1.** Formed from personal experiences.

_____ **2.** Often, you might be most severe on yourself in this role.

_____ **3.** A positive one benefits you at any age, especially now.

_____ **4.** Valuing people.

_____ **5.** Any new experience may be threatening to a person if this is low.

_____ **6.** The story of Jesus' return to Nazareth points out the need for this.

_____ **7.** An exaggerated love of oneself.

_____ **8.** A person with a positive self-concept will likely welcome a variety of these.

Since we are all created of the same substance, which has a beginning but no end, we may love one another with a single love. For all who know themselves know that they are of one immortal substance.

Saint Anthony of Egypt

Application

Read the directions and descriptions of each project to the students. Allow the students to choose their own project. Suggest the following steps: (1) formulate a plan, (2) complete the tasks, (3) share the initial project with a partner for comments. and (4) revise and finalize the project.

Putting Vocabulary to Use

1. self-esteem
2. critic
3. self-concept
4. God's kingdom
5. respect
6. acceptance
7. narcissism
8. experiences

Final Thought

Background

Saint Anthony of Egypt is known as the founder of monasticism. Born in 251, he left home at age twenty to live alone in various places in southern Egypt. He spent his time in prayer, study, and the manual work necessary to earn his living. Over the years, he attracted many followers to his way of life.

Focus On: Chapter 3

Decision-making is an important part of life. Some of the decisions that we make seem to be done almost by reflex; for example, we habitually decide which route to take to school or the way that we wear our hair. Other decisions have greater implications: whether or not to marry, or the choice of one career over another, for example.

Chapter 3 examines how decision-making affects our lives. What are some of the factors that affect the decisions we make?

1. Family, societal, and Christian values influence our decision-making process. How do we recognize these values?

2. What role does conscience play in making decisions? Chapter 3 introduces a process for using conscience when making a choice.

3. Finally, how can a person decide what God wants? The students will learn a discernment process that will help them discover God's will for them.

Plan Ahead

- Incorporate formal and/or spontaneous prayer into each lesson. A participatory prayer service is provided in the Teacher's Resource Book (TRB).

- Note the **Resources** suggestions in the TRB. These suggestions can be used to teach or extend the lessons of the chapter.

- Preview the **Application** project ideas from the Chapter Review. Refer to **Teaching Approaches** for suggestions on when to assign these projects. The projects may also be used as part of a lesson, section, or chapter review.

- Decide how you will group students for projects and discussions.

Choices for Life

Grace will assist us if we are not presumptuous about our own virtues, if we give thanks for what we already have the power to do, and if we support our prayer with fruitful works of kindness.

Saint Augustine

This chapter will help you to:

- Understand how decision-making affects your life.
- Appreciate the importance of freedom in making good decisions.
- Recognize the sources of personal values and how family, societal, and Christian values can influence decision-making.
- Examine how conscience operates when you make choices.
- Practice discernment as a way to discover God's will for your life.

Media Suggestions (Optional)

- *High Powder* (Paulist Productions). 27 minutes. A boy who braves peer pressure to report a friend who sells drugs pays the price for his actions.

- *Goal Setting* ((Priority One). 20 Minutes. Through the use of magic and humor the viewer learns how to set goals and turn dreams into reality.

Aims

1. To help students understand that decisions made through the course of history shape who they are today.
2. To help students define what is meant by *values*.
3. To help students understand how conscience operates in decision-making.

Begin the Section

1. Have students read the opening quotation from Saint Augustine. Ask: "What is a virtue? What does it mean to be 'presumptuous about our own virtues'?" Accept all answers.
2. Assign three groups to research the background of one of the following: Saint Augustine, Saint Ambrose, or Saint Monica. Ask the groups to report on at least one important decision each saint made in his or her life.
3. Introduce the section by summarizing or reading the first paragraph. Ask students to comment on Augustine's three skills needed to make good decisions.
4. Pray with the students this reflection from Saint Augustine: "Too late have I loved You, O Beauty of ancient days, yet ever new! . . . You were with me, but I was not with You . . . You touched me, and I burned for Your peace."

1. DECISIONS, DECISIONS

Saint Augustine learned the importance of good decision-making the experiential way. As a young adult, he made many reckless decisions and lived more like a playboy than a saint. He turned his back on his mother's Christian values, choosing to follow the prevailing social and political trends. He rejected a life of virtue for one of immediate gratification. Augustine eventually recognized the "error of his ways" due in great part to the prayer of his mother, Saint Monica, to the teaching of Saint Ambrose, and to a personal study of Scripture. In his *Confessions,* Augustine emphasizes the skills needed to make good decisions:

- Know the truth.
- Recognize how a Christian should act.
- Take action accordingly

43

Resources

Resource 3A from the Teacher's Resource Book provides biographical information on Saints Monica, Augustine, and Ambrose.

The Party

Lesson Overview

Making good choices is the main focus of this chapter. This lesson illustrates a choice faced by one high school student. Encourage the students to share similar decisions that they have faced.

Teaching Approaches

- Ask the students if they are familiar with the group "Students Against Drunk Driving." Allow volunteers to share what they know about the organization.

- Assign the story for reading. Have the students make note of the decisions that are made in the story. List the decisions on the board. Add any decisions that you think should be included. Have the students attempt to rank the decisions from most to least important.

- **Reteach**—Have the students do **Application** Project 2 in class. Share some of the stories with the entire group.

- **Extend the Lesson**—Arrange for a S.A.D.D. member to speak with the class and provide information about the organization. Encourage students to look for ways to begin a S.A.D.D. chapter. **Application** Project 1 may be done in conjunction with the S.A.D.D. presentation.

Talk It Over

For Question 3, assign small groups to role play this story or a similar dilemma faced by their own peers. Schedule time for the groups to act out their parts before the entire group. Discuss the activity with the students when the plays are finished.

The Party

Students had been talking about it for days: Jennifer's parents were away for the weekend and a huge party was planned. Jason knew that there would be beer at the party, but since he didn't drink, that wasn't his concern. Jason was going to this party in order to be seen by Michelle.

Jason and Martin could hear music from a block away as they drove up in Martin's car. Martin quickly poured a few beers from a keg and went off to find Jenny. Jason grabbed a beer (so that he wouldn't look out of place) and surveyed the crowd. This was some party.

Jason had a lot of fun. He talked skateboards and hockey most of the evening, met several new friends, and had a chance to speak with Michelle. He'd even pumped the keg in front of her in order to look cool!

As his curfew neared, Jason looked for Martin, who was not to be found. Jason was beginning to worry about making it home on time when Michelle asked if he needed a ride. "That would be great," Jason said, trying to hide his feelings.

Michelle stumbled a bit walking to the car, and then had difficulty finding her keys. Jason knew that she'd had several cups of beer. "Want me to drive?" he asked. "Right," she answered sarcastically. "I'm perfectly capable of driving. I only had two or three beers, and I'm certainly not drunk." She added, "If you want a ride, get in the car because I'm out of here."

Jason knew the dangers of drinking and driving. He'd seen the driver's education films, heard the lectures, and had even signed a S.A.D.D. contract with his parents, promising that he would not drink and drive or ride with anyone who had been drinking. He really didn't know what to do. He didn't want to offend Michelle, whom he liked a lot, but he also didn't want to break his promises.

"I think I'll find another way home," Jason decided, "but thanks anyway. Okay if I call you tomorrow?"

"Forget it," Michelle said as she sped away.

What can you do to prevent friends from drinking and driving?

Talk It Over

1. Identify issues that Jason faced in this story. Which decisions would you find most difficult to make? Why?
2. How would your parents react if you asked them to sign a S.A.D.D. contract?
3. Write or act out a role-play between Jason and one of his parents on the way home from the party.

Resources

Resource 3B is a sample S.A.D.D. contract. Discuss with the students how their parents would react to signing such a contract.

Well-Being

Teaching Approaches

- Present the following facts to students: After three or four alcoholic drinks a driver (1) is less able to judge distances, speeds, and turns accurately; (2) is unable to accurately judge his or her own ability; (3) has a greater tendency to take risks; (4) has impaired reflexes; (5) is prone to forgetfulness, such as failing to signal a turn; (6) will experience sleepiness, and the inability to concentrate.
- Have students suggest other consequences of drinking.

Well Being
S.A.D.D.

Students Against Drunk Driving (S.A.D.D.) is a national organization with chapters throughout the nation. It began at a high school in Massachusetts after the alcohol-related deaths of several members of the student body. Students and their parents sign the S.A.D.D. contract:

I promise to call home at any hour when a sober ride is not available.

(student's signature)

I promise to come and get my son or daughter at any hour, any place, whenever a sober ride is not available, no questions asked, and no argument at that time.

(parent's signature)

Students Against Drunk Driving tells students to be prepared for questions concerning their own behavior when they give their parents the contract. While the S.A.D.D. contract is a way for students to express their growing responsibility, they are warned not to be surprised if their parents accuse them of unacceptable behavior or judge them unfairly. Parents need time to adjust to the idea that their children can behave as adults.

Decisions Are Life-Giving

In almost any story, you will find that decisions are at the center of the action. Jason decided to sign the S.A.D.D. contract with his parents. He decided to go to the party, knowing that alcohol would be freely consumed. Later, he needed to make a decision either to call his parents for a ride home from the party or to take a ride with someone who had been drinking. His decisions in these matters could literally have had life-and-death implications.

Decisions have been made throughout history which have resulted in your being alive. Your parents came together in a very specific time and place. They participated in the decision to give you life, as did their parents before them. Ultimately, this decision reflects God's great love, through which all of creation occurred.

Of course, not all decisions have such earth-shaking consequences. Most decisions that you make are made without much conscious thought or attention and may even seem unimportant.

Choosing when to get out of bed, what to wear, or how much to eat for breakfast are generally decisions of little consequence. Other decisions require much greater concentration. How do you normally make an important decision? What criteria do you use to determine the importance of a decision?

It's not always easy to make good decisions, or, in fact, to determine what is good. There are skills that you can develop now that will improve the way you make decisions and help you to decide what is the best possible choice you can make. Before examining a decision-making process, let's look at the importance of values, freedom, and conscience on your ability to choose.

Recognizing Values

While values are behind every choice you make, good values are guides for how to live well. Good values help you to determine what is really important. For example, if you place a high value on doing well academically, you will most likely make choices that will help you reach your goals; you might choose study time before entertainment and reading over television.

Decisions Are Life-Giving

Lesson Overview

Values influence a person's every choice. A person who makes the choice to rise early in the morning to go to work or to school shows, by the choice, the value he or she attaches to those endeavors. This lesson explores values: their definition, their influence, and where they are learned. "How values affect our decision-making" is a major theme of this lesson.

Teaching Approaches

- Ask students to trace the origins of some of the decisions that had to be made in order for them to be born. This can be done by developing a family tree.
- Ask: "What is the most important decision that you ever made? What made the decision so important?"
- **Reteach**—Discuss how we might know whether a decision was good or bad.
- **Extend the Lesson**—Have students research historic decisions that have proven to be bad, such as the Bay of Pigs Invasion or the appeasement of Hitler before World War II. Have them report on why these decisions proved to be wrong.

Journal Assignment

"Write a reflection about a person that you know who has a problem with alcohol." Or: "Write a letter to your parent(s) explaining your honest feelings about teens, alcohol, and driving."

Teaching Approaches

- Collect newspaper articles that describe alcohol-related fatalities. Schedule classtime for student reports on current alcohol-related incidents.
- Begin a bulletin board display of the articles as a reminder of the dangers of alcohol consumption.

Recognizing Values

New Words

Value means "something precious, of great worth." Families, society, and the Church set standards about what is of value. Individuals, however, have the freedom to choose values which will guide their lives.

Virtues are good habits and practices that help us grow in holiness. We sometimes describe Catholic values in terms of the traditional virtues, such as faith, hope, love, honesty, and justice.

Teaching Approaches

- Present this scenario to the students: They are the founders of a new society. They are to come to a consensus on the six most important values for their new society. List them.
- After reading the section, ask the students to label the origins of their listed values as family, societal, or Christian values.
- **Reteach**—How have students' opinions changed during the past year?
- **Extend the Lesson**—Assign **Application** Project 3. If possible, provide the students with a Bible concordance to help them locate words associated with their chosen themes.

✠ **To Your Health**
Dangerous!

According to the United States Department of Health and Human Services, alcohol plays a role in the following statistics:

- 37 out of every 100 suicides.
- 70 out of every 100 murders.
- 50 out of every 100 arrests.
- Between 45 and 60% of all fatal auto accidents involving young adults.
- Over 50% of drowning victims.
- Approximately 50% of those who die in falling accidents.

In addition, drinking and driving is the number one cause of death for people between the ages of 15 and 24.

The English word "value" comes from the Latin *valere:* to be worth, be strong. It is used to refer to principles or qualities thought intrinsically valuable or desirable and that promote goodness. In modern society, the word "value" seems, at times, to mean whatever the person using the word wants it to mean. That is, it refers to what an individual values more than it refers to a predetermined set of qualities or principles.

For example: Martin drinks alcohol because it makes him feel good. Therefore, Martin values alcohol and feeling high. Unfortunately, because of his drinking, Martin now lies to his parents, is not dependable with his friends, and places many lives at risk by driving under the influence of alcohol. Martin's use of the word "value" has nothing to do with promoting human goodness, only selfish pleasure.

Opinions, like fashions, change quickly. Values change infrequently.

Resources

Resource 3C from the Teacher's Resource Book suggests a value's ordering game.

Background

According to the *Catechism of the Catholic Church,* 1804, virtues govern our actions in accord with reason and faith.

For Want of a Nail

Teaching Approaches

- Have students read Franklin's advice aloud.
- Ask for answers to the feature questions.
- Ask: "What are some examples that prove Franklin's point?"

What is the difference between an opinion and a value? Opinions are statements of thought or feelings that may or may not have any basis in fact. You can have an opinion on anything, whether you know anything about the topic or not. People have opinions concerning their favorite music, movies and teachers. Opinions change repeatedly, often for little or no reason. Your father's wide ties or your mother's mini-skirts from the 1960s may be fashionable again, although you would not have considered wearing them even six months ago. What accounts for this change of opinion?

While opinions change frequently, values rarely change. Values are based upon observable truth. Honesty is an important basic value, considered necessary for human interaction. Honesty is a basic value because it promotes goodness and truth, not because it is in fashion. Over thousands of years, experience has taught us that life is better when people are honest with one another than

Franklin gave good advice: "Use great care in everything you do!"

it is when people are dishonest. Experience has also taught us the importance of other basic values as well:

- Integrity.
- Justice.
- Honor.
- Patience.
- Courage.
- Mercy.
- Wisdom.
- Selflessness.

Such values are the foundation for decision-making and are also known as *Christian virtues* because they reflect the principles by which a person following Christ lives.

Values are learned from many sources. There are personal, societal, religious, and cultural values. The family is usually the first conveyor of values, although values are also learned quickly through the influence of popular culture and society, especially through the media. All of these influences affect your understanding and acceptance of values.

For Want of a Nail

Common decisions, made frequently without great concern, might seem unimportant, but Benjamin Franklin had other thoughts on this matter. His *Poor Richard's Almanack* (1758) begins with this statement: "For want of a nail, the shoe was lost; for want of a shoe, the horse was lost; for want of a horse, the rider was lost; for want of a rider, the battle was lost; for want of a nail, the war was lost."

What is the moral of the story? Why is it that even the most seemingly unimportant actions can lead to disastrous consequences? Franklin's advice: take great care in every little thing because every little thing matters!

Journal Assignment

"Write about a seemingly small decision that had very large implications." For example, the students may write of an important personal decision that was life-altering, or a decision that affected the course of history.

Family Values

Teaching Approaches

- Introduce the topic of value formation by having the students begin **Application** Project 4. They may list values as the family, societal, and Christian values are presented in these next text sections.
- **Reteach**—Discuss how family values have changed over the past fifty years.
- **Extend the Lesson**—Have students interview adults over the age of 50 to see how they think family values have changed since they were children. Student findings should be shared aloud in class.

▲ Family Living

Teaching Approaches

- Ask: "How does your family celebrate Christmas?" Note the differences in the way families celebrate.
- **Reteach**—What difficulties would students expect two people to have combining the traditions of their two families into one?
- **Extend the Lesson**—Have the students talk over the questions listed in the text with a partner or in a small group.

Societal and Cultural Values

Teaching Approaches

- Have the students choose one of these small group projects: (1) a role play starring society's "ideal" teenagers; (2) a written list of all the characteristics of the perfect teen; (3) a collage of advertisements that represents the media's definition of products that people value. Projects should be presented to the class.
- **Reteach**—Ask for volunteers to debate whether they or their parents are more influenced by societal or cultural values.
- **Extend the Lesson**—Ask the students to interview a parent or other adult who was an adolescent in the 1960s. What were the problems that they faced? What were their favorite things to do? Who were their heroes? Have the students share the similarities and differences between past and present adolescence with the class.

Family Values. A frequent comment is that values are "caught, not taught." This goes along with another saying, "actions speak louder than words." What do you think these sayings mean?

Generally, people are more likely to learn from experiences than from words. Families teach healthy values by acting with mutual kindness, communicating openly, sharing the responsibility for decision-making, and showing genuine affection. Families promote unhealthy values by being unreliable, indifferent, or hostile to one another. Children learn values from the way their families live.

As you know, your family's values affect many of the choices you make. Have you ever had the feeling that your mother or father is watching you even though they are nowhere near? This feeling is really a deference to family values: people tend to act in ways that are deemed acceptable by their families. What values are important in your family and how have they been communicated to you?

Societal and Cultural Values. The parents of a three-year-old boy made a great effort to teach their child about the importance of nonviolence and peaceful resolutions to problems. They did not spank their son. They did not buy him guns or war toys. Then, one day the boy pointed a piece of a branch at his father and said, "Say your prayers before I wipe you out!"

At first, the father laughed. Then, he wondered: Had the boy picked up such an idea from a television program or commercial? Or did he learn it from the playmate next door? The parents realized that their task in teaching values was much more complex than they had thought. There were more factors affecting their son's values than the parents could control.

▲ Family Living
What's Important In My Family?

All families are different. It follows, then, that the things that families value are different, too. Some families value neatness and order with everything in its place. Other families appear to live in disarray; only the individual family members seem to know where certain belongings can be found. Some families value a standard time for a family meal. Everyone must be in his or her place at the table by 6 p.m. Other families live by the "demand eating" principle; you eat when you are hungry.

You can imagine the confusion that ensues when a man and woman marry. Each may come from a family with a contrasting set of values. It is often said that you cannot predict the content of the first disagreement between husband and wife, but you can predict when it will happen. The answer is the Christmas season because each family usually has a variety of customs and values to be celebrated in a particular way. Both husband and wife rise up to protect their birth family's values.

Take some time to think about the things that are important in your family. This is a way to determine at least some of your family's values. Ask yourself these questions:

1. What is our most important family rule?
2. What is a piece of advice that has been told to me over and over since I was very young?
3. What are some subjects my parents believe to be either very right or very wrong?
4. On what does my family spend money?
5. How do members of my family treat other people?

Background

While values develop very early in a child's socialization process, usually, modeled on the example of one's parents, they eventually must become one's own. According to clinical psychologist, Charles M. Shelton, S.J., in order to become a mature adult, a person must reassess and analyze the values that he or she has been taught in order to develop a personal value system.

✳ Media Watch
Many Messages

Look carefully at these photos. Describe ways that society's values have coincided with the family values represented below. Write your ideas or share them with a partner.

Ask yourself, "What is being advocated here? Do these values resonate with my family and personal values? How am I influenced by images seen in the media?" Which, if any, of these images seems most appropriate for your personal value system?

You experience the values of culture and society as soon as you turn on a television, listen to music, watch a movie, look at a book, or greet a playmate at the back fence. Many of these values—good and bad—reinforce family values, while others contradict what the family has taught.

Peer groups exert pressure and shape your values through all stages of life, whether as an adolescent or as an adult. Even what your parents wear to work is greatly influenced by the expectations of their peers.

Studies suggest that unrealistically thin models establish the "ideal" weight for women, who then starve themselves in order to be slim and in style. What are some other ways in which adults are influenced by their peers? How do your peers influence your decisions?

Christian Values. For a Christian, determining what is of value cannot be accomplished without first understanding what God has communicated to the world through the life and teachings of Jesus Christ.

What did Jesus value? The answers come to us through the Scriptures and in the living tradition of the 2,000-year-old Church. Jesus was God's expression of truth *(John 14:6)*. He healed and forgave sinners *(Mark 2:1-12)*, and described a kingdom where the usual societal values of power, wealth, and control were unimportant *(Matthew 5:1-12)*. It follows that honesty, forgiveness, and morality are three examples of values founded in the life and teaching of Jesus.

Jesus summed up what was important to him when asked about the greatest commandment:

"You shall love the Lord, your God, with all your heart, with all your soul, and with all your mind. This is the greatest and the first commandment. The second is like it: You shall love your neighbor as yourself"
(Matthew 22:38-40).

✳ Media Watch

Teaching Approaches

- The media serves as a go-between, or a way of effecting or conveying a message. As the students examine these photos, make sure they are aware of exactly what is conveying the message, be it the postures of people or the items represented.

- Discuss the questions in class, or have students answer them in their journals.

Christian Values

Teaching Approaches

- Present the question, "What did Jesus value?" as an individual assignment to the students. Ask them to use the Scripture passages listed in the section for references. Have volunteers sum up their answers in single sentences.

- After the students have read the section, add, "How is God's love for you unselfish? How is God's love for you challenging?" Invite the students to share their responses.

- **Reteach**—The Beatitudes take their name from the first word of each statement: "blessed" (which also means "happy"). These offer a glimpse of a kingdom where those who depend on God for all their needs have more prominence than the rich, powerful, and respected. Help the students to identify people in their lives who represent the poor in spirit, the meek, and the other Beatitude values.

- **Extend the Lesson**—As homework, have students apply a Beatitude solution to a current problem. How would living as the Beatitude suggests change behavior and solve the problem?

The Importance of Freedom

Teaching Approaches

- Ask: "How did Jesus choose to freely express His love? Why can authentic love only be expressed in the setting of freedom?"
- Ask for additional elements of freedom. How do forces curtail student freedom at this time?
- **Reteach**—Compare present student freedoms to historical examples where freedom was limited (i.e, woman sufferage, age 21 to vote, slavery, no Catholics or Irish need apply signs, segregation).
- **Extend the Lesson**—Have the students write about what factors (peers, family, self-doubts) limit their own personal freedom.

Talk It Over

Assign the questions for small group discussion. Ask one person from each group to summarize the discussion for the rest of the class.

As a value, love stands above all others. Love helps us to be honest with others and be open to genuine communication. Through love we learn to trust others and gain the courage to make the risk of self-disclosure. As Christians, we are guided in love by our relationship with Christ and through the support of the Christian community. Love helps us to place everyday decisions into the context of the big picture: "How do we fit into God's plan."

Consider the following questions: How does your love reflect the love of Jesus? How can this relationship grow more in Christ? How can love help you to see ordinary decisions in a larger context?

The most basic Christian values are clustered around the relationship of the love of God, love of neighbor, and love of self. John's Gospel account states, "And the Word became flesh and made His dwelling among us, and we saw His glory, the glory as of the Father's only Son, full of grace and truth" *(John 1:14)*. What meaning can you draw from this passage? How have you experienced God's love for yourself and your family?

We have many witnesses today who challenge us to adopt Christian values. What does Mother Teresa's example teach us about love?

The Importance of Freedom

The gift to make choices freely is rooted deeply in Christian tradition. Put simply, freedom is a gift that works in union with God's grace and with our own ability to choose. According to Catholic teaching, God *activates* human freedom and *initiates* a response by people greater than their normal ability to respond. What does freedom mean to you?

This "partnership" between God and human beings was expressed in the First Letter of John, "Beloved, if God so loved us, we must also love one another" *(1 John 4:11)*. We were made with the freedom to choose or reject God's offer of friendship and love. Once accepted, we are called to share God's love with others. What are practical ways that you can share God's love?

Are there times when you are less free than others? For example, while you are free in school to learn, you are not free to disrupt the class. Are there people you know who are less free than others? How is someone who is shunned and teased less free to date or participate in social functions than one who is well liked? What about you? Do your emotions ever affect your freedom? How can feelings of loneliness and neediness influence the freedom of your behavior and attitudes?

The appropriate setting for making all decisions is one of freedom. By making such an affirmation, we add a new dimension to decision-making. This is a way to describe personal responsibility. Affirming one's freedom means one has to choose. Making good decisions means that one chooses what is good.

Background

According to the First Letter of John, the person who loves testifies to God's presence in his or her life. God's love, as represented by Jesus' giving of His life on the cross, is authentic, with no strings attached. In order to be one with God, the Christian must love others in the same manner.

Talk It Over

1. What are some things that are important in your family? What is your family's most important value?
2. What is the difference between personal values and traditional values?
3. What does it mean to say that values are "caught, not taught"? Discuss whether or not you agree with this statement.
4. At this time in your life, from which source do you primarily draw your personal values?

The Role of Conscience in Making Decisions

"Conscience" is probably a familiar word to you, but the meaning of conscience may continue to be unclear. Conscience is not "a little voice" from the outside or an unfriendly accuser who stands ready to point out any flaws in your behavior. Rather, conscience is a part of you that shapes your capacity to make good decisions—to think and act morally.

Your conscience has a general awareness that there are right and wrong actions and thoughts. It is also the part of you where values and principles are integrated. Finally, your conscience guides you to make the best decision in any particular situation.

How does conscience work? The best way to understand it is to look at an example of how conscience might operate in making a choice between right and wrong.

Tax Refund

Jack had an after-school job as a courier using his own car. Though he made only minimum wage, he also received 25 cents for every mile he drove. At the end of the year, Jack had to fill out his first federal and state income tax forms. Jack's brother suggested to him, "Why don't you claim the miles you drove at work as a business expense?"

In Focus
Discerning Life Choices

Reviewing thoughts and actions is an important part of maintaining a functioning and informed conscience. Many Christians devote parts of each day to examining their consciences. A helpful method was developed by Saint Ignatius of Loyola and is found in his *Spiritual Exercises*. It contains five steps:

1. Thanking God for the many gifts that have been received.
2. Asking God's help in facing the truth about oneself.
3. Reviewing the events of the day.
4. Asking God's pardon for the times God's gifts were not used well.
5. Making a resolution to grow in faith and do better.

"Can I do that even though I have already been paid for them?" Jack asked.

"Not legally," his brother said. "But everyone does it."

Immediately, Jack had **questions**. "Is it right to claim the mileage? What will happen to me if I am caught?" A list of mental questions is the first stage of your conscience in action.

Next, Jack's conscience formed **moral answers**, the second stage. "It's wrong to claim the mileage when I have already been paid for it." Jack's determination was based on years of living with family, societal, and Christian values that helped him recognize what is right and wrong.

The third stage of conscience is the hardest. After asking the right questions and receiving the right answers, it's time for **action**. Some people are able to do steps one and two, but may finally fail when it comes to acting in accordance with their consciences. Remember, people have freedom to

---

Background

The *Spiritual Exercises* are a set of directions on how to develop a closer relationship with Jesus. The *Exercises* include instructions in faith, warnings, meditations, examinations of conscience, and other religious practices.

Resources

Resource 3E lists examples of moral dilemmas that are suitable for role plays.

The Role of Conscience in Making Decisions

Lesson Overview

What is the role of conscience in decision-making? This lesson reviews the definition of conscience and explains how conscience works in helping a person make the choice between right and wrong.

New Words

Conscience is a person's sense of right and wrong, and the subsequent desire to choose good over evil. Conscience is not literally the voice of God, but it is our best judgment about right or wrong.

Teaching Approaches

- **Brainstorm** words associated with conscience.
- **Reteach**—Help the students to flesh out misconceptions about the word's meaning.
- **Extend the Lesson**—Develop a class definition for conscience.

In Focus

Teaching Approaches

- The five steps of the examination of conscience can be used as starting points for prayerful reflection in student journals. Encourage the students to be specific about what they write.
- Have students identify other ways they examine their consciences.
- When would a student feel obliged to examine his or her conscience?

Tax Refund

Teaching Approaches

- Assign the section for silent reading. Then ask: "Based on following one's conscience, which is the hardest stage to follow? Why?"
- Ask: "What did Saint Paul mean when he wrote, 'I do not do what I want, but I do what I hate'?"

Tax Refund

Teaching Approaches (continued)

- **Reteach**—Have students offer examples of how other problems can be solved using the question, moral answer, and action process.
- **Extend the Lesson**—Choose volunteers to role play this or another similar dilemma. Tell the students to dramatize their dilemmas up until the point where a character must act on his decision. Pause and ask the audience, "What should she (or he) do?" After a brief discussion, allow the group to finish their play in whatever way they see fit.

Following Your Conscience

New Words

Scrupulous derives from the Latin word *scrupus* which refers to "a small sharp stone." A scrupulous person has been compared to a traveller whose pebble-filled shoes makes every step fearful and hesitant.

Teaching Approaches

- After summarizing or reading the selection, ask: "What would the moral decision-making process be like without the component of healthy guilt?"
- **Reteach**—Assign **Application** Project 5.
- **Extend the Lesson**—Have students identify some examples from literature where conscience is ignorned (e.g. Poe's, *The Tell-Tale Heart*).

Talk It Over

For Question 1, encourage the students to develop a concrete example to explain the moral decision-making process (similar to the story of the "tax refund"). For Question 2, ask the class to brainstorm examples of healthy and unhealthy guilt. Point out that "healthy guilt" always reminds us of positive values and reinforces positive behavior.

---

make choices. Right or wrong, they must live with their decisions. As Paul wrote:

> "I do not do what I want, but I do what I hate… For I do not do the good I want, but I do the evil I do not want"
> *(Romans 7:15, 19).*

Following Your Conscience

Generally speaking, the best advice is for you to always follow your conscience in order to make a good decision. However, there is a danger that if your conscience is not properly informed, you could make an immoral choice.

When you do not follow your conscience, you will often experience *guilt.* Guilt is a feeling that warns you when you are doing wrong. Have you ever experienced feelings of guilt? What were the results of these feelings?

Feelings of guilt are natural and normal when they are healthy. It is possible also to experience unhealthy guilt. Do you know the difference between the two?

When you act in a way contrary to what you know to be good, you experience *healthy guilt.* This type of guilt is productive. It reminds you of your values and reinforces positive behavior.

Guilt is unhealthy when you feel guilty about something that is very normal and right, such as feeling sexually attracted to another person.

While some people may never feel troubled by their behavior, others feel almost paralyzed by guilt and, so, are afraid to do anything. (In extreme cases, people become *scrupulous,* afraid that everything they do is sinful.) Neither reaction is healthy. Finding a balance between these two extremes is a challenge everyone faces.

Guilt serves as a moral warning system for us, in much the same way as the nervous system does for our bodies. Pain and discomfort alert us that something is wrong with our bodies. Guilt signals that something is wrong with our behavior or attitudes.

As a warning system, guilt is not something that will operate on its own forever. Just as we can learn to live with pain until it's forgotten and ignored, we can learn to ignore feelings of guilt. Eventually, the warning system fails to operate properly. If a person continues to ignore feelings of guilt when making a decision, eventually his or her conscience will malfunction. He or she will be unable to tell the difference between right and wrong.

Talk It Over

1. Explain how your conscience works in making a moral decision using the three steps: questions, moral answers, and action.
2. Is guilt primarily a healthy or unhealthy feeling? Explain your answer. How do you know when you experience "healthy guilt"?

If you ignore your conscience long enough, it will soon cease to function appropriately.

Background

The development of a healthy sense of guilt is vital for the development of conscience and of other-centered values. Psychologist Charles Shelton suggests "focusing on what the future can become, on how their future lives might be different, on what they can do in light of their current failings, and on how their increasing self-knowledge from their present experience will aid them in responding more appropriately in the future" *(Morality and the Adolescent).*

II. DISCERNING LIFE CHOICES

You may have already made some essential decisions in your life:

- "Attending Catholic high school will prepare me for the rigors of college."
- "Wrestling requires a lot of time and energy. I'm willing to sacrifice money and a social life now so that I can possibly earn a college scholarship."
- "I know all about the dangers of cigarette smoking, but that doesn't apply to me. A little pinch of smokeless tobacco won't hurt."

These are each important judgments that reflect a process of decision-making. Practical ways of improving your decision-making process are presented over the next few pages. With practice, you can make them your own.

Discerning God's Will

Catholics believe that God takes an active interest in our lives, nurtures us, provides us with the grace we need to face difficult challenges, and even directs our lives toward goodness and holiness. Understanding God's will has always been a challenge for humankind, and will continue to be a challenge until the end of time.

Discernment is the ability to distinguish between wants and needs, desires and wishes, and reality and dreams. Used in a religious context, it refers to a way of discovering God's will in one's personal experiences. With the process of discernment, you can make crucial decisions by evaluating facts, weighing benefits and risks, and understanding emotions and desires as you attempt to recognize God's plan for you. Christian discernment helps to keep your life focused on Jesus and to coordinate your own wants and needs with what God wants and needs from you.

The tradition of discernment is well developed within the Catholic tradition. By the Middle Ages, discernment became synonymous with the virtue of prudence. Today, discernment is recognized as a practical way for making decisions using an individual's experience, intuition, and prayer.

When we consider our options, we can have a tough time reaching a decision, especially when more than one option is a good choice. How do you decide between something that is good for you now and something that might be good in the future? Is it better to save money for college or go on the senior class trip to Washington, D.C.? Compete on the swim team or dedicate your free time to your studies and a part-time job?

All of these choices are good and have potential benefits. Choosing between them (recognizing that you can't have or do everything you want) can be quite difficult. A discernment process can help you recognize the benefits in each situation and come to a decision that is most right for you.

✿ Prayer in Action
For the Glory of God

Saint Ignatius of Loyola (1491-1556) based his spirituality on what became the Jesuit motto, *ad majorem Dei gloriam,* "for the greater glory of God." He often suggested this prayer to those seeking God: "Receive, Lord, all my liberty, my memory, my understanding and my whole will. You have given me all that I have, all that I am, and I surrender all to Your Divine Will, that You dispose of me. Give me only Your love and Your grace. With this I am rich enough, and I have no more to ask."

Background

According to Saint Ignatius of Loyola, discernment is a process for working through options. In making decisions, everyone faces a variety of options. Not all of these options are unattractive. Making a decision may come down to choosing between more than one good option. The process of discernment—or "making out what is clear"—is a way for us to keep our lives focused on Jesus Christ.

II. DISCERNING LIFE CHOICES

Aims

1. To help students differentiate between "wants" and "needs."
2. To help students use a discernment process to make important life choices.

Begin the Section

1. Ask: "What does it mean to do God's will? How do we know if we are doing God's will?"
2. Introduce the section. Explain: "In this section, we will explore ways to discover God's will for our lives through a process called 'discernment'."
3. Summarize the section opening. Ask: "What will help to prepare you to make important decisions in the future?"

Discerning God's Will

Lesson Overview

This lesson provides the students with a way to make decisions using their own experiences, intuitions, and prayers.

Teaching Approaches

- Ask students to differentiate between "wants" and "needs." Point out that the discernment process helps us to clearly distinguish between the two.
- **Reteach**—Explain that discernment was once synonymous with prudence, the skill of being sensible or reasoned.
- **Extend the Lesson**—Students should find examples from current headlines where the virtue of prudence was followed or not followed.

✿ Prayer in Action

Teaching Approaches

- Allow the students time for silent reflection.
- Play a recording of the song, "Only This I Want" by the St. Louis Jesuits. **Resource 3F** provides the song lyrics.

A Process for Life

Lesson Overview

The *Spiritual Exercises* form a framework for the discernment process introduced in this lesson. The students are taken through eight steps of decision-making using this process. You may wish to apply these steps to a predetermined sample decision that is to be made.

Teaching Approaches

- Read or summarize the eight-step decision-making process.
- **Reteach**—Ask the students to brainstorm difficult decisions that might require using such a process.
- **Extend the Lesson**—Assign the students to make one large poster, or eight separate posters, listing the eight steps. Post them in the classroom as a reminder of this decision-making process.

Mastering the Skills

Teaching Approaches

- Have students consider each of the eight steps and provide an example that illustrates their understanding of the activity.
- *Define the Problem*—For the purpose of working through the eight steps with the class, choose one "problem" that can be tested in the process.
- *Gather the Data*—Assign small groups to collect data. After they have finished, collate what they have found into one class list.
- *Consider Alternatives*—Present the students with a simple problem or puzzle that could be solved in a number of different ways. Allow time for the students to solve the problems and share how they solved them.
- Point out the freedom that we have to solve problems and make decisions in our own way. Ask volunteers to offer alternative ideas to the class problem.
- *Consider the Consequences*—Besides speculating on the future, ask the students to recall how decisions they made in the past have had an effect on their present lives.

A Process for Life

The formal process for discernment commonly used today developed from the teaching of Saint Ignatius of Loyola in *The Spiritual Exercises*. The steps below have been adapted from those taught by Ignatius. When used along with your already developed decision-making skills, this eight-step process can help you make even the most difficult life choices.

Before making a difficult decision, consider each of the following steps:
1. Define the problem.
2. Gather data.
3. Consider alternatives.
4. Consider the consequences.
5. Consider in light of your values.
6. Seek advice and pray.
7. Choose and act.
8. Re-evaluate.

Mastering the Skills

Think of a skill that you have developed since childhood: playing a musical instrument, speed-reading, painting, playing sports. How much time and effort have you put into mastering this skill? How much more time and effort must you spend practicing in order to be truly proficient at your craft? The same dedication and perseverance that you've shown in developing your special skill will be necessary if you are to gain a personal mastery of the discernment process.

Let's examine the steps in the discernment process to see how you can begin to implement them in your life.

Define the Problem. You must ask yourself what exactly is the problem that needs solving. At times, several problems are lumped together into one, and it's not clear which one is being addressed. The problem, "Do I attend college after high school or seek a full-time job?" is loaded with hidden questions: "Can I afford it? Do I want to leave home? Am I capable of doing college level work? Do I need a college degree for my career?"

All of these secondary questions are important, but they confuse the main issue. The bigger questions are, "What do I want to do with my life?" and "What do I need to do to reach my goal?" Once you are clear on the major questions, then you can proceed to solve them one at a time.

Gather the Data. Gathering data means researching the consequences of each decision. What are the facts you need to know? What are your initial feelings concerning each choice? What guidance can Church teaching and Scripture offer about your options? How have adults you respect resolved similar situations? It is important to come to know your own thinking on these issues as well, not just the external facts. This is not the time for making the decision. It is the time for gathering and evaluating information.

Consider Alternatives. Where does the data you have uncovered lead you next? Have new solutions been suggested by what you've learned? Remember, you may reach your own unique solution to a problem. The story of the Gordian Knot from world history points to this kind of creativity. Alexander the Great solved a seemingly unsolvable problem. The knot that couldn't be untied was simply cut in two! There may be many more creative ways of addressing your problem than you have considered.

Consider the Consequences. What can happen if you make this choice? Role-play what your life will be like five years from now if you make this decision. How will your life and the lives of others be affected?

Consider in Light of Your Values. You're usually a careful driver. You've never had a ticket, attempt to stay within the speed limit, and always wear your seat belt.

You're driving a couple of friends home from soccer practice in your dad's T-bird. At the stoplight, a girl in a hot 4 x 4 revs up her engine, looks over at you, and smiles.

Just as the light turns green, she stomps on the gas, squeals the tires, and speeds off. What do you do? What pressures do you feel to take off after

---

Journal Assignment

Have the students describe a personal skill of which they are most proud. Make sure they include how much time and effort they have put into mastering this skill. Ask: "Why does it take time to become proficient at most things?"

Resources

Resource 3H includes samples of "unsolvable" problems for use with "Consider Alternatives."

Investment Chart

Parents usually make plenty of investments in their children's future. One way parents invest financially is saving for college. A recent magazine article suggested investing money in a saving's account or mutual fund starting from a child's birth as a smart way to save the estimated $100,000 that college may cost in the year 2000.

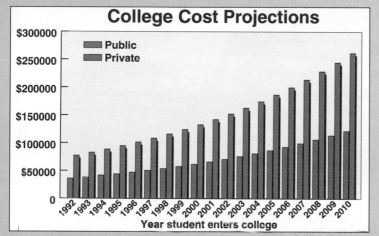

College Cost Projections

(Before you panic completely, realize that this figure covers private school tuition, room and board, transportation, books, and fees for four years; an average of $25,000 a year. While that is a great deal of money, you should also know that many colleges provide grants and loans to help cover the amount.)

Articles that discuss saving money for college usually provide charts based on a child's current age to determine how much needs to be saved each month in order to pay the future bills. For example, if the child is newborn, investing $100 a month will be enough to pay for college. However, if the child is five years old, $200 a month would need to be invested to reach the same goal. What stake do you have in your own future? What are you doing to prepare for it right now? What is the time and effort you've invested in high school worth? Answer the following questions, then determine how much extra you would need to invest to meet your goals.

1. What percentage of your time do you presently invest in preparing for your future? How much time do you feel you need to invest?

2. Which of your activities do you consider to be a wise investment of your time? Explain.

3. How are you investing your talent for the future? What are you doing to improve this talent? How do you expect to use this talent in the future?

4. How much of your own money do you save? What do you consider to be a wise investment? How do you plan to use these savings to meet your goals?

5. What other resources do you have to invest (i.e., baseball card collection, an idea for a new service or product)? How can you benefit from these resources in the future?

One thousand dollars invested now at six percent interest will be worth nearly $1,800 in ten years; your money is earning interest on the interest. Develop a plan to invest your time, talents, and other resources so that they produce the best return for your efforts.

Mastering the Skills

Teaching Approaches (continued)

- *Consider in Light of Your Values*—After reading or summarizing the section, have the students do **Application** Project 7. Allow time for a large group follow-up.
- Have the students write answers to the three questions at the end of "Consider in Light of Your Values," listed in the text on page 56.

Investment Chart

Teaching Approaches

- Summarize and comment on the activity.
- Have the students write a brief report, summarizing the answers to the questions presented.
- This would be an appropriate time to discuss students' plans for after high school: attend college, attend professional school, or go to work full time. What worries do students' have about paying for school? How are they and their parents preparing for the expense of continued education?

Resources

Resource 3G can be used to help students figure out other returns on their financial investments.

Mastering the Skills

Teaching Approaches (continued)

- *Seek Advice and Pray*—Ask: "What does it mean to 'bargain with God'?"
- Summarize the section. Point out the advantage of seeking advice of respected adults and of prayer in making good decisions.
- *Choose and Act*—Ask the class to come up with a consensus as to what type of action they will take to solve the problem.
- *Reevaluate*—Ask the students to discuss with a partner the questions listed in the text in terms of an important decision they made in the past. Ask: "How do you reevaluate that decision today?"
- **Reteach**—Work through several decisions using the discernment process. Discuss with students the difficulties they would have in using this process.
- **Extend the Lesson**—Assign students the task of using this method to reach a real or hypothetical decision. They should write down what they do during each step of the process.

What pressures do you feel when making decisions. How do these pressures influence your freedom and affect your decisions?

her as fast as you can? How free are you to choose one way over the other?

At times, personal values are overwhelmed by the immediacy of the moment and external pressures. How can you be true to what you believe when the entire situation is demanding another response?

In situations where you have barely any time to react, try to form answers to these three questions:

1. Why am I doing this?
2. What do I believe is the right thing to do?
3. Would I make the same decision if the situation were different?

Seek Advice and Pray. How is God involved in the choices you make? Through which choice are you acting most as a Christian? This is not a time for bargaining with God, or reading divine direction into coincidental occurrences. This is not a religious Ouija board where you wait for God to spell out the direct answers to your dilemmas. It is an opportunity to share your struggle with God, ask for guidance, and see how each avenue will support your Christian vocation.

Turn to your parents, counselor, or other trusted adults for guidance. You don't want them to give you answers (although that might be the easiest solution). Rather, you are looking for wisdom and understanding. How have they addressed similar situations in their lives and what were the consequences? From their experiences, you can gain more background to help you make your own decision.

Choose and Act. After going through all of these steps, you either know exactly what you want to do and how you should act, or you feel that either way you choose is acceptable. When you arrive at this point you are most open to knowing God's direction. The decision you make

Background

At the time of choosing and acting on a decision, a person is said to have reached a state of *indifference*. In this use, "indifferent" means "having or showing no partiality." To be indifferent means to be open to God's will for your life.

will gradually become clear. The decision will not be made for you, but many people find that their choice is obvious at this stage.

Now is the time to act. You know as clearly as possible what you should do. You've done everything you can to find the truth. You've consulted, prayed, and reflected. You've examined your motives and considered the morality of your choices. While you remain open to new information and ideas, it's now time to act. You step boldly into the future, trusting that God will support you and your decision.

Re-evaluate. Did you make the right decision? That's not an easy question to answer immediately, but it is always worth considering. You can still make a poor choice, even after such a rigorous process. So the final stage is to re-evaluate the decision. Are you satisfied with your choice? Is living out your decision a terrible burden or is it life-giving? Do you feel close to or far away from God because of the choice you made?

Important career or vocational decisions usually cannot be confirmed immediately. You may be extremely satisfied (or dissatisfied) with your decision during the first six weeks. Wait to see how you feel after six months or even six years. The consequences of your decision take time to play out.

Sharpening Your Skills
Reaching a Solution

Work with a partner or in a small group to think up a problem that needs to be resolved. Use these problem-solving steps to help you to reach a solution:

1. Clearly identify the problem so that it is well-defined for everyone.
2. Identify all the possible choices that can be made.
3. Consider and evaluate the consequences of each choice.

Questions to ask as you evaluate the results of your decision include:
- Am I growing in faith and love for Christ?
- Am I becoming a kinder and more considerate person?
- Am I enjoying life?
- Do I feel energized or burdened by my choice?
- Have I become more generous or more selfish?
- Do I like what I'm doing and who I am?

Until you make a final commitment, it's never too late to change your mind. Engagements can be broken even on your wedding day, new jobs can be found, and you can even leave religious life easily prior to receiving Holy Orders or taking final religious vows.

Learning How to Fall Gracefully

A yearly school function for the senior class was the ski trip. Although he had never skied before, Dan was really excited about going. People talked about what a great thrill skiing was, and the advertising made it look so simple. Dan was eager to give it a try.

At the ski lodge, the instructor helped the beginners with their skis and bindings. Then she said, "Your first lesson is how to fall without hurting yourself." Dan was amazed. For half an hour, most of the lesson in fact, they practiced falling down and getting up again. When the lesson was over, the beginners all headed for the "bunny" hill.

Skiing was a lot harder than Dan had originally thought. He became very adept at falling and getting back quickly to his feet. At first he was embarrassed, but that feeling passed as he hit the cold ground. Unless he wanted to freeze on the hill, he thought, he'd better pick himself up and get going.

Dan eventually learned how to ski. But if he had not known how to fall gracefully, he might have quit or been seriously hurt before his skills

---

The Choice Is Yours

Teaching Approaches

- Review the main points covered in this chapter.
- **Reteach**—Ask the students how they can apply the eight-step decision-making process to their personal choice of a life direction.
- **Extend the Lesson**—Discuss what happens to people when they make poor decisions. Develop an "advice board" based upon what students think people should do when they have made a poor decision.

Few people succeed the first time, everytime. When you make a mistake, learn from the experience, then get up and try it again.

developed. The same is true for decision-making. It looks simple, but effective decision-making actually requires a great deal of skill and practice. When you act in error:

- Admit that you've failed.
- Figure out what went wrong.
- Get up and try it again.

You will make mistakes. Everyone does, so don't let that stop you. You will make errors in judgment as you practice this decision-making process, but these errors will become less frequent with practice as you become more proficient at this skill. Be courageous and act on what you think is right.

The Choice Is Yours

You have made many correct decisions and will make many more in the future. These are not once-in-a-lifetime decisions either. You will continue to be called on to discern God's will for your life. By doing so, you will discover the meaning of Christian discipleship as it applies to the "one and only you."

The gift of freedom affords you many possibilities in making daily decisions and in making decisions about your future. The personal value system you are establishing through the influence of family, society, and Church provides a cornerstone for making good decisions. Your conscience

Background

According to the Encyclopedic Dictionary of Religion, "the freedom that can be reasonably claimed by man is the power and right of self-mastery, . . . to rightfully be guided by his own judgments, . . . make decisions for which he alone is responsible, . . . and direct his life toward goals recognized . . . by himself."

remains with you like a faithful friend, deliberating with you over big and little choices and helping you to make decisions based on the deepest, most honest part of your being. With practice, you will develop the skills you need to make the right decisions, and with God's grace, you will come to know the direction for your life.

Talk It Over

1. What has been your experience in learning new skills? Were you immediately successful or did you have difficulty? What did you do when you thought about quitting?

2. How do you make decisions now? How is it like the process described in this section? How is it different? What would you need to change in your present process to implement this new method?

3. How does discernment affect choosing a vocation? Explain your answer.

Chapter Summary

- Decision-making is life-giving. Your very existence comes from God's decision to create you.
- Freedom is a part of decision-making. Freedom works together with God's grace and your own capacity to make free choices.
- Values are guides for how to live. They can help you determine the good from the bad and make good choices.
- Conscience helps you make good decisions—to think and act morally.
- Three stages for making a conscience decision are asking questions, forming moral answers, and taking action.
- "Guilt" can be a warning to let you know that you have disregarded a value in making a decision.
- "Discernment" is a lifelong process. It helps you to separate your own wants and needs from what God wants and needs from you.

Talk It Over

Have the students discuss these questions with a partner or in a small group. Allow time to hear a sampling of their responses with the entire class.

Chapter Summary

- Before assigning the review exercises, ask the students if they have any questions or comments on the material covered in Chapter 3.
- Have the students read each statement. Or, you may wish to have the students read and discuss these statements in small groups before reporting back to the entire class.

Background

Catholics believe in the truth of "sufficient Grace." This means that God gives each of us the capability to act for goodness, but that we also have the ability and freedom of will to reject this grace. (See the *Catechism of the Catholic Church,* 1742.)

Chapter 3 Review

What Have You Learned?

Listed below are suggested answers. For many of the questions, the answers will vary.

1. People's parents and, in fact, all of their ancestors made decisions that eventually led to their birth.

2. According to Church teaching, God, through grace, activates human freedom and initiates a response by people greater than their normal ability to respond.

3. A person's freedom may be limited by any number of reasons such as time and place. For example, one can't holler "fire" in a crowded theater.

4. The sources of one's values affect a person's understanding and acceptance of them.

5. Some basic values are honesty, integrity, justice, honor, patience, courage, mercy, wisdom, and selflessness. These are considered basic because they form the foundation for human discourse.

6. A person maintains an informed conscience through reading, study, prayer, and practice.

7. Love stands out because it is our means for sharing in the life of God.

8. Your conscience guides you to make the best decision in any particular situation.

9. Guilt is healthy when it reminds you of your values and reinforces positive behavior. Guilt is unhealthy when you feel guilty about something that is normal and right.

10. The discernment process helps us to discover, over and over again, God's will for our lives. It can direct us in making important decisions throughout life.

11. Answers will vary. Answers should reflect the understanding that people need to make decisions freely.

REVIEW

What Have You Learned?

1. What are some ways that decision-making plays a part in creation?
2. What does it mean to cooperate with God's grace in making a free decision?
3. In what ways might a person be limited in his or her freedom?
4. Why is it important to be able to identify the sources of your values?
5. Name five basic values and explain why they are considered basic.
6. How does a person maintain an informed conscience?
7. How does the value of love stand out above all others?
8. What role does "conscience" have in decision-making?
9. How can guilt be a healthy feeling? How can guilt be unhealthy?
10. Why should discernment be a lifelong process?
11. What if God said, "I am Love. Love is wonderful. Therefore, I will make you love Me"? What is it like when someone imposes his or her will on others?

Application

1. Honesty is an important tool to open the lines to better communication. Sit down with a parent. Tell your mother or father about one or two things that are important to you. Ask them to share some of their important values with you.
2. Write a decision-making situation similar to the one faced by Jason at the party. Exchange yours with a partner. Comment on the possible choices that can be made in each.
3. Write a slogan for a personal value based on a Gospel passage.
4. Make a chart with three columns. In one column, list family, societal, and Christian values that you have already incorporated into your personal value system. In the middle column, list values you are still debating whether or not to make a part of your own. In the third column, list any values that you have presently rejected. Discuss your answers with a friend.
5. Talk about examples of healthy and unhealthy feelings of guilt with a partner or in a small group.
6. Explain how the discernment process can help you to keep your life focused on Jesus Christ.
7. Sometimes it is said that "people learn from their mistakes." Describe something that you have learned from a personal mistake.

Journal Assignment

Have students reflect on "What Have You Learned?" question 11. Students should write on the topic: "How does God guide me, yet allow me to act freely at the same time? How can I act accordingly in my personal relationships?"

REVIEW

Chapter Vocabulary

- freedom
- decision-making
- opinions
- values
- societal values
- family values
- conscience
- guilt
- honesty
- discernment

Putting Vocabulary to Use

Supply the missing word for each statement from the chapter vocabulary list.

_____ **1.** serves as a moral warning system

_____ **2.** every family has a different set of these

_____ **3.** statements of thought or feeling that may not have any basis in fact

_____ **4.** the media, books, and community standards help to form these

_____ **5.** the capacity that helps you make good decisions

_____ **6.** a healthy set encourages actions like mutual kindness, open communication, and genuine affection for one another

_____ **7.** a process to help you distinguish between wants and needs

_____ **8.** a gift that works in union with God's grace and with our own ability to choose

_____ **9.** steps that are followed to make a choice

_____ **10.** an important basic value

"We cannot solve life's problems except by solving them."

M. Scott Peck, M.D.

Application

Suggestions for using these **Application** projects are offered throughout the text. Have the students read the directions for each project. You may assign a particular project, or allow the students to choose a project they prefer. Allow class time for the students to share their completed project with others.

Putting Vocabulary to Use

Answers:
1. guilt
2. family values
3. opinion
4. societal values
5. conscience
6. values
7. discernment
8. freedom
9. decision-making
10. honesty

Final Thought

Background

M. Scott Peck is a clinical psychologist and author of the book *The Road Less Travelled.*

Unit 1 Review

Looking Back

Listed below are suggested answers. For many questions, the answers will vary.

1. To say that everyone has a vocation means that God has a plan for everyone.

2. Diversity assures a prominent and divinely chosen role for each person.

3. Prayer is used in decision-making to keep one's decisions rooted in God, leading to deep and personal satisfaction.

4. People marry for many different reasons. A good reason to marry is based on a joint decision of a man and woman to form the intimate partnership that is Christian marriage.

5. People prepare for Christian marriage today through the way they treat other people, especially people of the opposite sex.

6. People who receive a special call to the single life choose this vocation so that they can best respond with freedom to the needs of others.

7. The vocation to bring God's love to others is common to all Christians.

8. Self-concept refers to what you think about yourself. Self-esteem means how much you value or care for yourself.

9. A person's self-concept is formed from infancy; it is related to how the person is treated by others.

10. People with a positive self-concept seek the best for their lives.

11. Self-esteem can be improved by looking for positive reinforcements from those that you can trust. Concentrate on the things you do well. Learn from your successes and gradually build upon them. Love and respect yourself.

12. Some values are basic for human interaction because they insure safety and respect.

13. When self-talk is positive, it improves one's self-esteem. When it is negative it can damage one's self-esteem.

14. Using one's values, freedom, and conscience are key components of decision-making.

15. Discernment is the ability to distinguish between wants and needs, desires and wishes, and reality and dreams.

The Freedom to Be You

Looking Back

1. What does it mean to say that everyone has a vocation?
2. How does diversity improve the world?
3. How can prayer be used to help you make a decision?
4. Why do people choose to be married?
5. How can people prepare for Christian marriage today?
6. What does it mean to say that people receive a call to the single vocation?
7. What is a vocation common to all Christians because of their Baptism?
8. Define the words "self-concept" and "self-esteem." Write a sentence that explains how they differ.
9. How is a person's self-concept formed?
10. What is the importance of a positive self-concept?
11. How can you improve your self-esteem?
12. Why are some values considered basic for human interaction?
13. How can self-talk be beneficial and how can it be destructive?
14. List three key components of decision-making.
15. What is meant by the word "discernment"?
16. Why would a person practice discernment?
17. What are the steps in the discernment process?

Making It Real

One part of the discernment process is investigating a decision. Before you make any career decisions you should learn everything you can about the type of work you will be doing and about the employer. If one person has to investigate several different careers thoroughly, the process can become tedious, but if several people each research one career, the task becomes easier.

As a class, develop a *Guide to Careers* booklet. Each student is to choose one career and examine it thoroughly. The research should include educational and aptitude requirements (for example, two years of college and a willingness to travel are requirements for a career as an airline steward), the average number of positions available yearly, salary ranges, and where the jobs are most likely to be found. Check with the reference librarian at your local library for help in collecting this information.

---

16. A person would practice discernment in order to help make crucial decisions by evaluating facts, weighing benefits and risks, and understanding emotions and desires.

17. The steps in the discernment process are: (1) define the problem; (2) gather data; (3) consider alternatives; (4) consider the consequences; (5) consider in light of your values; (6) seek advice and pray; (7) choose and act; (8) re-evaluate.

A Time of Prayer

Many religious traditions use a string of beads as a tool for prayer. This strand is used to keep count of the numbers of prayers said and as a focusing tool. Fingering the beads helps the person praying to ignore distractions and concentrate on God. A standard set of prayers may be said while making the circuit, or simply touching the beads in silent meditation can be the prayer.

The Catholic tradition uses a strand of beads called a "rosary." The rosary is prayed by reciting the Hail Mary, Glory Be, Lord's Prayer, or Apostle's Creed as one touches the beads around the chain.

The rosary begins with the Sign of the Cross and the Apostles Creed, followed by the The Lord's Prayer, three Hail Marys, and one Glory Be. Next follows the first of five mysteries reflecting on Mary's role in the Incarnation of Jesus. After a period of meditation on the mystery, the Lord's Prayer is said, followed by ten Hail Marys and a Glory Be. This pattern of praying the Lord's Prayer, ten Hail Marys and a Glory Be continues around the rosary four more times (five times in all).

Practice this prayer together as a class and on your own as well. Many people around the world use this prayer as a source of guidance and strength. You can take comfort in "worrying the beads" even when you cannot actively pray them.

63

Making It Real

Teaching Approaches

- Read the directions to the class. Have the students choose the careers that they will research prior to discussing them to avoid duplicating work. If possible, arrange for a student or group of students to transfer the completed research onto a computer's hard disk for lasting reference.

- **Reteach**—Have students compare two or more careers using the following criteria: educational requirements, starting salary, working conditions, and stress level. Also have students explain if either career could be a vocation.

- **Extend the Lesson**—Arrange for a career guidance counselor to speak to your class, offering a general presentation on career planning.

A Time of Prayer

Teaching Approaches

- You may wish to assign small groups to look up Scripture references to correspond with each decade of a particular mystery.

- Have the students paint a large "rosary mural" on a piece of posterboard. Then, have them each write a special prayer intention in each bead.

- Explain that the "Marian Rosary" was popularized by a Dominican preacher named Alan deRupe in the fifteenth century in northern France. The devotion is directed to Mary, the Mother of God. A feast honoring Mary and the rosary is celebrated on October 7.

- **Reteach**—Pray one or more decades of the rosary together with the class. Allow as many students as possible to take the role of leader.

- **Extend the Lesson**—The rosary beads can be connected with other prayer forms. Have students develop creative ways to pray with the rosary.

Resources

Resource U1A from the Teacher's Resource Book provides suggestions to help plan a class Mass or other liturgical service suitable for a retreat or mini-workshop.

Resource U1B provides more information on praying the rosary.

Unit 2

At the Crossroads

A medical technician, looking back at his high school years, finds it easy to see the points that influenced him the most. He particularly remembers the biology course he once took in summer school: "It opened my eyes to a whole new world. My interest in disease prevention began with that one class."

Adolescence represents life "at the crossroads" between responsibility to family and responsibility to self. Unit 2 presents ways that students can build on the skills and relationships that are part of their lives now, so that they can make better decisions for their future.

The students will:

- Look at ways to make new friendships and maintain old ones.
- Recognize that dating relationships grow out of friendships.
- Be introduced to important dating issues and learn appropriate ways of behavior.
- Consider sexuality as a gift to be treasured and enjoyed, not repressed.
- Learn appropriate sexual behavior.
- Understand the goodness of sexual feelings while becoming more aware of the serious consequences that result from engaging in genital sex outside of marriage.

For a Christian, all of life's choices are to be made in imitation of the values of Jesus. This unit also introduces students to the values presented in the Beatitudes and helps them consider the meaning of Christian discipleship in light of career choices.

Unit 2 Overview

Chapter 4 Friendship and Communication
Learning the skills to make and maintain friendships can help you now and in the future.

Chapter 5 Dating
Dating is an outgrowth of friendship and a way to meet new people and have new experiences.

Chapter 6 Love, Sexuality, and Your Life
Sexuality is a good gift from God and a natural part of life.

Chapter 7 Fullness of Life
Discerning what God wants from your life is the best way to discover your personal vocation.

At the Crossroads

When I was a boy in New Jersey, I could in no way imagine the life that was ahead of me. But now, I can say that I consider myself one of the most privileged people I know. Why? Because of my vocation as a parish priest. I get to see God at work in people's lives for a living!

A priest is invited into some of the most deep down places in a person's life story. That's where God is powerfully at work—whether it's during times of sickness, conversion, trouble, or celebration. And one other thing: being a priest watching God at work in so many people's lives has led me, through prayer, to love the Lord and His people with a love that I cannot put into words.

64

Background

Father William Breslin is the pastor of Queen of Peace parish in Aurora, Colorado where he ministers to over four thousand families. Ordained for more than fifteen years, Father Bill is a native of New Jersey. An avid history and genealogy buff, he has traced his family tree in the United States back over two hundred years. He hosts a weekly television program where he answers call-in questions about religion.

NAME: *William Breslin*
CAREER: *Priest, Archdiocese of Denver*
VOCATION: *Priesthood*

65

Teaching Objectives

- To practice effective communication skills in relationships with others.
- To introduce an overview of the dating process.
- To help students understand how love is a part of all relationships.
- To help students develop appropriate ways to live out God's good gift of sexuality.
- To relate the call of discipleship to career choices.

Scope and Sequence

"Because people are capable of continual development, so are their relationships with God. Essentially, development in faith is the process by which one's relationship with the Father becomes more like Jesus' (cf. John 14:6ff): it means becoming more Christlike. This is not just a matter of subjective, psychological change, but involves establishing and nurturing a real relationship to Jesus and the Father in the Holy Spirit, through a vigorous sacramental life, prayer, study, and serving others" (*National Catechetical Directory,* #173).

Begin the Unit

1. Ask the students to relate the chapter titles of Unit 2 with the unit title, "At the Crossroads."
2. Read or summarize the unit objectives.
3. Point out that there are a variety of experiences connected with friendships and dating and that it is important to hear many different perspectives of these experiences.
4. Read and discuss the "priesthood" feature.
5. Ask: "What does the author mean when he says, 'A priest is invited into some of the most deep down places in a person's life story'?"
6. Ask: "What do you think Father Breslin likes most about being a priest?"
7. Point out the relationship between loving people and loving the Lord. Have the students share common experiences.

Background

In building and maintaining relationships, you lay the groundwork for a successful future.

"Jesus' words, 'You are My friends if you do what I command you' *(John 15:14),* . . . involves a relationship, a friendship between persons. As the quality of a friendship between human beings is affected by such things as their maturity and freedom, . . . so the quality of a friendship with God is affected by the characteristics of the human party" (*NCD, #173*).

Focus On: Chapter 4

By the time young people reach high school, they are very aware of the importance of friendships. During adolescence, friendships take on a crucial relevance. Friendships provide an avenue for teens to express triumphs and self-doubts. They also provide a climate for growth and self-knowledge that relationships with family members or even peers in general cannot.

Understanding the importance and dynamics of friendship is important to the students' futures as well. Learning to make and maintain friendships, to communicate effectively, and to handle conflicts in a constructive way are vital skills in any relationship.

In the coming years, these students will be meeting new people—at school, in the workplace, and in new social settings—and forming new relationships. Through these friends, students may well find spouses, or make the decision to live out the single or religious vocation. For these reasons, students need to develop the interpersonal communication skills presented in this chapter.

Plan Ahead

- Incorporate formal and/or spontaneous prayer into each lesson. A participatory prayer service is provided in the Teacher's Resource Book (TRB).
- Note the **Resources** suggestions in the TRB. These suggestions can be used to teach or extend the lessons of the chapter.
- Preview the **Application** project ideas in the Chapter Review. Refer to **Teaching Approaches** for suggestions on when to assign these projects. The projects may also be used as part of a lesson, section, or chapter review.
- Decide how you will group students for projects and discussions.

Friendship and Communication

A faithful friend is beyond price; no sum can balance a friend's worth.

Sirach 6:15

This chapter will help you to:

- Understand the importance of friendship.
- Develop good communication skills.
- Learn ways to maintain old friendships and make new ones.

Media Suggestions (Optional)

- *Friends* (Tabor) 30 minutes. Don Kimball talks with adolescents about the importance of friendship.
- *A Man Called Norman* (Augsburg Fortress) 50 minutes. A story of one man's friendship with his elderly, ignored neighbor that emphasizes the importance of overcoming fears and the rewards of reaching out to others.

Aims

1. To help students gain an awareness of the importance of friendship.
2. To help students improve their communication skills through the use of six rules.

Begin the Section

1. Ask the students to recall their first "best friend." Say: "Most children form their first lasting friendship when they reach school age. How old were you when you met your first best friend?" Or, you may wish to assign **Application** Project 1 at this time.
2. Make two columns on the board. Write a "plus" sign over one column and a "minus" sign over the other column. Ask: "What are the best things about friendships? What are the worst things about friendships?" Record the responses in the appropriate columns.
3. Preview the section by reading or summarizing the opening three paragraphs. Then, say: "We will be reading about a conflict in a friendship between two high school students and the importance of good communication between two friends."

I. THE IMPORTANCE OF FRIENDS

When you were younger, the relationship you had with your parents or the person who raised you was the most important one in your life. From them, you experienced love and care. You learned important lessons for living—how to get along in the world outside of your home and what it means to be loved—from this relationship.

When you started school, however, this relationship changed. You began to define yourself as more than a member of a family. It was not enough for your mother or father to think of you as the most beautiful or talented person in the world. You also needed the approval of other adults, like teachers, as well as that of your peers.

67

Background

The word "friend" is closely related to the Germanic word that means, "to love." Friendships most often develop out of loving, caring relationships.

Who Are Your Friends?

Lesson Overview

Communication skills, or the lack of them, contribute to the success or failure of any relationship. The ways that friends communicate most often determine the direction of their friendship. Friends who communicate poorly will not survive the first argument or difference of opinion. Conversely, those who communicate well have the possibility of a lasting, trusting, and loving, lifetime relationship. In this lesson, stress the connection between good friendships and good communication skills. The two definitely go hand in hand.

Teaching Approaches

- Ask the students to rank the importance of friendships with other aspects in their lives (i.e., school, work, family, activities, and volunteer efforts). Ask for a show of hands to the following questions: "Who ranked friendships as most important in your life? Who ranked friendships least important?" Call on volunteers from each category to explain their ranking.
- Read or summarize this material. Point out that this lesson will explore the connection between good friendships and good communication.
- **Reteach**—Have the students play a word association game with a partner using some or all of the qualities of friendship suggested in the text: rapport, empathy, trust, and respect. Ask them to share the first thoughts that come to mind about a good friend.
- **Extend the Lesson**—Choose pairs of students to role play a conflict between two friends. Then, have the class comment on the perceived goals and importance of this relationship to each "friend."

✠ To Your Health

Teaching Approaches

- Brainstorm with students other ways to deal with conflict. Have the students decide if these new ways are positive or negative.
- Apply the steps for dealing with conflict to the story of Karolyn and Martha in "Face to Face."

Into this equation came *friends*—individuals you liked and with whom you could share common interests. Over the years, you have probably shared much with your friends and have received much in return. Some of these relationships may have grown to the point where you may now be closer to these friends than you are to your brothers or sisters. You trust your friends with your life. Let's take a closer look at the importance of friends.

Who Are Your Friends?

For some people, friends are more important than anything else in their lives. They spend great time and effort in building and maintaining friendships. They revel in the shared experiences and personal interaction that are part of good friendships. When friendships go awry, these people are most deeply hurt.

To others, friendships are just one aspect of a full life that also includes schoolwork, an after-school job or activity, family relationships, and even volunteer work. These people are less likely to be devastated over the breakup of a friendship. They may also be less likely to experience the same great rewards from friendship. The saying, "you can get out only what you put in" certainly applies to friendships. How important is friendship to you?

Who are your friends? Friends can be older or younger than you, male or female, may live next door or far away. Your closest friends, however, are most likely to be from your peers. Strong friendships are usually built on rapport, empathy, trust, and respect. Forgiveness is another important element of friendship. Good friends do not let their first argument come between them. Friends learn to say "I'm sorry," and to accept an apology. Communication is a very important part of friendship.

✠ To Your Health
Dealing with Conflict

How do you respond to conflict? How do your personal goals and the importance of a relationship affect your response to conflict?

What are your goals? How would you like to settle the conflict? When the conflict is over, what will you want to have accomplished? Are you willing to reach a compromise solution?

What is the importance of this relationship? How badly do you want this relationship to continue? Is the conflict caused by something trivial or is there something fundamentally wrong? When the conflict is resolved, do you want the relationship to be stronger?

Learning how to manage conflict effectively can reduce tension. When you are not tense, you can relax and be yourself.

Face to Face

In the case of Karolyn, a high school junior, a lack of communication almost ruined her friendship with Martha.

Vanessa, an acquaintance of Karolyn, approached her one day near her school locker and said, "I thought Martha was your friend."

"She is," Karolyn answered.

"Then why is she spreading rumors about you?" Vanessa went on. "She said that the reason you go on so many dates is that you'll go out with any guy who asks you."

"Get away from me, Vanessa," Karolyn shot back. "I know that Martha didn't say that. That sounds like something you made up."

Journal Assignment

Say: "Write a story or reflection titled 'My Best Friend'." Do not provide any more information to the students. Allow them to interpret the assignment in the way they see fit.

Vanessa walked off with a smirk on her face. Karolyn, instead of forgetting the incident, started thinking about what she had heard. "Maybe Martha was talking about me behind my back. She hasn't been on very many dates. I wonder if she could be jealous?" By sixth period, when Karolyn saw Martha in the biology lab, she was convinced that Martha was jealous.

Karolyn kept her distance from Martha during the rest of the day, and she was quiet as they rode the bus home from school. That night, she did not call Martha on the phone as she usually did. The next morning, Karolyn did call Martha to tell her that she would not be riding the bus to school.

For Martha, that was the last straw. She spotted Karolyn in the hallway before first period. "What is bothering you?" she demanded.

"Were you talking about me to Vanessa and her friends?" Karolyn wanted to know.

"Of course not. Don't be crazy. You know Vanessa has a reputation for stirring up trouble," said Martha.

Friend or Acquaintance

People frequently refer to another person as a friend when actually what they mean is that the person is an acquaintance. A person is an acquaintance when the relationship has not developed beyond recognizing a person's name or face. Most of your classmates are probably acquaintances (hopefully friendly), as are most of the people with whom you work or attend church. How would you describe the difference between a friend and an acquantaince?

Karolyn's anger diffused. She looked carefully at her friend, and believed her. She was glad she didn't have to spend the rest of the day worrying about a problem that did not exist.

Gossiping is a bad habit. Left unchecked, it can damage even the strongest friendships.

Resources

Resource 4A provides a format to extend the story of Karolyn and Martha and asks the students to write about the friends' next conversation on the bus on the way home from school.

Face to Face

New Words
An *acquaintance* is defined as a person whom one knows, but not intimately.

Teaching Approaches
- Choose four volunteers to take the parts of Martha, Karolyn, Vanessa, and the narrator; then read the story aloud.
- Have the students list and comment on the communication difficulties presented in this story.
- **Reteach**—What real life examples can students offer of situations similar to the one in the text? How were these situations resolved?
- **Extend the Lesson**—Use **Application** Project 2. You may wish to assign several groups to role play additional situations.

Friend or Acquaintance

Teaching Approaches
- Read or have the students read the panel. Discuss the in-text question.
- Discuss: "Why is it important to distinguish between friends and acquaintances?"

Positive Confrontations

Teaching Approaches

- Discuss the impact of gossip on friendships. What do students think about gossip and the people who gossip?
- Ask the students to suggest other ways to avoid participating in gossip.
- **Reteach**—Read 2 Corinthians 12:19-13:9. What advice does Paul offer to those who gossip?
- **Extend the Lesson**—Encourage the students to put into practice the suggestions for ending gossip. Ask them to write a letter to someone they have offended by gossip and seek to reconcile the relationship. (They need not actually send the letter, although you may encourage them to do so.) Assign **Application** Project 3 at this time.

☀ Media Watch

Teaching Approaches

- Using Question 4, have students find ads that use friends to sell a product. What do students think about this practice? What makes this type of ad effective? How do these ads use or misuse friendship?
- Display other magazine ads or show several taped television commercials. Discuss questions 1, 2, 3, and 5 in relation to these.
- For Question 2, point out that about twice as much money is spent on television commercials as on other television programming.
- Invite a person who works with advertising to the classroom to join in the discussion initiated by these questions.

Talk It Over

If the students have previously discussed Question 1, you may wish to have them write a specific example for the question in their journals. For Question 2, have volunteers take turns acting out Karolyn's reaction. Discuss the first part of Question 3 with the entire class. Point out that there is really nothing positive gained by listening to gossip. For the second part, have the students brainstorm ideas. On a classroom chart designed as a stop sign titled "Stop Gossip," compile their ideas with those listed in the text. Post it in the classroom as a reminder.

☀ Media Watch
Keeping Tabs on Advertisers

Discuss these questions with a partner or write your responses in your journal:

1. What are some positive things advertising provides for consumers?
2. Why do you think more money is spent on television commercials than on television programming?
3. What are some ways that advertising uses friendship to sell a product?
4. Find an ad that clearly uses the idea of friends to market its product. What makes this ad effective? Explain why you think the ad uses or misuses the idea of friendship.
5. Explain why you think you would be more or less likely to pay attention to an ad that uses friendship.

Positive Confrontations

Have you ever lost a friend because of gossip or rumors? Do you think it's true that anyone who you hear talking about someone probably talks about you, too?

Gossiping is a bad habit that can cause harm. Saint Paul called it a moral disorder *(2 Corinthians 12:20)* that Christians should avoid if they hope to follow Jesus.

What can you do to stop gossip from ruining a friendship or hurting other people? One thing that you can do is to refuse to participate in gossip in any way. For example:

- Don't listen to rumors or gossip.
- Defend the reputation of people who are not present to defend themselves.
- Just walk away.
- Confront the person spreading the rumors. Ask point blank if what you heard was true. The person's knowing that you are aware of the situation may help to put an end to the problem.
- Don't spread rumors or gossip yourself.

Talk It Over

1. How important are your friendships to you? Illustrate your answer with an example.
2. How would you have reacted to Vanessa's rumors if you were in Karolyn's position?
3. Why do people listen to gossip? What are some other things you can do to stop gossip?

Learning to Communicate

Good communication requires dialogue; one person speaks while the other truly listens and attempts to understand what is actually being said. Friendships grow when both people work at these communication skills. They may often even be changed by the process. When friends can respond honestly to each other and share their insights and feelings on various topics without fear, they have a solid friendship. In these friendships, people are treated with respect, and real communication takes place.

There is no need to patronize someone or agree with everything that is said. Solid friendships demand that the truth be told with respect for the other person. Unfortunately, what passes for communication in many relationships is *shared monologue:* one person speaks and the other person thinks about what he or she will say when the first person finishes.

Faulty communication often breaks up friendships. For example:

◊ Jim tells Patrick that he has to stay home and study. Later that evening, Patrick sees Jim at the movies and is furious. Patrick doesn't stop to consider that maybe Jim finished his work early and came to the movie looking for him. Instead of trying to find out

Background

In 2 Corinthians 12: 19-13: 9, Paul alludes to the fear he has that the Corinthians have been swayed from "right thinking" by what Paul considers to be a satanic influence. The moral disorders—rivalry, jealously, fury, selfishness, slander, gossip, and conceit—are the results of this influence.

why his friend's plans changed, Patrick simply stomps away.

◊ Mary tells Amanda that she has no desire to date Edgar, and that Amanda can date him if she wants. The next day, Amanda sees Mary and Edgar studying together in the library. Amanda is hurt that her friend lied. And to think that she was going to ask Edgar to the next school formal. When Mary and Edgar finish using the same encyclopedia, they go their separate ways. Amanda doesn't know this, however. She's too busy feeling sorry for herself to find out the truth.

What are the communication problems in these scenarios? What would you do in a similar situation? How could better communication solve these problems?

Managing Conflicts

Conflicts can occur in any relationship and for any reason. In addition to communication problems, conflicts result from judging others. In Karolyn's case, she felt that Martha would probably not talk about her with someone else, but Karolyn did know that she and Martha had often gossiped about other girls in the school. Karolyn began to make a judgment based on that experience.

At times, conflicts occur because one person in the relationship is not as confident or does not have as positive a level of self-esteem as the other. The friend with the lower self-esteem may begin to take any comment that is brought up as a personal threat. At this point, tensions rise and conflict begins.

Conflicts do not have to be bad experiences in friendships. For example, conflict can make two friends aware of problems they need to resolve. A friendship may have become stagnant because of a lack of communication. Through conflict, lines of communication can be reopened. Also, conflict can lead a person to look more deeply at an issue. Finally, conflict can actually help to deepen and improve a friendship. It can strengthen a person's belief that the bond between friends is stronger than any issue that causes conflict.

Talk It Over

1. Agree or disagree: "Communication is the most important element of a friendship." Explain the reasons for your answer.
2. Give an example of how a conflict could help a friendship.

▲ Family Living
Learning at Home

People learn much about friendship at home. The strengths and weaknesses they exhibit with friends may well model the strengths and weaknesses of their families.

Dolores Curran, in *Traits of a Healthy Family,* lists 15 traits that are most commonly found in families considered healthy. The healthy family:

1. Communicates and listens.
2. Affirms and supports.
3. Respects one another.
4. Develops a sense of trust.
5. Has a sense of play and humor.
6. Shares responsibility.
7. Teaches right and wrong.
8. Has a strong sense of kinship with many traditions.
9. Has a balance of interaction.
10. Has a shared religious core.
11. Respects the privacy of one another.
12. Values service to others.
13. Fosters family table time and conversation.
14. Shares leisure time.
15. Admits to problems and seeks help.

How many of these traits would you expect to find in healthy friendships?

Journal Assignment

"Write about how an incident of faulty communication caused the breakup of one of your friendships."

Background

Dolores Curran is a nationally syndicated columnist and author of many books on family life, including *Traits of a Healthy Family* and *Stress and the Healthy Family.*

Learning to Communicate

Lesson Overview

The title of this lesson underlies part of the dilemma of good communication: people need to **learn** communication skills. Many people are under the impression that communication just happens, that communication skills are an in-born trait. This lesson examines some of the problems that result from miscommunication, and offers six rules to help improve a person's ability to listen, and hence communicate better.

Teaching Approaches

- Read or summarize the first two paragraphs. Ask a pair of volunteers to do an impression of the "shared monologue" form of communication.
- Read the rest of the section. Discuss the questions that follow the two scenarios with the entire class. Elicit several solutions for each communication problem.
- **Reteach**—What are other examples of times when relationships experienced difficulties because of poor communication skills?
- **Extend the Lesson**—Play the game "telephone." **Resource 4B** offers further suggestions and more detailed directions for playing the "telephone" game.

▲ Family Living

Teaching Approaches

- Have the students write a "Friendship Creed" based on some of these traits found in healthy families; for example, "A friend has a sense of play and humor."
- Encourage the students to add some of their own additional "friendship traits" to the list.

Managing Conflicts

Teaching Approaches

- Make sure that the students understand that conflicts can be either good or bad, depending on how they are handled.

Managing Conflicts

- What are examples of times when conflict is bad for friendships? When do friendships thrive on conflict?
- **Reteach**—Ask: "What must a relationship have to be able to thrive on conflict?"
- **Extend the Lesson**—Assign **Application** Project 4.

Talk It Over

For Question 1, have the students suggest other important elements of a friendship. Then, debate the relative importance of each. For Question 2, ask the students to think of personal examples. Ask volunteers to share their examples with the class.

Good Listener Exam

Teaching Approaches

- Assign the students to work individually on this activity. Ask volunteers to comment on what they learned from it.
- Students are to listen intently to the ways others communicate during a day. Have them keep notes on their observations. Are most of the interactions they observe healthy? Why? Why not? Allow time for them to discuss their findings and reactions in class.

Good Listener Exam

Indicate whether each statement describes you most of the time (M), some of the time (S), or never (N).

1. When listening, I assume I know what the other person is going to say.
2. I interrupt others when they talk.
3. I find myself thinking about what I am going to say while the other person is talking.
4. I don't make eye contact when listening to another person.
5. I do several things while I listen.
6. I find my mind wandering while someone else is talking.
7. I make quick judgments on what is being said.
8. I refuse to ask for things to be repeated.
9. I carry on several conversations at one time.
10. I don't ask questions, even when I haven't a clue what is being said.

Scoring. Give yourself 4 points for each M, 2 points for each S, and 0 points for each N.
- 0 to 10: You have very good listening skills.
- 11 to 20: You have some good listening skills, but could develop your skills more.
- 21 or more: Have you noticed people do not talk to you very much? It could be because of your listening skills, or lack of them.

Background

Discussions focused on the original problems are generally beneficial. Those that involve name calling or that use past events as weapons, are likely to harm a relationship. Conflicts can be constructive.

Resources

Resource 4C looks at some ineffective ways to manage conflict.

Six Rules for Improved Communication

Improving your ability to communicate is not easy, but it is possible if you are willing to work at developing better listening skills. Studies indicate that we spend 80 percent of our waking hours communicating, and at least 60 percent of that time listening. Unfortunately, most people are not good listeners. These six rules can help you improve your listening skills:

1. Give people your full attention when they are speaking. They, in turn, should do the same for you.
2. Try to understand what the other person is truly saying.
3. Stay calm.
4. Use "I-messages."
5. Show other people respect.
6. Think before you speak.

Let's look at these rules in more detail.

Give your full attention. Focus your attention on the speaker. You might consider actually looking the speaker in the eye. Don't be distracted by the television or radio, a book, or another conversation.

Be aware of the speaker's body language as well. Does he or she appear to be angry? happy? excited? defensive? Is he or she smiling or frowning? patting his or her foot impatiently? wringing his or her hands? bouncing up and down?

Understanding what people are feeling or thinking when they use words is difficult enough. Trying to decipher unspoken language is a real challenge. Friends often face this situation. Let's say that your best friend, Sam, stares right through you when you wave at him on the school steps before the start of class. The common human response is to jump to a conclusion: "What did I do wrong to make Sam mad at me?" Later in the day when you apologize for making him angry Sam responds, "What are you talking about?" When you explain the situation he laughs and says, "I didn't even see you this morning. I was trying to remember whether we needed our journals today."

One way to improve communication between friends is to give full attention to the speaker. What does this picture show about the communication skills of these people.

Six Rules for Improved Communication

Lesson Overview

Ask the students what they expect to gain from better communication skills. Point out that better communication skills improve the quality of relationships, increase self-confidence and motivation, and lead to better concentration, which in turn results in better decisions.

Teaching Approaches

- Read the first two paragraphs, introducing the six rules for improved communication. Say: "We will examine each rule in more detail."
- Read or summarize each of the six rules. Elicit questions and comments from the students to check their understanding of each rule. You may wish to have students memorize these rules.
- Discuss: "How would these rules improve communication?"
- **Reteach**—Complete **Application** Project 5 as a class or small group assignment.
- **Extend the Lesson**—Divide the class into groups of three. One person is to be the observer and to give feedback, one is to be the listener, and the third member has a problem that he or she is expressing. The observer should watch for the use of the six rules of good communication. The person with the problem confronts the listener with it. The listener's task is to practice the rules of communication. Rotate so that all the students have a chance to be the listener. Conclude with large group sharing about the successes and difficulties in communicating effectively.

Background

The average listener correctly understands, properly evaluates, and retains thirty percent of what was said 30 minutes after a ten-minute presentation. After forty-eight hours, retention will be less than twenty percent.

Journal Assignment

"Write a parable about the effects of using good or poor communication skills." As an example, remind the students of the story of "The Boy Who Cried Wolf."

In Focus

Teaching Approaches

- Read or summarize the text feature.
- Ask one or two volunteers to dramatize some of the examples of "body language" suggested by the text questions.
- Explain to students that nonverbal messages are often a truer reflection of the feelings of the person sending the message than what the speaker says verbally. It is easier to say something you do not mean than it is for your body to pass along a misleading message. People who are not being honest and open in their messages, will show the truth with their bodies. When verbal and nonverbal messages do not agree, people tend to become confused and begin to question the veracity of the speaker.

In Focus
Body Language

When you talk to a teacher, you may not stand as close as you do when you are conversing with a good friend. You may feel uncomfortable around strangers in a crowded elevator, while quite comfortable on a crowded dance floor. These examples illustrate the space people keep between themselves and others. This use of space is part of the communication form we call body language.

Think of recent conversations you have had with friends. Recall their posture. Think about whether or not they were attentive. Did they look at you rather than at the background or the floor? Did they nod their heads from time to time in agreement? Did they smile or frown at appropriate times? What did they do with their hands and their feet? These are all forms of body language.

Spend a few moments reflecting on how your family and friends express their love and concern for you. How do you know that they care? How do you show others what you feel or think?

Try to understand what the other person is truly saying.

The phone call you've been hoping for all week just happened. Glenda asked if you'd like to go to the concert on Saturday night, and you said yes! You can't believe your good fortune. You've wanted to see this group live for two years, but didn't have the money. Now this friend of yours has tickets. You arrive at her house on time and ready to rock and roll, but something's not right. Glenda's wearing her best dress while you have on sneakers and jeans. Glenda comments, "That's an odd way to dress for the orchestra."

Have you ever had the experience of understanding one thing when the speaker meant something else entirely? This type of confusion is common. If you have doubts about what the speakers mean, ask them for clarification, or restate what you heard in your own words. This works with both spoken and unspoken statements.

If you have doubts about what the speaker means, ask for clarification, or restate what you heard in your own words.

Background

According to Dr. Albert Meharbian, professor of psychology at UCLA, 55% of what we understand comes from body language, 38% from tone of voice, and 7% from the actual words spoken.

Resources

Resource 4D provides examples of various types of body language.

By clarifying what concert she meant, this problem could have been avoided. A clarifying reply to Glenda's offer of tickets to the concert might be, "You're inviting me to the rock concert?" Any miscommunication then could be resolved quickly. A corollary to this rule is *never be embarrassed to clarify your understanding*. What are some other ways to clarify a speaker's meaning?

Stay calm. Few conflicts are settled by yelling and screaming. When people are calm, they are less likely to say things they don't mean, and are less likely to use words that cause harm. A person who remains calm can often see new ways to resolve difficult problems.

Use I-messages. Speak about what you know or feel, not about what another has done or should do. For example, "You make me so angry" can easily become "I get so angry when you do that." The more you use I-messages in your conversations, the easier you will find it is to use them in a difficult situation. As you learn to think in I-messages, you will be less likely to be offended when others use "you-messages"; you will automatically translate them into I-messages.

Show respect. Treat friends as you wish to be treated, with the *dignity* that any person deserves. You know the appropriate time to talk about personal matters. How do you feel when someone asks you an embarrassing question in front of someone you want to impress? That is certainly not the proper time to talk about someone's complexion or weight gain! How would you feel if your friends raved about last weekend's great party—the one to which you didn't receive an invitation? In discussing problems or conflicts with a friend, choose a quiet time for discussion when there is little chance for interruption.

Think before you speak. Be prepared with what you want to say before you say it. Rehearse your ideas if you have time. Don't blurt out the first thing that comes to mind. Stay focused. Establish mental boundaries about what you will say. Discuss only the current problems. This is not the time to remember old hurts; they will only get in the way of solving the current difficulty.

Talk It Over

1. Look at the suggestions for improving communication. Make a list of those you already practice and a second list of those you want to practice. What do you need to do to improve your communication skills?
2. What are two other suggestions that you could follow to improve your communication?

Well Being
More Communication Tips

Here are additional suggestions for improving your communication skills:

1. Avoid conflicts based on personalities. Always remain specific when you have a disagreement with another.
2. Ask for advice when you are solving a problem, trying to decide what to do, or are sharing information about a current event. Avoid trying to impress someone with how much you know.
3. Show real respect for the other. Care about his or her joys and sufferings.
4. Don't hide your aims. Be honest about your motives. Always be up front about "what's in it for you" when you share an idea or suggestion.
5. Make requests, not orders. Never boss anyone else around.
6. When you give your opinion, admit that you are open to change. Never be so hardheaded that you refuse to listen to the other side of an issue.

Well-Being

Teaching Approaches

- If possible, have the students observe these additional rules for good communication in a role play situation.
- Point out that no matter how many rules or suggestions for good communication a person follows, there is no guarantee that communication problems will be solved. Communication is a two-way street. If the other person refuses to listen or to express his or her own real feelings, there is nothing else a person can do.

Talk It Over

Allow time for the students to compile the lists suggested in Question 1. Then, have them discuss both questions with a partner or in a small group.

Journal Assignment

The students can write their reflections to the questions, "How do you know that your family and friends care for you? How do you show others what you feel or think?"

II. QUALITIES OF FRIENDSHIP

Aims

1. To help students be aware that all relationships, including friendships, change over time.

2. To help students recognize ways to make friends and adapt friendships to new situations.

Begin the Section

1. If possible, arrange for the students to share photos of themselves as children with their friends. Ask: "What attracted you to certain friends?"

2. Read or summarize the first four paragraphs.

3. Ask: "Who is your most recent friend? How did you make that friendship? How would you compare your old friendships to your new friendships?" After some discussion, point out that these issues will be discussed further in this section.

Moving On

Lesson Overview

This story reflects the many emotions brought about by changes in one's life—sadness, excitement, jealousy, and love. Help the students to connect this story of friendship with experiences going on in their own lives.

Teaching Approaches

- Assign the story for silent reading.
- Allow time for comments. Ask: "In what direction do you think Dave and Jon's friendship will go from here?"
- **Reteach**—Use "Talk It Over" question 2 for discussion.
- **Extend the Lesson**—What would students do differently if this were their friendship?

II. QUALITIES OF FRIENDSHIP

Good communication skills can lead to strong friendships. Friends who communicate well are able to see each other as they really are, and can live with their faults and shortcomings as well. Friends who communicate well can accept their different opinions and attitudes. Some of their values and goals will not be alike. Yet, with honest communication, they can continue to enjoy the fruits of friendship. With honest communication, friends can better adapt to the inevitable changes that are bound to occur.

You may have had the same friends all your life. Dave met Jon in kindergarten and they have been best friends ever since. Friendships that last this long can bring a great deal of pleasure and satisfaction.

Some people, however, have moved frequently over the years and have friends in many different places. As your interests have grown and developed, your friendships have changed as well.

Most people continue to make friends as they grow older. It's hard to imagine, but some of your closest friends ten years from now may be people you have not even met yet. After you leave high school, you will leave some of your old friends behind and will form new acquaintances with people you meet in college or in the workplace. Some of these people may become friends. Consider what happened to the friendship between Dave and Jon. Could something like this happen to you?

Moving On

From the time Dave took a course in chemistry during his sophomore year, he wanted to be a pharmacist. Drake University, in Des Moines, Iowa, had an excellent program. The problem was that Dave lived in Florida. He couldn't imagine living so far from home, enduring harsh winters, and leaving his friends.

When he was awarded a scholarship, Dave knew that he would go to Drake even with all of his reservations. As his mom put it, "David, the opportunity is too good to pass up."

Dave remembered well the night his plane left for Des Moines. Jon, Dave's best friend, arranged a surprise party at a restaurant near the airport. Most of Dave's other friends came to see him off: Keith, Joni, Larry, and Sue, Dave's date to the senior prom. Just before Dave boarded the plane, Jon held up a clenched fist and called out, "Brothers forever!"

"Just plain friends forever," said Sue.

Dave felt like crying.

When Dave returned home at Christmas break, only his family was there to greet him at the airport. It took four days before he was able to reach Jon or any of his other high school friends who had gone camping. When they returned, Jon apologized. "Dave, we didn't know that you would be back so soon or we would have waited," he explained. "I wished you'd have written or called."

Changing Friendships

All relationships change over time, especially when people are separated and begin to have different experiences. In the years to come, you will change and so will your current friends. If you go away to college, your friends' lives are not put on hold while yours moves on. You will not be able to pick up exactly where you left off in the friendships when you return. You will have had new experiences, met new people, and made new friends without them, and they without you. Experiencing this for the first time can be very painful. Some people become so afraid

Journal Assignment

"Write a story about one of your changing friendships. Try to explain why this relationship is changing. How do you feel about these changes? What can you do to renew the friendship?"

Some friends make pledges to stay together forever.

of change that they are unwilling to try anything new.

Adjusting to the changes that occur in long-standing friendships and knowing how to make friends are important interpersonal skills. Learning these skills will make living with these new situations easier, and can be invaluable in other life choices as well.

One way that Dave and Jon worked out the changes in their relationship was by first acknowledging that changes were taking place. "Who knows? Maybe someday we will be neighbors and raise our families next-door to each other. But, for now, we need to admit that our lives are taking two different paths," Jon said.

Sometimes, a person will try to pit an old friend against a new one. For example, if Jon acts like everything his new friend says is funnier or more interesting than what Dave says, Dave will begin to feel unwanted. In doing this, Jon would be attempting to validate his new life as good while rejecting everything from his old life as bad. Friendship will never survive when forced into such a competition.

Reviving Friendships

How can a friendship be kept alive when faced with diverging life directions? Some friends actually schedule regular times to meet. Where in the past Dave and Jon's relationship was more spontaneous, now they call and arrange times to get together. As you get older, you may need to make similar appointments to meet with a friend.

Background

People tend to make friends with those people who share common attitudes and behaviors. Friends drift apart as their needs and interests change. To revive a stalled friendship, the two people must discover new sources of common concern.

Changing Friendships

Teaching Approaches

- Admitting that a relationship is changing, and developing a plan for taking the relationship in a new direction, are two ways to deal with changing friendships. Try to have the students pinpoint the reasons why some of their own friendships have persevered for many years, while others have ended.
- **Reteach**—Ask: "What is your experience of trying to bring your old friends together with your new friends?"
- **Extend the Lesson**—Ask: "How can learning to adjust to change be a valuable skill for the future?"

Reviving Friendships

Teaching Approaches

- Read or have the students read the section.
- **Reteach**—Discuss the in-text question: "How can a friendship be kept alive when faced with diverging life directions?"
- **Extend the Lesson**—Ask: "What do you think of Jon and Dave's plan to have a regular meal together? How will that help keep their friendship alive?"

Talk It Over

For Question 1, if possible, arrange for one of the students to bring the friend that he or she has had the longest to class. Ask them both to share the story of how they met. To extend Question 2, ask the students how they would feel if they were in the same predicament as Dave and Jon. Have the students brainstorm possible answers for Question 3. List their ideas on the board.

Making New Friends

Lesson Overview

Being able to make new friends is an important skill. The way students interact with friends now parallels in many ways the way they will interact in the future with their co-workers, supervisors, spouses, in-laws, and many other people. Some high school students are comfortable with and unwilling to move beyond their immediate (or current) peer group; they need to be reminded of the advantages of making new friends.

Teaching Approaches

• Read or summarize the section. Ask: "What are some reasons for making new friends? What are some reasons for not making new friends?" Lead the students to see that the advantages of new friendships are greater than the disadvantages.

• Divide the class into four groups. Assign each group one of the suggestions for meeting new friends. Have the groups practice and present a skit based on their suggestion.

• Be sensitive to the fact that some of your students may not have even one friend. Have students develop a general list of suggestions called, "How to make friends!"

• **Reteach**—Have the students begin keeping records as suggested in **Application** Project 6 (see **Resource 4E**).

Preserving friendships often means developing new tradtions.

When they were both in town, Jon and Dave committed themselves to dinner at least once a month. Each made sure they honored the commitment. Also, they never brought anyone else along. This night was theirs to renew old ties and catch up on new ones. The presence of a third person would change the dynamics of the conversation. For Dave and Jon, the dinners became a new tradition. Both could envision themselves getting together this way for years to come. This friendship would be preserved.

Talk It Over

1. Who is the friend you have had the longest? How did you meet?
2. How do you think Dave felt when he could not reach his friends? when he found out that they didn't wait for him before going camping?
3. What is another suggestion you have for maintaining friendships?

Making New Friends

One of the positive things about moving on to a new situation like college or career is that it affords you the chance to form new relationships and to make new friends. Unfortunately, some people do not think of making new friends as a positive event. Comfortable where they are now in their current friendships, some people dread the thought of having to make new ones.

Actually, making new friends can be fun, challenging, and rewarding. In your career, you will have to relate closely with people of all ages and both sexes. You will share your work with many people and probably have to report directly to a supervisor. The skills you practice in making new friends can help you in those relationships. If you plan to marry, you must first meet the man or woman who will become your spouse. Knowing how to make new friends can help you here, too. The marriage relationship, after all, is founded on friendship. People who marry become each other's best friend.

It's a given that making friends is not always easy. If you are quiet and unassertive, it may be very hard to get anyone to notice you. Even if you are confident in your ability to attract others, forming a new friendship is still difficult. Remember, a friendship always involves communication. Even people who host the best attended parties, go on the most dates, or win all the school elections, still must interact with others on a one-to-one basis. That is also where friendship really forms.

The best way to make new friends is to remember how you made old ones. When you were younger, you may have made friends by participating on a team or through an activity, like scouting. In your first years of high school, you may have made friends through common interests. Maybe there was only one other person in the school who shared your interest in snakes. You two were the ones who spent the most time in the biology lab.

Resources

Resource 4F includes suggestions for starting conversations that may lead to new friendships. Use these conversation starters with the "Extend the Lesson" exercise from "Making New Friends."

Your common interest led to initial conversation and then friendship. Did you ever make friends with someone new to your school or neighborhood? Sometimes all it takes to make a new friend is exchanging a kind word or friendly smile.

You don't have to reinvent the wheel in order to learn how to make friends. The same basic ways that you met friends when you were younger will work for you now, although they may need some modifications. Try these suggestions:

1. Join a club or group where there are people who you would enjoy knowing. In college, as in high school, there are many opportunities to participate in extracurricular activities. Generally, people who have the same interests as you do make good friends. If there happen to be no clubs or groups that meet one of your interests, consider forming your own. One student, who enjoyed science fiction movies, started a club called "Invader Videos." He reserved a classroom, video recorder, and television for lunchtime once a week. He advertised a scene from a sci-fi video in the school bulletin and invited anyone interested to come. The first few weeks, only a few people attended. Then, word spread that it was an entertaining way to spend the lunch hour and a good way to meet people. Within weeks, "Invader Videos" had a regular following.

2. Volunteer. Some of the most lasting relationships are formed when people work together on a common project. When Ben signed up to help build temporary housing for families who had lost their homes in a tornado, he did so to gain merit points for a scouting project. Little did he know that he would meet guys and girls from others schools who would become some of his closest friends.

3. Invite people to your home. Many people are lonely or shy and just need to be invited. Have someone over to study together, to have dinner, or to plan an activity for a group. This is a good way to really get to know someone.

4. Treat people as you would like to be treated. This is a good rule in any relationship, whether old or new. In forming new friendships, the friendly word or smile you share should bring the same to you in return. At that point, take the initiative a step further and begin a conversation. There are many general topics that can start a conversation.

Do you know anyone who does not have even one friend? That can be a miserable existence. What could you do to help this person make friends?

After you leave high school, the opportunities and needs to form new friendships increase. Be ready for the challenge. Set a goal to meet new people and make new friends.

Talk It Over

1. How easily do you make friends? Discuss how you go about making a friend.
2. Talk about what it would be like not to have any friends.

One way to meet new friends is to join a club where there are people who you would enjoy knowing.

Teaching Approaches (continued)

- **Extend the Lesson**—Choose one or both of these activities: (1) Have the students complete a questionnaire on their talents and interests. (For example, "What do you like to do on weekends?" and "What is your favorite hobby?") Keep the questionnaires anonymous. Then, collect them and list some of the responses on the board. Ask the students if they were aware that some of their classmates had similar talents and interests. Comment that by knowing more about other people, we are more likely to find the common ground necessary to begin a friendship. (2) Have the students work with a partner. They are to practice starting a conversation with someone who is new to the school. Instruct the pairs to take turns being the "new kid." Allow time for volunteers to share the problems they ran into as well as some effective conversation icebreakers.

Talk It Over

For Question 1, encourage students to offer suggestions for making new friends not previously mentioned. For Question 2, only call on volunteers to answer the question before the large group. Or, have all the students write their answers in their journals.

Background

According to various studies, friendships in the workplace are very important to a person's business success. They can influence one's productivity, creativity, problem solving, and even promotions.

Necessary Skills

Lesson Overview

By becoming incarnate, Jesus opened the way for a new type of relationship between God and humankind. As the Second Person of the Trinity, Jesus is truly God, yet He is also our Brother and Friend. In looking for ways to help the students come to a more tangible relationship with Jesus, encourage them to read the Gospels to become more familiar with Jesus' words. Also, point out how the communication skills learned for relationships with friends can also be used to communicate more effectively with God through prayer.

Teaching Approaches

- Read the first paragraph. Ask the students to agree or disagree with this statement: "Everybody needs somebody."

- Read or summarize the rest of the section. In small groups or with partners, have the students brainstorm a plan for making the six rules for good communication a part of their ongoing prayer life with God.

- **Reteach**—Assign **Application** Project 7.

- **Extend the Lesson**—Of the many Old Testament heroes, only one was referred to as a "friend of God"; the others were known as slaves. Have the students look up the following Scripture passages to discover which hero was called "friend of God": Moses *(Deuteronomy 34:5)*, Joshua *(Joshua 24:9)*, David *(Psalm 89:21)*, and Abraham *(Isaiah 41:8)*.

☙ Prayer in Action

Teaching Approaches

- You may wish to read this verse prior to a time of spontaneous, free-flowing prayer in which you allow the students to offer prayers of praise, thankfulness, and petition.

- Explain that Jesus is present in community, and "two or three" people are as small a community as one can have. While the common prayer of two or three people does not speak for the Church, it does call forth the presence of the living Jesus.

Necessary Skills

The skills you learn in making and maintaining friendships now will assist you in all your relationships in the years ahead, including your relationship with God. Acting as if you truly care for others is a good first step if you don't want to "go it alone." Everyone needs other people, even Saint Jerome, a noted curmudgeon who was a Father of the Church. While Jerome recommended that people live a life of complete solitude, he was never able to accomplish this himself. Though he fled society for the hermit's life, many people followed him into the desert. He also corresponded with many friends throughout his life.

The communication skills you've practiced can also be utilized in your relationship with God. Prayer is communication with God. One of the many surprises of Jesus' teachings was that we, as people, are friends of God. Jesus said:

> "I no longer call you slaves, because a slave does not know what his master is doing. I have called you friends, because I have told you everything I have heard from My Father"
>
> *(John 15:15)*.

How can your relationships with others help you to know God better?

☙ Prayer in Action
Time with Friends

We have a better chance to know one another when we share time together. How can prayer be a part of your shared time with friends as well? Through prayer, Jesus becomes a living and active member of your relationships. Read the words below. Consider their meaning in terms of some of your own friendships.

"Again, I say to you, if two of you agree on earth about anything for which they are to pray, it shall be granted to them by My heavenly Father. For where two or three are gathered together in My name, there am I in the midst of them"

Matthew 18:19-20.

As in other friendships, part of the communication problem many people have with God is that they do not listen enough. Most people will acknowledge that they pray, though their prayer may be mostly petitions; that is, "I pray to do well on this test" or "I pray for the good health of my parents." Only when we spend time listening to God do we have a chance to witness God's response. We can practice good listening skills in this relationship by taking notice of the ways that people act in our lives. You can ask yourself: "What is God saying to me through people?" This is one way to know God better. This is one way to deepen the friendship with God to which Jesus has invited us.

The Social You

There is a type of photography—Kirlian photography—that takes a picture of the energy being sent out of a given object. When your picture is taken by a camera with film sensitive to energy waves, your body will appear larger than life, be-

---

Background

Saint Jerome (345-420 A.D.) is best known for translating the Old Testament from Hebrew, and the New Testament from Greek into Latin. A mystic, he spent five years in the desert in prayer and penance living in Bethlehem in a cave thought to be the birthplace of Jesus. Jerome was reputed to be a curmudgeon and at times a very unpleasant person. Yet the people of his day looked to him as a holy man.

---

cause of the energy waves flowing out of it. A photograph of people standing next to each other, taken with this special film, would seem to show individuals blending into one another. In other words, if the picture were of you and some friends, it would show your energy waves entering the energy field of the persons next to you, and their energy field entering your own. You could say that something of you was in them and that something of them was in you.

When we relate with others, we share something of our lives. Have you ever thought that the kind of person that you are today is made up of bits and pieces of all the people you have met in your life? You are affected by every relationship, however brief.

Making new friends, keeping old friends, and improving communication between all friends is beneficial for your life now. These skills can also help you in the future. You have the power to be a positive influence on every person you meet in your life. If you marry, this influence can carry to succeeding generations through your children. If you become a religious or priest, this influence can literally touch God's People. And, in the workplace, the way you treat others will be noticed. By your actions you can be known as a living and working part of the Body of Christ.

Whatever you decide to do with your life, relationships will be a part of it. The better your

Sharpening Your Skills
Meeting the Right People

The best friendships often occur between people with common interests. If you are looking for a friend, ask yourself these questions:

1. What are my interests?
2. What do I value most?
3. What do I look for in a friend?

Look for friends in organizations or clubs to which you belong. Start up a conversation with someone who seems to share your sense of fashion by complimenting them on their taste.

communication skills, the more successful these relationships are likely to be. Improving your relationships with family members and friends now can help you in the future.

Talk It Over

1. How does your friendship with God compare with your other friendships?
2. Tell one specific way that the skills you have from making friendships benefits your life.

Chapter Summary

- Friendships are among the most important and influential relationships in life.
- Participating in a relationship with a friend can help a person to learn clear and honest communication skills.
- Practicing listening techniques is a way to improve communication skills.

- Conflicts can help a relationship to grow.
- Adjusting to changes in old friendships and knowing how to make new friends are important interpersonal skills.
- The skills used in making and maintaining friendships can be used in all types of relationships, including those with co-workers, spouses, and God.

The Social You

Lesson Overview

The whole idea of making "life decisions" can be a scary proposition at any age. Help the students see that with careful practice and with God's help, they will be able to move forward in life.

Teaching Approaches

- Read or summarize the section. Ask: "What are some important decisions that you will be making in the upcoming years? How can friendship and communication skills help you to make good choices? What part will God play in the choices that you make?"
- **Reteach**—Have students research Kirlian photography. Ask: "How is friendship illustrated by this type of photography?"
- **Extend the Lesson**—Use **Application** Project 8 as a tool to review the main theme of the chapter.

Sharpening Your Skills

Teaching Approaches

- Discuss: "How realistic is it to think that friends might pray together?"
- Ask: "How can prayer become part of your relationships with friends?"

Talk It Over

Have the students discuss both questions in a small group or with a partner. In a large group, have a leader from each group or pair share one idea from Question 3: a specific skill in making a friendship.

Chapter Summary

- Ask the students if they have any questions or comments on Chapter 4.
- Have students read and discuss these statements in small groups before reporting back to the entire class.

Journal Assignment

Have the students think about their best friend. Then, have them write their answers to the following questions: "What things do you like about your best friend? How would you describe your best friend to other people? In what ways does your best friend help you to feel good about yourself?"

Chapter 4 Review

What Have You Learned?

Listed below are suggested answers. For many of the questions, the answers will vary.

1. Though friends can be of any age or sex, a person's closest friends are likely to be drawn from his or her own peer group.

2. A friend is someone you like and with whom you share a common interest. An acquaintance is a person with whom you have casual contact.

3. Answers will vary. For example, gossip can be prevented by confronting the person spreading rumors.

4. Dialogue is an honest give-and-take of opinions, insights, and feelings. In shared monologue, one person talks while the other thinks up what to say next.

5. The six rules for good communication are: (1) give people your full attention when speaking; (2) try to understand what the other person is truly saying; (3) stay calm; (4) use "I-messages"; (5) show other people respect; and (6) think before you speak.

6. Answers will vary. Conflict occurs because people are different and have different tastes and needs.

7. Conflict can strengthen a relationship by making two friends aware of problems that need to be resolved.

8. Long-standing relationships can be maintained, for example, by admitting that the relationship must take a new direction and by then scheduling times when two friends can get together.

9. Some ways for making new friends include joining a club or group, volunteering, or inviting people to your home.

10. Answers will vary. Make sure the students are able to apply specific rules for using communication skills in other kinds of relationships.

REVIEW

What Have You Learned?

1. From what group are you most likely to draw your friends?
2. What is the difference between a friend and an acquaintance?
3. What is one way to prevent gossiping?
4. How is dialogue different from shared monologue?
5. What are the six rules for good communication?
6. Why do conflicts occur?
7. How can a conflict strengthen a relationship?
8. What are some ways to maintain a long-standing friendship?
9. What are some ways to make new friends?
10. How can the communication skills practiced in a friendship be utilized in other relationships?

Application

1. Record your personal recollections of how and when you met your best friend. Then, on another occasion, ask your best friend to record his or her recollections of the same event. Play the tape to the class. Enjoy hearing the similarities and differences in your two versions.
2. Role-play a scene involving gossip similar to the story of Karolyn, Vanessa, and Martha. Include a character who avoids gossip.
3. Debate the truth of this statement with a partner or in a small group: "Anyone who gossips about another to you will probably gossip about you to another."
4. Make a list of the common conflicts an adolescent experiences. Identify the causes and possible ways of handling these conflicts. Arrive at a consensus as to how the conflict might best be resolved.
5. Design a poster listing the rules for good communication. Display it at home or in the classroom.
6. How would you go about making a new friend this week? Use one of the suggestions listed in the text. Keep a daily journal of the experience. After a week, write your conclusion. Did you make a new friend or not?
7. Read the Scripture text from John 15:1-17. What does this say about your relationship with Jesus?
8. Share song lyrics that best describe the meaning of friendship to you.

82

Journal Assignment

Friendship is something that most people take for granted, and thus they never examine their own friendship skills. As a summary to this chapter, students are to evaluate their own skills by looking at their friendships closely. What are their strengths and weaknesses? What do they need to do today to improve their ability to make friends?

REVIEW

Chapter Vocabulary

- friends
- acquaintance
- gossip
- communication
- dialogue
- I-messages
- conflict
- shared monologue

Putting Vocabulary to Use

Write the vocabulary word that corresponds to the definition below.

_____ **1.** Speaking about only what you know or feel

_____ **2.** It plays perhaps the most important part of maintaining a friendship

_____ **3.** A person with whom you have some social contact, but with whom you are not particularly close

_____ **4.** Saint Paul called it a "moral disorder."

_____ **5.** Individuals you like and with whom you could share common interests

_____ **6.** Can lead two friends to examine what is causing a problem in their friendship

_____ **7.** One person speaks while the other truly hears and attempts to understand what is being said

_____ **8.** What far too often passes for conversation

No man is an island.

John Donne

Application

Have the students read the directions for each project. You may assign a particular project, or allow the students to choose a project they prefer. Allow some class time for the students to share their completed projects with others.

Putting Vocabulary to Use

1. I-messages
2. communication
3. acquaintance
4. gossip
5. friends
6. conflict
7. dialogue
8. shared monologue.

Final Thought

Background

John Donne (1573-1631) was an English metaphysical poet and clergyman. You may wish to assign students excerpts of his work to be read in class.

Focus on: Chapter 5

During adolescence, boys and girls begin to date. Dating may begin through a group encounter; many teens meet at a common location. Later, group dating may evolve into single or personal dating. Older teens may eventually date exclusively someone they like. This form of dating has been referred to as "going steady."

Whatever the students' dating experience, they need to be aware that the successful mastery of communication skills can help them improve their relationships with members of the opposite sex.

Dating partners are, first and foremost, friends. Though new dynamics develop in these relationships—mostly related to understanding their sexuality and the difference between males and females—the basic characteristics of a friendship are present. From this starting point, dating can grow in many different directions, possibly even to courtship and marriage.

This chapter provides ways for the students to proceed into the world of dating, acknowledging its appeal, yet ever mindful of the responsibility that dating demands. While many of your students may already date regularly, others may be reluctant to admit that they do not date. The basic information about dating in this chapter bridges the gap between these groups. Use the chapter as a springboard for deeper discussions of student concerns about dating.

Plan Ahead

- Incorporate formal and/or spontaneous prayer into each lesson. A participatory prayer service that is suitable for use on retreat is provided in the Teacher's Resource Book.
- Note **Resources** suggestions which can be applied to, or extend, the lessons of this chapter.
- Preview the **Application** projects in the Chapter Review. Refer to **Teaching Approaches** for suggestions on when to assign the projects. Or, the projects may be used as part of lesson, section, or chapter reviews.
- Decide on a method for grouping students for projects and discussion.
- Invite guest speakers who will participate in selected lessons in advance.

Dating

As a lily among thorns, so is my beloved among women. As an apple tree among the trees of the woods, so is my lover among men.

Song of Songs 2:1-3

This chapter will help you to:

- Recognize various dating arrangements.
- Realize that dating grows out of friendship.
- Discover ways to overcome shyness, meet new people, and arrange dates.
- Be aware of important dating issues.
- Practice the most appropriate ways for behaving on a date.

84

Media Suggestions (Optional)

- *Relationships with the Opposite Sex* (Priority One) 20 minutes. Young people share their fears of dating and thoughts about "going too far."

- *Anxious Hearts: Unified Version* (Tabor) 55 minutes. This video focuses on adolescents' responses to their feelings about growing up and entering into their new relationships.

Aims

1. To arrive at a common understanding of the various meanings of "dating" and related terms.
2. To simplify dating issues.

Begin the Section

1. Review some of the communication skills covered in Chapter 4. Ask how these skills can be applied to dating relationships.
2. Summarize the introductory paragraphs. Ask the students to share any other questions or issues they have about dating. Tell them that sexuality issues will be discussed in Chapter 6. (You may wish to move back and forth between chapters 5 and 6 as necessary to respond to students' needs.)
3. Say: "We have all had different dating experiences. As we discuss this chapter, please respect those differences. Everyone will have the chance to share his or her own perspective on dating. The first step in our journey is for everyone to consider what he or she knows about the dating process."

1. SOMETHING SPECIAL

Friendship is the basis of all relationships. It helps form strangers into a community and bonds people together with ties that are often stronger than family relationships. Friendship is also the starting point for *dating.*

"Dating" is the term that is used to express the special relationship that exists between a man and woman who spend intimate time together. Dating may occur in a group or as a couple.

In this chapter, we will look more closely at the dating process—from friendship to group dates to single dates to exclusive dates. Questions such as how to ask a person out on a date, what to do on a date, and proper behavior on a date will be examined.

Background

Dating is a topic that all students look forward to with great expectations. Students will often lack dating experience, but will, at the same time, act as if they do so as not to stand out among their peers as being different. Because students lack realistic expectations about what a date should be, they cannot accurately evaluate their experiences or feelings.

By Any Other Name

Lesson Overview

Times change, and dating customs change with it. This lesson looks at how dating today is different from what it was in the past. The lesson explores the language of dating and examines the physical and cultural reasons why people date.

Teaching Approaches

- Ask the students to suggest definitions for the word "dating." Write their ideas on the board. What does the word mean to them and their peers? Arrive at a generally accepted understanding of the term. (See "Talk It Over" Question 1.)

- What are the local dating customs: who asks? who pays? who decides? types of dates? dating activities? kissing on the first date?

- **Reteach**—Assign **Application** Project 2. Have students share stories about a special date of either their parents or grandparents.

- **Extend the Lesson**—Plan a social night (or set aside a class period) using a theme that represents the 1950s, 60s, or 70s. Include the proper music, dress, and a movie or TV program from that era.

◖ Well-Being

Teaching Approaches

- Define "developmental tasks" as "things that need to happen in order for you to continue growing toward a healthy, mature adulthood."

- Discuss these tasks. Which do students think are most important for them right now?

- Have the students make prioritized lists of these tasks for themselves and share them with partners. Point out that there are no right or wrong answers in this exercise, and that all of these tasks are important.

By Any Other Name

Have you ever wondered what your parents' or grandparents' experience of dating was like? Chances are that their experiences were quite different from yours today. That might explain why your parents seem so confused by your dating relationships.

Each generation usually has had a different experience of dating, so each has a different understanding of the term. For example, in the 1950s and 60s, dating was recognized as a part of the courtship process leading to marriage. *Going steady* was considered just one step removed from being engaged. Now, junior high school boys and girls exchange rings, pins, and jackets and say that they are going steady, even though most of them had never even been on a date. It's no surprise that parents are shocked when they hear that their son or daughter is going steady!

Dating seems to have many different meanings today, so precise definitions are not possible. Still, there is a need for a general understanding of the terms. "Going out" often refers to a boy and girl who date each other, but not exclusively, while "seeing" someone means that the relationship is more exclusive.

The term "dating" continues to be used as the generic, easily understood way to describe the way that males and females meet and get to know each other.

She's Just a Friend

What a day! Bryan found out from Mr. Shepherd, the school principal, at lunchtime that he had won the American history essay contest. He would be awarded a check for $100 at the school's spirit assembly later that afternoon.

Bryan felt his life was really going well. He had recently found a niche with a new group of friends. There were a couple of guys from his honors classes—Dustin and Sam—and Natalia, Desiree, and Charity who rode the bus to school from the other side of town. The six of them had together formed a comfortable group. He knew that some of his old friends were having trouble meeting and socializing with girls, so he felt really lucky.

At the assembly, the group sat together in the front row of the bleachers. Bryan was nervous. He worried that he might trip over a microphone wire as he crossed the gym to receive his award. But, as the assembly went on and other students came forward before him, he became less concerned.

◖ Well Being
Adolescence and Young Adulthood

Women and men face many developmental tasks during late adolescence and young adulthood. These include:

1. Forming more mature relationships with peers of both sexes.
2. Understanding what it means to be male or female.
3. Achieving emotional independence from parents and other adults.
4. Preparing for career, college, marriage and family life, or religious vocation.
5. Establishing career goals.
6. Adopting personal standards as a guide to behavior.
7. Learning how to live as a member of society.
8. Developing conceptual and problem-solving skills.

Resources

Resource 5A from the Teacher's Resource Book is a form to help plan the social night suggested in "By Any Other Name—Extend the Lesson."

Journal Assignment

"Write about a time when you were embarrassed by family members in a boy/girl situation."

Bryan and Desiree studied together, but that doesn't make them boyfriend and girlfriend. Or does it?

"Bryan Dugan, first place, American history." Hearing his name announced and the genuine applause that followed felt good to Bryan. Instinctively, it seemed, he turned and gave Desiree a kiss before getting up and going forward. The student body applauded louder. Bryan blushed, embarrassed and excited all at once about what he had done. He shook Mr. Shepherd's hand and jumped down from the podium. That's when Bryan saw his mom, standing near the gym entrance, waving to him. "They must have called her from work," he thought.

Boyfriends and Girlfriends

"Congratulations, honey," Bryan's mom said as he walked through the door after school. "I was very proud of you today. You worked hard for that award. By the way, was that your new girlfriend I saw you with today?"

The word "girlfriend" sounded strange to Bryan. Desiree was his friend and she was a girl, but …"No, she's not my girlfriend. She's just a friend," Bryan blurted out. He wondered what that meant. Maybe Desiree did mean something more to him. He wasn't sure.

The terms associated with male and female relationships can be confusing. Women sometimes refer to women friends as "girlfriends" but men seldom refer to other men as "boyfriends." For women, the term boyfriend usually refers to a romantic interest. For men, the same is true of the term girlfriend.

In this text, the words "boyfriend" and "girlfriend" refer to members of the opposite sex in whom you have a sexual or romantic interest. People with whom you socialize or are close to in other ways will simply be referred to as friends. Having a sexual interest in another person means that you are emotionally and physically attracted to that person.

Talk It Over

1. What are other terms that you and your friends use to describe dating? How do you define the words "boyfriend" and "girlfriend"? Do you distinguish between having boy and girl friends and having a boyfriend or a girlfriend?
2. How would you describe Bryan and Desiree's relationship?
3. Put yourself in Bryan's shoes. How would you feel if your mother saw you with your friends without you being aware of her presence? How would you respond to her question?

Resources

Resource 5B from the Teacher's Resource Book is a self-inventory that helps students look at the major developmental tasks in life.

She's Just a Friend

Teaching Approaches

- Choose one or two students to read the story aloud.
- **Reteach**—Have the students discuss "Talk It Over" Questions 2 and 3.
- **Extend the Lesson**—Role play the conversation between Bryan and Desiree after the assembly. How would Desiree feel about Bryan's surprise kiss?

Boyfriends and Girlfriends

Teaching Approaches

- Ask the students if they have ever heard young children say that they have "boyfriends" or "girlfriends." Ask: "How is a young child's understanding of those terms different from your own?" Discuss how students use these terms. (See "Talk It Over" Question 1.)
- Read or summarize the section. Make sure the students understand how the terms "boyfriend" and "girlfriend" will be used in this text.
- **Reteach**—Review with students their earlier definition of dating. How does this story fit into their definition?
- **Extend the Lesson**—Have groups of students of the same sex list questions they would like to ask members of the opposite sex about dating. Read the questions. Choose those that are most appropriate for class discussion. Pursue any topics the class finds especially interesting. You may wish to use some of the other topics as the starting point for future lessons.

Talk It Over

If not done as part of the lesson, have students discuss the many ways that they speak of dating. The students may write their answers to the other parts of Question 1 in their journals. Questions 2 and 3 are suitable for large group discussion. Call on a variety of students to share their responses for both questions.

The Opposite Sex

Lesson Overview

Part of the change in relationships during adolescence has to do with varying emotions. These changes may involve mood swings (feeling happy one minute and sad the next), feelings toward others (a person may view family and friends in a new way), and interest in the opposite sex (this desire may be confusing and frightening). Mention these changes to the students. Ask them how they might affect relationships between members of the opposite sex.

Teaching Approaches

- Read or summarize the opening paragraphs.
- **Reteach**—Ask: "What can it mean to say a person of the opposite sex is 'just a friend'?"
- **Extend the Lesson**—Discuss the questions in the second paragraph.

✳ Media Watch

Teaching Approaches

- Present segments of television programs that deal with dating from several different decades. Have the students comment on the differences in terms and customs used.
- Ask: "How do television characters handle the problem of rejection, or the fear of being rejected? How realistic are these portrayals with your experiences?"
- Use the discussion questions to stimulate discussion.

A Time of Great Change

New Words

Hormonal changes are related to the release of *hormones*, chemicals produced in the body that cause it to react in certain ways. Hormones also affect a person's emotional and social growth.

Teaching Approaches

- Read the section aloud. Pause to discuss the in-text questions.
- Ask: "What advice would you give to a friend who is concerned about his or her physical, emotional, or social development?"

The Opposite Sex

A few years ago the issue of dating may not have even been relevant to you. In grade school, most of your friends were probably of your sex. That situation most likely changed when you entered adolescence. You may now have as many close friends of the opposite sex as you do of your own. You may also have deeper feelings than friendship for a few, special people. These deeper feelings can cause your relationships with members of the opposite sex to be personally enriching or just plain chaotic.

How so? Why is it that you can be a close friend with a person of the opposite sex, yet have no romantic feelings for him or her, but at the same time be passionately "in love" with another person whom you barely know? Is there any logic behind these relationships?

A Time of Great Change

When you experienced puberty, you began relating to the opposite sex in a new way. You felt attracted to people whom you may have avoided just the week before. Your world of relationships was turned upside-down almost overnight.

From about age three until puberty, boys and girls rarely choose to play or work together. But during puberty, everything changes. Physically, boys and girls grow into men and women, becoming physically able to conceive children. The

You may find yourself passionately "in love" with someone you barely know.

hormonal changes of puberty also affect how you act and how you feel.

Embarrassment and fear are two of the most common emotions experienced during puberty. A rapidly maturing body can be awkward and embarrassing. Did you ever feel during puberty that everyone noticed your every mistake and blemish? Many people feel this way. Overcoming the erratic and clumsy growth and emotions experienced during puberty requires confidence, faith, and a sense of humor. Ask an adult to recall his or her puberty. Sometimes simply thinking of it will make a grown person shiver.

✳ Media Watch
Comparisons

Much of what teens expect from a date can be traced to how dating is presented in the media. In your media diary, for the next week see how television presents dating.

1. What happens on the first date?
2. How does the boy act? the girl act?
3. What makes the date successful?
4. What does the couple discuss?
5. Is there any connection between television dating and reality?

Take notice of the family rules for dating. Do the rules differ for males and females? Compare your dating rules with those you see on T.V.

Resources

"Ozzie and Harriet" (1950s), "The Brady Bunch" (1960s), and "Good Times" (1970s) are examples of currently syndicated shows that can be searched for dating themes. **Resource 5C** is appropriate here.

Resources

Resource 5D presents more information on the developmental changes associated with puberty.

✚ To Your Health
Changes

Males and females usually experience the following changes during puberty:

- Acne.
- Permanent teeth all in.
- Underarm and pubic hair.
- Perspiration increases.
- Long bone growth stops.

In addition, men experience receding hairlines, facial hairs, enlarged larynxes, deeper voices, broader shoulders, bigger muscles, and sperm ejaculations.

Woman additionally develop breasts, wider hips and narrower waistlines, and enlarged ovaries and uteruses. They also begin to ovulate and experience regular menstruation.

Hormonal changes give a person completely new emotions and attractions that aren't easily sorted out or understood. The emotional changes one experiences during puberty are swift and scary. Accompanied by physical changes, these internal developments result in a person's sexual attraction towards members of the opposite sex. Unfortunately, being attracted to someone doesn't entail knowing how to express or explore one's personal feelings towards the person.

Attracted

Why are you physically attracted to some people and not to others? That's a good question, but one that's impossible to answer conclusively. In many ways, the same attributes that attract you to friends will attract you to boyfriends or girlfriends. But it's more than that. We are also attracted by physical features, social behavior, and personal attitudes. There is no right shape, size, or hairstyle. There is no perfect attitude or behavior. People are attracted to different things.

Some people even believe that attraction is part of our biological makeup!

Knowing why we are attracted to some people and not to others may be difficult to understand, but our physical response to that attraction is very basic. When we feel drawn to someone we hardly know—"She's so funny" or "He is a talented artist"—we want to get close to him or her as soon as possible. Some people will watch from a distance until they work up the courage to speak to the person, while others will throw caution to the wind and introduce themselves immediately. Either way, attraction has done its job; it has brought two people together. What happens from there is up to the individuals. And that is why people date.

There is no right shape, size, or hairstyle. What attracts you to various people?

Background

The male sex hormone is called *testosterone* and the female sex hormone is called *estrogen*. Both of these hormones are present in each of the sexes, but at different levels.

Resources

Resource 5E lists stress management techniques.

Talk It Over

You may wish to have the students write their responses to all three questions before beginning. Then, allow volunteers to share what they have written with the large group.

Dating Considerations

Lesson Overview

Some people find the idea of dating frightening. Some boys may find themselves wondering, "How do I ask her? What if she says no?" Some girls may wonder, "What if I don't get asked out? Is it okay to ask the boy first?" Adolescents may also question their worth because of the dating process, especially if they feel unwanted, unasked, or rejected.

Assure the students that most people experience these or similar concerns. Point out that this lesson will explore suggestions for overcoming dating problems.

Teaching Approaches

- Have the students read the opening paragraph. Then, ask volunteers to take the role of the shy person described. Have him or her role play some of those feelings in front of the class.
- Include other characters in the role play to help the first person: (1) overcome shyness; (2) focus the limelight on others; (3) practice asking another out on a date; and (4) show respect for parental concerns.
- Use the text material as reference suggestions for each scenario.

The process of dating allows people to form, over time, meaningful relationships from these initial attractions. Although the "boy-meets-girl" formula in the movies is alluring, couples rarely live "happily ever after" following the first date, at least not until they develop an honest and committed relationship. Dating provides an opportunity for couples to share time, ideas, and experiences. Only through this kind of sharing can a man and a woman achieve the trust and love for one another that a sincere commitment requires.

Sharpening Your Skills
Why I Date

Below is a list of reasons people have for dating. What are possible positive and negative outcomes for each reason? Add additional reasons of your own to the list for why people date.

1. To have a good time.
2. To show off.
3. To be like everyone else.
4. To prove I am popular.
5. To have something to do.
6. To be with a person I like.
7. To learn something about myself.

Talk It Over

1. At what age do you think it's most appropriate for a person to begin dating? Why?
2. What attracts you to a member of the opposite sex? Explain. Why do you think this is true?
3. How do you respond when you feel attracted to another person? Why do you think you behave this way?

Dating Considerations

You've met someone who you would like to know better. But there is a terrible problem: you are not sure of what to do next. For one thing, you are shy. Even though you are attracted to many people, you have no idea how to go about meeting them. Even if you did meet someone special, how would you ask the person out? And, to top it all off, what kind of rules would your parents impose on your dating? You might wonder, "Is it all worth it?"

There are several things that you can do to simplify these issues. Here are a few suggestions:

1. **Overcome shyness.** Even the most outwardly confident people are shy at times. You can get over shyness by practicing social talk before you ask someone for a date or go on the date. Your parents or a close friend can help you. If it helps, arrange a date that won't require you to do all the talking. A first date at the movies might be more comfortable—and inexpensive—than going out to dinner. Better yet, plan your first few dates with a group.

2. **Focus the limelight on others.** Express an interest in what another person is doing. This is a good way to meet new people. For example, you might tell one of the cast members in the school play, "I enjoyed your performance." The compliment can serve as a conversation starter. By keeping most of the focus on the other person, you can get to know more about him or her. Oftentimes, you share a mutual friend with the person. Have that person introduce you, or ask to be included in a group activity along with that person.

3. **To ask or be asked on a date is your option.** In previous generations, only males asked females out on dates. Now, females do the asking, too. It basically comes down to whatever

---

Honoring your parent's rules is a good way to help them feel comfortable about your dating.

you are most comfortable doing. If you want to date, but haven't been asked, try doing the asking yourself.

4. **Respect for parental concerns.** On all dates, it is important to let your parents know where you are going, how long you will be there, with whom you are going, and what transportation you will be using. Honoring curfews is especially important. Nothing will instill more trust in parents than your keeping this rule. If you are going to be late for any reason, always call home.

Talk It Over

1. What rules have your parents established for your dating?
2. What other suggestions would you add to this list?

▲ Family Living
Parental Guidance

Many young adults don't like to talk to their parents about dating. It is often a subject that is too personal to discuss openly, and parents may often seem more concerned with rules than with their child's relationships. One way to involve your parents in your dating relationship is to develop with them your rules and guidelines for dating.

Set up a chart with three columns: "Area of Dating," "Rules and Guidelines," "How I Will Honor Them." Under "Area of Dating," list these words, "transportation, places to go, curfew, manners," and "other considerations."

By taking the lead in working out dating regulations with your parents, you show them that you are responsible and can be trusted.

Resources

Resource 5F in the Teacher's Resource Book provides a format for the suggested activity in "Family Living."

Teaching Approaches (continued)

- Have students role play other dating scenarios: (1) asking someone out and being rejected; (2) being asked out by someone you don't like and saying no; (3) being asked out by someone you don't like and saying yes out of the kindness of your heart (because you feel sorry for the person); (4) being the person who wants to be asked out, but never is; (5) being asked out by (or asking out) your best friend's love interest. After the role plays, ask students to describe what happens after their scenario ends (e.g. tell how the people feel and act after the event). What can people do to change the situations? What would students recommend in each of these cases?
- **Reteach**—Assign **Application** Project 4 as an in-class or homework exercise.
- **Extend the Lesson**—Have the students write a letter to "Dater's Anonymous," describing a real or imagined dating problem or concern. Have them sign fictitious names, seal the letters, and put them in a class mailbox for future discussion.

▲ Family Living

Teaching Approaches

- Discuss with students their current dating rules and guidelines.
- Establish a class chart as mentioned in the feature. The students should reach agreement on these matters.

Talk It Over

The students can discuss both questions in the large group. In addition, you may have to ask them which parental rules they do not feel are necessary. Make sure they are able to tell why they feel as they do.

II. OPENING THE DOOR

Aims

1. To clarify with students the various kinds of dating.
2. To raise special dating issues.
3. To develop with students a list of creative dating suggestions.

Begin the Section

1. Suggest that the students write answers to the in-text questions in their journals. If they wish, the students may even graph their dating history, noting their "highs and lows."
2. Read the second paragraph. Ask the in-text questions. Have the students compare what they have experienced about dating to what they hear about dating from others.
3. Allow volunteers the chance to share any comments the questions have raised.

Kinds of Dating

Lesson Overview

Let the students know that each of the dating situations mentioned—group dating, single or personal dating, and exclusive dating—has many advantages and disadvantages. One form of dating is not necessarily better or worse than another. And, the dating patterns discussed in this lesson are spoken of in general terms. A particular individual may never experience some of the situations presented.

Teaching Approaches

- Ask the students to comment on the opening scenario. Is it realistic or not?
- Introduce and briefly define each of the three types of dating situations.
- **Reteach**—Assign the students to read the text section on their own.
- **Extend the Lesson**—Write the words "dating situations" on the board. Ask the students to offer other words that they associate with dating. Write them below. Include other words from this section that the students failed to mention.

II. OPENING THE DOOR

What's your dating history? Think about that for a moment, maybe even jot down a chronicle of your dating experience. Who have you dated? When did you date? How many dates did you have? What types of dates were they? What expectations did you have? Were your expectations met? What have you learned from your dating experience?

Whether you've dated frequently or not at all, you probably know a great deal about the world of dating. From your own experience, or from listening to friends, you probably know how to ask someone out and what you should do on a date, the proper dating etiquette and behavior, and much more. This section will review the dating process. How realistic are these situations? What can you add from your experience or knowledge to enlighten this discussion?

Kinds of Dating

Here's a romantic scenario:

Girl meets guy and thinks he's nice. After learning all she can about him from her friends, she lets it be known that she'd like to go out on a date. She invites him to go skating, to which he readily agrees. They have a pleasant time together, and are soon a regular couple around school.

Meeting with guys and girls in a group situation is most teens first experience of dating.

Journal Assignment

"Write about your most memorable group dating experience."

Is that the typical way a dating relationship begins or are other alternatives also a part of your dating experience?

For many people, beginning to date is a much more gradual process. They might feel uncomfortable asking people they don't know very well for a date, and many more people might feel uncomfortable accepting. The aggressive approach to dating is not for everyone.

There are several types of dating situations commonly practiced by young adults. They include:

- *Group dating.*
- *Single or personal dating.*
- *Exclusive dating.*

Generally, these different types of dates follow a progression: people start with group dating, gradually move to single dating, and then, possibly to exclusive dating. There are positive and negative comments that can be made for each of these dating styles. No one style is better or more appropriate all of the time. Which dating style you choose depends on your personality, maturity, and preference. Let's explore each of these dating styles in more detail.

Group Dating

For many people, dating begins accidentally. They are like Gary and Sara, who gathered with a group of friends for support and encouragement. Neither Gary nor Sara knew each other before joining the group, but felt comfortable with this group of mutual friends. The group liked to play cards and volleyball, volunteered at the local food bank, and went to movies together. Gary and Sara both enjoyed spending time with this group of people, because they were there for friendship. There was no pressure to become especially intimate with anyone or find a date. Eventually, Gary and Sara became very comfortable being together, and began spending time together outside of group gatherings. Their personal relationship continued to grow within the security of the group. They still weren't quite ready to start dating personally, but they were comfortable together in the group.

This is one form of group dating. Another form is when people go out with a particular individual, but they don't go as a couple. A group date might be a guy and a girl who are dating, accompanied by several other friends, or maybe two couples out with several other friends. What are some other examples of group dates?

Why do people like group dates? For many people, group dates are a way to be comfortable in a strange and possibly embarrassing situation. If a person is not comfortable with his or her dating skills, a group date provides the perfect opportunity to practice these skills. When people are with other friends or couples, they don't feel as pressured to keep up a conversation or think of something fun to do.

For uncommitted individuals, going out with a group allows them to find out the kind of people that they get along with best, while those with dates may learn more about their companions through their interaction with others. Group dates are also a means of support. When they are with other people, a couple is less likely to become sexually involved. The presence of friends help them persevere in their beliefs.

Single or Personal Dating

Single or personal dating occurs when a male and a female go out together as a couple. Personal dating is the most common form of dating. As noted above, often single dating grows out of group dates. Many people also begin with personal dates. Once again, the right time to begin single dating varies from person to person. There should be no stigma attached to people who don't single date, but often there is.

Personal dates may be one-time things or they may lead to a longer relationship.

◊ Rocky had been friends with Mary Lou since freshman study hall. In the summer be-

Group Dating

Teaching Approaches

- Read or summarize the first paragraph. Ask students to suggest other ways that group dating situations develop.
- Have students read the second paragraph and name some of the advantages of group dating. Write these advantages on the board. Then, ask the students to suggest some disadvantages of group dating.
- **Reteach**—Ask: "When would you recommend to a friend that he or she group date?"
- **Extend the Lesson**—Set up two teams and debate the benefits and liabilities of group dating.

Single or Personal Dating

Teaching Approaches

- Have the students discuss, in general terms, some of the people they know who single date.
- Ask: "How do people arrange single dates?" After hearing a few examples, share the two stories from the text.
- Say: "Single dating begins at different times and in different ways, depending on the person. How is that true for you?"
- One stigma associated with people who do not single date is that they are considered "unpopular" or "uncool" by their peers. Have the students discuss this reasoning.
- Read the common misconceptions that often accompany single dating. Have the students fill in the words to make the statements true. For example, one date *does not necessarily* mean a person is interested in a permanent relationship.
- **Reteach**—Read and discuss the in-text questions concerning: expectations of a single date; meeting expectations; what can go wrong on a single date; and reacting to intimacy on a first date.
- **Extend the Lesson**—Encourage the students to develop an attitude about single dating that communicates, "I expect nothing on this date other than that we will enjoy our time together and that we will both be safe in each other's company." Unrealistically high expectations can lead people to experience major letdowns when things don't go as they had hoped.

Journal Assignment

"Finish this story: 'When I started dating, I expected . . .'"

Background

Relationships are always threatened by jealousy. When love and trust are strong, jealous feelings subside. You may wish to have the students share examples of jealousy and how they would cope with a jealous person.

Exclusive Dating

Teaching Approaches

- Ask the students to define "exclusive dating" in their own words. Then, read the text definition: "Exclusive dating is when two people decide to date only each other."

- Read or summarize the rest of the text section. Have the students comment on the in-text question.

- **Reteach**—Assign **Application** Project 5. Mention that a major disadvantage about beginning an exclusive relationship without any other experience of dating is that the person misses out on the chance to meet many different people, and have many different kinds of experiences. Have students suggest other advantages and disadvantages to exclusive relationships.

- **Extend the Lesson**—Assign students to write a short story or poem on the subject of exclusive dating.

Talk It Over

Question 1 can be used as part of a class brainstorming session. If possible, have the suggestions recorded, copied, and distributed to the students. Allow the students to choose a partner with whom to discuss Question 2, or have them write their answers in their journals.

✛ In Focus

Teaching Approaches

- Read the list of positive ways to end a relationship. Then, say: "Some people hold onto a relationship because they would feel jealous if the other person dated someone new. What do you think?"

- Ask the students to add other reasons couples continue to see each other, even when the relationship has gone sour.

tween junior and senior year, Rocky and Mary Lou finally went out on a date. They saw a movie and had a shake afterwards. They kissed good-night outside of Mary Lou's house, and went their separate ways. When school started, they picked up their friendship again, but they never had another date.

◊ Anthony and Karla had met through a mutual friend. They liked each other very much, and began dating. Over the next few years they saw each other regularly for a while, although they would still date other people. Eventually they began to date each other exclusively. Two years later, they were married.

Personal dating can be a lot of fun, but it can also cause a lot of pain. It affords people times of eager anticipation, delightful diversion, and emotional pleasure; it can also be a time of uncertainty and misjudgments.

What are your expectations of a single date? Are these expectations always met? What are some of the things that can go wrong on a personal date?

Some common misconceptions about single dates include:

- One date means a permanent relationship.
- Kissing means, "I love you."

- She asked me out, so she pays the bills.
- Because we are alone, it's okay to get very intimate.

Obviously, a personal date does not mean a permanent commitment. Questions about who pays is a point of local custom and honest communication. How would you react if a person tried to get very intimate on the first date?

Exclusive Dating

When two people decide to date only each other, they are exclusively dating. Exclusive dating is similar to the notion of "going steady" as your parents knew it. In this type of dating, people begin to form more committed relationships. Choosing to date only one partner is, in some ways, a prelude to married life; one person to share your life with can make every day more meaningful and satisfying. But to devote oneself completely to another person also entails a great level of maturity and discipline.

Exclusive dating has advantages and disadvantages, just like everything else. Some of the positive benefits of dating one person only include:

- Your relationship can deepen.
- You usually don't have to worry about having a date for an important function.
- You can relax and be yourself.

Negatively, there are:

- The pressures of keeping the relationship fresh and fulfilling.
- Reduced time for other friends and personal activities.
- Risk of sexual intimacy.

Exclusive dating most often follows after people date several others, although not always. Some people enter into an exclusive relationship without any experience of dating others. Why do you think this happens?

A common misunderstanding in personal dating involves who pays for the date. What is a person entitled to who pays for a date?

Background

Research suggests that females who go steady during early adolescence tend to marry at a younger age than do females who begin dating later in life.

An exclusive relationship can be the first step toward marriage. When a couple exclusively commits themselves to each other, they should be sure that they are ready to accept the responsibilities that come with the benefits.

Talk It Over

1. What are the advantages and disadvantages of group dating? Single dating? Exclusive dating?
2. What is your greatest concern about dating?

In Focus
Ending Relationships

The more serious the relationship, the harder it is to deal with its ending. When a relationship ends, here are some things that you can do to keep from hurting the other person too badly:

- Communicate your wishes to the other person honestly, but with gentleness.
- If the relationship is to end, you need to accept it. Dramatic and emotional scenes will only make matters worse.
- Look to the future. Send each other off with positive comments, and best wishes.

You will be able to use what you learned in this relationship in future relationships.

Dating Issues

It had been a difficult junior year for Cory. Because of school redistricting, Cory had had to change schools. She'd always been able to make friends easily, but she got off on the wrong foot at her new school by hanging out with kids who had serious problems. Some of them took drugs and one was expelled for stealing.

Cory's dad said, "Listen, honey, I know it was hard leaving your old school. But we didn't move.

You can still see some of your old friends. Better yet, you can still participate in the youth group. You switched schools, but Saint Rita's remains our parish."

Cory reluctantly agreed to go to the Thursday night youth group gatherings. She wondered what the kids there would say after she had made such a major deal about not attending any more once she became a senior.

Cory noticed Sean immediately. About her age, Sean had joined the group while Cory was away. When Sean laughed at all of her silly jokes, Cory felt special. Sure enough, a few weeks later Sean asked Cory out.

Cory was excited to tell her father that she had met a boy she liked from the youth group. He was an athlete and he was Catholic. Her father was sure to approve of their dating.

The night that Sean came to pick her up she introduced him to her dad. She could tell right away that something was wrong even though her dad didn't say anything about it in front of Sean. He just had that look he got when things weren't as he wanted them to be.

They excused themselves, saying good-night to her father, and went out to a baseball game with some of the other kids from the youth group. When Cory got home about ten minutes before her curfew, her father was waiting.

"What's wrong, Daddy?" Cory wanted to know.

"Oh, nothing," he said. "Well, I guess it's just that I'm not sure if I approve of your dating a white person. Yes, that's it."

Other Dating Issues

As Cory and Sean's dilemma points out, there are many additional dating issues to think about. Here are a few:

Mixed Dating. Mixed dating is used to refer to dates between people of different races, religions, and cultures. Though Cory and Sean are both Catholics, Cory is black and Sean is white. For many teenagers today, interracial, interreligious,

---

Resources

Resource 5G provides a list of steps that students can follow that will help in preventing rape.

Dating Issues

Lesson Overview

This lesson raises the complex issues of interracial dating, who pays for dates, abuse, date rape, and dating games people play. The text provides an introduction into these topics, but student discussion is essential if these questions are to be honestly addressed. Since many of these topics touch upon sensitive issues, use great discretion as you discuss them.

Teaching Approaches

- Choose four readers to take the parts of Cory, Sean, Cory's father, and the narrator. Have them read the story to the class aloud.
- Then, ask: "What do you think Cory said to her father in response? How do you think their conversation went on from that point?"
- **Reteach**—Discuss Question 1 from "Talk It Over."
- **Extend the Lesson**—Have students role play this scenario as they would expect it to happen in their community.

Other Dating Issues

New Words

Abuse means "to use something or someone in a way that causes harm." In a dating relationship, abuse may be inflicted physically, emotionally, or verbally.

Rape and *date rape*—sexual intimacy through force or threat—are acts of violence and are inexcusable and also illegal.

Teaching Approaches

- Read these examples of dating issues. Have the students explore how they would handle each situation.
- Explain that as is the case with many dilemmas, these issues are related. For example, the main issue in mixed dating is often not whether people of two races can get along, but whether they can withstand the pressure exerted on them by parents, friends, and society.
- Raise the issue of inter-religious relationships. What problems would students expect in these relationships?

(continued p. 96)

Teaching Approaches (continued)

- Ask: "Why would finances have a major effect on a relationship, especially at the outset?" Do students think that one partner may expect to "keep up" with what everyone else is doing and what everyone else is spending while the other partner may have less expensive ideas?

- Explain that the signs of an emotionally or physically abusive person may be present in a relationship long before they are acted out. For what signs would students think it important to look?

- **Reteach**—Encourage students to develop additional challenges and solutions to dating problems.

- **Extend the Lesson**—Use the suggestion from **Application** Project 6. You may also consider showing popular films about the subject of interracial relationships. Be sure to preview all films before showing them to your students.

Prom Pricing

Teaching Approaches

- Work on this assignment in pairs. Encourage the students to research the actual cost of the items listed in the local area.

- Have each group write and share a summary reporting on the problems and difficulties they had keeping their prom expenses under budget.

- Read this excerpt from an article by Father Joseph J. O'Hare titled "Ritzy Weddings Are Unchristian" (*U.S. Catholic*, January, 1984). "Simplicity in celebration is a fundamental way to acknowledge the conditions of the earth, the particular witness of Jesus, and the individual responsibility to those who are deprived. A lavish wedding—in fact, any excessively costly celebration—flies in the face of [Christian] values."

- Have the students comment on O'Hare's words in relationship to high school proms. Do they agree or disagree?

Prom Pricing

You are planning on going to the prom with your steady date, and you want to go first class. When you look at what prom expenses cost, however, you stop and think:

- $375 for a dress and shoes.
- $300 for a limousine.
- $175 for a hotel party suite.
- $150 for dinner.
- $100 for the prom bid and fees.
- $75 for a tuxedo and shoes.

When you add up the cost of going to the prom, you're looking at as much as $1,175. You've agreed to split all costs, but that's still a lot of money.

How much do you really need to spend on the prom? You and your date have agreed that you can each afford to spend $250. How should this money be split between you?

Use the following list to determine how you will keep the cost of your big night within budget.

Needs	Costs
Her Hair	_____
His Hair	_____
Makeup	_____
Tuxedo and shoes	_____
Dress and shoes	_____
Transportation	_____
Dinner	_____
Bid	_____
Post-Prom Expenses	_____
Photos	_____
Flowers	_____
Miscellaneous	_____
Total	_____

For occasions like the prom, its up to you and your date to determine the wisest use for your money.

96

Resources

   Resource 5H provides a format for completing this activity.

What are some other dating dilemmas a teen may face?

or intercultural dating is not a problem. In your parents' generation, however, most people only dated members of their own race, religion, culture, and social standing. Cory's father's concern was that outside pressures, including other people's lack of understanding, would make Cory and Sean's relationship difficult.

Finances. Dates cost money. Some people simply can't afford movie tickets or even a round of miniature golf. But finances should not keep you from dating someone you like. Suggest inexpensive activities for your date, and share expenses when possible. For a big event like a prom, plan way ahead. Save your money, and spend wisely. Whether or not you have a good time does not depend on how much money is spent. Being with someone you care for is the purpose of a date, isn't it?

Abuse and Date Rape. These are things that you might think could never happen to you, but it's always wise to be prepared for a threatening situation.

Unfortunately, some people will, at times, think that going out with a date gives them the right to take advantage of a person in some way. When these people do not get what they want, they may turn violent or harm their dates.

Abuse can be physical or verbal in nature. Putdowns, rude or vulgar remarks, and ridicule are all abusive.Remember, if you are not being treated with respect by your date, don't put up with any nonsense. Leave the person before you get hurt.

Rape is unlawful sexual intercourse by force or threat. When a person is forced to have intercourse or to engage in genital stimulation against his or her wishes while on a date, it is called *date rape*. Rape of any kind is a crime of violence that should always be reported. When a person says "no," it means no, and his or her wishes should be respected.

The Dating Game?

Some people treat dating as a game to be played, with little concern for other people's feelings or interests. They play by their own rules, and are concerned only with their own personal satisfaction. Do you know anyone who:

- Tries to steal someone else's date just for fun?
- Is more concerned with the number of different dates they've had than developing relationships?
- Uses dating to get revenge?

There always seems to be people who take advantage of other people. If you don't know anyone like this now, you are likely to run into him or her in the future.

Dating should be a time of great fun, a time to enjoy talking about new and different things with a person of the opposite sex. Through dating, people form healthy friendships and learn the skills and graces they need to pursue their chosen career and vocation. Don't let game players ruin the dating experience for you!

Talk It Over

1. What is your opinion about mixed dating?
2. Give an example of a fun date that doesn't cost much money.
3. The abuse of drugs and alcohol often play a part in abusive dates and date rape. Why do you think this would be true?
4. What are additional ways that people play games with the dating process? How do these game players affect the dating process?

The Dating Game?

Teaching Approaches

- Have the students comment on this statement: "Both men and women will share everything that happens on their date with at least one close friend."
- Read the section. Say: "Dating is meant to be fun. Don't expect too much from a date. Don't take the dating process too seriously. And, don't let other people have a good story at your expense. Always protect your reputation by being honest in your actions." Have students comment on your statement.
- **Reteach**—Review student dating rules developed earlier. Make changes as necessary.
- **Extend the Lesson**—Develop a campaign to discourage dating games. The campaign could include posters, student forums, outside speakers, films, or others elements that students consider important.

Talk It Over

Divide the class into four small groups. Have each group discuss one of the questions. Choose leaders to summarize and report on the highlights of their discussions to the rest of the class.

Journal Assignment

Students are to reflect on the causes of date rape and abusive dating situations. Ask them to examine their own behavior for its appropriateness. Ask: "How would you respond if you found yourself in such a situation.

On a Date

Lesson Overview

A radio announcer once asked a baseball player who had hit the game-winning home run what kind of pitch he hit, how he had adjusted to the new pitcher, and many other specific questions. The player responded, "It's simple: 'See the ball, hit the ball.'"

The point of this story is that life is easiest if it can be kept simple. Dating is a good example of this proverb.

Many of the tensions and pressures associated with teen dating could be alleviated if people accept dating for what it should be: a fun exercise in meeting new people and enjoying the company of others.

Teaching Approaches

- Read through the text section together with the students. Pause after each suggestion to allow the students the chance to share specific ways to implement the suggestions in their own dating relationships.
- **Reteach**—Assign either **Application** Project 7 or Project 8.
- **Extend the Lesson**—Discuss these suggestions for successful dating: (1) personal hygiene and grooming; (2) being prompt; and (3) using good manners. Ask them to add more of their own suggestions (see "Talk It Over," Question 1).

On a Date

Some dates are casual; you meet your date at the game or beach and spend time together. Some dates are formal; the homecoming dance and prom are examples of formal dates. As mentioned earlier, many dates are group dates; you might be with someone special, along with several other friends. Most dates are times for fun with someone you like.

What's supposed to happen on a date? If you were to ask all of your classmates, you'd probably hear many different answers. That is because every person has different expectations, interests, and ideals. Research shows that generally men expect physical closeness on a date, and women expect to feel wanted and needed by their partner. When expectations about dating conflict, problems result. Dating could be simplified if people would only talk about their expectations.

Good dates do not depend so much on what you do as on who you are with and how you relate to that person. Dating gives you time together so that your relationship can grow. The following suggestions for successful dating may help you deepen that relationship.

1. **Be Yourself.** If you are uncertain about your date's opinion of you, you may be tempted to cover your feelings by masquerading as someone who you're not. However, if you try to forget about yourself and concentrate on the other person, the feeling of uncertainty will subside. Just as you want to know what the other person is really like, so too, he or she wants to know the real you. Be willing to talk about your thoughts, feelings, and dreams.

2. **Be Sensitive.** Your time together should be a time of discovery and sharing. To do this, you must be sensitive to the other person's anxieties and expectations. A date should include time for shared dialogue. Try to find out how you and your date are alike and what you have in common.

Honest communication is one of the most important elements of successful dating.

3. **Be Honest.** In a way, this suggestion is much like the first, but the emphasis is on communication. Communication in dating means exchanging ideas, sharing experiences, and expressing your feelings. It's like giving the other person a map of yourself and how you perceive the world around you. While at first this may seem risky, the more spontaneous and candid you are, the more you will free the other person to reveal him or herself, too. This doesn't mean that your conversation has to be "deep" or "heavy," or that you have to solve the world's problems. It only means that you are willing to share who you are and what you like to do.

4. **Be Open.** Operate from a position of self-worth and trust. Let the other person know if you're enjoying yourself, and show as much concern for your date's enjoyment as you do for your own. Remember, a date is not a test in which you "fail" or "succeed." It is an opportunity to have fun and to be with a person you want to know better.

5. **Be Considerate.** You have to take into consideration your date's self-esteem, future, reputation, and personal health and safety on a

Journal Assignment

Have the students write about the kind of person they would like to date, ideas about where they would like to go on a date, and their responsibilities on a date.

date—as well as your own. Do nothing that could be embarrassing or put either of you at risk.

6. **Be Responsible.** Dating is an adult activity, not something done by children. Acting as a responsible adult means that you know about yourself and how you will act in certain situations. Part of that responsibility is to remember that pre-marital sexual intercourse is inappropriate. Catholics call it a *sin*—an action that destroys the special wholeness and peace with God. Responsible people do not place themselves in a situation where they may be tempted to have sexual intercourse.

This does not mean that individuals may not express their love and care for each other through warm embraces, kissing, and other expressions of love. Discuss these matters with your date. This is not to suggest a lengthy conversation about every aspect of sexual behavior, but some discussion is necessary. Confusion enters a relationship when neither person knows what the other expects. A responsible gesture would be to reveal to your date your expectations for your time together.

These suggestions are only means to an end—to have a relaxed and enjoyable time with someone you want to know better. Sometimes, you

---

Prayer in Action
Mutually Loving

Make this prayer part of your dating preparations:

"Let love be sincere; hate what is evil, hold on to what is good; love one another with mutual affection; anticipate one another in showing honor. Do not grow slack in zeal, be fervent in spirit, serve the Lord. Rejoice in hope, endure in affliction, persevere in prayer"
(*Romans 12:9-12*).

---

may be disappointed—things just won't work out. But at other times you will know the joy of sharing yourself and your thoughts with someone who cares about you.

Talk It Over

1. What can you add to these dating suggestions?
2. What is the greatest value in being honest with a date?
3. What are three qualities you hope for in a dating partner?

Chapter Summary

- Dating is a commonly understood term used to describe the way males and females meet and get to know each other.
- The hormonal changes of puberty contribute to making adolescents sexually attracted to people of the opposite sex.
- "Boyfriend" and "girlfriend" are terms that describe members of the opposite sex in whom a person has a romantic or sexual interest.
- Group dating, single dating, and exclusive dating are three types of dating arrangements.
- Good dates depend more on who you are with and how you relate to that person than on what you do.

Prayer in Action

Teaching Approaches
- Use as a part of their discussion for "Talk It Over," Question 1.
- Ask: "How is this Scripture passage an appropriate prayer for preparing for a date?"

Talk It Over
Discuss Question 1 with the entire class. Write their suggestions on the board. Questions 2 and 3 should be discussed in pairs or with small groups. In the large group, ask volunteers to share the relevant points of their discussions.

Chapter Summary
- This section lists the main points of summary of Chapter 5. To use as a review, you might have the students list examples from the text to illustrate each point, rewrite each point in their own words, or find creative ways to teach each point.
- Have the students share their review techniques with a partner.

Background
Students learn about dating from their peers and from the media. Neither source is very good at helping adolescents set responsible limits. Students need opportunities to develop and to practice responsible dating behavior. They need to know that it's okay to ask questions.

Chapter 5 Review

What Have You Learned?

Listed below are suggested answers. For many of the questions, the answers will vary.

1. Friendship is usually the starting point for dating. For this reason, most dates develop out of peer relationships.
2. Two of the most common emotions associated with puberty are embarrassment and fear.
3. "Boyfriend" and "girlfriend" refer to members of the opposite sex in whom you have a sexual or romantic interest. The terms do have other meanings.
4. Answers will vary, but people are attracted to people for different reasons.
5. A "group date" is when a group of males and females get together for a social outing. "Single or personal dating" is when a male and female go out together as a couple. "Exclusive dating" is when two people decide to date only each other.
6. Answers will vary. For example, a shy person can practice social talk before asking a person out on a date to overcome his or her fear.
7. People can build trust with their parents by informing them of all the details of the date: where they are going, how long they will be there, with whom they are going, and what transportation they will be using.
8. Interracial dating is an issue because outside pressures, including other people's prejudice, can make interracial relationships difficult.
9. Date rape is when a person is forced, while on a date, to have intercourse or engage in genital stimulation against his or her wishes.
10. Answers will vary. Honesty, consideration, and being oneself expresses self-confidence and self-esteem, manners, and presents the real person as he or she is without masks.

REVIEW

What Have You Learned?

1. How does dating grow out of participation in a peer group?
2. What are two of the most common emotions associated with puberty?
3. What are the meanings of the terms, "boyfriend" and "girlfriend?"
4. Why is it difficult to conclude why a person is physically attracted to some people but not to others?
5. Explain the difference in the terms, "group dating," "single dating," and "exclusive dating."
6. What are some things that a person can do to overcome shyness in order to meet new people and go on dates?
7. What are some ways that a person can build trust with his or her parents regarding dating?
8. Why is interracial dating an issue for some people?
9. What is the meaning of the term "date rape"?
10. How can being yourself, being honest, and being considerate help your dating experience?

Application

1. Read the ads in the dating column of a local newspaper. Then, on an index card, write a dating ad for yourself, pointing out your best qualities. Don't put your name on the card. Post all the dating ads in the classroom. Take time to read the other descriptions. Does anyone seem like a good date for you?
2. Interview your parents or other adults to determine changes in the dating practices over the years.
3. Think about a person that you are dating or would like to date. What are your reasons for wanting to date that person?
4. Make a list of dating suggestions that you would like to give to someone who has just started to date.
5. Work in two groups, male and female. Have each group come up with a list of advantages and disadvantages for exclusive dating, or "going steady." Compare the two lists.
6. Invite a spokesperson from a rape crisis center to speak to the class on ways to avoid date abuse and date rape.
7. Work with a partner or in a small group. Come up with creative ideas for dates that cost under $20.
8. List and rank the five most important characteristics that you look for in a dating partner.

Journal Assignment

Students are to answer these questions: "Why is responsible dating a sign of maturity? How would mature people act on a date?"

REVIEW

Chapter Vocabulary

- dating
- puberty
- intimacy
- boyfriend
- girlfriend
- group date
- single or personal dating
- exclusive dating
- abuse
- date rape

Putting Vocabulary to Use

In your own words, define each of the following words and use them in a descriptive sentence.

1. dating
2. puberty
3. intimacy
4. boyfriend
5. girlfriend
6. group date
7. single or personal dating
8. exclusive dating
9. abuse
10. date rape

I have come more and more to realize that being unwanted is the worst disease that any human can ever experience.

Mother Teresa

Application

Read the directions and descriptions of each project to the students. Allow the students to choose their own project. Suggest the following steps: (1) formulate a plan; (2) complete the tasks; (3) share the initial project with a partner for comments; (4) revise and finalize the project.

Putting Vocabulary to Use

1. Dating: Special relationship that exists between a man and woman who spend intimate time together.
2. Puberty: A time of physical change when males and females are first able to conceive children.
3. Intimacy: A feeling of closeness that often describes the relationship between a man and woman who are romantically involved.
4. Boyfriend: A man for whom a woman has romantic interest.
5. Girlfriend: A woman for whom a man has romantic interest.
6. Group Date: A group of males and females who spend time together in a dating situation.
7. Single or Personal Dating: When a male and female go out together as a couple.
8. Exclusive Dating: When two people decide to date only each other.
9. Abuse: Physically or verbally threatening actions.
10. Date Rape: Sexual intimacy by force or threat that takes place on a date.

Final Thought

Background

Mother Teresa's words are taken from *Words to Love* (Ave Maria Press, 1983).

Focus On: Chapter 6

Identity, self-image, and the images one has of others are included in a person's sexuality. Sexuality refers to one's body and to the particular way a person relates to life either as a male or a female. One's sexuality also influences a person's ideas, feelings, and attitudes. The term "sex" is used to refer to biological differences (male or female) or to genital intercourse. While sexuality and sexual acts are related, there are major differences between the terms. Sexuality is always a part of a person's life, whereas sexual activity happens only occasionally. In this chapter, the students will examine sexuality and some of the ways that sexuality can be expressed in healthy and appropriate ways. Also, the specific issues of sexuality will be explored, including the dangers of sexual intercourse before marriage.

Plan Ahead

- Incorporate formal and/or spontaneous prayer in each lesson. A participatory prayer service that is suitable for use on retreat is provided in the Teacher's Resource Book.

- Note **Resources** which can be applied to, or extend, the lessons of this chapter.

- Preview the **Application** projects in the Chapter Review. Refer to **Teaching Approaches** for suggestions on when to assign the projects. Or, the projects may be used as part of lesson, section, or chapter reviews.

- Decide on a method for grouping students for projects and discussion.

- Invite guest speakers who will participate in selected lessons in advance.

Love, Sexuality, and Your Life

Love is patient, love is kind. It bears all things, believes all things, hopes all things, endures all things.

1 Corinthians 13:4, 7

This chapter will help you to:

- Understand the gift of sexuality as a natural part of your life.
- Develop a Christian perspective on sexuality and love.
- Examine the many meanings of love and how love contributes to all relationships.
- Understand the virtue of chastity as a positive way to express sexuality.
- Appreciate the goodness of sexual feelings.
- Uncover some of the serious consequences of sexual activity outside of marriage.
- Use the virtue of modesty to accentuate the respect and dignity of human sexuality.

102

Media Suggestions (Optional)

- *Teens and Sex: Decide for Yourself* (Ligouri Publications) 30 minutes. Discussion of the problems teens face concerning sexuality. Several adolescents share their own perspectives on sexuality.

- *Teens and Chastity: A Talk with Molly Kelly* (Center for Learning) 60 minutes. Two 30-minute segments that consider pregnancy, abortion, AIDS, STDs, and contraceptives. Chastity promoted as a positive alternative.

Aims

1. To help students understand how sexuality differs from sex.
2. To examine a spectrum of love: from loving oneself to loving others.

Begin the Section

1. Read the opening quotation from the First Letter to the Corinthians. Ask: "Which of the definitions of love do you find most true for your own life? What are some other definitions of love?"

2. Have the students write or brainstorm a list of "Love is" statements. Collect them on the board. Do the same for the statement "Sexuality is." Write these on the board as well.

3. Compare the students' feelings about love with their feelings about sexuality. Ask: "Which of our images are more positive: those about sexuality or those about love?"

4. Read or summarize the opening paragraphs from the text. If possible, show or display advertisements (either from magazines or a videotape of a television commercial) that use sexual innuendo. Point out the basic conflict between society's and the Church's understanding of sexuality.

I. GIFT AND DILEMMA

Human sexuality is a wonderful gift from God. Your sexuality affects how you think and act, it attracts you to other people, and attracts others to you. Your sexuality shapes your emotions and desires. Through the gift of sexuality, the human race is continued in the setting of loving, lifelong, faithful marriages.

For you, sexuality may, at times, seem less like God's gift and more like your dilemma. The tremendous emotions many people experience during puberty are often accompanied by unexpected dreams and desires. These experiences may cause some people to feel uneasy or unsure about themselves. Others might feel shame or think that they are evil because they think about sex.

The conflicting messages people receive about sexuality certainly don't help matters. The messages one hears from peers and the media seem to say: "Sex is great; everybody is doing it; try it, there's nothing wrong with it." Adults and the Church are often pictured as saying: "Yes, sex is wonderful, but it is not for you until marriage, so don't look, don't touch, in fact, don't even think about it."

103

Background

Advertisers know that "sex sells." Most ads directed to teens and adults incorporate some type of sexual message into their pitches. Some of the ads blatantly promote sex while others use subconscious messages or subtle suggestions.

Loving

Lesson Overview

Bombarded with many conflicting images of male and female relationships, what do students consider appropriate ways for Catholic Christian couples to express their sexuality before marriage? This lesson explores the story of how one couple lived out their sexuality before marriage. It also defines and differentiates between terms associated with sexuality and sex. In discussing sexuality and sexual activity, note that male and female attitudes toward relationships and sex have been formed in different ways. In soliciting views on sex and sexuality, be aware of these differences between males and females.

Teaching Approaches

- Choose several volunteers to read the story aloud.
- Discuss whether the students consider the story to be realistic or not. Have students offer suggestions for making the story more realistic.
- **Reteach**—Assign small groups to role play a first-time meeting between a guy and girl who like each other. Have them share their role plays before the class.
- **Extend the Lesson**—Ask: "What do you think was different about the feelings that Dwight first had for Tanya and the feelings he had for her at the engaged couple's retreat?"

The Chastity Option

Teaching Approaches

- Ask: "Why do you think that so many men were attracted to Mary Meyer's ad?"
- Discuss the philosophy of Meyer's group: "Sexual intimacy within marriage is worth the wait."

How are you to know what to do? Is sexuality one of the most cherished gifts that God has bestowed on human beings or is it the forbidden fruit?

Loving

Stuck in traffic, Dwight and Tanya shared a laugh on the way home from their weekend retreat for engaged couples. "You know, hon," Dwight began, "all that talk about the gift of sexuality and how important sex should be in our marriage—are you sure we were at a Catholic retreat house?"

Tanya smiled. "It was a switch," she agreed. "In high school it seemed like all we heard was 'no,' and 'that is wrong.' I feel so good knowing that our love for each other is a gift from God and not something evil. Those talks we heard and the chance to discuss our relationship have made me feel so close to you."

Dwight felt very close to Tanya as well. Sitting there next to her, he couldn't help thinking back to when they first met. He was a senior and Tanya was a year younger. They were on a double date. The catch was that Dwight was dating Tanya's best friend, and Tanya was with Dwight's friend, Mike. Dwight was attracted to Tanya immediately. He called it love. It certainly wasn't the same feeling he felt for her today, he knew, but it was a strong and powerful attraction.

Several weeks passed before Dwight worked up the courage to talk to Mike about Tanya. Dwight was surprised when Mike told him it was okay. "Go for it, man," Mike said. "I think she likes you, too."

For some reason, Dwight felt terribly shy when it came to Tanya. Around school, he would look for her, and then when he would see her, he'd smile and head off in the other direction. He remembered feeling really good when she would smile back and really down if she didn't seem to notice him.

Right before Christmas, Dwight and Mike went to a school dance together without dates. Tanya would be there, also without a date. In the hours preceding the dance, Dwight felt nervous, excited, confident, shy, upbeat, and depressed. Most of all, Dwight felt that something special was going to happen.

As Dwight and Mike entered the gym, Dwight looked eagerly for Tanya. When he saw her, he felt like he'd been punched hard in the stomach. She was slow dancing with another guy!

Even years later, that memory was painful. Dwight prayed that he would never feel that way again. Then he laughed. He recalled how beautiful Tanya had looked in her Christmas gown, and how he had finally talked and danced with her for most of the night.

The Chastity Option

After the breakup of a relationship, Mary Meyer placed an ad in the singles column of a local newspaper: "Female wanting to meet a man who would like to marry. Celibate before marriage only." Over 100 men responded.

Encouraged by the response, Meyer founded the National Chastity Association, a nonreligious group for singles who want to reserve sex for marriage. The group agrees that premarital sex can get in the way of romance and that relationships that include sex before marriage inevitably burn out.

Meyer, who has been married and divorced, says: "People ask me, 'Don't you like sex?' Nothing could be further from the truth. In fact, I can hardly wait." The philosophy of Meyer's group is: sexual intimacy within marriage is worth the wait.

Background

Sexual intimacy outside marriage, in many cases, does not lead to commitment. Sexual intercourse early in a relationship confuses the physical closeness of sex with love. Other types of closeness needed in relationships—mental, emotional, spiritual—will often fail to develop.

When he saw Tanya dancing, Dwight felt like he'd been punched in the stomach.

Tanya, noticing Dwight's restlessness asked, "Are you all right?" Dwight squeezed her arm. Just a month from their wedding, Dwight couldn't help but think that being in love with Tanya was so right. He hoped he would always feel this way.

Understanding the Terms

The meaning of the word "sexuality" differs from our understanding of the word "sex." Sexuality is all-encompassing. We are sexual people—male or female—from the time we are born. Sexuality influences every dimension of our humanity. Physically, every cell in our body is sex-typed. From infancy, our sexual roles are influenced by our family and society. Even our thinking seems to be shaped by sexuality. Recent studies reveal that women think with a connective or relational emphasis, whereas men focus and respond more in terms of "problem-solving" or "information communication." Spiritually, there are unique characteristics of human beings based on sexual differences (for example, women seem more likely to be drawn to the practice of contemplation or deep prayer than men).

The word "sex" identifies the biological classifications of male and female. Gender refers to female (feminine) or male (masculine) behavior or attitudes. "Having sex" commonly refers to physical sexual activity involving the reproductive parts of the body or sexual intercourse.

Sexual Enjoyment

The pleasures of being a sexual person are many. There are definitely physical pleasures connected to sexual intimacy. Many researchers believe that, just as the body is equipped with pain receptors in the nerve cells that warn of danger, it also has pleasure receptors to encourage behavior beneficial to the survival of the human race. For example, we need food to ensure our survival. When we eat, our taste buds send pleasant sensations to the brain. These pleasant tastes encourage us to eat more.

Sexual intercourse is also essential to the survival of the human race. It is intrinsically linked to *procreation*—having children. It's no wonder then that acts related to procreation are sources of pleasure. And, it should come as no surprise then that we desire sexual intimacy.

Understanding the Terms

New Words

Sexuality is the quality of having been created male or female; a gift of God that has physical, emotional, mental, and spiritual dimensions.

The word *sex* is often used to mean *sexual intercourse*, the physical expression of love that is reserved for married people as their way to show love and to help God bring new life into the world.

Affection is the warm and tender feeling one has for another person. Showing affection is a part of intimacy. Unfortunately, during adolescence, young people are often confused about the proper ways to express affection. The expressions of affection that they have grown used to receiving from their parents may disappear as parents struggle to understand their children's changing bodies.

Adolescents who experience physical affection from parents and family members, along with the emotional fulfillment of family gatherings, celebrations, rituals, and traditions, are likely to become healthy, well-adjusted adults. According to Christine Gudorf, "Parents need to continue to express physical affection to adolescents. But they shouldn't impose it, as if they were offering affection as something that satisfies both parental needs to express love and adolescent needs to receive love. Learning to offer, not impose, affection at appropriate times means learning to read our adolescents' moods" (*U.S. Catholic*, September 1991).

Teaching Approaches

- Make sure the students clearly understand the difference between the meanings of "sex" and "sexuality."

- Explain that: (1) males and females are born with and are influenced by specific sex-typed hormones; (2) God intended for males and females to both achieve the highest sense of respect and dignity; (3) God intended their relationship to be harmonious, rather than competitive.

- **Reteach**—Assign **Application** Project 1 (see **Resource 6A**).

- **Extend the Lesson**—Assign the students to work in small groups to research more about the physical, emotional, and spiritual differences between males and females. Allow them time to share their findings in class.

Sexual Enjoyment

New Words

Procreation means to have children, and is the term used to describe a married couple's participation with God in the creation of new life through sexual intercourse and conception.

Teaching Approaches

- Make sure the students understand the difference between pleasure as a result of sexual activity and pleasure as the goal of sexual activity. How is one act selfish and one unselfish?

- Explain that: (1) Sexual activity can be a source of great pleasure; (2) A person's entire sexual nature is to be appreciated as a gift from God; (3) Sexuality is often misunderstood and thought of as a selfish means to gain pleasure; (4) Pleasure should be understood as a result of sexual activity, not as its goal—sexuality is then reduced to something one has, rather than an aspect of one's whole life; (5) Everyone is a sexual subject—there are no sexual objects.

- **Reteach**—Debate this topic: "When a person's basic reason for engaging in sex is personal pleasure, he or she is likely to use others as sexual objects."

- **Extend the Lesson**—Write an essay discussing how sexuality can be misused and can harm another person.

▲ Family Living

Teaching Approaches

- Discuss the panel with either "Understanding the Terms" or "Sexual Enjoyment."

- Ask: "How should affection be shown in families?"

Talk It Over

Question 1 can be used as a follow-up to check the students' basic understanding of the section. For Question 2, allow volunteers to share examples. Remind them that love is a deep and complex human emotion. Sex, on the other hand, can be simply a biological act. Sex is certainly not always an expression of love. For Question 3, have the students focus on other positive ways to show affection.

▲▲ Family Living
Wanted: Good Hugs

A sailor, at sea for seven months, was granted a surprise three-week leave. He arrived home, unannounced, in the middle of the night. His wife was still awake, and happy to see him, while his children were asleep.

He tiptoed into his daughter's room, admired her innocent face, gave her a kiss on the forehead, left quietly. He hesitated, however, before going into his son's room. They had argued about everything from haircuts to poor grades before he left and nothing had been resolved in their infrequent letters while he was away.

How he has changed, the father thought. Now sixteen years old, his son looked so much like a man. He quietly bent down and kissed the top of his son's head.

After his father had left the room, the boy wiped away tears. He hadn't been asleep when his father kissed him, the first time that had happened in eight years.

People, no matter how old they are, need hugs, embraces, pats on the back, and even friendly kisses from the people they love. These are not age-limited behaviors. Parents who appropriately express physical affection for their children communicate to them their deep love. This intimacy is an important aspect of sexuality. Such behavior communicates that physical affection is good and is a wonderful part of our lives.

Besides the physical enjoyment of sexuality, we also have a deep need to be with other people: to talk, to listen, to be wanted and reassured. Our sexuality encourages us to move beyond the narrowness of a private or isolated life to engage in loving interaction with others.

Talk It Over

1. How would you define the difference between sexuality and sex?
2. Describe how the words "love" and "sex" are defined by your peers.
3. What are some of the many ways people express their sexuality?

Sexual intercourse is intrinsically linked to procreation—having children.

Journal Assignment

Have the students write about the breakfast conversation between the son and the father the morning after "the kiss."

Resources

Resource 6C lists the addresses of many media outlets and agencies for use with "Media Watch."

☀ Media Watch
The Ultimate

Genital sex is just one part of your sexuality, but if you believe what you see on television, hear in music lyrics, or watch in movies, you might disagree. In the media, sexual intercourse is often presented as a common solution to problems: loneliness, poor communication with parents, the lack of meaning in life, and a host of other such "tragedies."

The media's opinions are based on a perception of life that is deeply distorted. For example, the producers of a popular television show decided that a lead character should lose her virginity. They said they wanted the popular show to be realistic. As one of the show's executives said, "If parents think that their sons and daughters are refraining from sex, they are very mistaken."

The producers were surprised when they received thousands of letters protesting the character's behavior. While they had assumed that all teens were sexually active, the letters maintained that most high school students have not engaged in sexual intercourse, and did not want their heroines to either.

☀ Media Watch
Teaching Approaches

- Have the students write letters to the producers or network executives of a current television program expressing their opinions on the way sexuality is portrayed on television.
- Develop a television script that students believe offers an honest portrayal of adolescent sexuality.
- Form small groups. Have each group videotape a segment of a television program that presents an issue of teenage sexuality, then write discussion questions on the episode that can be shared with the entire class after they have viewed the segment.

A Spectrum of Love

Love is the greatest of all virtues, lasting into eternity *(1 Corinthians 13:13)*. But what is love? And what does it have to do with sexuality?

The word "love" is used in many ways: "I love ice cream." "I love to dance." "I love my mom." "I love you." What is the common thread of experience in all these uses of the word "love"?

Love and sexuality are deeply interrelated. Unfortunately, one is often confused with the other: sexual intercourse is known as "making love." While it can be a sign of love, sexual intimacy cannot make love happen where it does not already exist.

Sexual intercourse is an act of passion that is soon over. Love is a strong attraction, a deeply felt emotion that binds us to another for a long period of time and in many different ways. Love makes a person want to spend his or her life caring for this special someone or something. Love encourages people to be dedicated, committed, honest, trusting, generous, kind, and compassionate.

"Love is patient, love is kind. It is not jealous, [love] is not pompous, it is not inflated, it is not rude, it does not seek its own interests, it is not quick-tempered, it does not brood over injury, it does not rejoice over wrongdoing but rejoices with the truth. It bears all things, believes all things, hopes all things, endures all things. Love never fails."

—as Paul wrote to the Christians in Corinth *(1 Corinthians 13:4-8)*.

You, like Dwight and Tanya at the opening stages of their relationship, may feel a deep and powerful attraction toward a person of the opposite sex. How much do you know about the different kinds of love or the spectrum of love?

Self-love

Self-love is a prerequisite for any other kind of love. It's difficult to love someone else if you don't first care for yourself. Self-love can be a problem, however, if it is conceited or *narcissistic*—that is, getting so caught up in loving oneself that there is no room for loving anyone or anything else.

A Spectrum of Love

Lesson Overview

Ask the students to define the term, "make love." Most likely, they will describe sexual intercourse. This lesson explores what love has to do with sexuality and sex. How are they related? How are they different?

Teaching Approaches

- Allow the students a chance to express various opinions on love. Ask them to share their answers to the in-text question.
- **Reteach**—Assign **Application** Project 2 at this time.
- **Extend the Lesson**—Have the students work individually or in small groups to find two other Scripture passages about love. A Bible concordance will help them with this assignment. Then, have them find two other sources that express a common theme about love—a poem, novel, short story, or song lyrics. Ask for a written or oral summary that explains why these examples were chosen.

Background

Love is the "greatest of virtues" because even the Trinity shares love. Also, in eternity, when faith gives way to sight, and hope to possession, love will remain. (See *Catechism of the Catholic Church*, 1822-1829.)

Journal Assignments

The students may write their answers to the "Well-Being" reflections in their journals. These entries should not be shared.

Self-Love

New Words

Narcissism is an excessive concern for one's appearance, comfort, importance, or abilities. Narcissus is a character from Greek mythology. Narcissus could love no one but himself. Echo, who loved Narcissus, was ignored by him. She died when her love was not returned. Narcissus was so caught up in himself that when he saw his reflection in a pool of water, he stopped and stared. Narcissus was so captivated by his own reflection that he could not leave the pool. He died staring at his reflection.

Altruism means "a devotion to others." People who are *altruistic* act for the sake of others, not for their own benefit.

Teaching Approaches

- Say: "Self-love means accepting yourself as a creation of a loving God."
- Ask: "How can knowing that God loves us, even more than we love ourselves, change our perspective on life?"
- **Reteach**—Make sure the students can differentiate between honest self-love and narcissism. Ask them to share examples of each.
- **Extend the Lesson**—Have students find examples in newspaper or magazine articles that describe people who act altruistically.

☾ Well Being
What Do I Believe?

Feeling comfortable with your own sexuality comes from an honest and positive understanding of yourself. Take time to reflect honestly on the following questions:

1. Do I use correct sexual terms, or do I use slang?
2. Do I have an appreciation of what the Bible and the Church teach about sexuality?
3. How do my sexual values compare to those of my parents?
4. What kind of "body messages" am I sending to others by the way I sit, stand, walk, dress, and act?
5. Do I use profanity?
6. Have I seriously considered my sexuality and sexual feelings?

Narcissism originates from the Greek legend. A handsome boy Narcissus saw his reflection in a pool of water, fell in love with his image, and starved to death because he could not bear to leave his reflection.

You may associate narcissism with people who constantly brag about or gaze at themselves in mirrors.

Honest self-love is quite different than conceit or narcissism. Honest self-love means looking at yourself as you are seen by God. In doing so, you find a person loved by the Creator. The love you have for yourself in the name of God keeps you from being limited by your strengths and by your weaknesses.

When you truly love yourself, you are able to share. You form friendships, and begin to live *altruistically*—for the sake of others. You begin to be "other-centered." Your friends' interests become your interests, their concerns your concerns. In doing this, you show that you love and care for others.

Loving Others

What does it mean to say that you "love" someone? The answer to this question may not be as simple as it appears. Love is often classified into three categories:

1. *Filial love.*
2. *Infatuation.*
3. *Romantic love.*

Look at these categories in more detail.

Filial Love. If you say you love your parents, siblings, or other relatives, you probably mean

Can you explain the difference between filial love, infatuation, and romantic love?

that you feel connected with them because of loyalty and affection. This is known as filial love, the love of a child for a parent or a parent for a child. This is the love we also have for a friend, a special teacher or coach, or a neighbor to whom we are close. Filial love is a special bonding that usually lasts a long time, but that is not erotic.

Infatuation. When we hear people say that they love someone they barely know we say that they are infatuated. Infatuation is usually caused by a strong physical or sexual attraction and is usually based on impressions rather than the full truth. Infatuated people are said to be "head over heels" in love, that is, it seems that their reasoning is turned upside-down, and that any decisions they make are more emotional than rational. Infatuated people can become obsessed with their feelings and develop a focus that controls their lives.

Fortunately, the strong feelings associated with infatuation usually diminish quickly. The strong physical attraction associated with infatuation is neither wrong nor improper. While we must learn to direct our actions, we cannot completely control them. Infatuation is a normal human response to an attractive individual. The real challenge is to recognize these emotions for what they are, and understand them and not be overwhelmed by them.

Romantic Love. In some cases, infatuation can lead to romantic love, a love that grows from the more intimate knowledge and experience one has of a person. While you can become infatuated with someone you see walking down the street, you can experience romantic love only after you come to know a person. Romantic love usually involves powerful emotions, sexual feelings, and a strong desire for intimacy. Romantic love does not equal sexual intercourse. Romantic love grows deep and involves all of the ingredients of a close friendship—strong communication, commitment, and enjoyment—along with sexual attraction.

Knowing the Difference. How do you tell the difference between infatuation and romantic love? Here's a clue: infatuation is concerned only with "how I feel," not with the feelings of the other person. When we truly love others, our

Loving Others

New Words

Filial love is the love suitable to, or due from a son or a daughter. In filial love, there is a tendency to show great care and responsibility for the one loved.

Infatuation is a love experience based on a sudden, intense attraction.

Romantic love is a thoughtful and spontaneous stage when one gets to know and cherish all the wonderful things about another person.

Teaching Approaches

- Have the students read the section individually or with a partner.
- Ask: "How do you tell the difference between infatuation and romantic love?"
- **Reteach**—Explain that those who experience the feelings of infatuation, most likely are attracted to just one feature, not to the whole person because of projection. We project on to others the images we would like them to be. If there are some similarities between the image we project and the people we meet, we experience a powerful sense of attraction to those people. We feel good if the people and our images are similar.
- **Extend the Lesson**—Have students look up or create other sayings to describe infatuation or romantic love: for example, "Love is blind" or "Love means never having to say you are sorry." Discuss the merits of each statement. Have students determine which statements they find most acceptable. Display the best sayings on posters around the classroom.

Resources

Resource 6E lists other sayings that describe infatuation or romantic love.

True Love

Teaching Approaches

- Write these statements on the board: (1) "It happens suddenly." (2) "You accept a person's faults." (3) "Feelings are based on one or two qualities of a person." (4) "Problems are faced together". (5) "Feelings endure separations." (6) "Thoughts are of your own needs and feelings." (7) "It fades fast." (8) "It lasts."
- Ask the students to identify which of the statements describe true love. **Answer:** 2, 4, 5, 8.
- Read or summarize the section.
- **Reteach**—Ask: "Why is it important to accept what another can offer in a relationship, and not demand more?"
- **Extend the Lesson**—Assign **Application** Project 6 with the lesson or as an extension to it.

concern is directed to their wishes. Generally, if the focus is more on oneself ("I feel so good in his/her presence.") rather than on others ("How are you feeling today?"), the experience is of infatuation, not love.

Even when infatuation leads to romantic love, it is still only part of the story of a loving relationship. Infatuation cannot sustain a relationship over the course of a lifetime. As mentioned earlier, infatuation is a fleeting emotion. In fact, many people "fall in and out" of love repeatedly.

True Love

You've looked at three ways in which the word "love" is used. There is a fourth way. What does it mean to say, "God is love"? How does using love in this context change our understanding of the word?

It is no accident that "love" is used to express both the attraction between people and as a description of God. We are created in God's image in such a way that we are attracted to God. The power of this attraction also draws us toward others.

After Jesus rose from the dead, He appeared to His Apostle and friend, Peter. "Simon, son of John, do you love Me more than these?" Jesus asks Peter. The most intimate Greek word for "love," *agape,* is used here by John *(John 21:15-19)*.

Peter answers Jesus, "Yes, Lord, you know that I love you." Peter's response here is *phile* another Greek word meaning love for a friend.

Again, Jesus repeats His question: "Agape, Simon?" Did Peter love Jesus this deeply and personally?

Peter responds, "Phile."

Jesus asks the question a third time. "Simon, son of John, phile?" Jesus has restated the question in Peter's terms. Jesus has met Peter directly. If he could not offer Jesus the kind of love Jesus was seeking, He would accept what Peter could give. Phile would have to do.

Jesus wanted Peter's complete love, but settled for what Peter was capable of giving.

Background

Peter's three-fold confession to love Jesus in John 21:15-19 serves to contradict his earlier three-fold denial. The First Vatican Council cited these verses in defining how Jesus gave Peter the power of supreme shepherd and ruler over the whole flock, the Church.

Being "in love" is a wonderful feeling. What can this couple do to build upon it?

🛐 Prayer in Action

Teaching Approaches

- Use the prayer reflection as a concluding prayer to the lesson. Choose several readers to read the prayer aloud in parts. If possible, accompany the reading with instrumental background music.
- Encourage students to add their own prayer reflections following the reading.

Talk It Over

Have the students share their answers to the questions with a partner or in a small group. At the end of their discussion, hold a large group roundup where volunteers can share some of the highlights of their discussion.

🛐 Prayer in Action
A Reflection

God,

There is something about love that I want to discuss.

I know something about the importance of loving others.

But I want You to know that I want to be loved!

I want to feel that I am lovable,

That someone will consider me very important,

And will tell me their thoughts.

I want that person to know

And love the real me.

Help me be open to hearing,

seeing, and feeling that love.

Help me also to return it

Honestly and enthusiastically.

Help me understand

That love is the meaning of life.

Amen.

The point is worth noting: true love means accepting another as he or she is. True love does not force another into something he or she is not ready to be or do. True love supports the dignity and holiness of others. It is joyful and life-giving and is an expression of everything that we are, including our deepest feelings, needs, and desires. Loving another person can lead to feeling compassion for everyone.

"Lord, you know everything; you know that I love you," Peter said, finally to Jesus. Jesus said to Peter: "Feed My sheep. And follow Me." Jesus accepted Peter's phile as the starting point for all the great things that Peter would eventually accomplish.

Talk It Over

1. Give three different examples explaining the word "love."
2. How do people prove their love for one another?
3. Why would it be difficult to love another person if you could not love yourself?
4. Describe the difference between romantic love and infatuation.
5. How does the story of Jesus and Peter point out the need for "give-and-take" attitudes and actions in a loving relationship?

Journal Assignment

Have students write their own personal prayer reflection, similar in length and tone to the one in the text. They may then share these reflections in the prayer as suggested in "Prayer in Action."

II. BEING SEXUALLY RESPONSIBLE

Aims

1. To help students understand positive ways to express their sexuality before marriage.

2. To help students become more aware of the consequences of sexual activity outside of marriage.

Begin the Section

1. Ask the students to brainstorm reasons people give for having sexual intercourse before marriage. Then, have them develop a list of reasons not to be sexually active before marriage. Write both lists on the board. Refer to the points on both lists when covering the material in this section.

2. Read the title of the section. Ask: "What do you think the phrase 'being sexually responsible' means?"

3. Recall that love and sexual intimacy are not the same thing, nor do they cause the other to happen. Love does not have to lead to sexual intimacy, and sexual intimacy does not automatically lead to love. Ask: "How can sexual intercourse be just another biological act? Why is sexual intimacy not always an expression of love? What would you say about a person who thought that sex was always an expression of love?"

To the Fullest

Lesson Overview

Ask: "What does it mean to live one's sexuality fully and completely?" Some of the comments may be future-oriented such as, "I cannot live my sexuality fully until I am married." As they read the lesson, the students will find that there are many healthy, Christian ways that sexuality *can* be lived out before marriage, and that there are positive benefits of doing so.

Teaching Approaches

• Assign the story to be read quietly.

• **Reteach**—Return to the original question: "How will you live your sexuality fully and completely?" Ask: "After reading the story, can you think of other ways that you now live your sexuality fully and completely?"

II. BEING SEXUALLY RESPONSIBLE

At puberty, a girl is able to bear a child and a boy is able to father one. After puberty, people are physically able to engage in sexual intercourse. The powerful drive to procreate can overwhelm all words of caution and cloud reason.

There is a widespread confusion in modern society about the proper relationship between love and sexual intimacy. This confusion leads to serious problems, not the least of which are teenage marriages, babies born to unwed mothers, abortion, *sexually transmitted diseases* (including AIDS), and suicide. A helpful way to overcome this confusion is to understand the healthy and holy relationship that exists between love and sexual intimacy.

To the Fullest

Tanya answered the question in her journal with an exclamation point. It asked, "How will you live your sexuality fully and completely?" She answered: "I already am; I always have!"

When she and Dwight were dating during high school, she told him what she valued about herself and included her feelings about sexuality:

"I expect to be treated with dignity and respect. I am a human being who cares deeply and can easily be hurt. I want to be held by you and touched by you, but I don't want to be treated like an object. I want to express my feeling for you, but I believe that sexual intercourse is for marriage."

Tanya remembered Dwight breaking into a surprised smile at her words. She could tell that he respected her for what she said, and loved her even more. What she didn't know at the time was that Dwight had the same views.

During their courtship they had many opportunities to yield to temptation. Dwight and Tanya often found themselves alone: on camping trips, in her mother's house, saying goodnight in the car. But because of the respect and love they shared for each other, they were able to work through these situations.

Dwight and Tanya had always found acceptable ways to express their sexuality.

Journal Assignment

For safekeeping, have the students write their lists of creative ideas from "Sharpening Your Skills" in their journals.

Background

For more information on the issue of responsible sexuality see the *Catechism of the Catholic Church,* 2331-2336.

Sharpening Your Skills
Be Creative

Expressing one's sexuality positively requires creativity. How can you express affection without engaging in sexual intercourse? What are creative ways of spending time with the person you love? Many young adults find volunteering together helps their relationship develop and mature. What could you do to help out at a day care center or at a nursing home? Are there crafts and hobbies that you would enjoy doing together?

Tanya looked back on a very romantic courtship. One summer, she and Dwight spent many Saturdays caring for an elderly woman in their neighborhood, a close friend of Dwight's family. They helped clean the woman's house and tended her yard. The lunch break always included time for a few hugs and kisses. Tanya especially enjoyed hearing the woman's stories about Dwight's family. Tanya loved those happy, peaceful moments. Her love for Dwight grew from those experiences. Now, seven years from the time they started dating, she looked forward to their marriage.

Love and Marriage

You've probably heard it a thousand times. No, make that two thousand! "Sexual intercourse is the fullest expression of married love and is reserved for married couples only." What's the big deal? What's wrong with "making love" to my boyfriend or girlfriend, you may ask?

A husband and wife share their lives, plan a family, discuss financial decisions, review what has happened at home or work, and communi-cate as close friends. These normal activities bond the couple together. The love they have for each other is then strengthened by their sexual union. Only in marriage can sexual intercourse be an intimate and full expression of love be-tween a man and a woman. Such sexual intimacy seals a relationship.

What's the value of waiting until marriage to have sexual intercourse? Many people argue that there is nothing wrong with having sexual inter-course before marriage. "This way," they say, "you know that you are sexually compatible." Others say, "By living together (*co-habitation*) before the wedding, you can decide in advance whether the marriage will work."

Actually, having sexual intercourse before marriage proves only that a couple is capable of having intercourse; living together proves only that they can live together, nothing more. Where is the promise of fidelity that offers hope for the future? the statement of, "I'll be there when you need me"? the trust that's necessary for a successful marriage? These commitments are non-existent in premarital intercourse or co-habitation.

Without the commitment of marriage, with-out the public promises a couple make to each other, something crucial is missing. Sexual in-tercourse loses its significance as a bonding and loving act, becoming merely a biological exercise.

Concretely, couples who are sexually involved or live together before marriage are more likely to divorce than are those couples who abstain from sex prior to marriage.

Abstinence has come to be associated with the virtue of chastity. To "abstain" means to not take part in an activity. In the case of sex-uality, abstinence means to refrain from sexual intercourse. People who practice abstinence don't have to worry about pregnancy or sexu-ally transmitted diseases. People who choose to refrain from sexual intercourse make a de-cision as important as any they will ever face.

Background

Pope John Paul II wrote that true conju-gal love "is realized in a truly human way only if it is an integral part of the love by which a man and woman commit themselves totally to one another until death" (*Familiaris Consortio*, #11).

- **Extend the Lesson**—Romans 12:9-12 lists seven guidelines to follow in per-sonal relationships: (1) love sincerely, (2) choose well, (3) show concern, (4) have respect, (5) remain joyful, (6) be patient, and (7) persevere. Ask the students to translate these guide-lines into a personal code of conduct for expressing their sexuality.

Sharpening Your Skills

Teaching Approaches

- Suggest these ways for handling sexual desire: (1) Make an agree-ment with yourself that you will not have sexual intercourse until you are married. Have a plan or thoughtful reason in mind to act differently when you are tempted; (2) Avoid tempting situations. Don't spend time alone with a date in the house or car. Plan ac-tivities with others; (3) Channel your energy into a sport, hobby, or volunteer activity. There is plenty of time after high school to form a relationship with the per-son who you will marry, but high school is perhaps your last and best chance to participate in a sport or activity that you enjoy.
- Use the idea suggested in **Application** Project 5 as a means to begin a long-term "chastity campaign."

Love and Marriage

Teaching Approaches

- Ask: "What does 'love' mean in a mar-riage? How is love defined in other relationships (for example, friendships or dating)?"
- Read or summarize the text section. Point out the connection between sex-ual intimacy, love, and commitment in marriage.
- **Reteach**—Refer the students to their lists of reasons to have and not have sex before marriage. Offer them the oppor-tunity to add reasons to either list.
- **Extend the Lesson**—Have students de-bate the merits of not having sexual in-tercourse prior to marriage.

- Read or summarize the section.
- Ask: "What qualities do you feel you have that help you find a 'middle ground' regarding sexual feelings and actions?" List some of the qualities on the board.
- **Reteach**—Assign small groups to come up with a plan to help develop the qualities that were listed.
- **Extend the Lesson**—Use the role play suggestion from **Application** Project 8.

Talk It Over

The questions can serve as a review. Have the students discuss all three questions with a partner. Summarize their discussion in a large group follow-up.

Finding Your Place

Your sexual feelings are part of God's gift to you. Nevertheless, these sexual powers can be easily misused. This does not mean that kissing is wrong, that holding hands is a sin, or that young lovers cannot be affectionate. It does stress the importance of learning self-control. How can you respect others and not use them for selfish gratification? How do your sexual feelings and desires honestly reflect who you are now? What can you do to control your behavior when passion seems to override your good intentions?

How can you balance your sexual feelings and desires with what you know to be proper moral behavior? Going to the extreme of avoiding relationships altogether won't work. That way, you will never learn to interact with members of the opposite sex. The other extreme—giving in to all of your sexual feelings without concern for anything but your own sexual satisfaction—may be even more harmful than the first. Such behavior can damage your physical and emotional health, as well as harm other people's well-being. Where is the middle ground between either of these two extremes?

Talk It Over

1. Why is it important to communicate your belief about sexuality honestly and openly?
2. What are some balanced ways to express your sexual feelings?
3. What do you think when you hear the word "abstinence"? What social pressures do you and your peers experience about being sexually active?

Sexual attraction often brings couples together. Long lasting relationships, however, only develop as couples find creative ways to be friends with each other.

Journal Assignment

Ask the students to define what it means to "be in control of your actions at all times." Encourage them to write about a specific experience when they felt that they were in control.

Background

"Woven through every search for genuine love, for personal maturity, and for interpersonal commitments, is a call to be chaste, sexually responsible, and appropriate for one's particular vocation in life" (*Human Sexuality*.)

Effective Communication in Marriage

The following suggestions have been identified as effective ways to improve communication in marriage.

1. Take time each day to share with your spouse what you have experienced during the day physically, emotionally, and spiritually.
2. Ask your spouse to share his or her experience. Listen attentively and show interest.
3. Write love letters to your spouse on a regular basis.
4. Whenever you have a disagreement, talk it out. Avoid the silent treatment.
5. Communicate imaginatively. Think of new and creative ways to say "I love you."
6. Settle your differences. Don't leave arguments unresolved.
7. Face your differences honestly. Be willing to compromise and don't be afraid to disagree.

How would you get these ideas out to married couples? You have been hired by an advertising agency to develop a campaign to promote these important rules. You may use any form of advertising that you wish, including magazine ads, radio jingles, bumper stickers, or television commercials. Plan your campaign and present it to the class as a pilot audience. Prepare a proposal for the ad agency explaining why your ad will be effective and how you plan to disseminate it around the country.

115

Effective Communication in Marriage

Teaching Approaches
- Read through each suggestion with the students. Ask them to offer specific ways to implement each.
- Assign the students to work with a partner or in small groups to complete the advertising campaign. Allow class time for them to share or display their finished work.

Resources
   Resource 6F provides a sample format for the suggested assignment.

Special Issues in Sexuality

Lesson Overview

The statistics and facts presented in this lesson are designed to emphasize the dangers of premarital sexual activity. Remind the students of their need to be in control of their behavior. Point out issues where a person may become a victim (rape and sexual abuse are examples) and ways to seek help for these problems.

Teaching Approaches

- "What does the term 'safe sex' mean to you?" If the students mention that the use of a condom classifies sexual activity as "safe sex" point out that studies have shown that condoms are not foolproof. They break during intercourse between five and thirty percent of the time. What level of risk are they prepared to take?
- Have the students read the section. Clarify the main point of the section: "Abstinence until marriage, and then a monogamous relationship with a spouse who has also practiced abstinence, is the only way to avoid unmarried pregnancy, STDs, and sexually transmitted HIV."
- **Reteach**—Show a video or slide presentation on STDs and AIDS.
- **Extend the Lesson**—Have students develop slogans promoting responsible sexual behavior.

Pregnancy

New Words

The *fertility cycle* is the time from the beginning of one menstrual period to the onset of the next, usually about twenty-eight days.

Fallopian tubes are a pair of tubes through one of which a mature egg, released from the ovary, travels to the uterus, or womb.

Ovum refers to the woman's fertilized egg, the beginning of human life. An egg is most likely to be present during the middle of a woman's monthly cycle. However, it is difficult and almost impossible, for an adolescent to determine when an egg is present. *Ovulation* may occur at any time in the most regular of cycles and even more frequently than once a month.

Few women have totally predictable *menstrual cycles*. It may take several years for an adolescent female to have anything close to a predictable cycle.

116   Chapter 6

Special Issues in Sexuality

Recent statistics report that:

- Approximately one million unmarried teenagers get pregnant each year.
- Young adults ages sixteen to twenty-four are more likely to become infected with a sexually transmitted disease (STD) than are any other age group.
- Sexually active young adults are considered a high-risk group for becoming infected with *HIV* (Human Immunodeficiency Virus), the virus that causes *AIDS* (Acquired Immune Deficiency Syndrome).

Responsible sexual behavior may differ for people based upon their maturity and moral development, but never includes premarital intercourse or intense petting, that is, the fondling of sexual organs. People with balanced approaches to sexuality:

1. Respect the feelings of others.
2. Control their actions.
3. Avoid behavior that would embarrass themselves, their dates, and their families.
4. Know their limits and stick within them.

Responsible sexual behavior does not mean "safe sex" or using a condom. Bluntly speaking, there is only one way to avoid pregnancy, STDs, and sexually transmitted HIV: abstaining from sexual intercourse until marriage, and then having a monogamous relationship with a spouse who has also practiced abstinence. Even if contraception is used, a person who has sexual intercourse with someone other than a faithful, monogamous spouse is at risk of acquiring an STD or HIV.

Living the virtue of chastity and practicing abstinence can be difficult, especially with the expectations of peers and society. And when passion is high, controlling one's behavior becomes more difficult. In order to persevere in your practice, you need to understand why abstinence is the only sure method of protection.

Pregnancy

You may have studied human reproduction in school or talked about it with your parents. In summary, at puberty:

- Males produce sperm and females produce eggs.
- Sperm fertilize eggs.
- Males produce sperm constantly, while women release eggs normally only once a month during the menstrual cycle.
- Fertilization normally takes place when the eggs are in a woman's fallopian tubes.
- Fertilization may occur after the man's penis has penetrated the woman's vagina during sexual intercourse, but it is possible for the sperm to reach the female's *ovum* (egg) even when the penis is not fully inserted into the vagina.

At puberty, males are able to father a child and females are able to conceive one.

Resources

Refer to **Resource 6G.** This chart shows the effectiveness of current birth control methods.

Journal Assignment

Ask the students to write a story imagining the chain of events that would take place, and the people that would be affected, if (1) they were pregnant or (2) they were the father of an unborn child.

- Fertility cycles differ. Some women will experience one cycle of 20 days only to have the next cycle be 40 days or more. (A cycle begins on the first day of menstrual bleeding and ends on the last day prior to the next menstruation.) Other women may have very regular menstrual cycles.

- An egg can be released at anytime during a cycle. Natural Family Planning, a form of birth regulation encouraged by the Catholic Church, charts a woman's morning temperature and mucus flow to help identify when she is fertile (an egg is released).

You probably also learned the falseness of these sexual myths: that a woman cannot conceive during her period; that a virgin cannot get pregnant the first time she has sexual intercourse; that douching after intercourse prevents pregnancy; and that birth control methods never fail, even when used incorrectly.

If believed, these falsehoods can cause serious problems. Conception *can* happen during menstruation; pregnancy *is* possible after only one sexual experience; douching *does not* prevent pregnancy; and *all* contraceptive measures can fail, even if used correctly.

Young unmarried women who make the courageous choice to give birth to their children face uncertain futures. A child's best hope for a healthy and productive life comes from being part of a stable and secure family. Teenage couples, including those who marry because of a pregnancy, lack many of the resources and skills needed for a child's optimal growth. Tragically, teenage pregnancy leads to thousands of abortions each year.

Respecting Others

Imagine a young couple who, soon after they meet, become physically attracted to each other. When they are alone, their attraction becomes so intense that they lose control and "make love." Sexual intercourse quickly becomes an expected part of their relationship, and then an obligation.

Eventually, one or both members of the couple begin to feel used by the other. Why would you think this happens?

The power of sexuality is very great and is often difficult to control. It is no wonder, then, that sex plays a major role in scandalous or abusive situations. Recognizing these situations and understanding why they occur can help you avoid them.

Sexual Abuse. People can and do use others for selfish gratification. Sexual abuse is a terrible crime. While most people are aware that young children can be sexually abused, few realize that many victims are junior high or high school girls abused by someone in their own home—a parent, stepparent, relative, or some other trusted authority figure.

A person who has been abused should seek help from a trusted adult or professional crisis center. There are many centers operated by the church.

Resources

Resource 6H provides more information about a woman's fertility cycle. **Resource 6I** lists several ways to communicate, "No, I do not want to be sexually intimate," to a dating partner.

Background

"The pain of sexual dysfunction, the effects of sexual abuse, the consequences of sexually immature decisions, and other forms of sexually-related hurt and harm can be discouraging" *(Human Sexuality, USCC).*

Teaching Approaches

- Have the students read about how the body changes during puberty.
- Conduct a brief quiz on the common myths about pregnancy?" Collect the quizzes.
- Have the students read this selection to find the answers to these questions.
- **Reteach**—Review with students their answers to the common myths about pregnancy.
- **Extend the Lesson**—Have students research the number of teenage pregnancies that occur in their community each year.

Respecting Others

Teaching Approaches

- Read or summarize the section.
- Ask the students to point out areas in their lives where they "can't control themselves." Point out that a person does have control over those areas of his or her life, just as he or she can control sexual desires.
- **Reteach**—Remind the students of the many factors that may influence the way they live out their sexuality from the media, their peers, and from society as a whole. Explain to the students that if they are secure in their self-esteem, their peers will not be able to talk them into taking dangerous risks.
- **Extend the Lesson**—Have the students answer these questions in their journals: "Who is more concerned about my well-being, me or the media? How do my peers influence me sexually?"

Sexual Abuse

New Words

Incest is sexual activity between persons who are closely related biologically.

Teaching Approaches

- Read or summarize the section.
- Stress the ways students can help someone who is a victim of sexual abuse.

Teaching Approaches (continued)

- **Reteach**—Point out that sexual abuse: (1) is often kept secret by the victim; (2) often takes place when adults subject children to fondling, incest, or rape, or when adults lure children into genital sexual activity; (3) often the person knows the molester; (4) the abuser may be a parent, a step-parent, a sibling, or some other person living in or visiting the home.

- **Extend the Lesson**—Have the students bring articles from the newspaper dealing with the results of sexual abuse. They should read the article, suggest causes of the problem, and offer ways that they could help solve it.

Pornography

Teaching Approaches

- What are the problems associated with pornography?

- Discuss the abusive nature of pornography and how it can be harmful to everyone.

- **Reteach**—Ask: "What can you do to help stop the spread of pornography?"

- **Extend the Lesson**—Conduct a debate between two groups on the issue of freedom of speech and artistic expression versus the danger of pornography.

In Focus

Teaching Approaches

- Read the facts presented. Ask: "Which fact do you find most disturbing?"

- Have the students personalize the question asked in the panel.

- Explain that in recent years, society has become increasingly aware of the occurrences of spousal abuse. The problem of battered spouses cuts across all levels of society.

Sexual abuse can go unreported for years. Sometimes abused children are threatened with severe punishment, embarrassment, ridicule, and even death if they tell anyone what has happened.

It is most important that victims of sexual abuse know that they are not at fault. They have done nothing wrong—it is the adult's behavior that is wrong. The proper course of action is for the victim to seek help. Talking to a trusted adult is the best first step for coming to grips with this problem.

Pornography. A compulsive interest in pornography can be a form of deviant sexual behavior. People, usually women and children, are portrayed in sexually explicit ways, turning them into objects to be used. Women, especially, are portrayed by pornography in demeaning and sometimes violent ways. Pornography encourages people to use others for their own sexual pleasure. It plants in the imagination of its users a distorted picture of sexuality. Pornography cannot contribute anything positive to the formation of a healthy relationship with another, the essential part of sexuality.

Sexual Orientations

One aspect of sexuality that we know little about is sexual orientation. What causes most people to be *heterosexual*—that is, to be sexually attracted to members of the opposite sex? What causes some people to be *homosexual* (gay or lesbian)—that is, sexually attracted to people of the same sex? Why are there what may be called degrees of heterosexuality and homosexuality, and sometimes a mixture of the two in one person (a bisexual)?

Many people experience a period of confusion about their sexual orientation. They may feel a strong sexual attraction toward someone of their own sex, or have someone of their sex demonstrate sexual feelings toward them. They may even engage in same-sex genital stimulation. None of these acts makes a person homosexual.

In Focus
Violence Against Women

Pornography often includes acts of violence against women, the most underreported crime in the United States. Consider these facts:

- On average, sixteen women are raped each hour; one every six minutes.
- Three to four million women are battered each year; every eighteen seconds a woman is beaten.
- Three out of four women will be victims of at least one violent crime during their lifetimes.
- More than one million women are battered and seek medical assistance each year.
- The United States has a rape rate 13 times higher than Britain's, nearly four times higher than Germany's, and more than 20 times higher than Japan's.

Why do you think our society still includes many destructive and unhealthy approaches to human sexuality?

Sometimes it isn't easy to sort out our feelings for other people. At puberty, when we begin to have adult sexual feelings, it is easy to confuse feelings and desires with other needs. For instance, a person seeking parental love may have a strong attraction to a same-sex adult. What appears to be a sexual desire can be a simple need for physical affection or approval. People also feel very strong bonds of friendship—without sexual attraction—toward an adult or peer of the same sex. That is normal. Have you ever had any of these feelings? What was your reaction to them?

People who experience a consistent homosexual orientation, needn't be alarmed. Homosexual orientation is not sinful, although the Church does

---

Resources

Resource 6J presents ways to recognize suicide warning signs that are reflected in a person's behavior and provides suggestions for getting help for people who are considering suicide.

Background

"We call on all Christians and citizens of good will to confront their own fears about homosexuality and to curb the humor and discrimination that offend homosexual persons" (*Human Sexuality*, USCC).

teach that homosexual intercourse (like premarital and extramarital heterosexual intercourse) is sinful because it denies the life-giving, creative part of sexual love.

Except for their sexual orientation, people who are homosexual are no different from any other people. They should be treated with the dignity and respect given to all human beings. Recall that Jesus went out of His way to protect from abuse those whom society considered sexual sinners. In following Jesus, we are to treat all people with love. People who are gay, lesbian, or bisexual are loved by God, are entitled to just and equal treatment by other human beings, and are to be granted loving acceptance by those who consider themselves Christians.

Masturbation

Masturbation may appear to be harmless. It certainly does not compare with the destructiveness of sexual abuse or pornography. While it does not hurt others, masturbation can erode one's self-esteem. In stimulating one's sexual organs to the point of sexual release—orgasm, the goal of masturbation—a person has acted selfishly, orienting an activity intended for loving human relationships and creation into a very self-centered act. This behavior can lead to a pattern of sexuality that is narcissistic, concerned only with satisfying personal needs and not with personal growth. Sexual pleasure may become so important to a person who masturbates that he or she does not form relationships or engage in activities with others.

Warning: Extreme Danger

Engaging in sexual intercourse outside of a committed married relationship can result in severe physical consequences, even more damaging than an unwanted pregnancy. In the case of AIDS, promiscuous behavior is a threat to your life.

If you engage in genital contact with a person who has a sexually transmitted disease, you may easily catch that disease. STDs are passed from one person to another through genital contact (not just intercourse). Some of the most devastating STDs are *chlamydia, gonorrhea, herpes simplex II,* and *syphilis.*

It is not always easy to tell when a person is infected with STDs; symptoms are not always visible. With some diseases, the symptoms appear for only a short time, and then disappear. A person may have a sore or odor around his penis or vagina that disappears after a few days.

Most STDs can be cured with antibiotics, although some forms of the diseases are resistant

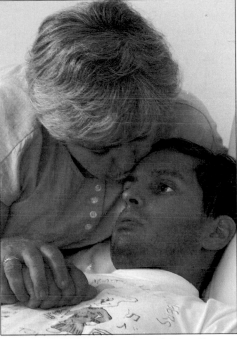

AIDS, like other STDs, is transmitted through sexual contact with an infected person. At this time, AIDS is always fatal.

Sexual Orientations

New Words

The terms *heterosexual orientation* and *homosexual orientation* refer only to the attraction a person feels, toward someone of his or her own sex, or toward someone of the opposite sex. In either orientation, the sexual feelings are meant to be controlled and directed to the appropriate behavior.

Teaching Approaches

- Read or summarize the section.
- Emphasize these points: (1) At puberty, it is easy to be confused by sexual feelings; (2) Experiencing sexual attraction for someone of the same sex does not make a person a homosexual; (3) People who are homosexual should be treated with the dignity and respect given to all human beings.
- Ask: "Why do people make disparaging remarks and jokes about people with homosexual orientations?"
- **Reteach**—Have students anonymously write questions about homosexuality. Collect their questions and use them to further the study of the topic.
- **Extend the Lesson**—Discuss: "Why are people afraid of homosexuality?"

Masturbation

Teaching Approaches

- Discuss how masturbation can lead to "a pattern of sexuality that becomes narcissistic, concerned only with one's own personal needs."
- **Reteach**—What myths have students heard about masturbation? Discuss them as a class.
- **Extend the Lesson**—Invite a psychologist to discuss the emotional aspects of masturbation.

Warning: Extreme Danger

New Words

Chlamydia, Gonorrhea, Herpes Simplex II, and Syphilis are all sexually transmitted diseases.

Human immunodeficiency virus (HIV) causes *acquired immunodeficiency syndrome* (AIDS).

Background

"In order to help an adolescent learner 'feel accepted in a communion of charity and freed from self-enclosure,' a parent, teacher, or counselor 'should undramatize masturbation. . . .' We encourage all educators and counselors to help those who masturbate to move toward better social integration, to be more open and interested in others, in order eventually to be free from this form of behavior." *(Human Sexuality,* USCC).

Teaching Approaches

- Introduce the section by discussing other communicable diseases; for example, chicken pox. Explain that the difference between chicken pox and an STD is that there is a social stigma or embarrassment attached to STDs. This stigma often prevents a person from seeking treatment, preferring instead to simply ignore the symptoms in the hope that the disease will go away. They hope in vain, however, because the disease just gets worse.

- Present this statement: "There is no safe way to have multiple sexual partners." Ask the students to share their opinion.

- **Reteach**—Discuss how "safe sex" is falsely promoted.

- **Extend the Lesson**—Use the students' letters from **Application** Project 7 as the starting point for a class discussion.

▲ To Your Health

Teaching Approaches

- Discuss the findings of this survey with the students, answering the in-text questions.
- Have students conduct a similar survey in their school.

Talk It Over

Have the students work in small groups to come up with the outline as suggested in Question 1. Follow up with a large group discussion. Combine the best of all the suggestions into one class plan. If possible, invite an abuse counselor to your classroom. Share the class's plan. Elicit his or her comments and feedback. For Question 2, the students may call out "sexual myths" as you write them on the board. For Question 3, arrange two opposing teams to gather facts in order to debate both sides of the statement.

---

to treatment and cannot be cured. If not treated early, the diseases can damage the reproductive system and eventually cause blindness, deafness, heart disease, and death.

AIDS can also be transmitted sexually. The Human Immunodeficiency Virus (HIV) destroys the body's T-cells, weakening the body's immune system until it can no longer fight other diseases. Inevitably, another disease, called an *opportunistic infection,* will attack. Without T-cells, the body is unable to fight off the disease. People with AIDS die from these opportunistic infections.

You can become infected with HIV in three ways: Blood-to-blood contact (sharing contaminated needles or from a blood transfusion, for example); through the exchange of bodily fluids (normally through sexual intercourse); or from an infected mother to a child (at birth and through breast feedings).

Condoms have been promoted as a way to protect a person against giving or getting an STD or AIDS from a sexual partner. Such advertising (either by business or special interest groups) is a dangerous and simplistic deception. While condoms may lessen the risk of catching a disease to

✚ To Your Health
Peer Pressure

In a recent survey, thirty-four percent of the girls polled said that peer pressure was the main reason teenagers are sexually active. Only eleven percent of the girls said that love was a reason. The boys also cited peer pressure as the number one reason. Curiosity, "everybody is doing it," and sexual gratification were also mentioned. For the boys, only six percent gave love as a reason. What do you think? Is the survey accurate? What is the main reason you think teenagers are sexually active?

---

some degree, they are not foolproof. Condoms break, especially when used incorrectly. When it comes to life and death choices, taking any risk is excessive.

If moral reasoning cannot convince you to practice abstinence (and not "safe sex") then allow healthy fear to influence you. Engaging in sexual intercourse outside of a monogamous marriage relationship is like playing Russian roulette with five bullets in a gun with six chambers. Take note of the lesson taught by "Magic" Johnson, one of the greatest basketball players ever, who contacted HIV: if you have sexual partners outside of a monogamous, faithful marriage, you may become infected, no matter who you are.

Talk It Over

1. Outline what course of action a victim of sexual abuse should take to stop the problem.
2. Name three other sexual myths that you have heard.
3. "Teenage pregnancies and STDs are basically results of personal behavior problems." Do you agree or disagree? Explain.

As It Was Intended

Your decision to say "no" to sexual activity is a public statement of your values. The Christian belief that sexual intercourse should be reserved for marriage is not something that you can keep to yourself. You can't say to yourself, "Well, I'm not going to have sex until I'm married," and then wait until a passionate moment during a date to communicate your beliefs to a dating partner.

What you believe about sexuality should be lived in the daily actions of your life. A very important help in managing your sexual feelings is moderation, or modesty. Modesty involves discipline and balance. Externally, it means wearing nonsuggestive clothing, behaving properly, and watching one's speech. In addition, modest

---

Resources

Resource 6K provides expanded definitions describing sexually transmitted diseases and HIV in more detail.

Teaching Approaches

- Have the students work with a partner to role play challenges to their decision to say "no" to sex before marriage. They may use the examples cited in this section and come up with their own. Choose two or three pairs to role play their conversations before the entire class.

- **Reteach**—Ask the students to suggest other ways to balance their sexual feelings through modesty.

- **Extend the Lesson**—Ask: What are some of the ways that modesty requires discipline and balance?

Chapter Summary

- Before assigning the review exercises, ask the students if they have any questions or comments on Chapter 6.

- Have the students read each statement. Or, you may wish to have the students read and discuss these statements in small groups before reporting back to class.

You communicate a lot to others by how you dress and act.

people have a common sense view of their own talents and limitations. They do not boast, brag, or call attention to themselves.

Your conduct speaks volumes about what you believe. In the same way, when you are on a date, and you initiate or approve of intense kissing, hugging, and petting, you are communicating to your partner something about your sexual attitudes. These are sexually stimulating activities. They help to prepare two people for intercourse. What do you communicate to a partner by participating in sexually stimulating behavior?

We are all challenged to live faithfully as disciples of Jesus. Living as a disciple will be considered in more detail in the next chapter. Learning to treat people as He treated people is certainly one way to live as a disciple. What does that mean for a person attempting to live a chaste life?

Chapter Summary

- Sexuality differs from sex.
- Love and sexuality are gifts from God.
- Chastity is the best way to express your sexuality before marriage.
- Sexual intercourse is an expression of love and commitment within marriage.
- Sexual feelings are good. Dealing with sexual feelings means finding an appropriate balance.
- Masturbation can be a selfish act that runs counter to the relational and creational aspect of sexuality.
- Modesty is a very important help in managing sexual situations.

Journal Assignment

Ask students to write on one of the following questions: "How does modesty in dress communicate a person's sexual intentions?" "How do you use dress, words, or gestures to indicate your feelings toward another?"

Background

The virtue of Chastity is fully discussed in the *Catechism of the Catholic Church*, 2337-2350.

Chapter 6 Review

What Have You Learned?

Listed below are suggested answers. For many of the questions, the answers will vary.

1. All of humanity is influenced by sexuality. Physically, every cell in the body is sex-typed. Sexual roles taught by the family and society typecast us emotionally. Even our thinking seems to be influenced by our sexuality.

2. The Catholic Church teaches that sexuality is always a part of your life, whereas sexual activity should only take place within marriage.

3. Romantic love is associated with strong feelings for a person of the opposite sex.

4. Answers will vary.

5. It's difficult to love someone else if you don't first love yourself.

6. Infatuation is usually based on perception rather than the truth. Romantic love is based upon knowledge and experience and is often self-centered. Genuine love grows out of romantic love and shows a great concern for the other.

7. The virtue of chastity helps you to express your sexuality in creative ways without engaging in sexual activity.

8. Jesus showed Peter that He was willing to accept the kind of love that Peter could offer.

9. Pornography encourages people to use others for their own sexual pleasure, and is a form of abuse. Masturbation is less harmful, though it may damage a person's self-esteem and make him or her more self-centered. It can also become addictive.

10. Many of the STDs can lead to serious physical ailments. In the case of AIDS, the result is death.

11. Modesty helps you to discipline and balance your sexual feelings.

REVIEW

What Have You Learned?

1. How does sexuality influence every dimension of humanity?
2. What is the Catholic belief about sexual intercourse outside of marriage? What is the Catholic belief about sexuality?
3. In what ways do love and sexuality go together?
4. To what do you attribute the many feelings that Dwight experienced on the day of the Christmas dance?
5. Why is self-love a prerequisite for any loving relationship?
6. What is the difference between romantic love, infatuation, and genuine love?
7. How can the virtue of chastity help you demonstrate a deep love for yourself and for others?
8. How did Jesus' use of phile show that he had accepted Peter for who he was?
9. What comparisons can you draw between sexual abuse and pornography? between pornography and masturbation?
10. What are the great dangers of STDs?
11. How can modesty be an aid in living out your Christian sexuality?

Application

1. Make a chart with three columns labeled "subject," "positive," and "negative." In the subject column, write the words "parents," "school," "media," and "Church." Write at least one piece of positive information and one piece of negative information you have heard about sexuality from each of the sources. Share your chart with a partner.

2. Create a collage of magazine photos and newspaper articles contrasting society's definition of sexuality and love with your personal definition.

3. Work with a partner to role-play two teenagers exhibiting a sense of self-love: one in a healthy sense, the other in a conceited manner.

4. In your journal, write about what it means to be infatuated. Comment on why the infatuation did or did not blossom into love.

5. Begin a campaign for chastity and moderation as ways to promote teenage sexuality. Elicit leaders in your parish or school to brainstorm ideas on how your group can promote those virtues.

6. Read John 21:15-19. What did Jesus mean when He told Peter to "Feed My sheep"? Find out some information about Peter's death. How does the way Peter died relate to John 21:18-19?

7. How would you respond to a friend who tells you that he or she has a sexually transmitted disease. Write a brief letter of response to that friend.

8. A friend is concerned that his girlfriend (or her boyfriend) is becoming too aroused on dates. What advice would you offer? With several other students, role-play your advice.

Background

Masturbation and pornography are closely linked. Pornography appeals to people's interest in private, personal sexual gratification. Neither encourages a person to develop as a human being. For more information on these offenses against Chastity, see the *Catechism of the Catholic Church,* 2351-2356.

REVIEW

Chapter Vocabulary

- sexuality
- sex
- self-love
- romantic love
- infatuation
- chastity
- agape
- sexual abuse
- pornography
- masturbation
- sexually transmitted diseases
- AIDS
- condoms
- modesty
- abstinence
- procreation
- phile

Putting Vocabulary to Use

Supply the following information.

1. Explain how self-love, infatuation, and romantic love might all factor into a developing relationship.
2. Write a plan for living your gift of sexuality in a positive way.
3. List one common sexually transmitted disease. Research how it is caused, what effects it has, and how it can be treated.
4. What does it mean to say that people with AIDS die from "opportunistic infections?"
5. Describe the biological process of how a woman becomes pregnant.
6. What did Jesus' use of the term "phile" teach about acceptance?
7. Explain how modesty involves discipline and balance.
8. Why is abstinence associated with chastity?

Christians need not fear sexuality but should rather appreciate it as one source for knowing and responding to God and human persons in ways that promote the justice, love, and community of the coming realm of God.

Christine Gudorf

123

Application

Have the students read the directions for each project. You may assign a particular project, or allow the students to choose a project they prefer. Allow some class time for the students to share their completed project with others.

Putting Vocabulary to Use

You may wish to assign some or all of these questions. Have the students answer the questions without referring to the text, if possible. Accept all reasonable answers.

Final Thought

Background

Gudorf's quotation is from the article "Are You Giving Your Kids Double Messages About Sex?" (*U.S. Catholic*, September, 1991).

Focus On: Chapter 7

Making a vocational choice is crucial. People will often choose careers based on financial reasons, only to find that they are not happy or satisfied with their job or career. From a Christian perspective, all important life choices—whether marriage, religious life, or a specific career—are to be rooted in discipleship to Jesus Christ. For people to do this, they must first have an established and well-maintained relationship with Jesus. No matter which vocational choice a Christian makes, he or she is called to a ministry of service that involves learning about and communicating God's Word, celebrating God's presence in life, and responding to the needs of others.

In Chapter 7, students will investigate ways to develop a more mature relationship with Jesus. They will examine Jesus' values as presented in the Beatitudes. They will consider the love of God and how God acts in their lives. This chapter will encourage the students to look for specific ways to incorporate this ministry into their own personal careers and lifestyles.

Plan Ahead

- Incorporate formal and/or spontaneous prayer in each lesson. A participatory prayer service that is suitable for use on retreat is provided in the Teacher's Resource Book.
- Note **Resource** suggestions which can be applied to, or extend, the lessons of this chapter.
- Preview the **Application** projects in the Chapter Review. Refer to **Teaching Approaches** for suggestions on when to assign the projects. Or, the projects may be used as part of lesson, section, or chapter reviews.
- Decide on a method for grouping students for projects and discussion.
- Invite guest speakers who will participate in selected lessons in advance.

Fullness of Life

Blessed are you who believed that what was spoken to you by the Lord would be fulfilled.

Luke 1:45

This chapter will help you to:

- Consider the meaning of discipleship in light of career choices.
- Understand the importance of using prayer, Scripture, and the faith tradition of the Church to discover a personal vocation.
- Practice living the Beatitudes in imitation of Jesus.
- Discover the Church's call to a "ministry of service."

124

Media Suggestions (Optional)

- *What Is Ministry?* (Tabor Publishing) Three 30-minute segments. Fr. Richard McBrien defines ministry and traces its development within the Church. (For the advanced viewer.)

- *Christian Virtues: Responding to God's Love and Reflecting on God's Ways* (Trehaus) 48 minutes. Provides basic insight into ministry and concrete examples of Christians living in ministry.

Aims

1. To communicate the meaning of discipleship and help the students apply it to their own lives.
2. To help students recognize how God is active in each of their lives.

Begin the Section

1. Randomly choose four or five students to share their answers to this familiar question: "What do you want to be when you grow up?" Comment on how easy or difficult it was for students to come up with an answer. Say, "It seems that some people have always known what they want to be, while others search for years before finding their call."
2. Read the opening paragraphs of the section. Ask volunteers to share their experience of "deep callings."
3. Discuss the photo. How can veterinary medicine be a deeper calling?
4. Point out the opening quotation from *Luke 1:45*. Ask: "To what kind of life is God calling you?"

1. DEEPER CALLINGS

The skills that you learn in friendship also affect your relationship with the world and with God. This statement might seem like a great leap of logic, but it is actually quite simple. Through friendship, you've learned communication skills, developed your ability to settle conflict amicably, and experienced the joy of a close relationship. You've also learned how to adjust your wants and needs to the wishes of others, learned that some sacrifice is often necessary to accomplish your goals, and recognized that what society, your peers, or even in some cases, family members, expect of you may not always be what you should do. These lessons will serve you in good stead as you begin to make career and vocational choices.

A recent survey revealed that almost 75 percent of Americans do not like their jobs. For them, work is synonymous with boredom and drudgery, hardly a vocation based upon personal interests.

Background

The picture above shows a veterinarian treating a farm animal. Many students might find it difficult to accept that a woman can be a vet. Many people avoid careers or vocations to which they are truly called because of just such misconceptions. Be prepared to help students confront their stereotypical cultural biases.

The Mind of God?

Lesson Overview

In this lesson, the students will learn more about the meaning of discipleship and what it means for them to be a follower of Jesus Christ.

Teaching Approaches

- Ask the students to describe times they were told by parents or other adults that something that seemed miserable or difficult was in fact "good for them." Follow up by asking the students to conclude if what they were told was true or not.
- Read or summarize the section. Explain that God communicated to Jesus those actions that were good, not only for Him, but for all of humanity.
- **Reteach**—Ask: "Do you ever think that you know exactly what God wants and expects of you? What does it feel like not to know what God expects? Explain your answers."
- **Extend the Lesson**—Each of the three predictions of Jesus' passion *(Mark 8:31-33, 9:30-32, and 10:32-34)* are followed by a misinterpretation of Jesus' mission by His disciples. Have the students explore these incidents further. Read the passages from the Bible. You may wish to have small groups role play one or more of these scenes. (See also: **Application** Project 1.)

Understanding

Teaching Approaches

- Ask: "How important is it for you to know what God wants of you?"
- Read or summarize the section.
- **Reteach**—Ask: "How does the reading of Scripture, the study of Church traditions (including the lives of saints), and prayer help us to uncover God's will for our lives?"
- **Extend the Lesson**—Students are to prepare a presentation on the life of a saint whom they admire, to whom they have a devotion, or by whom they feel inspired to emulate. Students may choose from canonized saints, or from other Christians who they think lived saintly lives (Dorothy Day, Thomas Merton, and Mother Teresa might be candidates for this latter category).

School counselors and teachers are often able to direct you to different surveys designed to explore your vocational interests based on what you enjoy doing and do well. You can use the results of these surveys as an indication of the vocation you should pursue.

Surveys, however, are simply tools. They can't show the whole picture or measure what's in your heart. You may already feel a call to a particular lifestyle or career. A girl who loves animals feels drawn to veterinary medicine. Her question is not which vocation but, "How can I turn my dream into a reality?"

The girl who always wanted to work with animals, or the boy who knew from an early age that he wanted to be an artist, probably doesn't need the help of a vocational survey in choosing their careers. Their vocations penetrate to the deepest part of their beings. They feel called or directed to a particular state of life.

In chapter 1, you learned that everyone, as part of God's plan, is called to a vocation that combines his or her interests with God's will. Sometimes people discover these vocations quite naturally and easily. They are like pegs that go smoothly into the proper hole. More often than not, however, choosing the right vocation is difficult to accomplish in the real world. The deep calling is still present, but may conflict with other perceived opportunities.

The Mind of God?

If you were asked to explain in one short sentence what God has in mind for you, would you be able to do it? Probably not. But that's just what Jesus did for His followers.

In Mark's Gospel account, Jesus "predicts" on three separate occasions what will happen to Him. He tells them: "The Son of Man is to be handed over to men and they will kill Him, and three days after His death He will rise" *(Mark 9:31)*.

The words couldn't be clearer; Jesus had spelled it out for them. Yet, each time the disciples heard this message, they shut their ears to it. Peter openly argued with Jesus. "How could this be?" he wondered. Jesus told him that he was "thinking not as God does, but as human beings do."

Jesus' followers were thinking of themselves. Perhaps they had great plans for an earthly kingdom of which Jesus would be the ruler. They would share in His power and riches. But Jesus

Jesus prayed to understand God's will for His life.

Background

In Mark's Gospel account, Jesus' three predictions of His passion mark the turning point of His ministry. The mystery of the messianic secret begins to be revealed, although Jesus sternly warns His disciples not to tell of His mission for fear that it will be misunderstood.

✳ Media Watch
Who Knows Best?

There was a popular television show in the 1950s called "Father Knows Best." You may have seen reruns of it. In a half-hour, a problem invariably was introduced, various solutions were suggested, and, in the end, father would prevail.

The media tends to invent and extend societal stereotypes to an extreme position. Television portrayed a father who went to work at the office and a mother who stayed home with the children. And, as in "Father Knows Best," the man was always the one capable of solving a major crisis.

However, television has greatly improved how it portrays most sexual roles in the last 40 years. The "Cosby Show," with both the mother and father working professionals, was a fine example of this. Unfortunately, many programs, especially those aimed at children and young adults, continue to reinforce sexual (and racial) stereotypes, of which "Married . . . with Children," "Dinosaurs," and "Home Improvement" are but recent examples.

In your media diary, examine how television programming portrays different types of human roles. Is what you see an accurate portrayal of how people really live? Which programs are the greatest offenders? Which provide the most honest presentations?

---

was not selfish. He did not choose to suffer: He prayed in the garden on the night before He died, "Abba, Father, all things are possible to You. Take this cup away from Me, but not what I will but what You will" *(Mark 14:36)*. He had come to understand God's plan for His life. Salvation for the world depended on His being handed over by the Jews to the Romans, being scourged and crucified, and then rising in glory. Crucifixion was not something He eagerly chose, but it was something He willingly accepted.

Jesus had truly put on the mind of God. Understanding God's will for His life, He would act on it.

Understanding

Discerning what God wants will be a lifetime challenge. What was easy for Jesus may seem difficult for you. After all, you say, even the Apostles found it impossible to follow Jesus' words completely, and they had the advantages of walking with Jesus personally and hearing His words.

Christians today are not at such a great disadvantage as you may think, however. We have almost 2,000 years of faith tradition to draw upon for support, along with the Scriptures and examples of Christian living handed down to us by members of the community of faith. When we wonder what God wants for our lives, we have these resources to turn to for help in understanding God's will.

The Meaning of Discipleship

As a Christian, living as God intends means that you accept the call to *discipleship*. You become a disciple when you enter into a relationship with Jesus Christ. This is helped through prayer and living the Christian virtues. Your developing relationship with Jesus is deepened through the sacraments.

✳ Media Watch

Teaching Approaches
- Assign the in-text questions.
- As a follow-up, ask the students to share their examples of accurate and inaccurate portrayals of life.
- Videotape a past or current half-hour situation comedy (perhaps even an episode from "Father Knows Best") and present it in class. Have the students take notes as they watch the program, looking especially for: (1) the main "problem" that is introduced; (2) how the problem is resolved; (3) which characters aid in the resolution; and (4) how it does or does not reinforce societal stereotypes.

The Meaning of Discipleship

New Words

Discipleship means "to follow." In a time when it is possible to stake out one's own way—no matter what the implications—to follow God remains as radical a lifestyle as it was for the first disciples.

Conversion is a necessary element of discipleship. Jesus demanded that His followers incorporate themselves into the ways of God. To do so implies a willingness to change not only once, but many times. Jesus spoke of this conversion when He said, "Whoever wishes to come after Me must deny himself, take up his cross, and follow Me. For whoever wishes to save his life for My sake and that of the Gospel will save it" *(Mark 8:35-36)*.

Teaching Approaches
- Have the students describe how their own relationships with Jesus have changed over the years. Use the in-text questions for discussion.
- Make sure the students understand the connection that exists between conversion and discipleship.

Resources

Resource 7A from the Teacher's Resource Book is a copy of the popular prayer "Footprints." Share a reading with the students. Ask the students to share what "walking with Jesus" means to them personally.

Resources

Resource 7B provides a blackline master for the activity suggested in "Media Watch."

The Meaning of Discipleship

Teaching Approaches (continued)

- **Reteach**—Consider the implications of following a master. Jesus is not a master to be obeyed, as a servant or slave must obey a master. Jesus, rather, is the master teacher. He knows what we need to do to live God's will and we follow Him to learn from Him. Stress the importance of freedom in following Jesus.
- **Extend the Lesson**—With the students, prepare a list of master/student relationships. "What does it mean to 'follow a master'? What does it mean to follow Jesus, the Master?"

✠ In Focus

Teaching Approaches

- Assign the feature to accompany "The Meaning of Discipleship" text.
- Read aloud or have students act out the Emmaus story found in Luke 24:30-32. Discuss with students the importance of the story for Christian discipleship.

Talk It Over

For Question 1, you may wish to have the students return to the timelines they completed with Chapter 1. Ask: "Where did you find God present in these events?" Have the students discuss the other questions in small groups. Allow time for each small group to summarize its responses for the entire class.

A disciple is one who has learned from the master. You can recognize the master in the student's work.

A disciple is one who learns from the master. The disciple's goal is to be like the master. A disciple of a famous musician will compose music that reflects the master's style and values. In the same way, a disciple of Jesus will live in a way that reflects His style and values.

Disciples are willing to change their lives in order to be more like the master. The life of a disciple is one of *conversion.* Conversion requires that a person change from one way of living to another. Conversion does not happen immediately, but is a gradual, lifelong experience. You can think of Christian conversion in terms of the development that takes place in a friendship. A friendship begins when people get to know each other. It grows as trust and understanding develop. Forgiveness and reconciliation are often required in friendships. Eventually, friends make a commitment to each other.

You have probably known about Jesus for most of your life. You have heard stories about Him, recited prayers to Him, and sung in praise of Him. As you seek freedom and independence from your family, and move to establish your own life, begin a career, or deepen a relationship with another, it can be helpful to take time to ask Jesus, "What now? What is it that I believe about You? Where does our relationship go from here? What is it that You want from me?"

✠ **In Focus**
Looking for Meaning

Jesus' suffering, death, and resurrection stand at the forefront of any consideration of discipleship. Jesus does not promise His followers an easy road to follow. There is no ignoring the fact that most of His followers deserted Him at the time of His arrest because they expected a savior who would save them from their troubles. Disciples today must be prepared to experience disappointment and even to have their expectations shattered.

The fact is, the Apostles were not abandoned by Jesus, and neither are we. Their experience of the Risen Jesus transformed them. Their hope returned, and their hearts burned within them even before they recognized Him in the breaking of the bread (see *Luke 24:30-32*). Jesus will fulfill expectations greater than any we can imagine. The process of conversion is one of challenge and hope!

Journal Assignment

Have the students write a letter to Jesus, reintroducing themselves and initiating ways to bring their relationships with Him up-to-date.

Background

Luke 24: 30-32 is a formational text for the Church. Jesus' passion was foretold by the prophet Isaiah *(Isaiah 42:13-43).* For the disciples, the resurrection experience would

Of course to receive answers to these questions, you can't seek out the same Jesus you knew as a seven-year-old. In some ways, that would be like asking a second grader how you should prepare for the SAT. Times change. Relationships change. It's time to bring your relationship with Jesus up-to-date. What can you do to develop a mature relationship with Jesus?

Talk It Over

1. Briefly describe how God has led you in the past. Where is God leading you now? In the future?

2. What are some advantages of faith that you have been given?

3. What can you do to be a better friend with Jesus?

4. How does the media influence your views of other people?

What would you answer if asked about your current relationship with Jesus?

On the Spot

As a senior Confirmation candidate, Kay was expected to attend Sunday Mass. "Everything else flows from sharing faith on Sunday at church," Father Lloyd had said.

Kay kept up her end of the deal. Even though her parents rarely went to Mass, Kay attended regularly. She came to the Family Mass every Sunday morning with her best friend, Tiffany.

One Sunday, Kay and the other seniors celebrated the Rite of Enrollment for Confirmation. During his homily, Father Lloyd asked if any of the candidates could share something of their personal relationships with Jesus Christ. Everyone was afraid to even glance up in fear of being put on the spot. Kay looked down and fiddled with a missalette.

"How about you?" Father Lloyd asked as he stuck a microphone under Kay's chin. "What does having Jesus as a friend mean to you?" Kay could feel her face growing redder by the second. "No," she whispered loudly. "Please, don't pick on me!" Moving across the aisle to someone else, Father Lloyd barely looked back.

Beginning that afternoon, Kay went on the offensive. She had given up every Tuesday night for

> ### Rite of Enrollment
>
> The *Rite of Enrollment* is a public ceremony in which adults who are seeking the sacraments of Baptism, Confirmation, and Eucharist formally profess their intentions to become part of the Catholic community. In turn, the community welcomes these people to the Church. This ceremony is part of the overall *Rite of Christian Initiation for Adults* or RCIA. Many dioceses have adapted the RCIA to use with high school aged students preparing for Confirmation.

On the Spot

Lesson Overview

If any of the students researched the incidents that followed the predictions of Jesus' passion from the Gospel according to Mark, allow them to share their information prior to beginning the lesson. Ask: "What action do you think is required of a disciple?" Point out that this lesson will help the students learn ways to deepen their relationship with Jesus.

Teaching Approaches

- You may wish to assign parts and have the students read the story aloud. Ask students how they would react in Kay's situation.

- Have the students identify the moments of conversion that take place in the story.

- Ask the students to comment on Jesus' definition of power from Mark 10:35-45.

- **Reteach**—Explain that in Matthew 20:20-28, the story of the disciple's ambition is altered so that the mother of James and John, not the Apostles themselves, ask Jesus the question about sitting at His right and left hand in the coming kingdom. Matthew's change was due, in part, to the important roles James and John played as Church leaders. Matthew spares James and John the embarrassment of revealing their misunderstanding of Jesus' role as Messiah.

- **Extend the Lesson**—Suggest the students attend a Scripture study offered by the parish. (See **Application** Project 4.)

> ### Rite of Enrollment
>
> **Teaching Approaches**
> - Read and summarize the panel feature.
> - If possible, arrange for the class to attend a Rite of Enrollment ceremony for catechumens.

---

transform them from being fearful to courageous. Ultimately, with the coming of the Holy Spirit *(Acts 2),* the Church was able to begin to fulfill Jesus' mission to take the Good News to the ends of the earth.

Journal Assignment

"Knowing Jesus seems to revolve around love and service." Students are to explain why they agree or disagree with this statement.

Prayer in Action

Teaching Approaches

- The feature accompanies "On the Spot."
- Assign **Application** Project 3.
- Have the students keep a log in their journals of their answers to the questions asked in "Prayer in Action." Use class time for volunteers to share their prayer suggestions.

Talk It Over

For Question 1, you may wish to take the part of Father Lloyd from the story. Randomly place a "microphone" under several students' chins and ask them to explain their friendship with Jesus. Explore Question 3 with the entire class as well. List brainstorm answers on the board. Question 2 is more personal. You may wish to have the students write their answers in their journals or share them orally with a partner.

the last year and a half in order to "confirm" her commitment to Jesus, but who was He? Kay prayed in her bedroom, something she hadn't done for years. "Jesus, I want to know You. Jesus, I want my faith in You to mean something." That afternoon, Kay continued her prayer by reviewing her day: there was Father Lloyd's embarrassing question, the juice and muffin she shared after Mass with her friends, and the ride home with Mrs. Henning, Tiffany's mom.

Kay thought about Mrs. Henning. She was always kind and giving. She had driven the girls around town for as long as Kay could remember. Kay recalled the first words of her prayer: "Jesus, I want to know You." Through the kindness of Mrs. Henning, Kay realized, she did know Jesus a little better.

At Confirmation class on the following Tuesday, one of the catechists began the session by reading a section from the Gospel according to Mark. "This will be the Gospel reading for next Sunday," he said. Kay had always found this part of the class boring. This time, though, she listened with new determination. It was the story of the Apostles, James and John, asking Jesus to grant them power. Jesus told them that His kingdom did not operate in terms of power and lording authority over others: "Rather, whoever wishes to be great among you will be your servant; whoever wishes to be first among you will be the slave of all" *(Mark 10:35-45)*.

The group talked over the meaning of the reading. Many of the kids laughed at Jesus' words. They dreamed of owning expensive houses and heading large corporations. Kay had another thought: "In one way, following Jesus' words would be very difficult. I know what it feels like to serve others from serving Thanksgiving dinner at the soup kitchen. But, in another way, being the slave of all would be so easy! There would be none of the pressures to buy designer clothes or to be rich by the time you're 30." Kay smiled at the idea, but then kept her thoughts to herself.

Kay continued to work at making her faith an important part of her daily routine. She

Prayer in Action
Reviewing YOur Day

As part of her prayer, Kay reviewed the events of her day. Little did she know that she had uncovered one of the most effective and popular ways to pray. Most people know that prayer means "communicating with God." But often forgotten is that communication also involves listening to what God has to say. Reviewing the events of your day is one way to discover God's presence in your life. Pray in a quiet place. Wait until your day is completed or nearly completed. You may wish to follow these other suggestions:

1. Identify three things that happened during the day for which you are thankful.

2. Think of your conversations during the day. Was anyone trying to tell you something that words could not express?

3. How did your God-given talents benefit you today?

4. When did you forgive another? When were you forgiven?

5. How were you touched by anything you heard or saw?

Conclude with the traditional evening prayer: "Lord, watch over us this night. By Your strength, we may rise at daybreak to rejoice in the resurrection of Christ, Your Son, who lives and reigns forever and ever. Amen."

Background

In Matthew's Gospel, the eight Beatitudes or "blessings" are spoken by Jesus at the Sermon on the Mount. The mountain placement was understandable to Matthew's audience, Jewish converts to Christianity. In the Hebrew Scriptures the most important pronouncement (the giving of the Law to Moses) was delivered from a mountain. In Luke's Gospel the Sermon occurs on the "Plain." In either case, Jesus favors the *anawim* or "poor in spirit." The message: those who depend on concluded that in many ways it was all effort and attitude. If you wanted to develop a Christian attitude, then you needed to try each day to know and respond to Jesus.

Later in the year, Kay's Aunt Ellen, her godmother and Confirmation sponsor, asked if she had chosen a Confirmation name. "Clare, my middle name from Baptism," Kay explained. "Then you should learn something about her," Aunt Ellen said. "Saint Clare was a friend of Saint Francis of Assisi who gave up a life of wealth to serve the poor."

Kay was beginning to understand clearly. Knowing Jesus seemed to revolve around love and service. Kay still wasn't sure how this new knowledge and faith would help her grow closer to Him, but it did, at least, provide some direction.

Talk It Over

1. If you were asked at Sunday Mass to tell what having Jesus as a friend means to you, what would you say?
2. How does your faith influence your choice of life goals?
3. If you reviewed your day (or week), what evidence would you find of Jesus acting in your life?

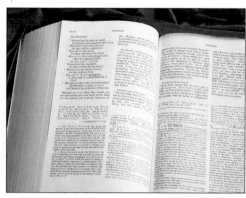

The Beatitudes express Jesus' teaching concerning the meaning of discipleship.

Value Based

Kay followed a three-step technique to understand how God was active in her life:

1. Prayer.
2. Reading and studying Scripture.
3. Following the tradition of the Church, as lived out by the example of past and present Christians.

To know what God wants for you, it is important that you know what Jesus valued. Disciples of Jesus try to live according to the values He expressed in the Beatitudes.

The Beatitudes are short sayings that articulate a different rationale for living for those dedicated to God's kingdom. They express the values of people who want to live by God's will, and tell what happens to those who do.

The Gospel according to Matthew records the Beatitudes as follows:

"Blessed are the poor in spirit, for theirs is the kingdom of heaven.

Blessed are they who mourn, for they will be comforted.

Blessed are the meek, for they will inherit the land.

Blessed are they who hunger and thirst for righteousness, for they will be satisfied.

Blessed are the merciful, for they will be shown mercy.

Blessed are the clean of heart, for they will see God.

Blessed are the peacemakers, for they will be called children of God.

Blessed are they who are persecuted for the sake of righteousness, for theirs is the kingdom of heaven"

(Matthew 5:3-10).

Do the Beatitudes reflect the values of society, or do they offer a different perspective on life? Are these statements to be considered realistic for people living today?

Value Based

Lesson Overview

This lesson introduces the Beatitudes as the basic code of values that were expressed and lived by Jesus. In turn, it asks the students to develop a plan to incorporate the values of Jesus into their lives. A three-step technique of prayer, reading and studying the Scripture, and following the tradition of the Church, is reemphasized. What are other ways to come to know Jesus more personally?

Teaching Approaches

- After reading or summarizing the section, ask for discussion on these questions: "How are you challenged by the Beatitudes?" and "How difficult would it be to live according to the values expressed in the Beatitudes, the values of Jesus, and those of the Church?"
- After reading Saint Paul's words from the Letter to the Ephesians ask: "Do you find these words more hopeful, challenging, or frightening? Explain."
- **Reteach**—Have the students cite examples from their own lives, or from the news, of ways the values of the Beatitudes are or are not lived out. Also, have the students begin working on **Application** Project 5.
- **Extend the Lesson**—Assign the students to share a brief oral report detailing (1) a favorite time, place, or way to pray, and (2) one Scripture passage that speaks to them about life and faith.

God for everything will prosper and come to full inheritance of the kingdom. This is the true meaning of discipleship: dependence on God. See the *Catechism of the Catholic Church,* 1965-1974 for a fuller presentation of how the Beatitudes express the new law of the Gospel.

Teaching Approaches

- Read the panel with the students and discuss the in-text questions.
- Say: "The first step toward improving yourself is knowing yourself. This means taking a good look at your strengths and weaknesses."

Talk It Over

For Question 1, have the students suggest ways they use to get in touch with God. To extend Question 2, ask: "What is preventing you from living according to the Beatitudes right now?"

Put simply, the Beatitudes tell us of the importance of putting God first. Imagine Jesus speaking to His followers today:

"Some say, 'Only the strong survive.' I say, 'Blessed are the meek.' Some say, 'Everybody must look out for himself. I have mine, go get your own.' I say, 'Blessed are the merciful.'"

The challenge of living the eight Beatitudes is that they contrast with many of the values of modern society. "Putting the needs of others first" stands in direct opposition to the mentality, "get ahead at all costs."

How are you challenged by the Beatitudes? How difficult would it be to live according to the values expressed in the Beatitudes, the values of Jesus, and those of the Church?

The first Beatitude speaks of people "poor in spirit" who live without the arrogance of the rich and who live dependent on God's providence. This is the same message that Kay was discovering. Following the will of God means living a life of service.

Kay recognized that living according to these values would require a great deal of effort on her part and a definite change in her attitude. Recognizing that there are alternative dreams besides being popular or powerful can be a challenge. What does it take to use one's individual talents

To Your Health
Changing Habits

As you adopt new attitudes, some of your old habits may no longer be appropriate and may need changing. Which of your current habits would you like to change? How would changing them make you a better disciple of Jesus? What is the first step in making this change?.

without having to choose jobs and careers that abuse others in the process? This challenge both shapes and is shaped by an attitude—a *be*-attitude, as others have called it—of friendship with Jesus.

Saint Paul wrote long ago about the need for a new attitude brought about through conversion:

"You should put away the old self of your former way of life, and be renewed in the spirit of your minds, and put on the new self, created in God's way in righteousness and holiness of truth"
(Ephesians 4:22-24).

Talk It Over

1. Discuss how you can get to know God better.
2. Describe how your life would be different if you lived according to the Beatitudes.

Some say, "I have mine, go get your own." I say, "Blessed are the merciful."

Journal Assignment

Students are to recast the Beatitudes for today. They may do this through a story, through art work, or through song. Ask, "How could the Beatitudes be portrayed today to communicate them better to the world?"

II. MINISTRY WITHIN CAREERS

We tend to compartmentalize our lives: a time for work, a time for fun, a time to spend with parents or children, and a time for God. During the other times, a person may have little or no thought about what else goes on in his or her life. For example, a person may spend one hour a week connecting with God, and the other 167 hours of the week living as if God didn't exist.

The Church challenges us to see all parts of life as important and *grace-filled* (touched by God). Work and career are to be viewed as necessary aspects of God's plan; together with vocation, they unveil the completeness of creation:

"For while providing the substance of life for themselves and their families, men and women are performing their activities in a way which appropriately benefits society. They can justly consider that by their labor they are unfolding the Creator's work, consulting the advantages of their brothers and sisters, and contributing by their personal industry to the realization in history of the divine plan" ("The Church Today," *Documents of Vatican II, #34*).

As you consider a career or college major, examine how they are compatible with your own dreams and talents, and how they offer ways for you to serve others. Your work will provide you with a way to make a living you enjoy, along with an opportunity to contribute to building God's kingdom on earth. In this way you can turn your career into a *ministry*.

It is not enough to worship one hour a week and forget about God the rest of the time.

Resources

Resource 7C is a model to help students develop a pie graph that lists the many roles they play in their own lives.

Background

We are all called to work for the common good. See the *Catechism of the Catholic Church*, 1905-1917.

II. MINISTRY WITHIN CAREERS

Aims

1. To help students find ways to combine ministry with career choices.
2. To help students understand that all Christians are called to a ministry of service and consider ways that they can begin to be of service now.

Begin the Section

1. Ask the students to imagine themselves many years in the future, on the day of their retirement from work. Have them try to put into words the most important accomplishment of their long career. Ask: "Why was this accomplishment so important to you?"
2. Read or summarize the opening paragraphs of the section. Explain that turning a career into ministry means using personal skills, talents and dreams in service of God's kingdom.
3. Begin to have the students consider ways that they can translate their own personal ideals into a way of life that can be beneficial not only to themselves, but to others as well.
4. Assign **Application** Project 6. Allow time for the students to share their graphs. (See **Resource 7C**.)

Ministries of Service

Lesson Overview

This lesson defines the essential parts of the Church's mission and points out that all Christians are called to a ministry of service to others.

New Words

Ministry means "loving service to others." Ministry has been used to refer to the various offices in the Church necessary for its maintenance as a hierarchical structure. Modern theologians speak of the ministry of all the baptized. At Baptism, all Christians are given the office or power to "announce with joy the Good News of Christ to all nations."

Teaching Approaches

• Have each student make a list of five of their personal talents and exchange the list with a partner. The partner should make one or two career suggestions based on the talents. Allow time for a discussion among the partners about their suggestions.

• **Reteach**—Read or summarize the section. How did the word "service" play a part in the students' discussion?

• **Extend the Lesson**—Say: "The Vatican has handed down a new decree: 'Being a once-a-week Catholic is no longer enough.' What does this decree mean? What do you think the Church now expects from its members?" Allow time for general discussion and comments.

Talk It Over

First, have the students share their responses to both questions with a partner. Then, in a large group, ask volunteers to summarize the highlights of their discussion.

Ministries of Service

There are three essential parts to the Church's mission:

1. Learn about and communicate God's Word.
2. Celebrate God's presence and involvement in life.
3. Respond to the needs of others.

This mission takes place through the *ministry* of its people. The word "ministry" is from the Greek word meaning "to serve." A minister is one who is in service to others. The Church has ministers of the Word (for example, priests, deacons, lectors, and catechists) and those who help in the celebration of faith (primarily the ordained ministers).

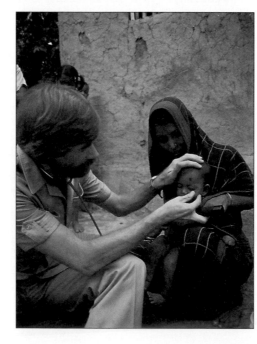

All Christians are called to the third aspect of ministry—service—by reason of their Baptism. No matter what a person's career, vocation, or age happens to be, each one is called to a ministry of service.

From its beginning, the Church has appreciated the diversity of its people, and encouraged the freedom of individuals to serve one another based on their special talents. Saint Paul wrote:

"There are different kinds of spiritual gifts but the same Spirit; there are different forms of service but the same Lord; there are different workings but the same God who produces all of them in everyone. To each individual the manifestation of the Spirit is given for some benefit"
(1 Corinthians 12:4-7).

You may have a clear understanding of your particular talents, that is, what you like to do and what you are good at doing. But, perhaps, you're not sure how these talents can be used in a career. In addition, how can your talents be used in service to others?

Talk It Over

1. What roles do you have in your life: son or daughter, student, friend? In which role do you find the most time for God? The least time for God?
2. How have you been shaped by your experiences of serving others?

All Christians are called to a ministry of service within their vocation.

Background

"Some of them (laity) do all they can . . . when sacred ministers are lacking or are blocked by a persecuting regime. . . . But all ought to cooperate in the spreading and intensifying of the kingdom of Christ in the world" *(Dogmatic Constitution on the Church).*

Career Inventory

One of the ways to determine how your interests and personality correspond to potential careers is to take a career interest inventory. Listed below are some sample survey statements. Do you fit any of the categories provided?

If you ...
... usually can mend or repair things
... like working with objects more than ideas
... are interested in agriculture, mechanical activities, the military, or outdoor work
... view yourself as conventional in most things,
then you are a **Practical Type.**

If you...
... like to find your own solutions to problems
... are interested in science, mathematics, medical science, or research
... like to learn about yourself and the world around you
... can solve complex problems,
then you are an **Intellectual Type.**

If you ...
...like to create things that are different
... can write creatively
... are interested in music, drama, art, or writing
...prefer to make your own plans for a project than to be given plans
then you arc a **Creative Type.**

Sample careers for

Practical Type:	Intellectual Type:	Creative Type:
Air traffic controller	Biologist	Actor
Emergency medical technician	Geologist	Journalist
Machinist	Engineer	Literature teacher
Dressmaker	Computer operator	Architect
Painter	Economist	Public relations person
		Religious life

If you find this survey interesting, arrange with your high school counselor to take a complete interest inventory.

Exploring Life Choices

Lesson Overview

Where our parents or grandparents often made vocation choices while adolescents, people today are delaying their choices. Before beginning the lesson, have the students debate the pluses and minuses of delaying vocational choices until a later age.

Teaching Approaches

- Read or summarize the section.
- Ask: "What are some ways that you have been taught to live independently?"
- **Reteach**—Discuss what prevents people from making a vocational decision. How much are students influenced in their choices by outside sources (peer pressure, family, popular myths, societal expectations)?
- **Extend the Lesson**—Have the students write a story titled, "Age 23." In the story, ask them to chronicle their life from age seventeen to twenty-four. Ask several students to share their stories. Comment on how many did or did not indicate that they had decided on a vocation by age twenty-three.

▲ Family Living

Teaching Approaches

- Ask the students to suggest other parental discipline techniques besides reward and punishment.
- Answer the question, "How can young adults and parents overcome questions of power and control? (Look to students to develop their own methods to deal with issues of power and control.)

Talk It Over

Allow time for the students to discuss both questions in a small group. Choose a leader in each group to summarize important points of the discussion to be shared with the entire class.

Exploring Life Choices

In the past, people would decide on a vocation early in life. They would join the full-time work force, attend college, make temporary religious vows, or start training programs to prepare for a particular career. Young adults today put off making a vocation choice to a much later age.

People now delay choosing their vocation for about seven years—or until their mid-twenties—for a variety of reasons. People have many more possibilities to consider before they actually choose a career or vocation: college degrees, professional careers, testing a number of different jobs, travel, and even volunteer service.

Delaying vocation choices for too long, however, can also be a way of avoiding difficult decisions. Some people, for example, will do anything to keep from breaking the bonds that tie them to their families. Others will take a series of temporary jobs or frequently change their majors in college to avoid commitments. Why do you think some people avoid making a vocational choice? Are they afraid? procrastinating? unsure of themselves?

▲ Family Living
Power Struggle

A young adult's conflict with his or her parents is usually over the control they continue to exercise over his or her life. Parents who use power to discipline their children often live by a strict system of reward and punishment. As they mature, teenagers are much less affected by this style of discipline. Teenagers do not fear parental power as younger children do.

People who were raised in a family that used this style of discipline often interpret a parent's suggestions as yet another attempt to control them. The suggestions—often any suggestions—are rejected simply because they come from the parent. How can young adults and parents overcome questions of power and control?

Talk It Over

1. What are advantages and disadvantages to postponing the start of a life vocation?
2. In what areas are you most willing to consider suggestions from your parents? the least willing? Explain why you feel the way you do.

Many people are delaying their permanent vocation choices in order to serve others who need their help.

Journal Assignment

Answer this question forthrightly, "What do you think of your parents' career suggestions for you? Which ideas have merit? Which don't?" This entry should not be shared.

Making It Happen

How do you translate your personal ideals into a way of life? There are several steps that you can take to make this transition happen.

1. **Identify your vocational goals.** You may have no clear idea of where your life is headed. That shouldn't stop you from setting goals, even if they are short-term. For example, if you are not sure whether you want to attend college or go to work, your short-term goal can be to make a decision about this choice within a certain time frame, say three months. If you want to be an astronaut, then set that as your goal. If you want to help other people, but are not sure in what profession, then a goal can be to find out as much as you can about specific careers in that area.

2. **Take control of time.** While you cannot control events, you can control how you use your time and energy. Ask yourself: "What should I be doing now to attain my goal?" Make a list of what needs to be done: write to colleges, talk with employment recruiters, make a résumé, set up *information interviews* with local employers. An information interview is an opportunity for you to speak with a company representative to find out the skills and talents needed to work in a particular field.

   A prerequisite for most careers today is a college degree. For some careers, a general degree is all you need. For a career in art, business, education, engineering, medicine, law, mathematics, music, or science, then a specialized or even an advanced degree is desirable.

3. **List the Steps for Accomplishing Career Goals.** What kind of degree would you need to fulfill the general requirements for your career goal? What colleges offer a program in your interest area? What are other factors that you need to consider in your choice of college and career (i.e., financial, location, and family conditions)? Are there other alternatives for vocational training (military, trade schools, employer-sponsored programs) in your career area?

Some of these steps require a great deal of research. Your high school counselor should be able to help you identify your vocational aptitudes and interests, and help you set long- and short-term goals about how to turn your interests into a vocation. The school counselor is hired to be your advocate, to work with you as you pursue your dream. The counselor's job is not to convince you of a career direction that meets your parents' or the school's expectations.

Sharpening Your Skills
Realistic Dreams

Your dreams and goals for the future may not be easily attainable. Did you know that fewer than one out of every ten thousand high school athletes in the country ever competes professionally? or that the average career for a professional football player is three years? Medical schools accept fewer than thirty percent of applicants; law schools, fewer than forty percent. To increase your chances of success:

- Know your gifts and talents.
- Hone them with constant practice.
- Apply yourself completely to the challenge at hand.
- Be realistic.

Aim high now. You can adjust your goals later, if needed.

Making It Happen

Lesson Overview

An earlier lesson introduced the concept of goals. This lesson develops that idea further, and provides suggested ways for students to develop their goal-making skills. Have the students consider the lists they made of their own talents and skills. Say, "Let's look at ways to put these personal talents to use."

Teaching Approaches

- Write the three steps: (1) "Identify your vocational goals;" (2) "Take control of time;" and (3) "List the steps for accomplishing career goals"—on the board.
- Have the students silently read the section. Then, ask them to brainstorm practical ways to implement each of the steps. List these suggestions in the appropriate column on the board.
- **Reteach**—Assign **Application** Project 7.
- **Extend the Lesson**—Have the students determine two goals they wish to reach this week. Have them assess their progress every morning. If they need more time to reach a goal, they may need to adjust their plan. Encourage them to be realistic, but tell them not to take more time just to avoid reaching the goal.

Sharpening Your Skills

Teaching Approaches

- Incorporate these suggestions with the steps presented in "Making It Happen."
- Use the "blue sky" process with students: they may dream any dream they wish about their futures for five minutes. What are their biggest dreams?

Background

More goal-setting suggestions: (1) Make certain the goal is in keeping with your deepest feelings, beliefs, and values; (2) Do a motivation check; make certain that the goal is what you want, rather than what someone else wants for you; (3) Set only those goals that nourish you, not to please others; (4) Do not become a slave to a goal; (5) Break long-term goals down into achievable steps; (6) Have a contingency plan in case your present strategy fails.

Teaching Approaches

- Provide the students with an appointment schedule for their school counselor. Make sure that they are aware of the times that their counselor is available for consultation.

- Have the students suggest other practical career and vocational-related questions that can be asked of a school counselor.

- **Reteach**—If your school has a career placement office, bring to class relevant brochures, scholarship applications, and other printed or video materials. Discuss these with the students.

- **Extend the Lesson**—Plan a "Vocation Day." See **Application** Project 8.

☽ Well-Being

Teaching Approaches

- Explain that a recent study indicates that exercise may help teenagers cope with the stress that might otherwise have ill-effects on their health. The study showed that those who did not exercise and who had suffered stresses (such as splitting up with a boyfriend or girlfriend, or moving), reported higher levels of physical illness and stress than those who encountered similar stresses but exercised regularly.

- Have students list ways that they handle the stress they feel in their daily lives.

Questions for Your Counselor

Remember, your school guidance counselor is on your side. Here are some questions to make sure that he or she can best serve your needs:

- What are the merits of the various career and aptitude surveys you offer?
- What type of aptitude survey will you administer? How will the results of the survey be used?
- How often am I able to meet with you? What kind of scheduling arrangements must be made?
- Am I taking the right courses to achieve my career goals?
- Does the school have any arrangements with community businesses for intern programs?
- What college or professional training program should I consider based on my qualifications and interests?

Open Doors

Some young men and women explore religious vocations after high school. College seminaries offer an academic setting where young men are able to discern whether or not the "deep calling" they have experienced is leading them to the ordained ministry as a priest. Other young women and men choose to inquire about living in a Christian community of sisters or brothers.

The common thread in these traditional religious vocations is a desire to know and love God better, and to work in service for God's people. This desire is not limited to these specific vocations; it is a common thread running through *all* vocations.

Discipleship in Jesus Christ is an alluring option. It offers a promise of peace, truth, and love. But with these great gifts there is a cost. A person must balance his or her desires with doing the will of God. Jesus said:

☽ Well Being
Planning and Your Health

Planning can help you manage stress. By recognizing that change can and often does occur, you can better deal with unexpected disappointments, frustrations, and delays. Rather than concentrating on living from moment to moment, think ahead. Don't worry about it, but do try to anticipate the future.

"Whoever wishes to come after Me, must deny himself, take up his cross, and follow Me. For whoever wishes to save his life will lose it, but whoever loses his life for My sake and that of the Gospel will save it. What profit is there for one to gain the whole world and forfeit his life?"

(Mark 8:34-36).

There are many doors open to you and many directions your life can take. As a Christian, you are searching for your own direction, looking for a career that resonates with your talents and interests. How will you include Jesus in your journey? Through prayer, the reading and study of Scripture, and the examples of other Christians, Jesus can help you choose your life's course if you include Him in your plans.

Talk It Over

1. What has been your experience of working with your school's counselors? How would you like to see these services improved?
2. What criteria would you use to judge your career or vocation aptitude? How can speaking with others help you make a wise decision

---

Resources

Resource 7F offers additional tips for student/counselor sessions.

Use **Resource 7G** to help the students learn additional stress management techniques.

Teaching Approaches

- Invite a college student or other recent high school graduate to your class. Ask him or her to share some of the adjustments that he or she has made in the first years after high school. (For an alternative idea, see **Application** Project 8.)

- **Reteach**—Ask the students to put Jesus' words, "What profit is there for one to gain the whole world and forfeit his life?" in terms of their own lives and careers. Ask: "Why is it important for you to make Jesus a part of your vocation?"

- **Extend the Lesson**—Have the students research the initial discernment processes suggested by college seminaries or religious orders in the local area. You may invite a vocation director of a diocese or religious order to your class to explain something of their own particular discernment process.

Devoting oneself to discipleship in Jesus Christ is an alluring option.

Talk It Over

Have the school counselor participate in a discussion with the students. Use these questions as a discussion starter.

Chapter Summary

- Before assigning the review exercises, ask the students if they have any questions or comments on the material covered in Chapter 5.

- Have the students read each statement. Or, you may wish to have the students read and discuss these statements in small groups before reporting back to the entire class.

Chapter Summary

- Discipleship is a lifelong process of following Jesus.
- It takes effort each day to put on the Christian attitude.
- Three techniques for understanding more about God and how God acts in our lives are: (1) prayer, (2) reading and studying Scripture, and (3) following the tradition of the Church, as lived out by the example of Christians.

- The Beatitudes tell us the importance of putting God first.
- Conversion is necessary at each stage of Christian life.
- Everyone is called to a "ministry of service."
- "How can I use my talents to serve others?" is a question that Christians should ask themselves when considering a vocation.
- Matching interests and aptitudes is one way to determine a vocation.

Journal Assignment

Have students evaluate their present career and vocation goals in light of what they've learned in this chapter. Have them also develop career and vocation questions that they feel comfortable discussing with a counselor.

Chapter 7 Review

What Have You Learned?

Listed below are suggested answers. For many of the questions, the answers will vary.

1. Jesus says, "The Son of Man is to be handed over to men and they will kill Him, and three days after His death He will rise" *(Mark 9:31)*.

2. Christians today have two thousand years of faith tradition, along with the Scriptures and examples of Christian living to draw on for support.

3. Both the friendship and discipleship processes include trust, understanding, forgiveness, reconciliation, and commitment.

4. Kay developed a plan that included prayer, the reading and studying of Scripture, and following the tradition of the Church, as lived out by the example of past and present Christians.

5. "Putting the needs of others first," as expressed in the Beatitudes, stands in direct opposition to the "get ahead at all costs" mentality often implied by society.

6. All parts of life are grace-filled; that is, touched by God and thus important.

7. All Christians are called to a ministry of service by reason of their Baptism.

8. Answers will vary. People put off choosing a vocation out of fear, some because of uncertainty, some want to stay with their families, and some simply need to wait longer for God's call. Delaying a vocational choice is not of itself bad, but can be a sign of other difficulties in a person's life.

9. At this time, a person can identify his or her vocational goal, take control of time, and make a list of steps for accomplishing career goals.

Application

Have the students read the directions for each project. You may assign a particular project, or allow the students to choose a project they prefer. Allow some class time for the students to share their completed projects with others.

REVIEW

What Have You Learned?

1. What did Jesus tell His disciples about His own vocation?
2. What resources do Christians have today for determining God's will for their lives?
3. How do the stages of discipleship parallel the stages of a growing friendship?
4. What are some things that Kay did to deepen her faith in God?
5. In what ways do the values of Jesus, as expressed in the Beatitudes, contrast with the values of society?
6. Why should all parts of life be seen as important?
7. In what part of the Church's mission are all Christians called to participate?
8. Why do some people put off finding their vocation?
9. What are some things that you control right now with regards to your vocation?

Application

1. Read and tell about another way Jesus' disciples reacted to His news that He must be handed over, suffer, and die. (See *Mark 9:30-37*).
2. Interview a primary grade child, a high school student, an adult, and an older person. Ask each to describe their relationship with Jesus. Write a report summarizing the similarities and differences in their answers. What might account for these?
3. Record the events of your day in a notebook. Then, prayerfully review the list. Look for times and ways that God acted in your life.
4. Attend a Scripture study at your parish. Apply what you learn to seeking out a personal vocation.
5. Find an example in news reports of someone who is living out a Beatitude value. Also, find an example of someone living out a contrasting value. Share your information in class.
6. Draw a pie chart. List the roles in your life, giving them the amount of space in relation to the time you spend on each. Write or tell how you can keep your faith active in each part of your life.
7. Make a list of one thing you can do today, one thing you can do this week, one thing you can do this month, and one thing you can do this semester to help further your vocational goals.
8. Arrange for people who experienced a calling to a particular vocation to speak to your class. You may consider asking an actor, artist, a priest, religious, doctor, chef, teacher, or police officer to take part.

Background

Application Project 4 calls for students to attend a Scripture Study program at their parishes. Students may also be encouraged to develop a Scripture Study at school. Students may gather at lunch or before/after school to read the Bible aloud and share what it means to them.

REVIEW

Chapter Vocabulary

- discipleship
- Rite of Enrollment
- Confirmation
- conversion
- prayer
- Scripture
- tradition
- Beatitudes
- ministry
- vocational goal
- information interviews

I know not what I shall become: It seems to me that peace of soul and repose of spirit descend on me, even in sleep.

I only know that God keeps me; I am in a calm so great that I fear nought. What can I fear, when I am with God?

Brother Lawrence

Putting Vocabulary to Use

Indicate whether each statement below is *true* or *false*. Correct the italicized word to make each statement true.

_____ **1.** Living as God intends means that you have accepted the call to *ministry*.

_____ **2.** *The Rite of Enrollment* is a sacrament of commitment.

_____ **3.** Sometimes, *prayer* can mean simply taking the time to review the events of your day.

_____ **4.** Being able to see Jesus face-to-face and having *Scripture* at their disposal were two advantages the first disciples had.

_____ **5.** *Tradition* with regards to faith means being able to draw on the experience of Christians past and present.

_____ **6.** The values of God's Kingdom are best represented by the *Beatitudes*.

_____ **7.** *Discipleship* means to serve others.

_____ **8.** Choosing a *vocational goal* is a lifelong process.

_____ **9.** *Information interviews* are an opportunity for you to speak with a company representative to find out the skills and talents needed to work in a particular industry.

_____ **10.** *Vocational goals* can help a person to change the pattern of his or her life.

141

Putting Vocabulary to Use

1. false (discipleship)
2. false (Confirmation)
3. true
4. true
5. true
6. true
7. false (ministry)
8. true
9. true
10. true

Final Thought

Background

A goal of prayer is to feel as comfortable in God's presence as Brother Lawrence feels. Such great trust is at the heart of true peace.

Unit 2 Review

Aim

To review and practice the key ideas and themes of Unit 2.

Looking Back

The following are suggested answers. For many questions, the answers will vary.

1. Answers will vary as to the important choices people make between the ages of seventeen and twenty-five, but may include college, career, and vocation.

2. Relationships may change after high school for many reasons. For example, people become more independent as they begin college or a career.

3. Answers will vary.

4. The Beatitudes express putting the needs of others—especially the lowly—first. In doing so, we express our desire to put God first.

5. The three essential parts of the Church's mission are: (1) learn about and communicate God's Word; (2) celebrate God's presence and involvement in life; (3) respond to other's needs.

6. A positive reason to delay a vocational choice is that people often consider many careers or vocations before deciding on one. A negative reason is that people avoid making a commitment to one career or vocation.

7. There are several steps to translating personal ideas into a way of life. An individual must: (1) identify vocational goals; (2) take control of time; (3) list the steps for accomplishing goals.

8. Answers will vary.

9. Forgiveness is an important tool for mending broken relationships because it is a statement of conversion; it expresses the commitment that you plan to make a change in your life.

10. A friend is someone you like and with whom you have developed a relationship through common experiences. An acquaintance is someone who you know by name or face, but with whom you do not have a relationship.

11. Answers will vary. For example, people date to meet new people, to try a new experience, because of an attraction to another, or because everyone else is dating.

12. The six rules for improving communication skills are: (1) give people your full attention when they are speaking; (2) try to understand what the other person is truly saying; (3) stay calm; (4) use "I-messages"; (5) show other people respect; (6) think before you speak.

13. Conflict is not always bad. For example, conflict can make two people aware of problems they need to resolve.

At the Crossroads

Looking Back

1. What are some important choices a person must make between the ages of 17 and 25?
2. How might relationships with friends, family members, and God change after a person graduates from high school?
3. Why is a relationship with Jesus Christ important to you?
4. How do the Beatitudes communicate the necessity of putting God first in your life?
5. What are three essential parts to the Church's mission?
6. What are some positive and negative aspects of putting off vocational choices until a later age?
7. How can you translate your personal ideals into a way of life?
8. List the ways one of your relationships with a friend or family member has recently changed.
9. Why is forgiveness an important tool in mending broken relationships?
10. What is the difference between a friend and an acquaintance?
11. What are some reasons people date?
12. What are the six rules for improving communication skills?
13. Why are conflicts with friends not always bad experiences?
14. What are some of the components of a good date?
15. How does "sex" differ from "sexuality?"
16. Why is self-love a prerequisite for any other kind of love?
17. How do you tell the difference between infatuation and romantic love?
18. What are some ways that the gift of sexuality is misused?
19. List some of the health dangers associated with having sex with multiple partners.
20. How can you communicate what you believe about sexuality through your daily actions?

Making It Real

Create a classroom bulletin board of dating ideas. Dating suggestions should be written on index cards and pinned to the bulletin board. Extra items like photographs of couples on a date, menus from restaurants, ticket stubs from amusement parks, and directions to places of interest can also be included to make the bulletin board your version of "Dating Central."

Use some of the ideas listed below to get "Dating Central" started. Add your own ideas to the list.

- Go fishing on a boat.
- Make a batch of oatmeal cookies together.
- Go window shopping. Each person may pick only one item.
- Get two baseball gloves and play catch.
- Attend Mass together.
- Baby-sit a younger family member.
- Go to the animal shelter for a visit.
- Host a barbecue for your friends.
- Take your parents out to dinner.
- Learn a musical instrument together.
- Make the yard sale circuit in your neighborhood one weekend looking for gifts for friends.
- Take a foreign language class together. Then, go to a restaurant where they speak your new language.
- Write poems to each other.
- Clean a neighbor's house or yard.
- Visit one of your grandparents.
- Say a decade of the rosary.

A Time of Prayer

God speaks to us in many ways, including through song. How many times has a song reminded you of a special person, a special place, or a special time in your life? Compose a prayer about someone, someplace, or something specific in your life. Then, set the prayer to music. Read the prayer to your classmates. Play the song as accompanying background music to create a more prayerful mood. Remember: any song that speaks to you will do!

143

14. Components of a good date include: (1) being yourself; (2) being sensitive; (3) being honest; (4) being open; (5) being considerate; and (6) being responsible.
15. Sexuality is all-encompassing, influencing every dimension of our humanity. Sex identifies the biological classifications of male and female. "Having sex" commonly refers to genital sexual activity.
16. You have to love yourself before you can love others.
17. Generally, if people focus on themselves rather than on others, the experience is that of infatuation, not love.
18. The gift of sexuality is misused in rape, pornography, masturbation, and promiscuity.
19. Dangers associated with engaging in sexual intercourse with multiple partners include: pregnancy, sexually transmitted diseases (including AIDS), and a loss of self-esteem.
20. Through modesty, which involves discipline and balance, you can communicate your concern for your sexuality.

Making It Real

Teaching Approaches
- Have a general class brainstorming session sharing dating ideas.
- **Reteach**—Play a version of the dating game. Have people in the class try one of the suggested dating ideas and report back on their experiences.
- **Extend the Lesson**—Encourage students to bring photos of their dating experiences to include in the display.

A Time for Prayer

Teaching Approaches
- Read directions to students.
- Set a time limit (for example, one to two minutes) to the reading of the prayer.
- Allow class time to share prayer and musical accompaniment.
- **Reteach**—Discuss with students the importance of putting prayer to music.
- **Extend the Lesson**—record prayers on tape for later use.

Resources

Resource U2A from the Teacher's Resource Book provides suggestions to help plan a class Mass or other liturgical service suitable for use during a retreat or mini-workshop.

Unit 3

For a Lifetime

So much of life is transitory: people move from place to place; friendships evolve or dissolve. Often, the most intimate of relationships, marriage, ends in divorce. People often change careers three or four times during a lifetime. Within their careers, people will work at many different jobs. Given this reality, the call to a lifetime vocational commitment may be difficult for the students to accept or even understand. Unit 3 examines what it takes to make a successful vocation—in marriage, religious life, or the single life.

Students will:

- Learn that each vocation is rooted in the Gospel counsels of poverty, chastity, and obedience.

- Recognize that allegiance to these counsels and to a relationship with Jesus and the Church community are sources of strength to people committed to a vocation.

- Examine the attractions, benefits, hardships, and rewards of each area of Christian vocation.

- Focus special attention on the issues of marriage preparation and the first years of marriage.

- Learn that Catholic marriage is a sacrament and an expression of personal faith and love.

- Recognize that a main objective in all vocations is to find ways for God's love to shine forth.

- Learn that whatever vocation they choose, they are called to deepen their relationship with God and to carry God's love to others.

Unit 3 Overview

Chapter 8 Callings and Commitments

All Christian vocations are rooted in the Gospel counsels of poverty, chastity, and obedience.

Chapter 9 Answering a Call

Religious life and the ordained priesthood are ways for people to radically accept Christ's call to discipleship.

Chapter 10 Preparing for Marriage

Couples considering marriage are given the help they need to prepare thoroughly.

For a Lifetime

My life is my response to God's love. I see my life and specifically my vows of poverty, chastity, and obedience as freeing me so that I can share with others the gift I have been given. Sometimes this means simply sitting down and listening to the heartaches of another person.

When I entered religious life, I did not see my vows as particularly freeing. I entered in my twenties and I felt that I had many opportunities ahead. I was then living in New Mexico, having just graduated from college with a degree in dietetics. I was awarded an internship, but turned it down because there was something in me which wanted to try religious life. I say "try" because I had decided that if it was not for me, I would not stay. Many of my friends were surprised at my decision, but I now view it as a work of God' grace.

As a Sister of Loretto, I see myself giving from the abundance I have received. This is a special aspect of the work of our religious community. We see ourselves as helping those in need, especially economically disadvantaged women.

I remain open to God's grace and am most grateful for the life I have been given.

Chapter 11 The Marriage Covenant

The sacrament of Christian marriage is an expression of personal faith and a sign of Jesus' love.

Chapter 12 The First Years of Married Life

Effective interpersonal communication skills help to make the transition to married life successful.

NAME:	Dr. Lydia Peña, Sister of Loretto
CAREER:	Teacher
VOCATION:	Religious Life

Teaching Objectives

- To familiarize students with a variety of different Christian vocations.
- To help students understand the importance of the virtues of poverty, chastity, and obedience to Christian vocations.
- To help students recognize the different kinds of religious vocations.
- To examine a process of preparing for Christian marriage.
- To help students understand the sacramental nature of marriage.
- To offer students effective ways of dealing with the adjustments that occur during the first years of married life.

Scope and Sequence

We can know, love, and serve God in a variety of Christian vocations.

"Married Christians, in virtue of the sacrament of matrimony, signify and share in the mystery of that unity and fruitful love which exists between Christ and the Church; they help each other to attain holiness in their married life and in the rearing and education of their children; and they have their own special gift among the People of God" (*Sacred Congregation of Rites*).

"Given the powerful individual and cultural pull toward self-centeredness and sin, each person must pursue a personal, lifelong journey of conversion by which one tries to 'consider, judge, and arrange one's life according to the holiness and love of God'" (*Human Sexuality*, USCC 1991).

Begin the Unit

1. Read the feature on Sister Lydia Peña. Ask: "Are you surprised that Sister Lydia did not enter religious life with the idea that it was 'for a lifetime'?"
2. Read the chapter titles and objectives.
3. Ask: "What are some of your lifelong interests? What are some things that are a part of your life right now that you think will last a lifetime?"
4. Ask students to interview a man and woman religious and answer these questions: "How old were they when they entered religious life? What career or profession were they involved in before they entered religious life?"

Background

Sister Lydia Peña is a professor of art history in the "University Without Walls" program at Regis University in Denver, Colorado. She teaches about sculpture and is extremely fascinated with Pre-Columbian and Latin American art. She has been a Sister of Loretto for over twenty-five years. Sister Lydia deeply values her Hispanic heritage and culture.

Focus On: Chapter 8

The word "vocation" is often used to explain the call a man or a woman has to join religious life. Once the person's motives, qualifications, and skills are examined, and a series of preparatory steps are fulfilled, the man or woman embarks on a life of service. As a sign of this life, he or she makes public promises, or vows, that are usually connected to the virtues of poverty, chastity, and obedience.

During the past twenty years, vocations to the priesthood and religious life have decreased. Ironically, over the same period of time, the Church's general membership has grown in record numbers. One positive element of this vocation "crisis" is that the Church has further developed its understanding of vocation.

The Church recalls from Scripture that each person is called by God to communion with Jesus Christ: "God is faithful, and by Him you were called to fellowship with His Son, Jesus Christ our Lord" *(1 Corinthians 1:9)*. This is the primary Christian vocation. Each person has a responsibility to seek his or her personal way to fulfill it.

In this chapter, the students will explore a number of life choices—including marriage, single life, and religious life—under the heading of vocation. They will come to understand that commitment and faith are prominent elements of any chosen vocation.

Plan Ahead

- Incorporate formal and/or spontaneous prayer in each lesson. A participatory prayer service that is suitable for use on retreat is provided in the Teacher's Resource Book.
- Note **Resource** suggestions which can be applied to, or extend, the lessons of this chapter.
- Preview the **Application** projects in the Chapter Review. Refer to **Teaching Approaches** for suggestions on when to assign the projects. Or, the projects may be used as part of lesson, section, or chapter reviews.
- Decide on a method for grouping students for projects and discussion.
- Invite guest speakers in advance who will participate in selected lessons.

Callings and Commitments

Then I heard the voice of the Lord saying, "Whom shall I send? Who will go for us?" "Here I am," I said. "Send me!"

Isaiah 6:8

This chapter will help you to:

- See how the traditional virtues of poverty, chastity, and obedience support the Christian vocations.
- Witness to the beauty of sexual intimacy in marriage by practicing the virtue of chastity.
- Cultivate the virtue of obedience.

- Become familiar with a variety of Christian vocations including religious life, single life, and married life.
- Understand that commitment and faith go hand in hand with vocation.

Media Suggestions (Optional)

- *Work of Love* (Ikonographics) 25 minutes. A reflection of Mother Teresa's work and vocation with the poor.
- *Without Reservations* (Mars-Hill Productions) 25 minutes. Four teenagers, victims of a fatal car crash, find themselves suspended in time and space. They are able to observe those left behind and preview what is ahead. They challenge us to share our faith and to examine our relationship with Jesus.

Aims

1. To identify the roots of the traditional vows of poverty, chastity, and obedience as they relate to vocation.
2. To examine ways to put the vows of poverty, chastity, and obedience into practice.

Begin the Section

1. Present the students with this dilemma: They have been arrested and accused of being a Christian. Ask: "What evidence is there to convict you?" You may wish to have the students first write, and then share, the "evidence."
2. Point out that there are no minimum requirements for being a disciple of Jesus. Rather, the requirement is to seek out the personal way, or vocation, that God has intended for an individual.
3. Summarize or read the first three paragraphs. Ask the students to comment on Saint Ignatius's words: "If we are not completely ready, through Him, to die in order to suffer like Him, His life is not in us."
4. You may wish to use either **Application** Project 2 or Project 3 as a part of the section introduction.

I. WITNESSES

For three centuries, Christianity was outlawed in the Roman Empire. A person identified as a Christian risked persecution and even execution. During the periods of persecution, a great number of Christians were put to death.

The early Christians who died for their faith came to be known by the Greek term *martyr,* meaning "witness." As the years and persecutions continued, martyrs were remembered with great honor: they had faithfully lived out the highest ideals of discipleship by imitating Christ fully.

Saint Ignatius, the early second-century bishop of Antioch, was arrested during the persecution of the emperor Trajan. In his writings, Ignatius expressed a complete willingness to give his life in the name of Christ: "If we are not completely ready, through Him, to die in order to suffer like Him, His life is not in us." In A.D. 107, after a long and treacherous journey to Rome, Ignatius was taken to the public amphitheater where he was thrown to the lions.

147

Vows

Lesson Overview

Explore the students' understanding of the vows of poverty, chastity, and obedience. By the end of the lesson the students should be aware that all Christians are called to incorporate these virtues into their lives, no matter what their specific vocational choices, or whether they actually profess specific vows.

New Words

A *vow* is a deliberate, voluntary promise made to God, by which one obliges oneself to do something that is pleasing to God.

The *diaconate* is the first of the major orders of holy orders.

The word *deacon* originally referred to a table waiter or waitress but expanded to mean "servant." The word was commonly used in Greek to refer to any servant.

Teaching Approaches

- If necessary, familiarize the students with the terms "diaconate" and "vows" and the difference between a transitional and permanent deacon.

- Read or have the students choose parts and role play the story.

- **Reteach**—Have the students play word association with the virtues of poverty, chastity, and obedience. Ask: "How important are these virtues to you now?"

- **Extend the Lesson**—Arrange to interview a seminarian who is approaching ordination. Ask him to explain and share his personal feelings on the vows of poverty, chastity, and obedience. (See **Application** Project 6.)

Christianity spread and prospered when it was legalized in A.D. 313 by the emperor Constantine. Ironically, when the persecutions stopped, Christians had to find new ways to express their commitment as disciples of Jesus.

Vows

"It's not priesthood that scares me, it's the diaconate," Michael Evans told Saint Mel's youth group.

"The diacowhat?" Ana Villalobos wanted to know. She had never heard the term before.

Michael was a Jesuit seminarian working as a parish intern for a semester at Saint Mel's. He'd come to the weekly meeting of the youth group to talk about vocations—his and theirs.

"Diaconate," Michael repeated. "It's when I'll be ordained a deacon. Next March 12, to be exact. A few years ago, when seminarians like me came to work in parishes, they had already been ordained deacons. I'm sure glad that rule has changed. These past five months have really helped me understand what parish ministry is about before I take vows," he added.

"Take what?" Mark Verge wanted to know. "My Dad's been a deacon for years. What did he have to take? A test?"

Even Michael laughed before waving Mark off. "Vows. Promises. That's what I have to take. Poverty. Chastity. Obedience. Your dad took one of those vows—obedience. He's a permanent deacon. I'll be a transitional deacon—meaning I will eventually be ordained a priest."

"I thought you didn't take vows until you were ordained a priest," Peter said.

"No," said Michael, "I make these promises when I enter the diaconate."

"Oh," said Ana seriously. She seemed to understand now what Michael was facing next March 12.

"I don't see how you can promise those things!" Mark said to Michael. "I know I never would want to sacrifice that much. I never could, anyway."

Michael was upfront with his concerns about promising to live the vows of poverty, chastity, and obedience.

Journal Assignment

After Jesus tells the rich official, in Luke 18:18-22, to sell all that he has and give it to the poor, the man was "quite sad, for he was very rich." Ask the students to speculate on what became of the man. Have them write the rest of his story in their journals. How does having one's deepest values challenged affect a person?

♣ Prayer in Action
"Here I Am"

The First Book of Samuel *(1 Samuel 3:1-10)* offers an example of how you are to respond to God's call. Samuel was a young boy working as a servant to Eli. One day, while he was asleep, Samuel heard the Lord call him. Samuel was not familiar with God yet, so he assumed Eli had called him. Eli, however, was still asleep. Only after Samuel woke him three times did Eli realize that Samuel was being called by God. Eli said to Samuel, "Go to sleep, and if you are called, reply, 'Speak, Lord, for your servant is listening.'" When Samuel next heard God, he listened and obeyed.

What can be learned from Samuel's call?
1. Realize that God calls when people least expect it.
2. God's call may be confused with messages from other sources.
3. Everyone needs the wisdom and guidance of the community (Eli was Samuel's help) to understand God's call clearly.
4. Our response is first to listen, and then to understand.

"You better learn how," Michael responded. "Maybe not to poverty, chastity, and obedience, but sometime in your life you will be asked to make a commitment. Couples promise to love and care for each other faithfully for a lifetime. People who choose the single life are called to live chastely. And all Christians are called to be responsible stewards. How they use money, their bodies, and their loyalty is part of their baptismal commitment."

Michael could tell he was losing them. What meaning do vows, responsible stewardship, and baptismal commitment have for a group of high school students?

New Understanding

Every Christian, through Baptism, receives the vocation to spread the kingdom of God as a disciple of Jesus. We are asked to hear Jesus' Good News presented through the Scriptures, understand His message, and apply it to our lives. As disciples, we try to live justly, use God's gifts wisely, and follow God's commands faithfully. Living as a disciple requires effort and discipline things, which many people experience difficulty practicing.

Jesus recognized that living the basic challenges of faith would be difficult enough for most people. Remember the story of the rich young man from Luke, chapter 18?

Jesus was asked, "What must I do to inherit eternal life?" *(Luke 18:18).* His reply identifies the challenges we are all called to live: "You know the commandments, 'You shall not commit adultery; you shall not kill; you shall not steal, you shall not bear false witness; honor your father and your mother'"*(Luke 18:20).*

The young man replied, "All of these I have observed from my youth." *(Luke 18:21).* Here was a person who felt called to do more than what was required. He recognized that he needed to go beyond ordinary expectations for his own life.

Jesus responded, "There is still one thing left for you: sell all that you have and distribute it to the poor, and you will have a treasure in heaven. Then come, follow Me" *(Luke 18:22).* Jesus' message is that there is always more to do for those who wish to be His disciples. People experience this call still today.

Gospel Counsels

Poverty, obedience, and chastity are called the Gospel counsels. They are the traditional vows of a Christian vocation. Men and women who enter religious life bind themselves to these counsels

Resources

Resource 8A from the Teacher's Resource Book provides a blackline master for the questions listed in "Prayer in Action."

New Understanding

Teaching Approaches

- Read or have the students read the section.
- If you wish, you may have the students read the entire story of the official's question and Jesus' answer from Luke 18:18-30.
- **Reteach**—Have the students discuss the question posed in **Application** Project 1.
- **Extend the Lesson**—Explore the idea of people choosing to do "more than what is required" in a variety of endeavors from schoolwork to sports to friendships. Ask: "What motivates people to do more? In what area of your life do you feel called to do more?"

♣ Prayer in Action

Teaching Approaches

- Have the students recall that "vocation" means "calling." Tell the students that Samuel was called to his personal vocation as prophet. He was the prophet who was responsible for the enthronement of David as king of Israel.
- Set the mood for quiet prayer.
- Choose one or two students to read the revelation to Samuel from 1 Samuel 3:1-10.
- Continuing in the atmosphere of quiet prayer; read aloud each of the following questions, pausing between each to allow for personal reflection: When has God spoken to you when you least expected it? When have you confused God's message? Who can help you to interpret God's call? Listen to God speaking to you right now. What is God saying?
- As a follow-up to the prayer, have the students discuss the things listed that can be learned from Samuel's prayer.

Gospel Counsels

New Words

Poverty is a vow that religious take renouncing their right to own property. The scriptural meaning of poverty involves acquiring a spirit of sacrifice.

Chastity is the virtue contrary to lust. Chastity is practiced by living a life of sexual virtue in accordance with one's state in life. A married couple practices chastity by refraining from sexual intimacy with anyone but their spouse while men and women who profess the vow of chastity refrain from sexual intimacy with anyone.

The vow of *obedience* taken by a religious obliges him or her to obey the will of God as expressed by one's superior. The counsel of obedience is the denial of self in order to combat pride.

A *monastery* is the communal residence of religious who live in seclusion, lead a life of contemplation, and recite the Liturgy of the Hours in common.

Traditionally, the *abbot* is the superior of a religious order of men. An *abbess* is the superior of women. Today, however, many orders have abandoned the title. For example, Franciscan superiors are called "guardians" and Jesuit superiors are called "rectors."

Teaching Approaches

- Read or summarize the section.
- **Reteach**—Make sure the students can trace the evolution of poverty, chastity, and obedience from Gospel counsels to public vows taken by religious.
- **Extend the Lesson**—Ask: "Which Gospel counsel would you find the hardest to commit to publicly? Why?"

The vows of poverty, chastity, and obedience have traditionally been associated with people who made commitments to the religious life.

when they profess vows. How did the practice of professing vows develop?

An elaborate code of behavior evolved among the first generation of Christians. The Acts of the Apostles reminds us how the "community of believers was of one heart and mind, and no one claimed that any of his possessions was his own, but they had everything in common" *(Acts 4:32).*

Paul wrote specifically of the virtue of virginity (chastity):

> "I have no commandment from the Lord, but I give my opinion as one who by the Lord's mercy is trustworthy... I should like you to be free of anxieties. An unmarried man is anxious about the things of the Lord, how he may please the Lord... An unmarried woman or a virgin is anxious about the things of the Lord, so that she may be holy in both body and spirit."
> *(1 Corinthians 7:25, 32, 34)*

Over time, two of the counsels gained special influence: chastity (foregoing marriage, sexual intercourse, and children) and poverty (renouncing ownership of personal property and other possessions). Traveling preachers, missionaries, and hermits (men and women who lived solitary lives

---

Resources

Resource 8B lists suggestions for practicing the virtues of poverty, chastity, and obedience.

Background

According to the *Catechism of the Catholic Church,* Christ offers the Gospel Counsels to every disciple. See 915-918.

in the desert) accepted these virtues as essential to their religious practice.

Eventually, many of those who lived these strict disciplines came to live together; men in monasteries and women in convents. These were places where Christians could practice discipleship under the guidance of a learned teacher, the abbot for men or the abbess for women. The third Gospel counsel took on new importance in these situations. Rooted in Jesus' words, "I came down from heaven not to do My own will but the will of the One who sent Me" *(John 6:38),* obedience came to mean obeying the abbot or the abbess, who made the decisions on how life in the monastery or convent was lived.

Over several generations, poverty, chastity, and obedience became the promised vows for everyone who made a commitment to religious life, whether or not they lived in monasteries or convents. Unfortunately, the significance of these counsels for all other Christians was lost.

We recognize today, as seminarian Michael Evans hinted to Saint Mel's youth group, that these Gospel counsels do offer guidance to all Christians as they actively participate as disciples of Jesus in a variety of ways. We are challenged, like the rich young man who sought to do more than simply follow the commandments, to incorporate the Gospel counsels freely into our own vocations.

Talk It Over

1. What's your reaction to Michael's suggestion that the vows of poverty, chastity, and obedience are promises that you are called to live out in your life?
2. Why would you think the Gospel counsels became more significant after Christianity became legal?
3. A Catholic writer, G. K. Chesterton (1874-1936), wrote, "The Christian ideal has not been tried and found wanting. It has been found difficult; and left untried." What does this statement say about Christian discipleship?

▲ Family Living

Teaching Approaches

- Be sensitive to the students who cannot find examples of the Gospel counsels in their own family lives. Ask the students to share concrete examples from "their own families or families they have witnessed."
- Do the students see these counsels lived out in their parishes?

Talk It Over

Extend Question 1 by having the students suggest realistic ways that they can begin to practice the virtues of poverty, chastity, and obedience. For Question 2, the students should understand how the Gospel counsels became the "highest" form of discipleship after martyrdom was no longer a likely option. For Question 3, ask students to discuss Chesterton's remarks.

▲ Family Living
Gospel Counsels in Your Home

How does your family model the Gospel counsels of poverty, chastity, and obedience?

- The spirit of poverty recognizes that material goods can be sacrificed for others' benefit. What is the importance placed on material things in your home? Do you discuss the importance of material things in relation to other things of value? What sacrifices does your family make so that others in need might have food, shelter, clothing, and a chance for an education?

- The spirit of chastity promotes the goodness of the human body. How do you respect other family members? How does *your* behavior and dress encourage personal modesty? What have *you* learned about the importance of marriage vows, including those of bringing children into the world and raising them lovingly?
- The spirit of obedience witnesses a sense of humility; the attitude that others may know more about a subject than you do. What are some concrete examples of how *your* family lives the spirit of obedience?

Background

The Church also celebrates the order of "virgin." These are men and women who vow to live chastely for life, for the sake of the kingdom, yet do not become consecrated religious or priests. This state of life is considered a special gift from God. (See *Catechism of the Catholic Church,* 922-924.)

Living the Counsels

Lesson Overview

Living the Gospel counsels may be easily perceived by your students as a burden that they would be unwilling or unable even to try. In fact, the counsels are a natural and normal extension of a Christian's chosen course of discipleship. Stress to the students how the Gospel counsels can be a witness to the world of "kingdom values."

Teaching Approaches

- Read the opening paragraph.
- Discuss with students their impressions of the vows of poverty, chastity, and obedience, along with their thoughts on why anyone would want to make vows of any kind.
- **Reteach**—Ask: "Why must a person be free before he or she can commit to vows?"
- **Extend the Lesson**—Assign **Application** Project 4. Allow time for the students to discuss.

Living the Counsels

The vows that Michael Evans was preparing to profess publicly reflect much of what the Church has learned over the past 2,000 years about living out the Gospel message. Vows are not meant to punish, nor can vows be forced upon someone who is unwilling to accept them freely. Rather, vows are promises people make willingly, commitments people choose to accept that free them to live the Good News of Jesus.

Avoiding Excess, Sharing Talents

Megan felt very fortunate. When she graduated from college, most of her student loans had already been repaid. The trust fund that her grandmother had established at Megan's birth paid for most of her debts. Without the pressures of having to repay loans, Megan decided she could spend a year working with people as a volunteer, before starting her career as a journalist.

Five years later, Megan was still a volunteer. She had worked in a shelter for battered women in Los Angeles for several years, then spent three years in Guatemala establishing a woman's refuge. Megan realized that while she was not truly poor—she had the resources of her parents and her own education to fall back on—living her personal vow of poverty had given her the freedom to pick up and go where she was needed without worry. She had no car payments to make, no life insurance, no rent; she was really free. Her poverty allowed her to become part of a larger family among people who had few possessions, where the wealth she had left behind would have cast her as an outsider.

There are no special blessings in being poor. Why would a person choose to live in poverty? How does living a vow of poverty help the poor?

Background

Saint Paul took his duty to serve the poor very seriously. In his Letter to the Galatians, he wrote that "we were to be mindful of the poor, which is the very thing I was eager to do" *(Galatians 2:10)*. Students will be interested to know that Paul was never paid for his services to the Gospel, but made his living as a tentmaker.

How can you share your "wealth" with people who need what you have to give?

Like the other Gospel counsels, the vow of poverty reminds us that we live in a transitory world. People who live out the vow of poverty renounce the personal ownership of material possessions. They live simply, often on a minimal income, so that they are free to proclaim the Gospel without fear of losing their excessive material possessions. Some, like Megan, live as members of volunteer organizations. They do not take formal vows of poverty, but simply live the Gospel counsel at this time. Others, professed members of religious communities, promise to live faithful to the vow forever.

Religious are able to live their vow of poverty without concern for money because they are financially supported by their communities. The priests, sisters, or brothers who are part of the community turn whatever salary they earn for their labor over to the community treasury. They, in turn, receive a monthly stipend or allowance for personal use. Most of their transportation, housing, food, and medical expenses are paid for by the community out of the common treasury. Free of financial worries, men and women religious are able to go wherever and whenever they are needed.

What's the first picture that comes into your mind when you hear the word "poverty"? You probably visualize homeless people, soup kitchens, or inner-city crime. There is little doubt that people who are poor struggle to survive. Obviously, there are no special blessings in being poor. People who are poor often cannot find work that pays a livable wage, and so they earn little money. Without money they eat little food and live in substandard housing. No one should have to live like this.

Through living the vow of poverty, people bring the issues of the poor to the attention of society. People conditioned to owning many possessions tend to forget others who have little in the way of wealth. A vow of poverty serves as a reminder that there is no reason to own more than we really need. People vow poverty as a challenge to all of us so that we do not forget those people who live day to day hoping only to survive.

Pope Paul VI wrote of those who share the example of poverty with others:

Resources

Resource 8C lists several differences between wants and needs.

Journal Assignment

Students are to reflect on how their lives would be changed if they "lived simply" all of the time.

Avoiding Excess, Sharing Talents

Teaching Approaches

- Ask the students to comment on the bumper sticker slogan: "Whoever dies with the most toys wins." Have them cite examples they have witnessed of this type of mentality.

- Ask the class to brainstorm a list of things they want. Write their suggestions on the board. Then, go back through the list and have them label each a "want" or a "need." Put a line through each want. Comment on the things that are left.

- Read or summarize the section.

- **Reteach**—Assign the students to work with a partner to develop a plan for living simply.

- **Extend the Lesson**—Dedicate a week to "living simply." Donate all savings of money, clothes, and food to people who need it to "simply live."

Freedom to Serve

Teaching Approaches

- Discuss with students their attitudes about the vow of chastity. Would they expect to have difficulty in living out this vow? Why do they think people choose to live such a vow?

- Have the students read the section on their own.

- **Reteach**—Develop ideas for how the following people can live the vow of chastity: a teenager, a married couple, and a vowed religious.

- **Extend the Lesson**—Invite a priest or religious to the classroom. Ask him or her to share some of the challenges and rewards of living a life of consecrated chastity.

"At a time when there is an increased danger for many of being enticed by the alluring security of possessions, knowledge, and power, the call of God places you at the pinnacle of the Christian conscience. You are to remind men and women that true and complete progress consists in responding to their calling 'to share as sons and daughters in the life of the living God.'"

A modern phrase that explains the life of freely chosen poverty is "Live simply so others can simply live." All Christians are called to live out this example. How can you put this challenge into action now?

Saint Paul begged the Corinthians to continue in the gracious actions of self-giving. He reminded them "that for your sake, Jesus became poor although He was rich, so that by His poverty you might become rich" *(2 Corinthians 8:9)*. What can you do that reflects the Gospel counsel of poverty at home? school? in the community?

Freedom to Serve

Consecrated chastity is the promise a person makes to remain celibate for life. In the public testimony of marriage, people recognize the goodness of sexual relations. In consecrated chastity, this good gift is offered back to God.

Consecrated chastity is not for everyone. In speaking of those who gave up marriage for the sake of God's kingdom, Jesus said, "Not all can accept this teaching, but only those to whom that is granted" *(Matthew 19:11)*.

However, chastity is a part of every Christian life. Chastity is even a part of marriage. Couples refrain from sexual intercourse at certain times in their marriage for important reasons. Couples promise to remain chaste with people other than their spouses out of loving fidelity. People who are not married refrain from sexual intercourse out of chastity.

Those who are called to accept the vow of consecrated chastity are dedicated solely to living

While consecrated chastity is not for everyone, everyone is called to live chastely. You can have fun and remain chaste as well.

Background

There are two kinds of chastity: (1) *Conjugal* chastity is the "control and moderation of legitimate acts of the sexual relations of married persons"; and (2) *Continence* is chastity exercised by the unmarried, and includes the control of inappropriate sexual acts.

Living within a Budget

Although you may never take a vow of poverty, you will continually face the challenge of living within your means. No matter how much money you make, it is important for you to know how your money is spent. One way of keeping track of your spending is by keeping a budget. Here are some tips for preparing a budget:

1. **List your goals.** Include the things that you want to do and buy. If the list is long, underline those things that are most important to you. Now, cross out everything on the list that you don't need. Any money left over after taking care of your needs can be spent on these other items.

2. **Group your needs** under such headings as food, housing, education, and clothing. Keep a record of the amount you spend under each heading each day. Your chart might look something like the chart below.

   Keep your expenses for a week. Since your expenses may vary, it's good to also keep a monthly and yearly account of your spending.

3. **Estimate your monthly income.** Multiply your weekly income by four. Multiply that number by twelve to get an estimate of your yearly income. Add in any extra money you expect to earn or receive as gifts during the year. You now know how much money you have to live on during the year.

4. **Estimate your monthly expenses.** Multiply your weekly expenses by four. Add in any monthly expenses you regularly pay, such as car insurance or credit card bills.

5. **Make a yearly budget.** It would contain all of the same information as your monthly budget, multiplied by twelve. Remember to add in any yearly or one-time expenses.

   If you estimate that you will spend more money than you earn, you can either increase your income or cut back on spending.

   Prepare your own personal budget for the next year. Determine how you would change your spending to bring it into line with your expected income. How would your spending habits change if you made a lot more money? if you made a lot less money?

Date	Gifts or Contributions	Food	Housing	Education	Clothing	Savings	Transportation	Medical Care	Recreation	Insurance
1/6	$	$ —	$	$	$	$	$	$	$ 2.00	$
1/7		3.00					5.00			
1/8		.50			10.00					
1/9	2.00	1.50								
1/10		1.50				5.00				
1/11		.50							11.00	
1/12		4.00					1.50			
Total	2.00	11.00			10.00	5.00	6.50		13.00	

Teaching Approaches

- Have the students each keep a budget as if they were living alone.
- Allow time for the students to discuss and question each other's budgets. Have them focus on needs versus wants.
- Discuss with students the importance of keeping a budget. How do students think that they might benefit by living on a fixed budget?
- Review students' personal budgets with the entire class or small groups. Have the other students evaluate (not judge or criticize) whether the budget reflects reality. Encourage questions, not challenges or comments.

Resources

Resource 8D is a sample of a high school student's personal statements on chastity.

Resources

Resource 8E provides a worksheet for the activity suggested in the activity, "Living within a Budget."

Listening to God's Call

Teaching Approaches

- After the students have read the section, ask them to explain what the vow of obedience has to do with hearing what God intends.

- **Reteach**—Ask: "Why might vowed religious find obedience to be their most 'intimidating' promise? What would you find intimidating about the vow of obedience?"

- **Extend the Lesson**—Obedience is related closely to trust. Conduct a "trust walk." Have the students team up with a partner. One person is blindfolded while the other leads him or her on a walk. Allow enough time so that both partners can experience both roles. In a large group, ask the students how they felt in their roles.

Talk It Over

Have the students discuss all three questions in small groups. You may wish to have group leaders summarize the responses to the questions and submit them to you. Correlate the best answers and type them on a worksheet. Make copies of the best answers and return them to each student as a reference for practicing the virtues of poverty, chastity, and obedience.

God's life. As Paul explained to the Corinthians, people who are married are, "anxious about the things of the world" *(1 Corinthians 7:33)* while those who are unmarried are "anxious about the things of the Lord" *(1 Corinthians 7:32)*.

Consecrated religious are, theoretically, able to devote themselves to a life of prayer to God and service to God's People. And, in the religious community, the consecrated religious find a stability in relationships that are able to nurture them in the work to be done for the kingdom of God. How would a vow of chastity help support stability in relationships?

Listening to God's Call

People who take the religious vow of obedience often find it to be the most intimidating of all their promises. They pledge to follow the wishes of a superior, either the leader of the religious community, or in the case of diocesan priests, the local bishop. Such a promise requires confidence in God and trust in the religious superior. Instead of being limited by the promise, however, many people find it a source of freedom.

"My whole life as a priest would have been vastly different, and probably less productive, had I been able to do what I wanted to do, instead of what I was assigned to do," explained Father Theodore Hesburgh, the former president of the University of Notre Dame. "On three occasions early in my priestly life, I was asked my preference in possible alternate assignments. I voiced my wish and each time I was assigned to the alternative. Somehow, it worked out for the best. In a curious, almost contradictory way, I have always felt unusually free."

As a Gospel counsel, obedience is patterned on Christ's response to the will of His Father. In the garden on the night before He died, Jesus prayed that the cup of suffering might be taken from Him. However, Jesus' addition to the prayer was "but not what I will but what You will" *(Mark 14:36)*.

Jesus' obedience to God's will, even to death, was heroic. When emulated by the Christian, it can lead to similar suffering. But obedience to God's will in a particular vocation also brings its own rewards.

The virtue of obedience is not the same as blindly following what someone tells you to do. The word "obedience" comes from the Latin word meaning "to hear." Hearing what God intends of you often means taking time to listen carefully to what others say.

Obedience entails recognizing that you may not know everything you need to know about yourself or a particular situation. Being willing to listen to another shows humility and self-confidence. You recognize that you can learn from others, and can grow from their wisdom.

Talk It Over

1. What are some practical ways that you can live simply and share your resources with others?

2. How can young adults live chastely? What does chastity mean to you?

3. As a student, how are you called to obedience? How does this differ from simply obeying orders?

Journal Assignment

Ask the students to listen to how God speaks through the people and events of their day. Have them record some of their thoughts.

Background

The counsel of obedience is represented in Jesus' call to discipleship: "If anyone wishes to come after Me, he must deny himself and take up his cross daily and follow Me" *(Luke 9:23)*.

II. CALLINGS

On his journey to Damascus, Paul was blinded by a light from the sky. It was Jesus. "Stop persecuting and follow Me," the message went. Though not all vocations are communicated in such a dramatic way, all Christian vocations carry within them the possibility of sainthood, just like Paul's. As Paul wrote,

> "There are different kinds of spiritual gifts but the same Spirit; there are different forms of service but the same Lord; there are different workings but the same God who produces all of them in everyone".

(1 Corinthians 12:4)

Answering God's Call

God calls us towards goodness in many different ways. No one particular vocation is better than another or a clearer sign of holiness than any other. No one particular vocation is a surer road to heaven. All vocations demand that we listen to and answer faithfully God's call.

There are many choices that can be made (with God's help) for a lifetime vocation within the callings to the priesthood or religious life, to the single life, or to marriage. There are new people to meet along the way. Relationships are to be formed and love will blossom. There will be many ways within each of the callings to work for God's kingdom and to serve those in need. Making this choice is an ongoing struggle made easier by the belief that God will call you to a vocation that is appropriate for you.

Priests do much more than lead the community in prayer. What are some of the other roles priests perform?

The "Religious Life"

Under the umbrella of "religious life," there are typically two kinds of vocations: the sacrament of Holy Orders and the sacramental profession of religious life. Each fulfills an important role in making God's kingdom present.

Both priests and religious brothers and sisters take the traditional vows of the Gospel counsels as a sign of their commitment to their vocation (though priests who work in a diocese are not required to take a vow of poverty). At the heart of the religious vocation is a deep desire to know and love God better and to serve God's People.

Resources

Resource 8F provides a list of religious communities for men and women and their special focus of ministry.

Background

The title deaconess was given to women deacons. Because of the aspect of nakedness in baptisms of immersion, deaconesses helped in the baptisms of women. The practice was discontinued by the Council of Nicaea in 325.

II. CALLINGS

Aims

1. To examine the similarities and differences of many kinds of Christian vocations.

2. To help students see how faith and commitment are important factors in any Christian vocation.

Begin the Section

1. Invite several adults to take part in a vocation panel. Include men and women of a variety of vocations from the married, single, and religious life. Ask each person to give a short opening statement about his or her vocation (i.e. calling, practices, rewards, and difficulties). Then, open up the session for questions.

2. Read the opening paragraph. Assign students to read the entire text of Paul's conversion from Acts 9:1-22.

3. Ask the students to cite other examples of dramatic callings to a Christian lifestyle—either from the lives of saints or someone in today's world with whom they are familiar.

Answering God's Call

Lesson Overview

Dramatic or not, all Christian vocations are worthwhile and good. To accept the calling that God has offered means a person has chosen the best possible vocation for him or herself. Emphasize this opportunity of a unique and free choice.

Teaching Approaches

- Read or summarize the opening paragraph.

- With a show of fingers (five means strongly agree and one means strongly disagree), poll the students on their feelings about the following statement: "God will call me to the vocation that is right for me."

- **Reteach**—Assign **Application** Project 5 at this time.

- **Extend the Lesson**—Ask the students to reflect on the heart of their vocation by looking at the talents and interests to which they have been attracted from childhood.

✛ In Focus

Teaching Approaches

- Read this feature to accompany the "Ordained Ministry" lesson.
- Invite a priest to come to your classroom. Ask the priest to explain how he participates in the life of the Church.

✴ Media Watch

Teaching Approaches

- Assign small groups of students to review one movie or television program that depicts religious life. Have them summarize their answers to each question and share their findings as part of a large group roundup.
- Screen sections of movies featuring religious men and women for the class. Discuss how religious are featured in the media. At appropriate times, pause the video to discuss the religious stereotypes presented.

The "Religious Life"

Teaching Approaches

- Write these terms on the board: "priest," "deacon," and "religious." Call on students to list one name of a person for each category. Ask: "How are these vocations the same? How are they different?"
- Read or summarize the sections on ordained ministry and on religious life to help clarify the students' responses.
- Ask the students to comment on roles they associate with the priesthood.
- **Reteach**—Review the differences between ordained ministers, and religious sisters and brothers.
- **Extend the Lesson**—From a diocesan directory, find several names and addresses of permanent deacons in your area. Have the students write letters to these men inquiring about their ministry.

✛ In Focus
Sacramental Ministry

In the early Church, the primary celebrants of the sacraments were the bishops. Soon, the presbyters, or priests, were ordained to assist the bishops. Like the bishops, their primary role was to communicate the Good News of Jesus.

Today, the role of the priest is to lead and unify the community through proclaiming the Gospel. The priest is charged with helping create those conditions where the celebration of God's life can happen throughout the world.

Ordained Ministry. The ordained priest serves in the presidential role for the community of believers. The priest is the leader of the Eucharistic celebration. The priest has many other roles in the Church as well—counselor, person of prayer, preacher—but a major part of the priest's life involves the celebration of the sacraments. What are some of the roles you associate with the priesthood?

Unlike most other types of religious life, the ministry of the priest is marked by a sacrament: Holy Orders. From its earliest days, the Church has had an ordained ministry, which traces its roots back to Jesus' selection of the Apostles as Church leaders. Jesus said to the Apostle Peter, "You are Peter, and upon this rock I will build My Church. I will give you the keys of the kingdom of heaven" *(Matthew 16:18-19)*.

The deacon is also an ordained minister. Deacons may officiate at Baptisms, marriages, and funerals, as well as proclaim the Gospel and preach at the Eucharist. But the deacon's primary role is that of service; thus, deacons are ordained to care for those in need.

The diaconate has its roots in the early Church *(see Acts 6:1-7)*, but until the Second Vatican Council the role of the deacon had diminished. Now, men, whether single or married, may serve

---

✴ Media Watch
Going Our Way?

Make a list of examples of men and women religious you have seen depicted on television or in the movies. Answer the following questions concerning these characters:

1. Are these character depictions accurate or do they stereotype the behavior of priests and religious?
2. Are men and women religious shown as normal people doing normal activities or are they pictured as other-worldly?
3. Do any of these presentations reflect your understanding of a Catholic religious vocation? Do any of the presentations make you think about being a priest, brother, or sister?
4. What is the character's role in the production? Do they present a significant message, or are they used to develop the moral fiber of the main character?
5. How would the story change if the person presented were not a priest or religious?
6. From the way the priest or religious is presented, how would you describe the attitude of the writer, director, or producer toward Catholicism?
7. Are priests or religious shown having a normal life: having fun, going to the theater, being with family, eating, celebrating with friends? Why would these behaviors be important to see?

Background

Father Locordaire said of priests: "To live in the world without wishing its pleasures; to be a member or each family, yet belonging to none; to share all suffering; to penetrate all secrets; to heal all wounds; to go from men to God and offer Him their prayers, to return from God to men to bring pardon and hope; to have a heart of fire for charity and a heart of bronze for chastity; to teach and to pardon, console and bless always—what a glorious life!"

as permanent deacons. These men hold regular jobs and have families, but they also carry out their vocational missions. Other men, like Michael Evans, serve as deacons for a short time before being ordained as priests.

Brothers and Sisters. Men or women who take vows as part of a religious community, but do not celebrate the sacrament of Holy Orders, are called brothers, sisters, or monks. There are many different kinds of religious communities, each with a different focus for mission and service. Many of the communities of religious men and women were originally founded by well-known saints or gifted Church leaders. Saint Francis of Assisi, for example, was the founder of the Franciscans.

The Single Life

The vocation to the single life can either be temporary or permanent. Some people feel called to marriage, but because they have not yet met suitable partners, or because age or circumstance do not yet allow marriage, they live as singles. There are many people who are single much of their life because of chance, not by choice. They would prefer marriage, but for some reason or other, that option has not yet been realized. A single person in transition may also be considering a life as a vowed religious or priest.

People who have chosen the single vocation have come to a prayerful conclusion that the single life affords them the best chance to love God and serve others. For these people, the single life is a vocation similar to that of the religious life. It originates with a call and grace from God.

The single life can assist a person to live guided by Christian values, fully dedicated to people, a group, a cause, or a project in a way that a married person would find difficult. There can also be great freedom in the single life. This freedom makes it possible for the single person to respond readily to a community problem, a natural disaster, or a plea from a family member or a friend who is in need of special care. The single person is willing and able to respond personally to the needs of others.

Marriage

Matrimony is unique in that it is the only sacrament conferred by the participants themselves; the priest or deacon acts only as a witness and as a representative of the community. The man and woman exchange and confer the marriage vows with and on one another.

The vocation of marriage is a call to incorporate God's undying love into the spousal relationship. It is God's love, as well as the couple's

---

Well Being
Reasons for Single Living

There are more single adults now than ever before. There are many reasons for living a single lifestyle, including:
- **Independence.** Many single people appreciate being able to come and go as they please, especially after having to answer to family rules for much of their life.
- **Career.** Being single allows for more flexibility. Singles can move and change jobs as needed or desired.

- **New opportunities for women.** In the past, women were dependent on men for financial support. Today, most women are encouraged to work and achieve financial independence on their own.
- **Delayed marriage.** Many singles want to be married eventually, but are postponing the event until they are financially and emotionally ready.

Background

Almost ten percent of the people over 18 in the United States today have never been married according to the 1990 U.S. Census. This number will continue to grow according to surveys taken among teens, many who say that they do not plan to marry.

The Single Life

Teaching Approaches
- Point out that the single life as a lifestyle is increasing. Ask the students to speculate on why they think this is occurring.
- **Reteach**—Discuss how choosing to live a vocation as a single person is different from simply being single.
- **Extend the Lesson**—Invite a person who chooses to live the single vocation to speak with the students.

Well-Being

Teaching Approaches
- Discuss the reasons why people remain single as presented in this feature.
- Ask: "What attracts you to living a single life?"

Marriage

Teaching Approaches
- Ask the students to share their experiences of attending Catholic weddings. Ask: "What happens at a Catholic wedding? At what part of the ceremony does the couple confer vows?" (The couple confers vows after the Liturgy of the Word.)
- Read or summarize the section.
- **Reteach**—Point out that while the marriage covenant is between the man and woman, God is the author of marriage: "It is not good for the man to be alone" (Genesis 2:18) so a suitable partner was created.
- **Extend the Lesson**—Discuss how "God's love is manifested in the union of two people."

Talk It Over

Have the students discuss all four questions in a small group. Choose one person in each group to moderate the discussion, making sure that each person has the opportunity to speak to each question.

Faith and Commitment

Lesson Overview

People who dream great dreams are often able to make a commitment to do whatever is necessary in order to accomplish those dreams. For example, a person who wants to be a doctor must put in the time and effort needed for study, or a person who wants to be a professional dancer must put in the time and effort needed for practice. This lesson looks at how dreaming great dreams (faith) ties to continued effort (commitment).

New Words

A *commitment* is a promise, pledge, or trust to do something. Commitments beget trust in relationships and allow the committed parties to come to a better knowledge of one another. This is true, too, in one's relationship with God. A person who, as a sign of commitment, takes vows of poverty, chastity, and obedience opens himself or herself to the possibility of a deeper relationship with God.

Teaching Approaches

- After reading the section, ask the students to explain why committing to the vows of poverty, chastity, and obedience makes no sense unless accompanied by faith. See "Talk It Over," Question 1.
- **Reteach**—Assign **Application** Project 7.
- **Extend the Lesson**—To help the students research the projects, invite members of a local parish council to assist by providing information about parish hospitality, opportunities for volunteer service, and the dynamics of the working relationship between clergy and laity in the parish.

love, that is expressed in the words: "I take you, for better or worse, for richer or poorer, in sickness and in health, until death do us part." When these promises are made with full knowledge of their meaning, God's love is manifested in the union of two people.

Talk It Over

1. Share something about the priest or religious sister or brother whom you know best. How is he or she a model of Christ for you?
2. How can freedom within the single life be productive? unproductive?
3. Discuss the rewards and difficulties you imagine accompanying the married life.
4. Think of a happily married couple that you know. What do you think it is about their relationship that makes them happy?

Faith and Commitment

"You don't seem to have any doubts about your vocation," Mark Verge said to Michael Evans.

"Well, most of the time I don't," Michael responded.

"Then, what's the problem?" asked Mark.

Michael answered quickly, "Commitment."

Commitment is the issue most people doubt in their own vocations, as well. An engaged couple will almost always wonder if they can really be faithful forever to their marriage vows. Religious novices will doubt their ability to be obedient. Seminarians question whether they can be faithful to the vow of chastity. Making any lifetime promise and then sticking to it is a difficult proposition.

Commitment means a "pledge of trust." In the sense of a religious vocation, this pledge is accompanied by faith. Practically, committing oneself to vows of poverty, chastity, and obedience in any form may seem to make little or no sense.

Religiously, commitment to a vocation makes a great deal of sense when seen through the eyes of faith.

Your basic Christian vocation has already begun. Baptized into the life of Christ as your first step, eventually you must choose and commit yourself to a particular life. In the years ahead, you will have the responsibility and the privilege of examining these possibilities, and in time, choosing a direction you feel is best for you.

Part of your responsibility is to make sure you're aware of all your options. How can you investigate the religious life, the Christian single life, or the vocation to marriage now, before you make a choice?

Sharpening Your Skills
Participation and Service

Explore ways that Christians participate more fully in their vocations by serving the needs of others. On your own or with a group of classmates, work on these project ideas:

1. Suppose you were put in charge of a parish and asked to make it a closer community of friends where all people would feel at home and be able to use their gifts and talents. Write your plan of action.
2. Compile a list of volunteer organizations and community programs that would offer a high school student the opportunity to serve others. Choose one project from that list and see what it takes to get involved.
3. You have been asked to further develop the role of the laity in the Church. What changes would you make and how would you go about implementing them?

Journal Assignment

"Write a diary entry as it might be written by an elderly widow or widower; a divorced person; a young person who has returned to the family nest; a career-minded individual; or a person who has made a commitment to the single life. How would the values and practices of Christian living be practiced?"

Talk It Over

1. Why is faith a necessary ingredient in making a Christian commitment?
2. Formulate a list of questions about the various vocations. Share these questions with a friend, family member, or trusted adult.

Priests take vows as a sign of their commitment to their vocation.

Chapter Summary

- Living out the vow of poverty means avoiding excess material possessions so that you may share your time and talents with those in need.
- Chastity is a virtue to be practiced by all Christians; consecrated chastity is the promise to remain celibate for life.
- The Gospel counsel of obedience is patterned on Christ's response to God.

- Vocations to the religious life are the ordained ministries of priesthood and diaconate, and the religious community model lived out by sisters and brothers.
- The vocation of marriage is a call to incorporate God's faithful love into the spousal relationship.

Talk It Over

For Question 1, ask the students how committing to the vows of poverty, chastity, and obedience only makes sense when looked at through the eyes of faith. Assign the students to jot down a list of questions as asked for in Question 2. Then, allow time for volunteers to discuss how they would implement some of their ideas. Categorize the ideas in terms of specific vocations. Save them to be addressed during the next unit.

Chapter Summary

- Before assigning the review exercises, ask students if they have any questions or comments on the material covered in Chapter 8.
- Have students read each statement. Or, you may wish to have the students read and discuss these statements in small groups before reporting back to the entire class.

Resources

Resource 8G presents a breakdown of the single population in the United States and asks the students questions that speculate on the reasons for the figures.

Journal Assignment

Finish this sentence: "To me, the ideal marriage would be . . ."

Chapter 8 Review

What Have You Learned?

Listed below are suggested answers. For many of the questions, the answers will vary.

1. At the time of his ordination to the transitional diaconate, Michael Evans would make public vows of poverty, chastity, and obedience. Permanent deacons may be married men; they usually also hold regular jobs while carrying out their vocational mission. Transitional deacons serve as deacons for only a short time before being ordained priests.

2. Saint Ignatius of Antioch said that Christians must be willing to suffer and die in the name of Christ.

3. Gospel counsels (poverty, chastity, and obedience) are codes of behavior that developed from the Good News of Jesus Christ.

4. Christians came to monasteries to be alone to find God. Monastic life soon led to the practice of the virtue of obedience and following the wishes of an abbot or abbess.

5. The virtue of poverty reminds us that there are more important things than money and possessions.

6. In consecrated chastity, the good gift of genital sexual relations in marriage is offered back to God.

7. Priests or religious who take a vow of obedience pledge to follow the wishes of a superior, either the leader of the community, or in the case of diocesan priests, the bishop.

8. Vocation means "calling."

9. A priest's ministry is sacramental, a religious brother's or sister's is not.

10. In both the single life and the diaconate, service to others is a crucial element of the vocation.

11. Matrimony is the only sacrament in which the sacrament is conferred by the participants themselves.

12. From a religious sense, commitment means "a pledge of trust accompanied by faith."

Background

REVIEW

What Have You Learned

1. Why was Michael Evans concerned about the diaconate? How does the permanent diaconate differ from the transitional diaconate?
2. According to Saint Ignatius of Antioch, what must a disciple be willing to do in the name of Christ?
3. What are the Gospel counsels?
4. Why did Christians living the Gospel counsels of poverty, chastity, and obedience come together in monasteries and convents?
5. How does the virtue of poverty serve as a reminder that we live in a transitory world?
6. How does consecrated chastity witness to the goodness of sexual relations in marriage?
7. In taking a vow of obedience, who does a priest or religious pledge to follow?
8. What is the meaning of vocation?
9. Explain a difference between the religious vocation of a priest and that of a religious sister or brother.
10. How is the single life similar to the diaconate?
11. What is unique about the sacrament of Matrimony?
12. What does commitment mean in a religious vocation?

Application

1. Peter said to Jesus: "We have given up our possessions and followed You" *(Luke 18:28)*. Read Jesus' response in Luke 18:29-30. What do Jesus' words mean for your life?
2. Investigate the life of Saint Ignatius of Antioch. Find out why he had special prominence in the early Church.
3. Research the emperor Constantine and his mother, Helena. What did each have to do with the legalization of Christianity in the Roman empire?
4. Write a short essay explaining how you can incorporate one of the Gospel counsels into your life right now.
5. Make a collage with photos representing many Christian vocations. Use it as a part of a "Vocation Awareness Week."
6. Arrange for a seminarian or a candidate from a religious community to visit your class. Ask how this person has felt God's call to service.
7. Write about one Christian vocation. Mention any benefits one might expect to receive from living this vocation.

Background

While priests are ordained in the sacrament of Holy Orders, and married couples celebrate the sacrament of marriage, religious brothers and sisters do not receive a specific sacrament for their lifestyle. They, instead, are "consecrated" in their vocations. (See the *Catechism of the Catholic Church*, 925-927.)

REVIEW

Chapter Vocabulary

- diaconate
- martyr
- Gospel counsels
- monastery
- vow
- consecrated chastity
- poverty
- obedience
- commitment
- priesthood
- religious
- permanent singles

Perhaps I am most afraid of the strength of God in me. Perhaps I would rather be guilty and weak in myself, than strong in Him who I cannot understand.

Thomas Merto

Putting Vocabulary to Use

Complete the following statements by supplying the missing word from the chapter vocabulary list.

1. The _____ is an ordained ministry with a presidential function in the Church.
2. _____ is a most difficult pattern of Christian living modeled on Jesus' acceptance of God's will for Himself.
3. _____ is a public testimony that shows the goodness of sexual relations between a husband and wife.
4. The _____ is an ordained ministry for married or single men.
5. A _____ is a promise of commitment made by Christians.
6. In a religious sense, "a pledge of trust accompanied by faith" is called a _____.
7. Teachings that came from Jesus' recommendations for behavior that were not unconditionally demanded of everyone are called the _____.
8. _____ are people who choose to commit to a lifestyle that affords the freedom to serve the needs of others personally.
9. _____ is a Greek word meaning "witness."
10. _____ is a vow that serves as a reminder that there is no purpose in having more things than we really need.
11. People who live in religious communities are called men or women _____.
12. A _____ is a place "to be alone."

163

Application

Have the students read the directions for each project. You may assign a particular project, or allow the students to choose a project they prefer. Allow some class time for the students to share their completed projects with others.

Putting Vocabulary to Use

1. priesthood
2. obedience
3. consecrated chastity
4. diaconate
5. vow
6. commitment
7. Gospel counsels
8. permanent singles
9. martyr
10. poverty
11. religious
12. monastery

Final Thought

Background

Thomas Merton was a Trappist monk and perhaps the best-known twentieth century contemplative. He wrote many books including his autobiography, *Seven Storey Mountain.* He died in 1968.

Focus on:
Chapter 9

A young man considering religious life admitted his doubts to an older priest. "There seems to be so much inconsistency," the young man said. "I know priests who drive expensive cars and travel the world staying in the best hotels. They hardly seem the model of discipleship." The older priest nodded. "I know some religious men and women like that myself," he said. "But, please remember this: those people are the exceptions we notice. Most of the people in religious life sincerely want to know God better—to pray, to work with God's people, and to live in community."

While all Christians are called to prayer, work, and community living, the ordained priest, the religious brother, and the religious sister, dedicate their lives to this calling. They give up everything else in order to pursue this life of faith.

Attempting a vocation to the religious life or priesthood seems more radical today than ever before. Yet, God still calls many young men and women to these vocations. What are the signs of a religious vocation? How would a young adult know if he or she was called to a religious vocation?

Chapter 9 examines the attraction of religious life. It distinguishes between the roles of religious brothers, sisters, and the ordained minister, the priest.

Plan Ahead

- Incorporate formal and/or spontaneous prayer into each lesson. A participatory prayer service that is suitable for use on retreat is provided in the Teacher's Resource Book.
- Note **Resource** suggestions which can be applied to, or used to extend, the lessons of this chapter.
- Preview the **Application** projects in the Chapter Review. Refer to **Teaching Approaches** for suggestions on when to assign the projects. Or, the projects may be used as part of lesson, section, or chapter reviews.
- Decide on a method for grouping students for projects and discussion.
- Invite guest speakers who will participate in selected lessons well in advance.

Answering a Call

He said to them, "Come after Me, and I will make you fishers of men."

Matthew 4:19

This chapter will help you to:

- Understand what attracts men and women to the religious life.
- Recognize the priest's ministry as both sacramental and pastoral.
- Investigate the religious life or priesthood as a personal vocation.

164

Media Suggestions (Optional)

- *Priestly Work: Nothing Human is Beyond God's Touch* (Franciscan Communications) 28 minutes. The film investigates the particular aspects of priesthood.

- *Religious Women* (Franciscan Communications) 29 minutes. These five vignettes focus on the different apostolates of religious women.

1. A ROAD LESS TRAVELED

Ministry is a part of every Christian's vocation. Those who participate in vowed religious life as sisters, brothers, or ordained ministers have chosen to live their ministry full-time. People who choose these vocations are responding to God's call to serve the Christian community. This radical acceptance of discipleship is not the response to faith chosen by most Christians. The poet Robert Frost wrote:

Two roads diverged in a wood, and I—
I took the one less traveled by,
And that has made all the difference.
from *"The Road Not Taken"*

Women and men who choose to respond to God in the vowed religious life have chosen a road less traveled. What is it about their lives that, indeed, makes "all the difference"?

165

Aims

1. To help students recognize that all Christians are called to live religious lives and reach for the attainable goal of sainthood.
2. To help students understand some of the fundamental differences between the laity, vowed religious, and ordained ministers.

Begin the Section

1. Ask the students to think about friends or peers who always seem bent on doing everything their own way. Ask: "What similar qualities do you find in these people and in priests or religious brothers or sisters who you know?" Make the point that living as a vowed religious requires a lifestyle different from that lived by most people.
2. Read the opener to the section. Ask: "What is appealing about taking the 'road less traveled'?"
3. Randomly pair the students. Have each student write a bold prediction for the future for his or her partner on an index card. Tape the index cards to a large piece of butcher paper, designed in the theme of many divergent roads. Title the banner, "Our Roads to Be Traveled."

Background

According to the Second Vatican Council, although the religious state of life established by the profession of the Gospel counsels "is not part of the Church's hierarchical structure," it "decidedly belongs to her life and holiness." (*Lumen Gentium,* 44) The Revised Code of Canon Law considers all people who are not ordained to be lay. That is the interpretation used in this text.

Called to Be

Lesson Overview

Through the stories of three famous Christians—Thomas Merton, Saint Thérèse of Lisieux, and Mother Teresa of Calcutta—this lesson examines what motivates and attracts people to religious vocations. A distinction is made between ordained ministers and lay people who profess vows as religious brothers or sisters. Students may have many questions about the subtleties of religious life. Allow time for them to present these questions. You may address the questions at your convenience throughout this chapter or invite a member of a religious community to answer them.

Teaching Approaches

- Introduce the story by sharing some biographical information on Thomas Merton: Thomas Merton was born in France in 1915, the son of artists. His mother was a Quaker. After she died when he was ten, Merton and his father settled in a small village in France. Almost everyone there was Catholic except Merton, who did not rush headlong into the faith.

    A writer and teacher of English at Columbia University in New York, Merton was baptized at age twenty-three. Shortly after his baptism, Merton decided to enter the monastery at Gethsemani, Kentucky and become a Trappist monk. As a monk, he wrote on many themes, particularly on a life of poverty, being a monk, and against war. Thomas Merton was accidently electrocuted in 1968, while on retreat in India. His spiritual writings are well-known today.

- Choose one or two good readers to read the story aloud.

- **Reteach**—Ask: "What are some qualities of a saint? What would you have to do to become a saint?"

- **Extend the Lesson**—Assign for reading and discussion specific chapters from Merton's autobiography, *The Seven Storey Mountain* (New York: Harcourt, Brace and Company, 1948).

Called to Be

Thomas Merton, who became a Catholic as a young adult, learned through a conversation with his friend, Lax, about the Christian attraction to holiness. A holy person is one who is filled with the presence of God. Merton, who soon after this conversation entered the religious community known as the Cistercians, recognized that the way to holiness for him was as a monk, and finally as a priest.

"What do you want to be, anyway?"

I could not say, "I want to be Thomas Merton, the well-known writer of all those book reviews in the back pages of the *Times Book Review,*" or "Thomas Merton, the assistant instructor of Freshman English at the New Life Social Institute for Progress and Culture," so I put the thing on the spiritual plane, where I knew it belonged and said:

"I don't know; I guess what I want is to be a good Catholic."

"What do you mean, you want to be a good Catholic?"

The explanation I gave was lame enough, and expressed my confusion, and betrayed how little I had really thought about it at all.

Lax did not accept it.

"What you should say," he told me, "what you should say is that you want to be a saint."

A saint! The thought struck me as a little weird. I said:

"How do you expect me to become a saint?"

"By wanting to," said Lax, simply.

"I can't be a saint," I said, "I can't be a saint." And my mind darkened with a confusion of realities and unrealities: the knowledge of my own sins, and the false humility which makes men say that they cannot do

Merton chose to follow his path to holiness as a Cistercian monk.

things that they *must* do, cannot reach the level that they *must* reach; the cowardice that says: "I am satisfied to save my soul, to keep out of mortal sin," but which means by those words: "I do not want to give up sins and my attachments."

But Lax said: "No. All that is necessary to be a saint is to want to be one. Don't you believe that God will make you what He created you to be, if you will consent to let Him do it? All you have to do is desire it."

The next day I told Mark Van Doren:

"Lax is going around saying that all a man needs to be a saint is to want to be one."

"Of course," said Mark.

All these people were much better Christians than I.

from "The Seven Storey Mountain"

Resources

Resource 9A from the Teacher's Resource Book lists samples of writings by Thomas Merton expressing one's vocation to a life with God.

Background

"The term *laity* is here understood to mean all the faithful except those in holy orders and those in a religious state sanctioned by the Church. These faithful are by Baptism made one body with Christ and are established

Actually, becoming a saint is the attainable goal of all the baptized. A saint is someone whose very life exemplifies the goodness of God on earth and in heaven. Holiness or sainthood is at the very heart of Christian life. For those who choose life in a religious community or as an ordained minister, the focus on holiness becomes a public goal—one struggled with, win or lose, in the presence of the rest of the community.

Understanding the Differences

The term "laity" refers to all of the baptized. It comes from the Greek phrase, *laos tou theou*, "the people of God." Within the laity are people called to special roles. Some are ordained for special activities in the Church, primarily related to its sacramental life. Priests and deacons are men who receive the sacrament of Holy Orders. Other men who profess vows, but who are not ordained, are known as religious brothers. Vowed women are known as religious sisters. Sisters and brothers are members of the laity just as you are.

It is the mission of all the laity to minister to the world through their daily lives. Priests and religious perform this ministry through lives of dedicated service to the Church; a way of life greatly different from those lived by most of the laity. The form of discipleship chosen by a man or woman who becomes a vowed religious is radical; that is, at the heart of Christian discipleship.

Religious sisters, priests, and brothers take the same vows in religious communities, and live similar lifestyles. Ordained priests who are members of religious communities, also serve as priests in their sacramental ministry. Sisters and brothers are neither ordained ministers, nor do they have the same roles in the Church that priests do.

Choosing Religious Life

Why would a young adult in the last decade of the twentieth century choose to live the vowed religious life? Tricia asked herself that question. After college she'd worked for a few years and was making a great deal of money, but she wasn't satisfied. She dated regularly and participated in her parish's singles group, but that, too, wasn't enough. She longed for good friends with whom she could share her dreams. The singles group had dances and a Bible study group that met once a week, but Tricia still wanted something more. Tricia felt the need for a supportive prayer community.

Tricia decided to quit her job and work for a year at a shelter for runaway youth. During her year, Tricia realized that, while her work was now more satisfying, her life still seemed empty. Seeing a notice in the parish bulletin, she went on a weekend retreat offered by the Sisters of Mercy.

Although Tricia left her job to work with troubled youth, she realized that something else was missing from her life.

among the People of God. They are in their own way made sharers in the priestly, prophetic, and kingly functions of Christ. They carry out their own part in the mission of the whole Christian people with respect to the Church and the world" *(Lumen Gentium)*.

Resources

Resource 9B from the Teacher's Resource Book examines the attitudes of Catholics towards ministry and Church leadership.

Understanding the Differences

Teaching Approaches

- Have the students read these paragraphs individually or with a partner.
- Ask questions to review the students' understanding. Have them write their answers to the following questions on scratch paper: Are religious brothers and sisters ordained ministers? Are religious brothers and sisters lay people? Do priests of religious orders and religious brothers and sisters profess the same vows? Are priests and religious holier than lay people?
- Check and discuss their answers.
- **Reteach**—Discuss how living a vocation as a lay person is different from that of a priest or religious.
- **Extend the Lesson**—Have the students develop a class mural depicting life on the edge between this world and the next.

Choosing Religious Life

Teaching Approaches

- Ask: "What do you do when you want to get to know a person who you like more intimately?" Take several suggestions. Then, ask the students to apply these ideas to their relationship with Jesus.
- Provide biographical information, as needed, on Saint Thérèse of Lisieux and Mother Teresa: Saint Thérèse of Lisieux was born Thérèse Martin in Lisieux, France in 1873. She entered the Carmelite convent at age fifteen. She modeled her "little way" of service on the littlest of flowers that serve God's creation. Before she died, at age twenty-four, she wrote: "I want to spend my heaven doing good on earth."

  Mother Teresa was born Agnes Boyaxhui in Skopje, Yugoslavia in 1910. In 1946, she left the Sisters of Loretto when she "heard the call to give up all to follow Him into the slums and to serve among the poorest of the poor." She is the foundress of the Missionaries of Charity.
- Read or summarize the text section.
- **Reteach**—Assign **Application** Project 2 for individual reports.
- **Extend the Lesson**—Invite a person preparing to enter religious life to visit and speak with the students.

Talk It Over

All three questions may be used as journal entries. If the students do write their responses, allow time in small groups or with the entire class for those who wish to share what they have written.

Living the Difference

Lesson Overview

God's kingdom exists outside of time; time has no bounds on it. The thought of this realm beyond a world controlled by time is appealing to many people.

Part of the attraction of religious life is to a lifestyle that exists in and for the kingdom. Prayer, work, and community living take on a different significance when done for the kingdom. Discuss the attraction of religious life with the students. Ask them what they think they could accomplish if their lives were devoted to God as a religious.

Teaching Approaches

- Read or summarize the opening paragraph.
- **Reteach**—Ask: "How are prayer, work, and community living a part of your life right now?"
- **Extend the Lesson**—Ask: "How much time do you spend each week in prayer, working, and building community life?"

In Prayer

New Words

The word *contemplative* traditionally has been used to describe a person who lives a cloistered existence. Through his or her practice of prayer, self-mortification, and work, everything is directed toward God.

The *Divine Office,* or *Liturgy of the Hours,* is the public prayer of the Church. Its daily recitation is the sacred duty of most religious and priests. In the revised Liturgy of the Hours, the prayers are shorter than in past editions. The psalms are prayed over a four-week period instead of during a week. Additional readings are also included from the Church Fathers and the lives of the saints.

Humility and an unconditional obedience to God are characteristics of Benedict's rule—summed up by the saying *laborare est orare.* Work and prayer alike are to be carried out with a profound sense of God's presence.

She was attracted to the experience she had on the retreat. She especially was moved by the idea of living with other people who felt called by God. Six months later, after much prayer and soul searching, late night conversations with friends, and guidance from the Sisters of Mercy's Vocations Director, Tricia made the decision to enter religious life.

Tricia's journey to religious life is not unusual. Many of the men and women who accept a vocation to religious life or priesthood tell similar stories. They are not satisfied by their work, they miss having a supportive community, and they experience a great longing for prayer.

For centuries, people have been drawn to religious life by the call of intense prayer, work, and community living. A person who chooses vowed religious life is usually attracted to a religious community because of its lifestyle of service and its focus on spirituality. But the ultimate attraction is Jesus. Religious seek to deepen their relationships with Jesus, just as a married couple seeks to deepen their relationship with each other.

What do you learn about the desire for religious life from these stories:

◊ Shortly after Saint Thérèse of Lisieux took her final vows as a Carmelite nun, she was visited at the convent by her recently married cousin, Jeanne. Jeanne told Thérèse about her deep love for her husband. Thérèse was stirred by her cousin's words. She said to herself; "It's not going to be said that a woman will do more for her husband, a mere mortal, than I will do for my beloved Jesus." Thérèse retired to her room and composed a wedding invitation announcing the union between Jesus, "the King of Kings and Lord of Lords and Little Thérèse Martin." Thérèse is remembered for having celebrated this union throughout the rest of her life.

◊ Mother Teresa of Calcutta, the founder of the Missionaries of Charity, explained that the vocation of her community "is to belong to Jesus with the conviction that nothing can separate us from the love of Christ." In Jesus, the religious prays, works, and builds community both at home, with his or her brothers or sisters, and in the Church and world at large. Mother Teresa writes, "Just as God sent Jesus to be His love, His presence in the world, so today He is sending us."

Talk It Over

1. How would you respond to Lax's reasoning that "all that is necessary to be a saint is to want to be one"? What are some obstacles that young adults experience while trying to achieve this goal?
2. What are some of the ways people "live on the edge" besides the religious life?
3. In what ways can you now deepen your relationship with Jesus?

Living the Difference

As mentioned earlier, three practices that set vowed religious off from the rest of the People of God are their devotion to prayer, work, and community living. All of these aspects are, of course, essential to the life of all the baptized. Vowed religious, however, commit their lives to these practices in a special way.

In Prayer

Prayer is essential to religious living. A life of good works, not rooted in communication with God through Jesus Christ, is incomplete. Prayer brings God to the heart of the work and finishes it. Prayer keeps the work focused, in and for God.

Resources

Resource 9C provides relevant quotations by Saint Thérèse of Lisieux, Thomas Merton, and Mother Teresa.

Background

See the *Catechism of the Catholic Church,* 925-927.

Many vowed religious spend approximately three hours a day in prayer. The time is divided between participation at Mass, praying the daily prayers of the Church, and praying alone. Men and women who have committed themselves to *contemplative* religious communities spend even more of their day in prayer. Members of these communities focus their lives on contemplative, meditative, and reflective prayer. Thomas Merton became a contemplative monk. His quest for a fuller life brought him to seek admittance to the Cistercian monastery at Gethsemane, Kentucky.

The founder of communal religious life was Saint Benedict. Benedict wrote a rule for monks, inviting them to pray seven times each day from the early morning until late at night. Together they prayed from the *Divine Office,* a collection of psalms and readings from Scripture. In between, they would perform the work necessary to sustain them. *Laborare est orare*—"to work is to pray"— is one of Benedict's most memorable sayings.

There was also time assigned for suitable recreation and relaxation. When they retired to their rooms, literally small cells, for rest, they would continue in private prayer. It was once said that "The monk in his cloister is like the cow cared for in the stable: he ruminates constantly on Jesus Christ as the cow on the hay brought to the manger."

Most religious men and women today, although they don't belong to a contemplative community, still are dedicated to this life of prayer. Mother Teresa has explained how her order, though active in service of the world's "poorest of the poor," were actually contemplatives who lived their prayer in the heart of the world:

> "The work we do is only our love for Jesus in action. And that action is our wholehearted and free service to Christ in the distressing disguise of the poor. If we pray the work—if we do it to Jesus, if we do it for Jesus, if we do it with Jesus—that's what makes us content."

✿ Prayer in Action
How I Pray

You may ask me how I pray, what I say to God. My form of prayer is very simple. I'm afraid I do not know how to pray and so it is very difficult for me to speak of prayer, but I will tell you how we pray. Very often I go to the chapel because our lives are interwoven fully with the Mass, Holy Communion, and our poor people. Christ in the Blessed Sacrament and Christ in the distressing guise of the poor is the same Christ for us and so we try to pray always by 'praying the work.' Very often I go to chapel and I tell the Lord, 'I don't know how to pray; you pray in me to the Father.' And I think He does it better than me. We try to pray the work because Christ cannot deceive us, and it is He we touch all the time in the poor!"

Mother Teresa

Christ's Work

What distinguishes the people who are members of religious communities from people who simply share a house or a job? Do they work any harder to accomplish their tasks? Have they been given special help by God (grace) that is denied others?

One thing that sets religious communities apart from other groups is that they are joined together by a shared vision to work toward a common purpose. Like the Missionaries of Charity who are directed by Mother Teresa's command to "see Christ in each person you meet," religious men and women focus on meeting a specific need or solving a particular problem.

Most religious communities were founded by a man or woman who felt called to care for God's people in a particular way. The vision of these

---

In Prayer

Teaching Approaches

- Assign the students a simple task—for example, rearranging the desks or chairs in the room. Tell them that their work must be done in complete silence. After they have finished, say: "One part of religious life means combining physical work with prayerful reflection." Then ask: "How would living like this be difficult? Why do you think combining prayer and work would be considered important?"

- Read or summarize the section from the text. Clarify the meaning of new words and phrases.

- **Reteach**—Explain that the rule of Saint Benedict is practiced today by communities of men and women. According to 1985 data, there were 9,453 monks living in 383 houses in the United States, and 7,911 nuns living in 351 American communities.

  In daily prayer, Benedictines recite the Divine Office (often in English), celebrate Eucharist, spend hours in adoration of Christ in the Blessed Sacrament and in personal prayer in the form of *lectio divina,* or reflective reading. The schedule of prayer is balanced by work and study activities. Benedictines farm, give retreats, publish magazines, make altar breads and church vestments, work as artists, care for the sick, fight for justice, teach, perform prison ministry, and serve in parishes, along with many other ministries.

- **Extend the Lesson**—Choose two groups to debate this statement: "There is no more important action in the world today than prayer."

✿ Prayer in Action

Teaching Approaches

- Ask: "How does this prayer of Mother Teresa express the combined action of work and prayer?"

- Have the students devise a way to "work and pray."

Resource

Resource 9D provides a copy of part of the rule of Saint Benedict.

Background

St. Thérèse of Lisieux wrote, "For me, prayer means launching out the heart towards God . . . a cry of grateful love, from the crest of joy or the trough of despair."

Christ's Work

Teaching Approaches

- Have the students discuss the meaning of the phrase "deeds rather than words." Then, choose several students to read the text section aloud. Ask: "How did witnessing to the practice of deeds, rather than words, affect Saint Dominic's life?"

- Using a directory of religious communities, have the students match one of their own particular talents or interests with an order that specializes in that apostolic work.

- Recall for students the parallel lives of Saints Dominic and Francis. Both men founded religious orders near the turn of the thirteenth century. In 1210, Francis had asked Pope Innocent III for approval of his way of life. Dominic founded his *Order of Preachers* in 1214 at Toulouse, France. In 1218, the Dominican Rule was established. The main focus of this order has always been "educated preaching." Both the Dominican and Franciscan orders emphasize the virtue of Christian poverty.

- **Reteach**—Assign **Application** Project 4.

- **Extend the Lesson**—Provide the students with names and addresses of vocation directors of a variety of religious communities for men and women, including all of those active in your diocese, if possible. Have the students write and request information on the specific ministries performed by members of the order. (See also: **Application** Project 3.)

In Focus

Teaching Approaches

- Read and comment on the information presented.

- If possible, arrange for the students to interview or write a letter to a religious brother. Have the students inform the religious of the survey and elicit their comments. This assignment may be used with **Application** Project 1.

---

founders continues to shape the actions of their followers long after the founder's death. One example of this is Dominic Guzman.

Early in the thirteenth century, Dominic became aware of the Albigensians. (The name comes from "Albi," a town in the south of France.) These people falsely believed in two gods: a good, spiritual god and an evil god who made all material things. The Albigensians believed that human souls were held prisoners in their bodies. The only way to escape from evil was to renounce all material possessions. Those who did so were honored as gods themselves.

Dominic preached among the Albigensians and converted them from their error. Dominic became convinced that this was his life's work. At

---

In Focus
Religious Brothers

A recent study by the Center for Applied Research at Georgetown University in Washington, D.C. shows that personal contact with a brother helps foster religious vocations. Unfortunately, there is less contact between brothers and male students than in the past, and so fewer vocations to the brotherhood.

According to the study, morale is high among the brothers. They chose words like "caring," "hardworking," "approachable," and "generous" to describe each other. Students who participated in the study picked "kind and caring," intelligent," "dedicated and generous," and "religious man" to describe brothers they know.

Ninety-seven percent of brothers said they were proud of their vocation, 95 percent were proud to be teachers, and 90 percent said that one of their closest friends is a member of their congregation.

---

the same time, he wondered thoughtfully why the priests in the area had not been able to correct the Albigensians. Dominic concluded that the local priests' lifestyle interfered with their message. When the local priests came to preach, they were accompanied by many servants. Dominic realized that he could reach the Albigensians, when the Cistercians could not, because of his life of poverty.

Dominic gathered a group of men around him to preach the Gospel. These men used prayer, penance, preaching, informal discussions, and public debates to reach the Albigensians. Where the Cistercians had once traveled with swords, Dominic and his followers wore rosary beads.

Dominic and his followers lived in extreme poverty, depending on charity for their food and clothing. This order of preachers became known as *mendicants* or beggars. Their public witness and preaching revived the faith of Europe.

Dominicans today (priests, brothers, and sisters) continue to follow the vision of Saint Dominic. Their approved charter (or constitution) says, "Our order was specially instituted from the beginning for preaching and the salvation of souls." For more than 800 years, men and women have kept Dominic's idea alive by preaching and witnessing to the power of God's Word.

There are hundreds of religious communities (also known as religious orders or religious congregations) in the Church, most founded by charismatic leaders, like Dominic, for the purpose of meeting a need not being met by anyone else: educating children, caring for orphans, tending the sick, and many other concerns. For example, Franciscans follow the vision of Francis of Assisi, Vincentians, that of Vincent de Paul, Claretians, that of Anthony Claret, and the Sisters of Charity, that of Elizabeth Ann Seton.

For religious today, service comes under many titles and is done in many traditional and nontraditional ways. Men and women religious are teachers, nurses, and missionaries, but also farmers, engineers, public servants, publishers, and college presidents.

Resources

A Guide to Religious Ministries for Catholic Men and Women (New York: The Catholic News Publishing Company) provides an in-depth list of religious communities and their apostolic works.

The freedom provided by their lives as religious affords them countless opportunities to serve the needs of humanity.

With Community

◊ The day begins with a breakfast shared with some of the members of the local community. By 6:45 [am], eight or ten of us gather... [for] common prayer. Though some days it is difficult to find the coffee pot in the morning, let alone be ready to pray at 6:45, it is a very important part of a day which should be dedicated to doing the Lord's work. The school day at Bourgade Catholic High School begins at 8:15... During some seasons of the year, school business takes me away from some community gatherings, but the opportunities to be with the community for meals, prayer, or just informally, gives meaning to all the rest, and provides the spirit and incentive with which to continue.

Father Donald Fetters C.S.C.

What does it mean to live as a member of a community? What is it like for you to live in your family? According to Father Donald Fetters, a religious priest of the Holy Cross order and a teacher at a Catholic high school, family life and community life often have a lot in common. "How was school today?" your father might ask. From the kitchen you hear, "Whose turn is it to do the dishes?" "Not mine, I cooked dinner," you shout proudly. "Can anyone help me with this problem?" asks your sister. In the same way members of religious communities share household responsibilities, discuss the events of the day, and assist each other to solve problems.

Your family is a small Christian community in a way similar to that of religious orders. In the case of religious, everyone is a responsible adult and no one is the parent. The members of the community establish the incidental rules for daily living needed to maintain order. The vision of the founder, the constitution, and the order's rules cover the major activities of each individual small community.

The need for shared friendships and affirmation from those who have taken the same vows and share in the same work was never lost on the founders of apostolic orders. The religious brothers and priests of the Holy Cross, for example—whether a teacher like Father Fetters, a retreat director, or the director of a medical facility—live together in local community settings for this friendship and affirmation.

Traditionally, religious men lived together in monasteries or rectories, while religious women lived in convents. Community living today allows for much more flexibility than experienced in those previous options.

Sometimes, because of a variety of jobs and places of employment, large numbers of religious are not able to live together. Sister Jane Kelly and Sister Ann Veronica are Religious Sisters of the Holy Names of Jesus and Mary who live together in a house, not in a convent with other sisters.

Women religious today often live in small communities.

With Community

Teaching Approaches

- Present the students with these two different scenarios: (1) You won $1,000 dollars at a raffle; (2) Your doctor informs you that you will need exploratory surgery. Ask: "With whom would you share these experiences? How would these experiences be different if you had no one with whom to share them?"

- Read or summarize the text section. Ask volunteers to comment on the importance of living in community—of having someone with whom to share experiences—for religious life.

- **Reteach**—Explain that the Second Vatican Council referred to Scripture in describing the importance of the community life for religious: "As Christ's members living fraternally together, let them excel one another in showing respect *(cf. Romans 12:10)*, and let each carry the other's burdens *(cf. Galatians 6:2)*. For thanks to God's love poured into hearts by the Holy Spirit *(cf. Romans 5:5)*, a religious community is a true family gathered together in the Lord's name and rejoicing in His presence *(Matthew 18:20)*" *(Decree on the Appropriate Renewal of Religious Life,* #15).

- **Extend the Lesson**—Families are natural communities. Religious communities, much like schools, must form around the people who belong. What are some of the difficulties students have with forming community within the school? How would people in religious life face the same challenges?

Journal Assignment

Complete this sentence: "The times I need someone most are when . . . "

Talk It Over

For Question 1, brainstorm a list of suggestions with the students. Use some of these suggestions in the development of future lessons. To extend Question 2, have the students research how Christians are presently active in ministry. For Question 3, ask volunteers to role play their answer before the class. If possible, they may even dress in religious habits.

☀ Media Watch
Brand X Versus Brand Y

The basic message in advertising is always the same: buy our product and your various needs will be met. Your problems will vanish. In other words, material things can take care of your personal and interpersonal problems.

What about advertising for membership in religious orders? What do these ads try to sell? A few years ago, a religious order of priests ran ads with Father Guido Sarducci of "Saturday Night Live" fame. His claim was "Be a priest. See the world. Eat in the finest restaurants." Effective or not? A religious order of men ran a different ad in "Playboy" magazine in which they tried to reach those men struggling to find meaning in their lives. The order received many letters complaining that advertising revenue supported pornography. What do you think about this approach? How does where advertisements appear affect their messages?

Carefully examine the "vocation ads" pictured here. Analyze them. Determine which ads provide the most information about the religious order. Which ad interests you to the point that you might seek to find out more about the order? Discuss your ideas with a partner or in a small group.

After making her profession of vows as a Holy Names, Sister Jane taught theology at a Catholic high school. Today, she conducts workshops on healing near Ventura, California.

Sister Ann Veronica has been a Holy Names sister since 1941 and has taught virtually every grade, including 15 years as a high school business instructor. She's also served as a parish minister offering support to the families of deceased parishioners.

Jane and Ann share a two-bedroom house. Ann has set up prayer and mini-retreat rooms for the people Jane counsels. They find consolation in each other: "We do often miss the celebrative atmosphere of living in the larger community. But we are still with the rest of our group in spirit and prayer. And, Annie and I have formed a remarkable kinship. We are community."

Talk It Over

1. How can you incorporate the motto "to work is to pray" into your own life?
2. What are some of the most important needs that might be addressed by followers of Christ? What do you think is the role of religious men and women in meeting these needs?
3. Imagine yourself as a religious brother or sister. Discuss what would be the greatest challenge for you in that life.

Ordained Ministers

Priests can also be members of religious communities, which can be confusing. Here's the explanation: A *diocesan* priest is not a member of a religious community. He is ordained to serve the Church, usually in the well-defined geographic area of a diocese. He does not take the vow of poverty. At ordination, the diocesan priest promises celibacy and obedience to the bishop. Most often, a diocesan priest (also called a secular priest) works in a parish. But he may also work as a teacher, as a chaplain in a hospital or prison, or as a campus minister.

A religious order priest, like a vowed religious brother or sister, is a member of a religious community. The difference between him and the other religious is that a religious priest is ordained: he receives the sacrament of Holy Orders. Unlike diocesan priests, his service is not restricted to a particular diocese or bishop. His obedience is promised to the superior of his order, and he may be called to serve anywhere around the world. Religious order priests promise to live the vows of poverty, chastity, and obedience within a supporting religious community. Because each religious community has a special mission or focus, aspirants to religious life can choose an order

Priests are ordained to lead the community in worship. Priests are sacramental ministers.

Background

Celibacy presumes a perfect and complete love and absorption in Jesus: "Celibacy is not a natural phenomenon; it can be a charism. A charism is a grace, a supernatural gift, not dependent on, or even accessible to, human will alone. A charism is not chosen but is received as a special calling" ("Double-talk on Celibacy," Dr. Richard Sipe, *The Tablet*, May 16,1992).

Ordained Ministers

Lesson Overview

Understanding the difference between a diocesan priest, a religious priest, and a religious who is not ordained is one focus of the lesson. Also, the students' main experience of priesthood may be sacramental. Emphasize the pastoral aspect of a priest's ministry. Point out that, as with other religious, a priest's special ministry is most often dependent on his particular gifts and talents.

New Words

Diocesan priests finish high school, four years of college, and then four and a half more years of graduate study before ordination. The graduate study is usually completed at a seminary.

The *sacramental ministry* and *pastoral ministry* of the priest are intimately and unbreakably united. The purpose of both ministries is "the glory of God the Father as it is to be achieved in Christ" (*Decree on the Ministry and Life of Priests,* #2).

Teaching Approaches

- Ask a Catholic—lay person or priest—familiar with the Church before the Second Vatican Council, to share with the class how the role of the priest has evolved during his or her lifetime.
- Read or summarize the first paragraph. Make sure the students understand the distinctions between religious, religious priest, and diocesan or secular priest.
- Finish reading the section.
- Ask the students to list specific sacramental and pastoral ministries. Write their suggestions in appropriate columns on the board.
- **Reteach**—Explain that priests of the Latin rite are celibate, meaning that they do not marry. This practice began in the fourth century and was mandated during the twelfth century. A special dispensation has been granted to married Anglican priests who become Catholic, so that they may be ordained Catholic priests, yet remain married.

  Eastern rite priests may marry, but they must do so before they are ordained to the diaconate. They may not marry after ordination. Eastern rite bishops are celibates.
- **Extend the Lesson**—Discuss the importance of celibacy to the role of priesthood. How would the role of a priest change if celibacy were not required?

Holy Orders

Teaching Approaches

- Check the students' understanding of the divisions of Holy Orders as you cover the different levels of ordained ministers.
- **Reteach**—Ask the students to recall the story of Michael Evans from Chapter 8. Ask: "What is the difference between a permanent and transitional deacon?"
- **Extend the Lesson**—Have students prepare a report on the pope and their local bishop.

based on how their talents and gifts will be used in ministry. Men who wish to teach, but feel called to priesthood, often become members of an order that considers teaching their special ministry.

The ministry of priesthood is twofold: *sacramental,* and *pastoral.* It is sacramental because priests officiate at the celebration of sacraments, and receive the sacrament of Holy Orders. The priest's ministry is also pastoral. "Pastor" is a word that means "shepherd," or "one who cares for sheep." In this sense, a pastor is someone who cares for the needs of parishioners. The pastoral nature of a priest's ministry is service *oriented,* taking as its origins the image of Jesus as the servant who washed the feet of His disciples *(John 13:1-20).*

Holy Orders

The sacrament of Holy Orders is divided into three levels:

1. Episcopacy.
2. Presbyterate.
3. Diaconate.

Episcopacy. The word bishop comes from the Greek word "episkopos," meaning "overseer." Through the episcopacy, bishops are granted, along with the pope, the fullness of authority from the Apostles. Bishops ordain priests and deacons, confer the sacraments, and participate in other ministries within their dioceses. Bishops are responsible for the spiritual welfare of all the people within their dioceses. They meet in councils and Synods with the pope to provide guidance for the Church. The pope is the Bishop of Rome, selected from among other bishops as the leader of the Church.

Presbyterate. Priests, or presbyters, are ordained by the bishop to proclaim the Gospel and

minister personally to the People of God. People generally are more familiar with the role of the priesthood than they are of the role of bishop. Priests administer parishes, counsel people in need, visit the sick, celebrate the sacraments, raise money, conduct wedding rehearsals, lead wake services and bury the dead, and do just about anything that can be imagined. Priests are also teachers, community organizers, public speakers, lawyers, doctors, research scientists, scholars, and photographers, just to name a few professions not normally considered when one thinks about the priesthood.

Diaconate. A new opportunity for Christian service was made available in some dioceses with

Permanent Deacons are often married. The wife of a permanent deacon often participates in ministry with her husband.

Resources

Resource 9E provides a format for reviewing Holy Orders. Answers: (1) episcopacy, presbyterate, diaconate; (2) overseer; (3) the Apostles; (4) true; (5) answers will vary (For example, administer parishes, visit the sick, celebrate the sacraments); (6) charity, word, and sacrament; (7) false; (8) the deacon assists at eucharist, celebrates the sacrament of Baptism, witnesses and blesses marriages, officiates at the Rite of Christian burial, and presides at prayer services.

the restoration of the order of Permanent Diaconate. Deacons are not "little priests," nor are they the "priest helpers." Deacons are responsible to the bishop, serving in the ministries of charity, word, and sacrament. The ministry of charity is the main focus of the deacon's vocation. The services he performs depend upon his own abilities as well as the needs of the Church. He may serve the handicapped, the imprisoned, the chemically dependent, or others who need Christ's love. There is hardly a category of needy people not being served by deacons. In his ministry of the word, the deacon proclaims the Gospel and preaches and teaches the Gospel message, just as do priests and bishops. In his ministry of sacrament, the deacon assists the priest or bishop at the eucharistic liturgy, distributes Eucharist, celebrates the sacrament of Baptism, witnesses and blesses marriages, officiates at the Rite of Christian Burial, and presides at prayer services.

Formation for Religious Life

How long does it take to become a diocesan priest? Is that time different for religious order priests? How about being a sister or brother? The answers to these questions differ according to religious community and dioceses, but the following answers normally apply.

Most priests are required to successfully complete four years of graduate study after college, or eight years after high school, the same as for many professions. Many dioceses also require an extra year of internship so that the seminarian (priest candidate) can gain experience at parish ministry. The internship year also allows the seminary to evaluate the student on his ministerial skills. The final period of time prior to priesthood is spent as a deacon. This period may last anywhere from three months to several years.

Called transitional deacons, these men are ordained and function just as permanent deacons do. Few of these men remain deacons long,

however. Most are ordained to the priesthood within a year or less.

Men preparing for the priesthood as members of religious communities go through an additional formation process, similar to that of sisters and brothers. The following generally applies to all men and women preparing to enter religious life.

When men or women join religious communities they are called candidates. During this time of initiation, they begin to learn about the congregation directly. They may live as a member of the community, or continue to live on their own. A person may remain a candidate for a few months or even for several years.

Following candidacy, men and women enter the novitiate, a year or more of self-assessment and deep study into the religious congregation's charism and history. During this time the community also comes to a better understanding of the novice.

At the end of this period, the novice and community decide if it is right for them to continue together. If so, he or she makes temporary vows of poverty, chastity, and obedience for a set number of years. The individual lives the life of a religious until he or she makes final vows. These men and women will usually continue their studies or work in a religious ministry while in temporary vows. They may leave the community at any time while under their temporary vows. They make a permanent commitment when they profess their final vows, often three to five years after pledging their temporary vows. Seminarians who are also members of a religious community are usually required to make final vows before they are ordained to the priesthood.

Talk It Over

1. In your own words, explain the meaning of the words "religious," "religious priest," and "diocesan priest."
2. When you think of the priesthood do you focus more on sacramental or pastoral ministry? Explain your answer.

Formation for Religious Life

New Words

The *candidacy* or *postulancy* period usually occurs during or after college. The candidate may spend a short period of time living with the community in order to become exposed to the spiritual and community life of the members.

The *novitiate* marks the official entry into the community. During the novitiate, the novice prays and studies to learn more about his or her relationship with God and the community, and comes to a greater understanding of what it means to be committed to this religious order.

Teaching Approaches

- Discuss this selection with the students. What image do they have about religious formation?
- Have the students write one question they have about the priesthood or religious life on a slip of paper. Answer the questions as you can, or incorporate them into future lessons.
- **Reteach**—Compile the questions on a list and present them, as appropriate, to a priest and a religious. Ask them to write their answers to the question.
- **Extend the Lesson**—Invite local vocation directors to address the class and share their answers to the questions personally with the students.

Talk It Over

Use Question 1 for review. Randomly check students for understanding. For Question 2, allow students to share a variety of ideas and explanations with the large group.

Background

Bishops are the successors or representatives of the Apostles. Bishops have the fullness of the priesthood. Priests are under the jurisdiction of the bishops. Bishops can ordain priests and other bishops. Also, as apostolic successors, bishops are charged with proclaiming Christ's teaching in their dioceses.(See the *Catechism of the Catholic Church,* 1554-1571.)

II. WELCOMING GOD

As members of the pilgrim Church we are members of the communion of saints that bridges heaven and earth. But what of our varying degrees of sainthood? What follow-up is required of us to answer the question: "Do I want to be a saint?"

Ultimately, it is God's providence that directs the course of our lives. The gifts of the Holy Spirit, poured out in different ways determines who we are to become. But we are co-participants in this plan.

If we are to be saints, we must listen carefully to God's call, no matter what our eventual earthly vocations entail. The decision to marry, to profess religious vows, or to receive Holy Orders, is not entirely our own decision. It is a call from God, a "vocation" to which we respond. It is a call that is communicated to us through the Holy Spirit. It is a call that will not and cannot be silenced until we give an answer.

Shared Priesthood

A key word for priests today is collaboration. By virtue of Baptism, all Christians share in the priestly, prophetic, and kingly mission of Jesus. This understanding of a shared priesthood, practiced by members of the first-century Church, has been reemphasized in the past 30 years. Priests

and laity collaborate by sharing roles as ministers at Eucharist, as well as in the pastoral work involved in serving God's People.

The *priest*, in the Hebrew Scriptures, was the one who offered sacrifice. For Catholics, the priest offers the sacrifice during the Eucharist. The priest is also the leader of the community, especially in prayer. Historically it was the priest who *offered* the sacrifice of the Mass for the community with little or no lay involvement. Now, through the special ministries of the Word and Eucharist, the laity have more visible and better defined roles at the Eucharistic celebration. The community at large is an active participant, offering with the priest a prayer of thanksgiving.

To be a *prophet* means to share the Good News of the kingdom and to interpret it in light of the signs of the time. The priest does this by preaching the Gospel and challenging us to live each day as disciples of Jesus. He also does this through his promise of celibacy. By not marrying or having children, the priest reminds us that the kingdom of God is more important than anything else on earth. The community shares this role of prophet, too, when it places kingdom values above the world's values.

The *kingly* function of priesthood is that of authority and services. The priest speaks in the name of the bishop (or superior), and through him, in the name of the Church itself. We can trust in the priests' guidance, even though we recognize that they are simply men. Because we share in the kingly nature of Christ, Christians have the responsibility to make decisions of conscience for themselves.

In any collaborative effort, there must be a center of focus. The ordained priest provides the focus for both the sacramental and pastoral ministry of a parish. This function of the ordained minister has not wavered since Jesus first chose the Apostles to help Him initiate God's kingdom on earth.

Sharpening Your Skills
To Be a Priest

Read the following Scripture passages and note the qualities in each which should mark those ordained for service in the Church: Matthew 4:19, 5:14-16, 10:2-6; Mark 10:28-31; Luke 4:32, 22:26; John 10:14-15; and Hebrews 5:1-6.

- **Reteach**—Discuss how priests can also be prophets.
- **Extend the Lesson**—Use the suggestion from **Application** Project 5 at this time.

Sharpening Your Skills

Teaching Approaches

- Have the students write one or two adjectives for each Scripture citation that describes "qualities" of those ordained for service.
- Jesus' call of the Twelve Apostles *(Matthew 10:2-6)* is the clearest sign of a chosen priesthood. Many people may debate about who is qualified for priesthood, but few doubt that Jesus intended someone for the role of an ordained leader.

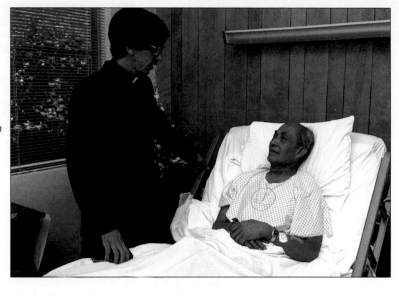

Why are priests often treated with great respect.

Images of Priesthood

Ask several adult Catholics to offer their descriptions of the priesthood, and you will hear several images described. According to college professor Father Robert Schwartz, "Many adults grew up understanding the priest primarily as a cultic figure endowed with *mystical powers* imparted at ordination." How would you describe a priest? a business figure extraordinaire? a person responsible for church property and activity? a person who says Mass and hears confessions? a fundraiser and accountant?

Priests are often treated with great respect. Father Schwartz recalled visiting an elderly parishioner in the hospital who had been unconscious for weeks. Before he left, Father Schwartz offered to give the man a blessing. Suddenly, reverently, the man carefully made the Sign of the Cross. He never responded to any other gesture.

Some adults have more negative images of priests. To them, a priest signifies the voice behind a screen that scolded them as youngsters in the confessional. Or their image of a priest may be associated with Church rules that condemn their sexual behavior.

Your own image of the priesthood, hopefully, is somewhat more balanced. You may know the priest as a leader of sacramental worship and as an active member of your parish community. Your main image of a priest may focus on his practice of celibacy or the fact that all Roman Catholic priests are male. These images shape an individual's understanding of priesthood. They also play a part in the priest's own acceptance of his special role in the Christian community.

There is great concern in much of Europe and the Americas concerning the shortage of vocations to the priesthood and religious life. In the United States, there is also great concern because of the rising age of priests and religious. There are many more priests and religious over 50 than there are under 50. What happens when these older men and women retire or become too ill to work full-time?

Images of Priesthood

Teaching Approaches

- Have the students write a poem, personal memory, or reflection expressing their images of the priesthood.
- Ask volunteers to share their images of priests. Compare these images with those of pre-Second Vatican Council Catholics.
- Say: "Having a proper image of the priest means focusing on the priesthood of Jesus, rather than on the priest as a man; the one who is merely His representative."
- **Reteach**—Have the students write or share their answers to the in-text questions.
- **Extend the Lesson**—Discuss: "Why would anyone choose to be a priest today?"

Rather, the priest at the altar acts only in virtue of an *office* committed to him by the community.

Resources

Resources 9F lists the text of the Scripture passages suggested in the "Sharpening Your Skills" panel.

✚ To Your Health

Teaching Approaches

- Ask: "What would you do on your day off if you were a priest? Are there any activities that would be inappropriate?"
- What would you expect priests or religious to do on their day off?

A Model for the Future

Teaching Approaches

- Read or summarize the section on Saint John Vianney. Tell the students that John Vianney was first rejected as a seminarian because he could not read or write.
- **Reteach**—Ask: "What does John Vianney's perseverance say about responding to a vocational call?"
- **Extend the Lesson**—Assign pairs or small groups to research other inspirational words of John Vianney. Have them share these words with the class. Include these sayings on a class poster.

In many areas of the world, parish communities live without a regular priest. Some of these parishes have a religious sister or a lay pastoral administrator who runs the parish, visits the sick, prepares people for the sacraments, leads the people in prayer, officiates at weddings, baptizes new members, counsels those in need, and even buries the dead. These administrators do much of the work traditionally performed by priests, but they cannot grant absolution in the sacrament of Penance, celebrate the Eucharist, or celebrate the Anointing of the Sick. In many cases, a priest will come to the parish every week or two to hear confessions and celebrate the Mass. For the rest of

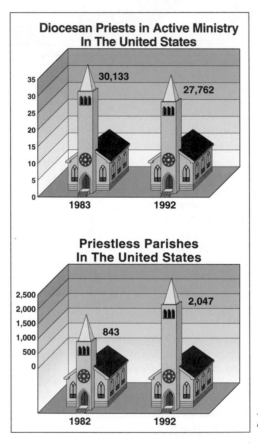

Diocesan Priests in Active Ministry In The United States

30,133 — 1983
27,762 — 1992

Priestless Parishes In The United States

843 — 1982
2,047 — 1992

✚ To Your Health
What Do You Do?

Priests and religious are asked many questions about their lifestyle. Here is one of the most common questions and its answer:

Do priests and religious get time off, and, if so, what do they do with it?

Priests and religious have approximately the same amount of leisure time as most adults. Today, they are free to do whatever is legal, moral, and reasonable for adults in religious life. Obviously, because priests, brothers, and sisters are unique individuals, they don't all choose the same types of recreational activity, and none of them chooses the same activity every time. Some of the more common choices are sports, movies, TV, reading, visiting friends, enjoying the outdoors.

the time, the parish is dependent upon the parish administrator.

What would it be like to live in a priestless parish? What would it mean not to have ready access to the sacraments of Penance or the Eucharist?

A Model for The Future

Father John Vianney was the pastor of the small, antiquated parish in Ars, France. He quickly became known as a kind and considerate confessor. John would spend hours listening to, advising, and forgiving people, sometimes up to 18 hours a day. People came to him burdened and left feeling totally free.

The number of priestless parishes increased 143% in 10 years. There are now approximately 280 parishes administered by lay leaders.

Journal Assignment

"Write a profile of a person who you believe best personifies the qualities of the priesthood."

Resources

Resource 9G lists quotations from Saint John Vianney.

His reputation soon spread, and tens of thousands of pilgrims came from Paris to Ars seeking spiritual healing. Other priests of the diocese, noting John's lack of education, protested that he had no background to be conducting spiritual direction. A petition was circulated to that effect. John was one of the first to sign it in agreement. When the protests reached the bishop, they claimed that John was mentally deranged. "I wish," the bishop responded, "that all my clergy had a touch of the same madness."

Saint John Vianney, the *curé de Ars,* or pastor of Ars, is the patron saint of parish priests. He was a true shepherd and is now a model for a priesthood that extends into the future. He appreciated the strength of a community gathered together in prayer. He said, "Private prayer is like straw scattered here and there: if you set it on fire it makes a lot of little flames. But gather these straws into a bundle and light them, and you get a mighty fire, rising like a column into the sky; public prayer is like that."

Talk It Over

1. In what ways does your parish share in collaborative ministry with the priest?
2. How can you live out your baptismal role as priest, king, and prophet?
3. Describe your image of the priesthood.

Well Being
Freedom to Love

The Church has always had priests who were celibate. Jesus, in fact, spoke of those who would give up having wives and homes for the sake of the Gospel *(Matthew 19:29).* Different customs developed regarding celibacy. In the Eastern Church, married men were ordained to the priesthood. In the Western Church a similar practice existed for a thousand years but eventually it was decided by the Church that only men who made a permanent commitment to celibacy could be ordained. In neither the East nor the West was a man permitted to marry after receiving the sacrament of Holy Orders.

Signs of a Vocation

Do you possibly have an interest in a vocation to the vowed religious life or the priesthood? Whenever the question is posed, many people immediately refuse to consider even the possibility. One of the main reasons for this immediate reaction is that people think that they will receive no support for the idea from friends and family members: "My parents would never understand. They expect me to raise a family." Or, "My friends would think I had lost my mind! They would never want to speak with me again!" What do you think people would say to you if you expressed an interest in religious life? What would you say to someone who expressed such an interest to you?

If you think you might have a religious vocation, you may be concerned with whether or not you can meet the entrance requirements for a program of religious formation or the seminary. If you are an average student, are physically and emotionally healthy, and are reasonably mature, this worry should not be a major concern.

Generally, the requirements fall under six categories:

1. Intellectual.
2. Physical.
3. Religious.
4. Psychological.
5. Moral.
6. Motivational.

Background

According to the United States Catholic Bishops: "In practice, living out the commitment to forego the experience of conjugal love can be very difficult. Because celibate persons are called to love and serve . . . their vocation, like that of all Christians, is one of being fully human and fully alive . . . authentically and deeply in friendship" (*Human Sexuality,* USCC).

Talk It Over

For Question 1, ask the students to cite specific examples. If possible, invite parishioners involved in parish ministry to come to the class to speak on this issue. For Question 2, have the students apply their answers to the explanation of each function given in the text. If the students did not complete the journal assignment, allow them time to discuss Question 3 either with a partner, in a small group, or with the entire class.

Well-Being

Teaching Approaches

- A common theme of Jesus' preaching was the idea of giving up worldly pleasure for heavenly treasures. Have the students read the text of Matthew 19:29.
- Ask: "How does Matthew 19:29 relate to a priest's choice of celibacy?"

Signs of a Vocation

Lesson Overview

Recall for the students that "the first attraction to religious life is the desire to deepen one's relationship with God and to serve the Christian community." This lesson asks the students to explore more deeply their attraction to religious life and to familiarize them with some of the requirements for seeking religious life.

Teaching Approaches

- Read the first paragraph. Ask: "What would be your greatest concern about seeking a religious vocation?"
- Read or summarize the rest of the text section.
- **Reteach**—Ask the students to write their responses to the following: "What special talents and gifts do I have for the religious life? How do I meet the requirements—intellectual, physical, religious, and moral—for a religious vocation?"
- **Extend the Lesson**—Assign the students to research the specific entrance requirements for a number of different religious orders and diocesan seminary programs. This assignment may be done in conjunction with **Application** Project 6.

Talk It Over

First, have the students write brief answers to each question. Then, have them share what they have written with a partner. Emphasize that making any vocation choice alone, without consultation can be damaging. While people don't usually run away from home to join a religious community, it does happen. People considering a vocation decision should discuss their decisions with trusted friends, advisors, counselors, parents, and even their parish priest.

What are your sources of motivation? What are you willing to sacrifice to reach your goal?

Each religious order has its own requirements, depending on its ministries. A teaching or nursing order, for example, would normally require a college degree. For a traveling missionary order, you must be in excellent health. For ordination to the priesthood, an undergraduate and graduate degree is usually required.

Religious are expected to have a committed prayer life, an active practice of the faith, an exemplary moral life, and the temperament to live a vow of chastity. Candidates to priesthood and religious life are also given career and psychological testing to evaluate their personal maturity and motivation for seeking the religious life or priesthood. Are they willing to devote their lives to the service of others as disciples of Jesus Christ. Are *you*?

Deep in your heart you may experience an invitation, a call, a desire, or a yearning that points you in the direction of the priesthood or religious life. Don't reject it automatically, out of fear or embarrassment. What would it cost you to speak with people you admire who already live out a similar calling? Priests and religious are not like military recruiters who try to get you to sign up or enlist you on the spot. No one will try to talk you into anything. Talking with a priest or religious about their life might help you clarify your thinking and set your goals.

Talk It Over

1. What is your inclination about the kind of life the Holy Spirit is calling you to?
2. What do you think your friends and family would say to you if you told them that you were considering a religious vocation?
3. Where can you go for help in making a decision about a vocation?

Journal Assignment

Have students respond to the following question: "How will you be able to identify in your heart that a call, a desire, or a yearning that points to religious life or priesthood comes from God?"

Knowing Your Diocese

How much do you know about your diocese? Research the following questions using Catholic directories or diocesan newspapers. You may also interview diocesan or parish leaders to help you answer the questions.

1. What year was your diocese established? Of what diocese was it previously a part?

2. Who was the first bishop of the diocese?

3. Who is the current bishop of the diocese?

4. What is the diocese's official name? boundaries?

5. What is the name of the diocesan cathedral? When was it built? Where is it located?

6. How many diocesan priests serve the diocese? how many religious priests? Besides parish ministry, in what other ministries do priests serve? What is the projected number of priests for your diocese ten years from now?

7. How many religious men and women are active in the diocese? What are the names of the different orders represented? What ministries do they perform? What is the projected number of religious for your diocese ten years from now?

8. What religious communities have their headquarters in your diocese?

9. Does your diocese have a local seminary? What is its name?

10. How many people were baptized in the diocese last year?

11. How many marriages were performed in the diocese last year?

12. What is the Catholic population of the diocese? Has it grown or shrunk during the past ten years? What percent of the general population in your diocesan area is Catholic?

13. Choose one ministry in your diocese and research how people proclaim the Good News through it.

181

Knowing Your Diocese

Teaching Approaches

- Have the class work in small groups on the activity.

- Much of this work can be researched in libraries that have copies of the diocesan directory or newspaper. Students may also interview a diocesan or parish leader who can help them answer the questions.

- Have each student write a project summary, expressing his or her opinion on the most interesting fact uncovered in the research. Given their information, what will the diocese be like for them as adults?

Background

According to the *Encyclopedic Dictionary of Religion* a diocese is "a territorial unit of the Church, governed by a bishop ruling in his own name and not as delegate of another." The second Vatican Conference defines it as "the portion of God's people which is entrusted to a bishop."

Teaching Approaches

- Allow the students to choose their own groups of six for the role plays. Encourage the students to include a variety of responses to the announcement of a vocation, both positive and negative.

- Reserve class time for the groups to act out their role plays in front of the class.

Answering

Lesson Overview

Although advertising slogans suggest otherwise, it's impossible to "just do it" when it comes to answering the call to a religious vocation. The process demands much prayer and reflection. This lesson presents suggestions for coming to conclusions about choosing a religious vocation.

Teaching Approaches

- Write the four suggestions for making a decision about religious life on the board: (1) Pray (especially read Scripture and participate in the Eucharist); (2) Read about the lives of saints; (3) Talk with parents, trusted friends, and a man or woman religious for guidance; (4) Consult the vocation director of a religious order or diocese.

- Read or have the students read the entire section.

- **Reteach**—Ask: "What does Blessed Theophane Venard say about making vocational decisions? What can you add to the list?"

- **Extend the Lesson**—Assign **Application** Project 8.

▲ Family Living
"You've Decided What?"

One of the most rewarding things a family can experience is for one of its members to choose a vocation to the religious life or priesthood. Yet, some religious vocation candidates don't experience much acceptance for their decisions from their families.

With classmates or friends, dramatize the family roles listed below. Pretend that you have just come home with the news that you have been accepted into the preparation program for a religious community or into the seminary. What is the family's response to your announcement?

The characters:
1. You
2. Your parent(s)
3. Your 20-year-old sister
4. Your 12-year-old brother
5. Your grandmother
6. Your best friend

Answering

Father Tom Duffy, a Holy Cross priest from the University of Notre Dame, encouraged eighth-grade graduate Ted Hesburgh to come to Indiana to attend the order's high school seminary. Ted's mother refused. Her reasoning: South Bend, Indiana, was much too far from Syracuse, New York, especially for a ninth-grade boy who would be living away from his family. Instead, Ted would attend the local Catholic high school.

Father Duffy had a warning: "If he doesn't come and go to high school at Notre Dame, he may lose his vocation." Mrs. Hesburgh looked the priest straight in the eye and said, "It can't be much of a vocation if he's going to lose it by living in a Christian family." After four years of high school, Ted entered the college seminary at Notre Dame.

The point of this story is that calls to a particular vocation do not go away. Eventually, they must be answered. What can you do to answer God's call?

A decision about any important life choice should never be reached alone. A decision to marry, for example, is reached by talking and planning with your prospective partner, your parents and friends, a priest, and with God. A call to the life of a vowed religious or priest should be answered with the same care. Prayer, especially through reflection on Scripture and participation in the Eucharist, is of great benefit. Reading the lives of saints may also help you to understand how others have responded to God. Talking with parents, trusted friends, or a priest is also important. Each religious community and diocesan office has a vocation director who will be happy to assist you.

Finally, consider the advice of Blessed Theophane Venard, a French missionary to Vietnam who was martyred for his faith in 1861. Theophane wrote to his younger brother, Eusebius, encouraging him to make a vocational choice. Imagine that you have received this letter. How would you respond?

◊ Well, you are wondering about your future. Pray simply, humbly, and fervently to know God's will, and your path will be made clear. Then you must follow the inspiration divine Mercy puts into your heart. Some say, "I will be a priest," or "a soldier," and they add, "Oh, such and such studies are not necessary for this or that profession." This is the reasoning of pure idlers. Others go on about piety: "Piety! It's only for priests and nuns. God does not expect so much from us!"

Background

From 1854 until 1860, Blessed Theophane Venard was a French missionary serving the persecuted Christians in Tonkin, China. He was captured, chained in a cage, and, a short while later, beheaded for his faith. He was beatified in 1900.

Catholic worship centers around the Eucharist, with the priest the presider over the celebration.

(How do you know?) These are the arguments of cold and calculating natures. Now I want you to say to yourself, "I am, above all, a man, a rational being, created to know, love, serve, and glorify God. I come from God. I go to God. I belong to God. My body is His. My mind is His. My heart is His. I shall be judged according to my deeds, according to the way I have corresponded with the grace given me. Well, then, by God's help, I shall use this body, this mind, and this heart as much as I possibly can for His greater glory, honor, and love."

Life, well-employed, consists in this: A faithful correspondence to grace and a good use of the talents we have been given. This rule of life applies equally to all.

Chapter Summary

- Ministry is a part of every Christian's vocation.
- Religious brothers and sisters are lay people who live in community and take the vows of poverty, chastity, and obedience.
- Prayer, work, and community living are essential parts of religious life.
- A diocesan priest serves the Church in a specific area called a diocese.
- Through Baptism, all Christians share in the collaborative ministry of the priesthood.
- A decision about a vocation should be reached with the help of others.

Chapter Summary

- This section lists the main points of summary of Chapter 9. To use as a review, you might have the students list examples from the text to illustrate each point, rewrite each point in their own words, or find creative ways to teach each point.
- Have the students share their review techniques with a partner.

Journal Assignment

Say to the students: "You are Eusebius, the brother or sister of Theophane Venard. Imagine that you received his letter. How would you respond?"

Chapter 9 Review

What Have You Learned?

Listed below are suggested answers. For many of the questions, the answers will vary.

1. Religious brothers and sisters take the same vows as ordained ministers. They do not, however, have the same role of sacramental and pastoral leadership as priests.

2. People are attracted to religious life because of its emphasis on prayer, work, and community living done for the glory of God.

3. According to Benedict's Rule, monks prayed seven times a day, primarily from the Divine Office.

4. The mendicants' ministry to the Albigensians was successful because the mendicants lived a life of poverty.

5. A religious receives support and companionship from his or her religious community in much the same way a person does from his or her family.

6. Sacramental ministry means that a priest officiates at the sacraments; pastoral ministry emphasizes a ministry of service.

7. People have many images of the priest. He may be treated with the reverence of a god by some, while to others, he may connote the negative image of a parent scolding a child. There are many other images in between.

8. Lay people are called to share in the sacramental ministries (for example, as eucharistic ministers) and in pastoral ministries of service to the community.

9. Saint John Vianney was a nineteenth-century parish priest in France. He was known for his insights as a confessor. He is the patron saint of parish priests.

10. A person considering a religious vocation should pray; talk with a parent, trusted friend or priest; read the lives of saints; and consult a vocation director for a religious community or diocese.

REVIEW

What Have You Learned?

1. What are some similarities between religious and ordained ministers? What are some differences?

2. What are some of the things that people find attractive about religious life? What is the ultimate attraction?

3. What was a part of Saint Benedict's rule concerning prayer?

4. What made the mendicants' ministry to the Albigensians successful?

5. Why is living in a community a part of vowed religious life?

6. How are a priest's sacramental and pastoral ministries different?

7. What are some of the varying images of the priest?

8. How are lay people called to share in the collaborative ministry of the priest?

9. Who was Saint John Vianney?

10. What are some things a person should do if he or she is considering a religious vocation?

Application

1. Arrange to interview a religious sister, brother or priest. Develop a list of questions to ask prior to your interview. Share your interview with the class.

2. Find more information about all of the following: Thomas Merton, Saint Thérèse of Lisieux, and Mother Teresa.

3. Use a national or local Catholic directory to find the names of religious communities for men and women. Write to the vocation director of one order requesting information. Share the information about the order with the class.

4. Imagine that you, like Saint Dominic, are asked to help someone return to the faith. How would you do it? What techniques would you use?

5. Invite a priest to your classroom. Ask him to share his impressions of the changing priesthood.

6. Write a letter to a college or graduate seminarian. Ask him to describe his daily schedule and what motivated him to enter the seminary.

7. Browse through Catholic periodicals for advertisements that encourage vocations to the priesthood or religious life. Report on the effectiveness of the advertising techniques.

8. Write a letter of response to Theophane Venard.

184

Background

Saint Dominic resolved the tension between contemplation and preaching by substituting study for manual labor, strict poverty, and democratic government. The original rules of the order were from Saint Augustine.

REVIEW

Chapter Vocabulary

- Albigensians
- ordained minister
- lay people
- contemplative
- curé de Ars
- Divine Office
- mendicant
- collaboration
- *laborare est orare*
- shepherd
- diocesan priest
- religious brother
- sacramental ministry
- pastoral ministry
- Hebrew Scriptures
- Cistercians

And we must recognize that we are heard not for our speaking, but for our purity of heart and tears of contrition.

From the Rule of Saint Benedict

185

Putting Vocabulary to Use

Note the highlighted words below. If the statement is false, substitute the correct word(s) from the chapter vocabulary.

1. Dominic founded a religious order known as *Albigensians*, a term meaning "beggar."
2. The priest's ministry is a *pastoral ministry* because of the priest's leadership in sacramental worship.
3. *Curé de Ars* is a term developed by Saint Benedict meaning "to work is to pray."
4. To serve the Church as a *religious brother* means that a man has received the sacrament of Holy Orders.
5. A *diocesan priest* pledges allegiance to a bishop and usually serves only in a particular area.
6. Religious brothers and sisters are *lay people;* yet they are often viewed differently by other lay people.
7. Monks prayed from the *Hebrew Scriptures,* a collection of psalms and readings from Scripture.
8. *Cistercians* is another name for "shared priesthood."
9. Members of a *mendicant* religious order generally spend the majority of their day in prayer.
10. "Pastor" is a word that means *priest.*
11. A priest's *pastoral ministry* has its scriptural origins in Jesus' washing of His disciples feet at the Last Supper.

Application

Read the directions and descriptions of each project to the students. Allow the students to choose their own project. Suggest the following steps: (1) formulate a plan; (2) complete the tasks; (3) share the initial project with a partner for comments; (4) revise and finalize the project.

Putting Vocabulary to Use

1. false (mendicant)
2. false (sacramental ministry)
3. false (laborare est orare)
4. false (ordained minister)
5. true
6. true
7. false (Divine Office)
8. false (collaboration)
9. false (contemplative)
10. false (shepherd)
11. true.

Final Thought

Background

Have the students apply these words to their relationships with others. Why would it be important as witnesses to Christ that our hearts be pure and that we recognize our sinfulness?

Focus On: Chapter 10

Preparing for marriage has never before been such a vital issue. Present trends show that families are smaller, divorce and remarriage more common, and in most marriages, both partners are employed outside of the home. If Christian marriage is to survive as we know it, it must be able to adapt to these and other social changes. In order for marriages to adapt, young people will need to develop a vision of marriage based on unselfish love and mutual growth.

This chapter focuses on some of the practical skills necessary for determining and developing the mature love that is necessary in a successful marriage. A distinction is made between the popular, romanticized ideal of marriage and the realistic issues and expectations that a married couple and a couple considering marriage will face. Students will learn about the requirements for a sacramental marriage, and will begin to consider if, when, and how married life is for them.

Plan Ahead

- Incorporate formal and/or spontaneous prayer in each lesson. A participatory prayer service that is suitable for use on retreat is provided in the Teacher's Resource Book.

- Note **Resource** suggestions which can be applied to, or extend, the lessons of this chapter.

- Preview the **Application** projects in the Chapter Review. Refer to **Teaching Approaches** for suggestions on when to assign the projects. Or, the projects may be used as part of lesson, section, or chapter reviews.

- Decide on a method for grouping students for projects and discussion.

- In advance, invite guest speakers who will participate in selected lessons.

Preparing for Marriage

It was not you who chose Me, but I who chose you and appointed you to go and bear fruit that will remain, so that whatever you ask the Father in My name He may give you. This I command you: love one another.

John 15:16-17

This chapter will help you to:

- Understand the responsibilities that are involved in deciding to marry.
- Determine whether or not you and a prospective marriage partner are compatible.
- Practice the skills needed to develop a mature love.

- Question a prospective marriage partner about the issues and expectations that are vital to a relationship.
- Determine whether or not your love for another is genuine and can be incorporated into a committed married relationship.

186

Media Suggestions (Optional)

- *Loving, Lasting Relationships* (Dallas Christian Videos) Eight 30-minute programs. The goal of these presentations is to develop relationship skills.

- *Helping Young People Get Married* (Tabor) 90 min. The importance of courtship and typical feelings about love and marriage are addressed in the three 30-min. segments by Charles Gallagher, S.J.

Aims

1. To learn how marriages were arranged in previous generations.
2. To understand how men and women choose marriage partners today.
3. To take a closer look at the courtship process.

Begin the Section

1. Choose students to read the first three paragraphs aloud. Ask for volunteers to briefly share the story of a romanticized marriage they have read about or seen on television or in the movies. Ask: "What makes these stories so enjoyable?"
2. Have students describe their criteria for a successful marriage. List the points on the board.
3. Read the final paragraph. Explain that romantic attraction is just one factor in a successful marriage. Ask: "What are some other factors necessary for a successful marriage?"
4. Say: "Most people consider marriage at some time in their life and, in fact, most people eventually do marry. What can you do to prepare for marriage? In this chapter, we will examine the skills needed in preparing for a successful marriage."

1. A MOST IMPORTANT DECISION

"I know that there is one special person in this world who is meant for me."

Marriage is by far the most popular Christian vocation. Since most people consider marriage at some time in their lives, it is safe to say that most everyone has had thoughts like the one above. A popular understanding of marriage today often revolves around the romantic belief that suddenly, magically, Mr. or Miss Right will appear to whisk you, "happily ever after," into a dreamlike world of marital bliss.

Imagining an ideal marriage with your perfect mate at your side is a thought worth holding. You picture yourself meeting your future husband or wife on a chair lift at a ski resort. Or you imagine coming to school one day to find that it's love at first sight between you and a new student at the next locker!

187

Background

According to the *Catechism of the Catholic Church,* 1603, the vocation of marriage is part of humankind's very nature as an act of God's will, and not a purely human institution. As said by the Second Vatican Council "The well-being of the person and of human and Christian society is intimately connected with the healthy state of marriage and family" (*Gaudium et Spes,* 47).

Other Times, Other Ways

Lesson Overview

"Choosing" one's marriage partner is a relatively new practice. Arranged marriages were prevalent in most cultures until this century. As the students are presented with the information in this lesson, remind them that arranged or not, the Church still understood marriages to be sacramental, holy unions. Men and women both had to work hard in the hope of establishing a relationship where God's love could be visible.

New Word

A *contract marriage* is a bond, a formal agreement between the husband and wife, and oftentimes their families as well. A new form of contract marriage today includes a contract called a "prenuptial agreement." This contract puts in writing such issues as how property and income should be divided if the couple ever separates or divorces. People marrying in the Catholic Church may not sign written contracts of this kind. An oral recitation of vows does take place during the wedding ceremony.

Teaching Approaches

- Discuss the benefits and problems of arranged or contract marriages.
- Have the students individually read the section.
- Discuss how parents today do "exert powerful influence on the decision process" of who their children will or will not marry.
- Explain that in biblical times, typical contract marriages were arranged either by the parents or by the bridegroom and his future father-in-law. Sometimes a brother of the bride would do the negotiating. The gift of the dowry was in anticipation of the bride's usefulness to the family of her husband and the loss of services to her father's clan. The offspring of the wife would become part of the labor force of her husband's family. Also, as part of the contract, if the husband should die prematurely, it was the responsibility of his family to find the widow another husband, normally the eldest living brother of the one who died.
- **Reteach**—Assign **Application** Project 2 at this time.
- **Extend the Lesson**—Have the students write a position paragraph on arranged marriages.

Romantic dreams are fun to have. They call our attention to what is possible in marriage. But it's important to recognize that much of the lore of romantic dreams ("love at first sight," "there is one person in the whole world just for me") is pure fantasy—straight from popular magazines and the entertainment industry. Rarely do these scenarios actually happen as they are depicted.

There is no denying that romantic attraction is a strong factor in bringing two people together. But romance is only one part of the love that is necessary to sustain a relationship between wife and husband. In this chapter, you will examine the process for finding a marriage partner and look at the responsibilities that are involved in deciding to marry. You will seriously consider important questions to ask before marriage. Choosing a compatible marriage partner is a crucial decision. The cost of choosing poorly may be dissatisfaction, financial turmoil, divorce, or all of these.

Other Times, Other Ways

In the Western world today, most first-time marriages follow a simple pattern: a couple decides to get married, they announce the news to their parents, they plan the wedding, and then "tie the knot." It is a choice made by the couple on their own with little concern for the approval of society, the Church, or their families. The marriage may be based upon relationships that range from mere physical attraction to mature commitment. You may be surprised to learn that this understanding of marriage is of very recent origin.

Through much of history, marriages were arranged by parents and families. That is, families entered into an agreement that promised the daughter of one family to the son of another. A man's children were considered his property to do with as he pleased. Boys were often prepared

Marriages in many countries today are still arranged. What do you think of this custom?

Resources

Resource 10A from the Teacher's Resource Book provides a list of past and current engagement and marriage customs.

to take over the family business. Girls were taught how to care for a home, and the needs of the husband and children.

Marriage was seen as a way to build alliances between families and make them prosperous. A payment, or *dowry*, was often made by the family of the bride to the husband at the time of the wedding. In some cultures the dowry actually belonged to the wife as a guarantee to the husband that she would not be a financial burden on him. Usually, families tried to promise children of similar age to each other, but often the man would be much older than the woman.

In arranged marriages, the couple often did not even meet until immediately before the wedding. If a loving relationship developed, wonderful, but that was not necessary for the marriage to be successful. The couple was joined together more by cultural and parental expectations than by any personal expectation of happiness. In most cases the woman was considered subservient to the man, having few rights or privileges of her own.

These marriages were considered *contract marriages,* with their main purposes being bearing and raising children. In these marriages gender roles were very sharply defined: men worked to provide food and shelter, while women gave birth, nurtured the children, and cared for the home. Unfortunately, under this system women had few rights and often were victims of abuse.

Saint Monica, for example, was one of the few wives living in Tasgate, North Africa whose husband did not beat her. For this she was grateful. Monica's husband Patricius, a nobleman who was seventeen years her senior, was abusive in other ways, however. He shouted at her in frustration over his family's diminishing finances. He embarrassed her with his numerous affairs. Yet, Monica remained with him as a wife and mother for their two sons and one daughter. In her fourth-century world, she had little choice: in most cases, women could not divorce their husbands. However, husbands could divorce their wives.

Prayer in Action
Monica's Prayer

Saint Monica prayed unceasingly for the religious conversion of her husband, Patricius. According to her son, Augustine, Monica "learned not to resist an angry husband, not in deed only, but not even in word. Only when he was smoothed and tranquil, and in a temper to receive it, she would give an account of her actions."

Her prayer also centered on her children; she is remembered for her influence on Saint Augustine, who had once lived a decadent life. Augustine said, "It was her earnest desire that You, God, rather than my father, should be my Father, and in this You did aid her to prevail over her husband."

Arranged marriages were prevalent in most of the world until this century. In many cultures, such as those of India and Japan, the practice of arranged marriages continues today. And, though most families in our society do not have the definitive say in who their children marry, they do exert powerful influence on the decision-making process of their children.

Talk It Over

1. Why are the phrases "love at first sight" and "there is one special person in the world just for me" closer to myth than to fact? How does this realization affect your understanding of marriage?
2. How do parents or family members today affect a person's decision to marry?
3. What are the advantages and disadvantages of arranged marriages? How would you feel about having your marriage partner selected for you?
4. Which of your values would be contradicted or violated by an arranged marriage?

Marriage Today

Lesson Overview

Ask the students to think about several qualities that they would find most important in a spouse. Write their ideas on the board. Discuss the importance of compatibility between marriage partners. Review the list of qualities. How many relate to compatibility? Point out that more issues of compatibility will be introduced in the lesson.

Teaching Approaches

- Read or summarize the first paragraph and the quotation.
- Ask the students to compare Jesus' command of love from the chapter opener with the words from the Second Vatican Council document on modern marriage.
- **Reteach**—Ask: "Do you think this statement is true: 'Love is a good starting point and ending point for determining a suitable partner for marriage'?"
- **Extend the Lesson**—Debate the statement: "Who I marry is my business and nobody else's."

A Changing Process

New Words

Besides *bigamy* (entering into marriage while still legally married to another), there are other terms for illegal marriages.

Polygamy involves a marriage between a husband and two or more wives.

All states forbid *consanguinity,* the marriage between blood relatives.

Some states have laws concerning *affinity,* the marriage between people who are related by marriage only. The Catholic Church prohibits all of these types of marriages.

Teaching Approaches

- Ask: "What does the old saying 'look before you leap' have to do with getting married?"
- Read or summarize the first three paragraphs. Point out how the decision of who a person marries will affect one's happiness, one's life, and even what one's children are like.

Marriage Today

Today, the choice of who you marry is most often a personal one. The system of arranged marriages has been replaced by the dating process, which is the means people use to meet and get to know someone of the opposite sex more intimately. Instead of a contract, contemporary marriage is based upon a personal commitment to love. Both the husband and wife should be nurtured and fulfilled in the marriage relationship.

According to the Second Vatican Council:

> "Such love, merging the human with the divine, leads spouses to a free and mutual gift of themselves, a gift proving itself by gentle affection and by deed. Such love pervades the whole of their lives. Indeed, by its generous activity it grows better and grows greater… Firmly established by the Lord, the unity of marriage will radiate from the equal personal dignity of wife and husband, a dignity acknowledged by mutual and total love" (*Pastoral Constitution on the Church in the Modern World*, Chapter 1, verse 49).

A Changing Process

Although it might seem that people have unlimited freedom to choose who they marry, in practice most people's number of potential partners is limited by age, background, interests, and proximity. Most people marry someone from their own town, race, and economic class. This effectively limits their choices.

Through dating, a person learns about someone in great detail: what he or she likes and doesn't like, how he or she feels, and why the other acts as he or she does in various situations. As a relationship develops, a person can visualize a shared life. The initial physical attraction is joined with a growing love.

Choosing a marriage partner through dating requires many more individual decisions than did the process of arranged marriages. But it's not totally accurate to conclude that today's couples have gone from parental control to making their own choices about who they marry. It's not like buying a car, where you go to the lot and choose one car from among several. In many ways, this

How is choosing a marriage partner different than choosing a car?

Background

Emotional and social maturity are important factors for successful marriages. Maturity can be described as the ability to establish and maintain relationships, to give as well as receive, and to perceive others' feelings. Mature people are personally stable and live by established values.

Who Can Marry?

Although, at first glance, marriage would seem to be a right that anyone can exercise without restriction, there are actually many laws and prohibitions concerning marriage. The most basic requirement found in the law is the need for mutual consent: no valid marriage can exist if either the man or woman does not freely choose to marry. If one person is under the influence of drugs or alcohol at the time of the marriage, or if a person is pressured into the marriage by family or friends, the marriage may be invalid.

There are other marriage laws as well. Most states have two age requirements for marriage; one defines the age a person can marry with parental consent, and the other when a person can marry without parental consent. Many states will not permit a marriage if one of the partners has a sexually transmitted disease; a blood test must be taken to prove the health of both partners.

Also, under the law, a marriage may involve only one wife and one husband. A person who is still legally married and enters into another marriage commits the crime of *bigamy*. Other laws prohibit marriages between close blood relatives.

The Catholic Church prohibits marriage in eight cases. Many of these impediments can be removed with the special permission from the local bishop, called a *dispensation*.

The Church's prohibitions on marriage are:
1. Girls must be at least 14 years old. Boys must be 16 years old.
2. Permanent deacons and priests may not marry unless they have received a dispensation of their promise of celibacy from the Vatican.
3. A religious brother or sister may not marry unless first released from the professed vow of chastity.
4. Brothers and sisters can never marry. Close relatives such as first cousins need a dispensation in order to marry.
5. Close relatives through marriage (for example, a stepfather and stepdaughter) may not marry.
6. Persons who have established legal relationships through adoption may not marry.
7. Catholics are prohibited from marrying without the presence of a priest. If they do so without the proper dispensation, the Church may consider the marriage invalid.

Who Can Marry

Teaching Approaches
- Read through the list of state and Church regulations for marriage. Pause for questions or comments.
- Which prohibitions do the students find most difficult to accept? Discuss their reasoning as a class.

is the "Velcro age"; you meet many people and eventually become attached to one. For unknown reasons, your "hooks" stick to the other person's "loops." Modern marriage is founded on developing a relationship with another person so that all of these little connections are made.

There are many variables that affect relationships. Because no two people are alike, no two relationships can be alike. For that reason it's impossible to predict whether any relationship will last or not. Success depends both on the choices

that lead to marriage and the choices made after the marriage as well.

While predicting the success of relationships is impossible, there are some general principles that can be used to more effectively insure success or failure.

Common Interests. A couple who share similar values and beliefs enjoy a head start in their relationship. Because of their common interests, they will feel more comfortable sharing important things about themselves sooner than if they have

Resources

Resource 10B provides a format for the activity suggested in "Extend the Lesson."

Resource 10C provides a state-by-state list of marriage laws and regulations for use with the feature, "Who Can Marry."

Common Interests

Teaching Approaches

- Read or summarize the section. Ask the students to explain the "opposites attract" principle in their own words.
- **Reteach**—Have the students think about the importance of common interests in forming friendships. Ask them to speculate on how having common interests with a marriage partner would also be important.
- **Extend the Lesson**—Arrange for a married couple to come to class and discuss how they adjust to living with a spouse who is in some ways similar to and in some ways different from themselves. (See "Talk It Over," Question 1.)

Readiness for Marriage

Teaching Approaches

- Read or summarize the section.
- Have the students suggest ways to determine the readiness of another for marriage.
- Point out that one way to determine readiness is to look at the level of commitment the person exhibits in other areas of his or her life. Have the students suggest other ways.
- **Reteach**—Discuss: "Why is it important that the man and woman be at similar levels of maturity?"
- **Extend the Lesson**—With the students, develop a "Readiness for Marriage" instrument using the points already developed in this chapter. Have students interview people using this instrument and gauge their "Marriage Readiness Quotient (MRQ)." People of all ages and states in life should be interviewed.

People who share common interests often make very compatible marriage partners.

to search desperately at finding something to discuss. And, when it comes time to share more important interests and values, a couple who shares common friendships, careers, and favorite recreational activities, have at least experienced what it is like to agree. They have made successful shared decisions together. They have a point of reference for attempting to work out the more major decisions influencing their relationship. Together, they have made discoveries about themselves, life, and their relationship with each other.

Relationships that start with little in common are likely to fail. Human relationships are a blend of similarities and differences. People will often be attracted to partners who are in many ways quite different from themselves: one person's strengths are the other's weaknesses, and vice versa. For example, a shy woman may be most comfortable with an outgoing, vocal man. An assertive woman may find happiness with an easygoing and accepting man. These relationships prosper when the couple finds a balance with one another and supports each other's deficiencies. If a balance is not found (the stronger person begins to dominate the weaker person), the dissimilarities can be a source of tension. The couple will soon realize that they are incompatible.

Nina may like Mozart, while Miguel prefers heavy metal. These two people can develop a strong relationship even with such differences. However, if their values and beliefs are as incompatible as their tastes in music, usually the relationship will experience great tension. While marriages are built on love and the acceptance of differences, the building blocks for permanence also include common beliefs and values. The more important the value and belief, the less likely it is that the relationship will last with such differences. Miguel and Nina will have a stronger relationship when they share common expectations about marriage, finances, children, family life, and respect for the other's uniqueness.

Background

A great deal of research has been conducted to try and understand why people choose the marriage partners they choose. One major influence on a person's choice appears to be a person's parents. Apparently, people often unconsciously search for a mate who reminds them of their own mother or father.

Common cultural experiences are also important. This is particularly true in the case of interracial marriages. The pressures of dealing with cultural differences may be too demanding for a relationship to endure. The pressures of cultural differences are intensified for an interracial couple because society is often slow to accept relationships between people of different color, nationality, or race.

Readiness for Marriage. Another factor affecting who you marry is the other's readiness for marriage. A man and woman may feel very compatible and have similar goals and values. But all of that is for naught if both are not at a stage in their lives where they are ready to commit to a permanent, faithful relationship that leads to marriage. School or career obligations can cause the couple to be physically separated for long periods of time. Pressing family matters may make it impossible for the man or woman to consider marriage at that time. Often, because of these situations, a couple will separate rather than try to continue the relationship.

Readiness for marriage can also refer to psychological or emotional maturity. People who are extremely jealous, who habitually lie, steal, or cheat, or who have psychological or emotional problems, will have considerable difficulties in forming lasting relationships. They may desire a permanent mate, but may not be mature enough to follow through on their intentions. It follows that one sign of maturity is one's capacity to live by a commitment.

A couple should be adequately mature, with the man and woman at similar levels of maturity. Because marriage is a commitment between two people, there must be shared levels of understanding and trust. A person unable to fulfill his or her promise of commitment may be immature and not ready for marriage.

To Your Health
Meeting Your Own Needs

In order to love in a mature way, a person must first develop a mature relationship with him or herself. Maturity has many meanings, but generally a mature person will:

- Be able to form and maintain trusting relationships with others.
- Be able to offer and receive support.
- Have adequate self-knowledge and self-identity.
- Have established personal values based on the experiences of family, friends, and Church.
- Be emotionally secure and not totally dependent on another.

While it's vital to know as much as you can about your partner before marriage, it's even more important to know yourself—everything from how you react to certain situations, to your dreams for this life and beyond.

Strange, but True

After 15 years, Gabriela still delights in telling the story of how she met her husband, Ed. She was 16 years old and going on the last of her family's annual trips to Yosemite National Park. She had protested to her parents about having to go on the family vacation when all of her friends would be home for the summer. Once at Yosemite, she took off to be by herself as much as she could.

One night Gabriela was standing on the bridge over the river that ran through the heart of the valley. Although just yards from the campsite, the only light was from the moon. Looking down from the top of the bridge, Gabriela could not see the water below. Through the darkness, Gabriela heard someone approaching on the gravel path. Even though the light was dim, she had no trouble seeing this walker. What was such a cute guy doing here?

To Your Health

Teaching Approaches

- Review the list of maturity factors.
- Have the students do a self-reflection exercise by commenting on some or all of these factors in their journals.

Strange, but True

Teaching Approaches

- Choose one or two students to read the story aloud.
- Discuss the story. How realistic do students think the story is? (This story actually happened as described. The couple is married and have three children.)
- **Reteach**—Have students tell other stories about crazy ways that people meet.
- **Extend the Lesson**—Have the students interview two or three married couples and ask them to tell about their first meetings. Save time during a future class meeting for volunteers to share some of their favorite stories. (See also: **Application** Project 4.)

Journal Assignment

Ask the students to write a story similar to "Strange, but True" from one of the stories shared with them by a married couple. You may wish to substitute **Application** Project 1 for this suggestion.

Talk It Over

If the students have not already completed the assignment suggested in Question 1, you may wish to invite a married couple to the classroom to be interviewed concerning these items. For Question 2, refer to some of the important factors listed in this section. Some additional questions would be: (1) How does he or she react in an emergency situation? (2) How does your prospective partner respond to unpleasant situations? (3) Does this person face problems with patience and determination or become frustrated and quit? (4) How does your loved one act when you are not at your best? (5) How do you respond to this person's moods and emotions? Query the students on Question 3 to see if their opinions of the "opposites attract" principle have changed since the beginning of the lesson.

"I'll be back in five minutes to introduce myself," he said to her. Before she could speak, the guy leaped over the side of the bridge into the night. Splash!

Gabriela's concern turned to laughter when he returned a few minutes later, fully soaked. "The name's Ed," he said.

For the next two years, Gabriela and Ed communicated mainly through letters. After graduating from high school, they attended the same college. Eight years from the time they met, they married. They honeymooned at Camp Curry in Yosemite. For old time's sake, Ed did one more night jump off the bridge.

Every married couple is able to tell a unique story about how they came to be married. Some will tell of a long friendship before they decided on marriage, while others will describe a whirlwind series of events that led to their wedding day. But all the couples will describe a process of shared discovery during which they eventually concluded that they would be able to commit to a lifetime together.

Talk It Over

1. Choose a married couple whom you know well (parents, relatives, or friends) and ask them how they are similar or different in the following areas: age, background, interests, and how close they lived to one another at the time they were dating.
2. List five important factors to consider in choosing a marriage partner. Rank them. How do your responses compare to those of your friends?
3. Reflect on the saying, "opposites attract." Do you think this is really true? Can two people who hold greatly different fundamental beliefs form a lasting relationship?

Every couple has a unique story to tell. Every courtship is different.

Background

While people who hold fundamentally different beliefs can form lasting relationships, it is quite uncommon. Marriage is best built by couples who share common beliefs and values. They may be different in personality, but its best that they are similar in the more crucial matters.

Courtship

What Ed and Gabriela experienced is known as "courtship." The act of "courting" is designed to win another person's heart. Dating is an essential part of the modern courtship practice. Modern courtship differs greatly from some of the other practices that have been followed throughout history. For example, women are no longer considered property to be captured or bought. Men no longer pay the father of the bride a *betrothal* or *bride price*. While courtship through dating has its problems, it is certainly more civilized than capturing or purchasing a bride. More importantly, women now have a say about who they marry!

Although dating is now the common practice, every courtship is different. Each reflects the personality of the individuals involved. There are, however, stages that are common in most courtships.

Being In Love

In the first stage of the process, the **falling in love** stage, each person recognizes that the other is extra special. This recognition leads to beginning thoughts of themselves as a couple. Gradually, others become aware of their secret. This mutual attraction may be based on physical appearance, shared interests, or personality.

The early stages of a love relationship may be somewhat self-centered. Each individual may think first of his or her own personal satisfaction and enjoyment rather than the relationship. At the beginning of a relationship, there may be only modest concern for the other person's interests.

What does it mean to be "in love"? How would you think falling "in love" would be different from other kinds of love? For example, how is a parent's love for a child different from his or her love for a spouse? While a parent will love his or her child from birth, we do not say that the parent has fallen in love with the child.

There are at least two factors to consider about the experience of falling in love:

Falling in love can be a wonderful experience. What are some signs that tell you that a friend is in love?

1. Falling in love usually involves sexual attraction.
2. The experience of falling in love will almost always evolve into another experience.

The romance of falling in love is neither wrong nor bad. The initial selfish desire which may be present at the beginning of this stage is not necessarily harmful. In fact, it is the attraction between the couple that brings them together to forge a relationship. This powerful feeling helps people overcome shyness or anxiety about interpersonal relationships. By working through the emotions and somewhat self-centered desires of this stage, a couple may develop a mature love capable of supporting a relationship.

Courtship

Lesson Overview

In using a term like courtship, it's important for the students to understand how *courting* and *dating* are related. Dating is part of the courtship process, but all dating does not necessarily lead to courtship. Courtship is the kind of dating that occurs when a couple begins to consciously consider the possibility of marriage.

Teaching Approaches

- Define the term "courtship."
- Read the opening paragraphs of the lesson.
- **Reteach**—Discuss how courting practices have changed.
- **Extend the Lesson**—Many people consider the word "courtship" to be out of fashion. What word would students use today instead of courtship?

Being In Love

Teaching Approaches

- Play a word association game with the students using the phrase "in love." Then, work with the class to come up with one acceptable definition.
- Read or summarize the section. Compare the class's definition with the one listed in the text. Make sure the students can explain why being "in love" may also be self-centered, especially in the initial stages.
- **Reteach**—Write the two factors of being "in love" on the board. Have the students develop a role play or write a short story to illustrate these factors. Choose volunteers to share with the class.
- **Extend the Lesson**—Ask: "Could a marriage survive if it were possible for a couple to always remain in the 'in-love' stage? Why or why not?"

Getting to Know You

When people come to know more about each other, the second or **trusting** stage of love begins. It is during this stage that trust develops and is tested. This is the stage of more honest communication and personal revelation. In order for this to happen, each person must reveal him or herself to the other. A common concern becomes: "If you really knew me well, would you still like me? If you knew all about me, my hopes and fears, my good points and weaknesses, would you still want me to be your friend?"

To counteract this fear, some people may put on masks. They become the person they think others want them to be. In the story of Gabriela and Ed, it turned out that Ed really did have a crazy sense of humor; his jumping off the bridge was not done simply to get Gabriela's attention. Ed once took Gabriela to a formal dance wearing his tuxedo backwards! Ed's pranks continue into their married life. Gabriela still roars with laughter each time Ed pulls one of his wild stunts. She dearly loves Ed's sense of humor.

Have you ever known people who do crazy things or act boisterous to attract attention to themselves? Some people, in order to hide their deeper feelings, camouflage them with outlandish behavior, while others remain silent. Still others wear the mask of being cool and in control, rarely sharing anything personal about themselves.

Everyone wants to be liked. It's not unusual to hide features about oneself, especially out of fear that others may not like what they see. Many people are not even aware that they put on masks when they are being unauthentic in their attempt to impress another.

Unfortunately, people sometimes marry without knowing all about their partners. Because it is only natural to think the best of the people we care for, it becomes relatively easy to avoid looking for a partner's hidden secrets.

In order to move into the deepest stage of love, however, both people must have an accurate and deep knowledge of each other. They will try to be honest about who they are and show that their words are consistent with their actions. At this point, they are ready for the stage of love.

✷ **Media Watch**
All You Need Is Love

Your understanding of the phrase "falling in love," has probably been shaped by the popular media. Many of your preconceived notions about love have been influenced by television, movies, and especially through popular music.

How much is your understanding of romantic love influenced by popular music? Take a survey to find out. Keep a radio log during the next week. Make a note of each song that you hear and the time it was played. Also write down each song's theme and the number of times the word "love" is mentioned. At the end of the week's log, determine the average number of love songs you heard during this period. Analyze what the songs say about love. How do you feel about their understanding of love?

All commercial radio stations make money from advertising revenues. Do you see any connections between the songs a radio station plays and the type of advertising they play? Keep track of the commercials in your log as well. When a commercial advertising a local restaurant always follows a song about true love, what do you think it's trying to accomplish?

Journal Assignment

Have the students write about people they know who act differently, depending on who they are around, or change part of their behavior in order to attract attention to themselves. Ask them to use fictitious names.

☾ **Well-Being**

Teaching Approaches

- Read the panel feature to add to the discussion on the second stage of love. Use the students' journal assignment to help answer the in-text questions. Have the students discuss the questions in a small group and summarize as part of a large group roundup.

- If possible, show a videotape of a "Leave It To Beaver" episode featuring the many faces of Eddie Haskell.

☾ Well Being
Zero to One

Television in the 1950s personified the person who wears a mask in the character of Eddie Haskell on the series, "Leave It To Beaver." Eddie was two-faced, acting one way with parents (kind and considerate) and totally the opposite with his peers (a rude troublemaker). While many of the parents accepted the Eddie they knew, kids knew that Eddie couldn't be trusted.

Not every person who wears a mask is an Eddie Haskell. Many people are outgoing around friends, but become very shy when a person of the opposite sex is around. Other people behave one way at school and another way at home. A mature person will generally behave consistently in all situations and, therefore, will be less likely to wear a mask.

What are some of the masks that you see people (adolescents and adults) wearing? Make a list of these masks and describe why, in your opinion, people wear them. How can you spot someone who is wearing a mask? What does it tell you about a person when he or she wears a mask?

Passing the Test

Teaching Approaches

- Introduce the third stage of love as the "testing stage." Read or summarize the section. Why do students think it is referred to by that name?

- **Reteach**—Assign **Application** Project 3. Have the students work individually or in small groups to write test questions for couples considering marriage based on the categories listed. Summarize, share, and compile into one class list.

- **Extend the Lesson**—Find a couple to take the class's test. Score their results and discuss them with the students.

Passing the Test

In the third or **testing** stage of love, couples often seriously consider each other as a future marriage partner. Think of the two-part tests that you take in school as an analogy. Before a man and a woman consider marriage they need accurate and comprehensive knowledge about each other. They need to know what the other feels about earning and spending money, sexual intimacy, religious practice, politics, values, the use of alcohol and drugs, raising a family, the importance of individual careers, and other important issues.

The second part of the test would be similar to an essay question. Based on the feelings of the two people, each person must ask: "Is there genuine, honest love between us? Is our love strong enough to last a lifetime?"

Talk It Over

1. Why do people wear masks?
2. Describe what might happen in a marriage when one or both partners continue to hide behind masks regularly.
3. List some other important issues that must be discussed by couples considering marriage.
4. Is it necessary for couples to agree on every issue before being married? List five important issues that a couple should discuss before marriage. On which issues should a couple agree if they hope to have a successful marriage?

Knowing how a potential spouse will react in a given situation is information that should be understood before marriage.

Talk It Over

Questions 1, 3, and 4 can be used as review questions. First, have the students write their answers. Check by calling on volunteers to share their answers in a large group roundup. For Question 2, encourage pairs of students to develop short skits based on this scenario.

Background

A couple cannot look for signs in the clouds or in a crystal ball to determine their love for each other. People know that they have found someone special when they can honestly admit they really *know* that person. Knowing a person includes understanding his or her likes and dislikes, but also includes being aware of what is in the other's heart.

Aims

1. To uncover some of the most common false expectations in marriage.
2. To help students consider questions that are to be asked prior to marriage.
3. To help students understand the meaning of committed love.

Begin the Section

1. Show the students photos of four or five different men and women of all ages and cultures. Ask them to speculate on what each person's expectations of married life would be. Discuss any stereotypical images that students raise.
2. Ask: "Why do people have different expectations of marriage?"
3. Read the introduction to the section. Allow the students to share what they consider to be important expectations of marriage. Write their ideas on the board. Plan to comment on them as you cover the lessons of this section.

Expectations

Lesson Overview

Recall with the students the marriage expectations they assigned to each of the people pictured in the opening of the section. Point out the differences in expectations, fictional or not. Say: "For every couple and every person within a couple, there are different expectations for marriage. Being aware of your own and your partner's expectations in many key areas of married life can increase your chance for a successful marriage."

Teaching Approaches

- Have the students read the issues raised in this section. Have them jot down some of their personal expectations in each of these areas. For example, "If I marry, I expect my spouse to treat me like an intelligent adult."

- Have the students rank the issues from most important to least important. Have volunteers share why they ranked them as they did.

II. PREPARING FOR A LIFETIME

People buy new cars expecting safe, dependable transportation. People attend movies for entertainment. But what about marriage? What do people expect from marriage?

Everyone who considers marriage will have many different expectations, even some of which they are not aware. Our expectations come from observing marriage, especially our parents' and relatives', or the marriages seen on television and in the movies. Knowing your expectations of marriage and those of your spouse is crucial for establishing a successful, happy marriage.

Expectations

No marriage is ever perfect. What a couple can hope is that they have an enduring, happy marriage. And that is enough. Perfect marriages—that is, marriages that never experience problems and that fulfill all of the needs of both partners—if they did exist, would be very boring! All marriages experience a certain amount of problems and frustrations. Even the most stable, loving marriages are filled with challenging experiences. The success of a marriage ultimately depends on the attitudes and actions of the couple.

It is a painful, yet accurate, statistic that approximately fifty percent of all marriages in North America end in divorce. Why is it that some marriages fall apart while others succeed? Marriages often fail because of false or unrealistic expectations:

1. **Sexual Intimacy.** Some people enter marriage thinking that all of their intimacy needs will be met through genital sexual activity. In reality, sexual intercourse is the *result* of sexual intimacy, not the cause of it. People who marry only for sex will soon be disappointed. Healthy marriages require much broader foundations than sexual intercourse can provide.

2. **Change.** Some people mistakenly think that marriage will automatically change the attitudes or behavior of the people they plan to marry. "He'll stop drinking after we're married." "She'll like my mother after the wedding," they say. What they find is that most people don't change easily. They recognize

If you are unhappy with a person's behavior now, don't expect it to change after marriage.

Journal Assignment

Say: "Write a story about a couple who did not discuss all the important issues before marriage. Tell what happened to their relationship."

Sharpening Your Skills
Breaking Up I Hard to Do

Ending a relationship is often a painful experience. Breaking up with a person who you have dated, and of whom you have grown particularly fond, can be heartbreaking, even when you know the relationship has actually ended. Knowing the skills to end a relationship properly can help ease the pain. These skills are valuable for people of all ages, but especially for adolescents. Romantic attachments and breakups are frequent events during young adulthood. Here are some things *not* to do when you are breaking off a relationship. (Positive suggestions are listed in the parentheses.)

● Just stop calling. Also, when you see the person at school, go the other way. (Actually, one last call would be appropriate. Arrange on the phone to meet the person face-to-face. An in-person meeting is the place to inform the other that you wish to end a relationship.)

● Make up a reason. (Making up a reason just leaves a person confused and can create more problems for you. Always be direct and honest, yet kind.)

● When your boyfriend or girlfriend tells you that the relationship is over, throw a tantrum and say rude, hurtful things about this thoughtless person. (Stay calm. Listen to what he or she has to say. Don't try to argue back or plead your undying love. Be pleasant. Say how much you valued the relationship.)

● Break it off slowly. You know you eventually want the relationship to end. So you start seeing other people behind your partner's back. (Make a clean break, and don't go back with the person because you are bored or you think the other person is hurt. That just prolongs the misery.)

Develop additional good advice for ending a relationship gently.

---

the truth only when the drinking continues and the arguments with the mother-in-law become even more bitter. The traits and behavior that drive someone crazy before the wedding usually worsen after marriage. Marriage brings out both the best and the worst in people.

3. I'll Be Treated Like Royalty. Some people marry expecting their spouses to be their live-in maid, janitor, banker, accountant, cook, laundress, gardener, and housekeeper. Unfortunately for them, this does not happen, especially in modern marriages based on mature relationships. There is a big difference between being loved and being pampered. People who are primarily interested in how they will benefit from marriage are in for a

rude awakening. Relationships among immature people, or people with great differences in their level of maturity, usually fail. People who insist that their needs are more important than their spouses' needs are immature. Men who expect to be mothered by their wives, or women who expect their husbands to put them on a pedestal, face many problems. Each person only has the right to expect that realistic needs will be met in a marriage. The operative word to consider here is realistic. Selfish wants and desires are not realistic.

In marriages that last, couples attempt to share roles and responsibilities in equal measure. When marriages are happiest, people think of their spouses before they demand that their own needs be fulfilled.

● Read or summarize the rest of the section.

● If possible, call one boy and one girl to the front of the class. Ask them to bring their written statements on the personal expectations they have for marriage. Choose one issue. Have each person read his or her statement. Have the class vote as to whether or not the two are compatible on the issue.

● **Reteach**—After going through this exercise for each of the issues with different couples, ask: "How would a couple be able to work out different expectations prior to marriage?"

● **Extend the Lesson**—In 1900, there were 709,000 marriages in the United States and 55,751 divorces. In 1985, there were 2,425,000 marriages and 1,187,000 divorces. Have the students compute the percentages of marriages that ended in divorce in both years (1900 - 7.9%, 1985 - 49%). Why do they think the percentages have changed so much over this century?

Sharpening Your Skills

Teaching Approaches

● Introduce the topic by asking the students to share some of the common causes for breakups of relationships.

● Discuss the right and wrong solutions for breaking off a relationship. Ask: "Why are they right? Why are they wrong?"

● Have two sides debate the following: "Someone who says, 'We are so in love that we never argue,' probably has a really good relationship."

Resources

Resource 10D provides more marriage and divorce statistics.

Talk It Over

Use questions 1 and 2 as part of the class discussion. You may wish to assign Question 2 as a journal activity.

Meeting Expectations

Lesson Overview

A couple considering marriage will likely be presented with a list of questions like those presented in this lesson by either a marriage counselor, priest, or retreat leader. Have the students reflect on and develop personal answers for each question. Also, have them formulate some more questions that should be raised.

Teaching Approaches

- Divide the class into five groups. Assign each group one of the questions to read and discuss.
- Read the last paragraph of the section. Ask: "Why are these issues important? What are some other important issues?"
- **Reteach**—Have the students in each group decide on a way to summarize their discussion for the rest of the class. For example, they may choose to debate the issue, act out a skit, share written reflections, or lead a large group discussion based on their topic. Provide follow-up remarks as needed.
- **Extend the Lesson**—With students, develop additional questions that a couple should consider before marriage and discuss them as a class.

4. **Finances.** Problems that deal with money and how to spend it are near the top of the list of those things which weaken a marriage. A recent study showed that the more people went into debt to pay for their wedding, the more likely the marriage would end in divorce within five years. The pressure of paying off debts can kill the marriage before it has a chance to get started.

While a married couple may be able to live more cheaply than two people who live in separate apartments, a certain amount of money is still required to live. Young adults who marry are often at a financial disadvantage because they usually don't have the education or skills they need to earn adequate salaries. People who simply expect that there will be enough money to live on, or who assume that their spouses will agree with them on how money should be spent are deluded.

What other unrealistic expectations would you expect people to have concerning marriage?

Talk It Over

1. What are other expectations that people might have about their spouses? How can these expectations help or harm a marriage?
2. How would you judge the difference between realistic and unrealistic marriage expectations. What can you do to help people change their expectations of you?

Meeting Expectations

Consider the issues raised by the following questions:

Are we willing to support each other's career interests?

One person might be planning to serve the poor in a faraway mission while the other dreams of owning an expensive home. What problems could arise if these expectations were not clearly understood? How might this situation be resolved?

 Family Living
Religion and Marriage

An interfaith marriage occurs between a Catholic and a person of another Christian faith. In an interreligious marriage, a Catholic's spouse is from a non-Christian religion. A marriage between a Catholic spouse and a person of no religious background is considered a mixed marriage.

Religion and religious practice seem to have a significant impact on whether or not marriages are successful. Consider the following statistics taken from the 1990 U.S. Census:

- One out of two marriages in the U.S., or 50 percent, ends in divorce.
- For couples who are married in a church wedding and who participate in church services together, the divorce rate drops to 1 in 50, or 2 percent.
- For couples who are married in a church wedding, who participate in services together, and who practice their religion and pray together at home, the divorce rate drops to 1 in 1150 or .08696 percent!

These statistics apply to all religions, not just Catholicism. There is no explanation on how the statistics apply to interfaith and interreligious marriages; the report put all types of religious marriages into one category. Other studies suggest that interreligious and interfaith marriages have higher divorce rates than do same faith marriages.

Background

Other important issues to question before marriage include the need for personal space, the ways arguments are settled, common interests, and whether or not the couple likes each other's friends.

What are the roles for the man and woman in marriage?

Many people have strong feelings about gender roles in marriage. One man might expect his wife to stay home and raise the children while he goes to work, while the woman expects to work, leaving her husband to care for the children. A woman who has been transferred to another city feels that her husband should give up his job for her career. How might a marriage be affected if one person's career is more financially successful than the other's?

What are our religious beliefs? How do we practice our religion?

Sometimes, when young people are dating, they do not consider religion to be an important concern. Even if one partner is religious and the other is not, the one who is might think, "I will be able to convert him/her to my way of thinking in time." Because you already know that expecting your partner to change is unrealistic, this difference in religious expression is sure to be a source of conflict. This issue usually becomes critical when children are involved.

Are we able to maintain our autonomy?

While dating, some couples do everything together, often because one or the other partner is possessive or jealous. A possessive person may feel threatened when his or her partner pursues other interests or spends time with friends. People who feel that they cannot do anything without their partner may lack self-esteem. Marriage involves a sharing of lives and interests; it is not the fusing of two lives into one.

Are we using marriage to solve a problem, or as a way to leave an unhealthy family situation?

Marriage is not an escape route from a past way of life. For example:

◊ Twenty-two-year-old Nancy could not afford the monthly rent for an apartment, so she lived at home with her mother and father. Nancy often argued with her parents about the hours she kept, her choice of friends, and her lack of financial independence. When Len proposed marriage, Nancy's first thought was that it was a way to get away from her parents.

◊ At the time of his marriage to Maria, 26-year-old Luke was an alcoholic who denied he had a drinking problem. Luke, who had recently been convicted of drunk driving and had lost a job because of his drinking, pictured marriage to Maria as a way to stabilize his life and correct his problem.

Nancy's and Luke's marriages each lasted less than a year.

Prospective marriage partners must take an honest look at each other's lives, as well as their own, to make sure that marriage is not being used to solve a problem.

How do we feel about children? What size family would we like to have?

A discussion about children and attitudes about child-rearing is a must before marriage. A

What size of family would you like to have?

Background

Marriages between Catholics and people who are not baptized are called *dispartiy of cult* marriages by the Revised Code of Canon Law.

▲ **Family Living**

Teaching Approaches
- Read or summarize the panel and familiarize the students with the terms for different kinds of marriages before they discuss "Talk It Over," Questions 3 and 4.
- Ask: "How important to you is marrying someone of the same religious faith?"

Talk It Over

If Question 1 has already been discussed with the large group, have the students write their own answers, or a summary of the class discussion in their journals. For Question 2, recall the volunteers who shared their opinions on issues before the class and the solutions discussed. Ask the students to determine ways to correct some disagreements and the advisability of correcting many disagreements. Questions 3 and 4 may be used as starting points for debate on the importance of religion in a marriage.

Growing Love

Lesson Overview

This lesson reviews the importance of commitment to a lasting marriage relationship and looks again at questions couples should consider before choosing to marry. Finally, the lesson ends by encouraging students to be honest in their relationships as a matter of principle and of common sense.

Teaching Approaches

- Have the students describe how people they know—whether they be their parents, grand-parents, neighbors or friends—continue to communicate their affection and love after many years of marriage.

- What are some of the challenges a relationship might encounter over the course of many years. How will love have to adapt to remain fresh in the relationship.

- **Reteach**—Have students role play a situation when a young couple realize that they cannot have children of their own. These role-plays should reflect the many different emotions a couple would feel including anger, sorrow, frustration and denial. Ask them to eplain how their response to these feelings will shape their relationship.

- **Extend the Lesson**—Invite several older couples into the class and ask them how they have managed to stay in love for so long?

Catholic Christian marriage has two purposes: to unify the couple in loving relationship and to assist God in the couple's role as co-Creators of new life with God. Besides exploring a partner's willingness to have children, a discussion on parenthood must also include opinions about child-rearing, financial needs, and birth control.

These issues are certainly not the only ones to be discussed. Practical questions such as how each partner handles arguments, where each prefers to live, and how holidays will be spent can be classified under the heading, "Are we compatible?" or "Can we really live together as wife and husband?" These questions need to be settled long before the wedding takes place.

Talk It Over

1. Why is it important to know a prospective spouse's answers to questions concerning children, finances, career, and gender roles? What additional questions do you feel need to be asked and answered before marriage?
2. How would you respond if you and your potential spouse disagreed on a few important questions? on many important questions?
3. What is the importance of religious practice in marriage? Why do you think that religious practice makes such a difference on the divorce rate?
4. What special problems would you expect interreligious and interfaith marriages to experience?

Growing Love

Have you ever seen your grandparents hold hands on an evening walk? Or your mother surprise your father with a weekend away from home for their wedding anniversary? The expression of love is much more than an expression of feelings, as in the first stages of love. Couples who express their commitment to love, do so intentionally.

When two people make a conscious decision to love, they create a relationship that will not be destroyed by the inevitable disagreements, differences, and disappointments that occur in marriage. A person whose love for another is based on a committed decision is strengthened to resist the temptations that can lead to infidelity or acting out of anger.

What do you think it takes for love to last a lifetime?

Compatibility?

Couples preparing for marriage in the Catholic Church are usually asked to complete a compatibility survey. Survey results are used to help the man and woman see how well they agree on important marriage issues. Where the survey identifies serious disagreements on an issue, the woman and man are asked to try and understand why they differ, and to determine how they might reach a solution to their differences.

This survey can be beneficial in other ways as well. By knowing the relationship's strengths and weaknesses, a couple can begin to resolve problems before they arise, and the survey results can help a couple realize that they disagree on too many things to marry. Couples have been known to postpone or even cancel their weddings after realizing how differently they felt about important issues.

Listed below are twenty issues that a couple should consider before marriage. On which of these issues, do you think, is it most important for the couple to be in agreement? Rank them from 1-20 (with 1 being most important) according to their importance to you, then answer the questions at the end of the survey. Discuss your rankings in class. Be prepared to explain your order of preference.

1. _____ The ability to get along with my future spouse's friends.
2. _____ Share common religious values.
3. _____ Drug and alcohol use.
4. _____ Acceptance by my future spouse's family.
5. _____ Understand the man's and woman's roles in a marriage.
6. _____ Views on parenting models.
7. _____ How many children do we wish to have?
8. _____ Where will we live?
9. _____ Techniques for conflict management.
10. _____ An understanding of the importance of sexual intimacy.
11. _____ An ability to offer and accept forgiveness.
12. _____ Concerns about one's future spouse's relationship with members of the opposite sex.
13. _____ The ability to completely trust one's future spouse with the most intimate details of life.
14. _____ Something from the couple's past continues to affect the relationship.
15. _____ A willingness to develop personal autonomy.
16. _____ The decision to marry is based on the expectations of others.
17. _____ Agreement on spending and saving money.
18. _____ Religious instruction and training of children.
19. _____ The skill of good communication resulting from good listening habits.
20. _____ The type of family planning method to be used.

- Which issue did you rank first? Why is this issue most significant for you?
- Which issue did you rank last? Why is this issue so insignificant?
- What other issues would you expect to see in a compatibility survey? Why would these issues be important?
- What does this survey reveal about your priorities?

203

Compatibility?

Teaching Approaches

- After the students have marked the survey, divide the class into small groups. Choose group leaders who will monitor the discussion and make sure that everyone gets a chance to share.
- Each person should share his or her opinion on one of the questions listed at the end of the activity.
- Allow time for a large group discussion. The group leader should share some of the significant points of discussion with the entire class.

Resources

Resource 10E provides a format for the activity suggested in "Compatibility?"

Teaching Approaches

- Review these ten considerations in making a commitment to love. Have students rank them in order of importance.
- Discuss what criteria students would use to determine if their love was genuine.
- **Reteach**—Have students evaluate their present relationships in light of these considerations.
- **Extend the Lesson**—Present this list to a married couple and have them comment on its usefulness. What would they add? What would they change?

What's Next

Teaching Approaches

- Assign the section for individual reading. Then, ask the students to comment on the stories of Jason and Georgina and Doug and Lynette.
- **Reteach**—Ask: "How would you deal with the issues presented in their changing relationships?" Also, you may wish to have the students debate the issues presented in **Application** Project 6.
- **Extend the Lesson**—Share some more information or have the student's research the Church's position on premarital cohabitation and sex. Have the students report to the class on these subjects.

Talk It Over

All three questions can be discussed in a small group. Allow time for the students to formulate their answers before sharing them with the small group.

What to Look For

A major part of preparing for marriage is to test the depth of love and to ask, "Am I willing and able to make an honest decision to love my partner every day, no matter where life's course takes us?" In order to answer that question honestly, you must discern whether or not your love for your partner is genuine. The following is a list of signs that your relationship has the potential to succeed as a marriage. These signs are only guides and are not to be used to determine a passing or failing grade. The list will, however, help you sense the range of considerations involved in making a commitment to love.

1. You should feel comfortable with one another.
2. You should be honest, candid, and at ease saying what's on your mind and in your heart.
3. You should feel respected and understood.
4. You should feel like your values are respected and supported.
5. You should respect the values of the other.
6. Although your relationship should excite you, it need not be that way all the time. Look for a balance in your emotions and in your feelings.
7. Although certain features of the other person might attract you, it should be the whole person that you find attractive.
8. Both of you should be genuinely interested in each other's past, present, and future.
9. You should both consistently seek to help the other feel good about himself or herself.
10. You should enjoy doing things as a couple or simply being together.

In Focus
Role Model

Jesus is the model for all vocations, even though He never married or became a clerical member of any of the religious communities of his day.

Jesus was eventually called a priest by the early Church, but the term was used in a new way for him. He offered a sacrifice to God as all priests do, but that sacrifice was Himself—an expression of the priesthood quite different from the view of His contemporaries.

Throughout the history of the Church there have been various ways of living the Christian life. Each of these ways of life was patterned in some way after "the way" lived by Jesus, the foundation of Christian life. Every Christian has to decide, through reflection and prayer, what particular way he or she should best follow Jesus.

What's Next?

You may find yourself in a committed relationship right now. For years, the phrase was "going steady." If so, where do you see it leading? Is this the marriage partner who will help you accomplish your life plan?

Couples who plan on attending different colleges after high school graduation usually have difficulty keeping committed relationships alive. Nevertheless, some people try.

◊ Georgina and Jason dated during the last two years of high school. Georgina went to college 200 miles from home, while Jason stayed in town working as a fire ranger for the local state park. For the first three months of school, Georgina and Jason tried to keep the relationship going. Either Jason would drive to see Georgina at school on weekends, or she would come home. At Christmas, when Georgina came home, Jason found out from a friend who attended the same school that she had been dating other guys during the last month of the semester.

Jason confronted Georgina, "All you had to do was tell me that you wanted to

Background

The Church's teaching on premarital sexual intercourse is consistent. Intercourse finds its full meaning only in the faithful commitment of a married couple. All other acts of sexual intercourse achieve only a part of the whole, and so are violations of the sanctity of the marriage union. "Outside this 'definitive community of life' called marriage, however personally gratifying or well intended, genital sexual intimacy is objectively morally wrong. Relational misunderstandings and breakups, start seeing other people. I kind of felt that way, too, you know."

The two remained friends, but their exclusive relationship ended.

◊ The situation was different for Doug and Lynette. Right after high school graduation, Doug was going to work in his father's auto repair business. Though Lynette's father's job had been relocated to another state, she was going to stay and attend the local junior college. After dating for their entire senior year, Doug and Lynette both wanted the relationship to continue. They had even talked about marriage someday.

The immediate problem was where Lynette would live once her family left town. "Why don't we get an apartment and live together?" she asked Doug. "It would cut down on our expenses. And besides, we could see what it is like to be married."

Doug didn't like the idea. He knew his parents would never approve, and he didn't think he was ready to find out "what it is like to be married." He felt as if Lynette was trying to trap him.

You set the direction for your own relationships. The Church would agree with Doug that living together—and the premarital sexual intercourse that may ensue—is wrong. The Church teaches that sexual intercourse is an expression of a full and committed relationship, the kind which exists only in marriage.

In making any decisions concerning your relationships, the most important thing to remember is to be honest. You need to come to a clear understanding of your dreams and expectations for married life. You have to ask yourself if the person you are dating in a committed relationship now fits into those dreams. Once clear in your own mind, you need to communicate how you feel and what you think to the other person. Couples can operate under false assumptions because of mixed messages. One person may be thinking marriage, while the other has a completely different idea.

Keep in touch with your dreams and goals. Be honest with yourself. Communicate honestly with your partner. These are simple steps to healthy relationships.

Talk It Over

1. Why do you think it is important to make a committed decision to love rather than to just rely on feelings?

2. What other signs would you look for to determine whether a relationship might lead to marriage?

3. From your observations, how well do romantic relationships formed in high school continue after graduation? Use examples to support your answer.

Chapter Summary

- There is more to choosing the right marriage partner than is often the hint of romantic dreams. Choosing the right partner takes considerable time and skill.
- Most people choose marriage partners with similar interests, backgrounds, and values.
- "Falling in love" is a romantic attraction. Mature love is needed for a lasting relationship.
- Couples contemplating marriage need to answer the questions, "Are we compatible?" and "Can we really live together?"
- Genuine love is needed if a couple is to make a committed decision to marriage.

the sense of being used or betrayed, the trauma of unexpected pregnancies, sometimes followed by abortion of the young, constitute some of the real personal harm that can result from sexual intimacy expressed apart from the bonds and fidelity of marriage" (*Human Sexuality,* USCC).

Chapter 10 Review

What Have You Learned?

Listed below are suggested answers. For many questions, the answers will vary.

1. Rarely do the romantic dreams, as portrayed in songs or movies, actually happen. Marriages require much work to succeed.

2. A man and a woman from the past would have different expectations than people have today because most marriages prior this century were arranged.

3. Couples with common interests generally find it easier to share about themselves early in the relationship. One advantage of marrying a person with opposite interests and beliefs, is that each person can fill in some of what is lacking in the relationship. The disadvantage comes if dissimilarities become a source of tension.

4. People are attracted to partners who are, in many ways, quite different from themselves. This method of choosing a partner is only effective when the couple finds a balance with one another and supports each other's deficiencies.

5. "Falling in love" usually involves sexual attraction, and the experience of being in love always fades.

6. Some people pretend to be the people they think their partner wants them to be.

7. The testing stage helps the couple determine the attributes of a potential marriage partner.

8. A person's expectations of marriage are formed by the way the person has grown up, by the media, and by the influence of peers.

9. When people have made a committed decision to love, love is present whether the feeling of love is present or not.

10. Comfort with the other, honesty, supported values, respect, balanced emotions, and genuine interest in the other are signs of genuine love.

11. Being honest keeps relationships from going off in wrong directions. False expectations are avoided, and trust is developed.

REVIEW

What Have You Learned?

1. How can romantic dreams mislead a person about what it takes to make a relationship work?

2. How would a man and woman's expectations of marriage have been different in the past?

3. What are the advantages of marrying someone with similar values and interests, and from a similar background?

4. What is meant by the saying "opposites attract"? How effective is this principle in deciding on a marriage partner?

5. What are two things to consider about the phrase "falling in love"?

6. Why do some people hide part of their real selves when forming a relationship?

7. How does the testing stage help to determine whether or not two people should really be considering each other as marriage partners?

8. How are a person's expectations of marriage formed?

9. What is the difference in a person's actions when one thinks of love as a feeling, versus when one views love as a committed decision?

10. What are some of the considerations involved in determining whether or not your love for another is genuine?

11. Why is being honest with oneself and others important in any relationship?

Application

1. Write a fictional account of a couple that gets caught up in a fast-moving relationship based on love at first sight. Leave your story open-ended. Then, ask two people to read your story and add possible endings. Note the direction they envision for the relationship. In general, how do you think people feel about love-at-first-sight relationships?

2. Research the marriage customs of different periods in history, or of different places in the world today. In your report, include some details of the wedding of a well-known person from that time or place.

3. Make a list of the important characteristics you would expect in a marriage partner. Then, rank them in order. Write a paragraph explaining why you ranked the particular characteristics as you did.

4. Interview a married couple. Ask them to tell you how they met or an interesting story from when they were dating. Share their story with your classmates.

5. There are many disguises we wear to protect us from being known as we really are. Name some of the common ones used by your peers. Prepare physical costumes or masks to illustrate these disguises. Share your efforts with the class.

6. Have a class debate on the issue of living together before marriage. Research facts and use individual case studies to back up your point of view.

Journal Assignment

Have students reflect on the difficulty they have in being honest with themselves What are some of the pressures they experience to lie to themselves? How would they benefit from telling the truth?

REVIEW

Chapter Vocabulary

- arranged marriage
- autonomy
- betrothal
- committed relationship
- compatibility
- dowry
- "in love"
- marriage partner
- masks
- mature love
- romantic dreams

"God, the best maker of all marriages,
Combine your hearts in one."

Shakespeare, "Henry V"

Putting Vocabulary to Use

Supply the missing words for each of the sentences below.

1. During high school, a person may be _____ many times with many different persons.
2. For years, a _____ was described as "going steady."
3. A _____ is a payment that was often made by the family of the bride to the husband at the time of the wedding.
4. Many _____, such as "love at first sight" and "there is one person in the world for me," are bound up in myth.
5. Today, more than at any time or place, the choice of a _____ is a personal one.
6. A _____ was once considered the price paid for a bride.
7. An important question couples preparing for marriage should ask is, "Are we able to maintain our personal _____?"
8. People who wear _____ tend to camouflage their feelings with outlandish behavior, or they simply do not tell others what they really think.
9. It is the presence of a _____ that develops from the initial period of romantic attraction that allows a relationship to grow.
10. The marriage of Patricius and Saint Monica was an _____.
11. Couples preparing to marry in the Catholic Church usually complete a survey to help them judge their _____.

Application

Read the directions and descriptions of each project to the students. Allow the students to choose their own project. Suggest the following steps: (1) formulate a plan; (2) complete the tasks; (3) share the initial project with a partner for comments; (4) revise and finalize the project.

Putting Vocabulary to Use

1. "in love"
2. committed relationship
3. dowry
4. romantic dreams
5. marriage partner
6. betrothal
7. autonomy
8. masks
9. mature love
10. arranged marriage
11. compatibility

Final Thought

Background

Interview a married couple about God's role in "making" their marriage successful.

Focus On: Chapter 11

It is impossible to consider the sacramental nature of marriage without focusing on its similarities with the life of Jesus. In a sacramental marriage, God's life is shared in the relationship between husband and wife. The passage from the First Letter of John sums up the living presence of God in all who love: "God is love, and he who abides in love abides in God, and God in him" *(1 John 4:16)*. Likewise, the relationship between Jesus and His Church mirrors the relationship between husband and wife. To say that Jesus loves the Church also expresses His love for individuals and families. A husband and wife actively and lovingly participate in each other's lives. Their lives become one.

The first section of this chapter helps the students to understand the sacramental nature of marriage. The second section looks at the practical issues involved in preparing for marriage, especially during the engagement period.

Plan Ahead

- Incorporate formal and/or spontaneous prayer in each lesson. A participatory prayer service that is suitable for use on retreat is provided in the Teacher's Resource Book.
- Note **Resource** suggestions which can be applied to, or extend, the lessons of this chapter.
- Preview the **Application** projects in the Chapter Review. Refer to **Teaching Approaches** for suggestions on when to assign the projects. Or, the projects may be used as part of lesson, section, or chapter reviews.
- Decide on a method for grouping students for projects and discussion.
- Invite guest speakers who will participate in selected lessons well in advance.

CHAPTER 11

The Marriage Covenant

This one, at last, is bone of my bone and flesh of my flesh; ... That is why a man leaves his father and mother and clings to his wife, and the two of them become one body.

Genesis 2: 23-24

This chapter will help you to:

- Recognize marriage as a sacrament of intimacy between a woman and a man, together with God.
- Understand the sacred nature of marriage through the story of the Wedding at Cana.
- Envision Christ's union with the Church as deeply related to Christian marriage.

- Experience the many different and important ways couples prepare for the sacrament of Marriage.
- Appreciate Christian marriage as an expression of personal religious faith and love.

208

Media Suggestions (Optional)

- *Christian Marriage* (Tabor) Three 30-minute videos. Presentations are on the topics: "Marriage in the Old Testament," "Marriage and the New Testament," and "Christian Practices Today."

- *Building a Christian Marriage: Marriage Enrichment Resources* (Liturgical Press) This video and its accompanying text are designed to help couples who are preparing for marriage.

Aims

1. To help students see that Christian marriage is modeled on the love of Jesus for the Church.
2. To help students understand how marriage came to be celebrated as a sacrament.

Begin the Section

1. Review the seven sacraments—Baptism, Confirmation, Eucharist, Penance, Holy Orders, Marriage, Anointing of the Sick. Ask: "What are some things all the sacraments have in common? How is a Christian marriage a 'visible sign of God's presence'?"
2. Read the section opener. Address the in-text questions.
3. Develop a working definition of marriage with the class. Write it on the board. In a second column, allow the students to suggest words and images associated with marriage. Write these suggestions on the board, too. Refer to and adapt the definition and images as you cover the lessons in this section.
4. Answers to Resource 11A are as follows: A sign of healing presence (Reconciliation, Anointing of the Sick); A vocation of service (Marriage, Holy Orders); Initiation (Baptism, Confirmation, Eucharist); Holy Meal (Eucharist); "Repent and be forgiven" (Baptism, Reconciliation); Mercy (Reconciliation, Anointing of the Sick); New Life (all seven sacraments); Grace-filled (all seven sacraments); A union of love (Marriage); Rooted in Jesus' experience (all seven sacraments); Celebrated with community (all seven sacraments); Given new understanding since Vatican II (all seven sacraments); Christian vocation (Baptism, Marriage, Holy Orders).

I. CALLED TO GOD'S LOVE

Marriage means different things to different people. Marriage is understood best when it is recognized as a special way to experience God's love through a lifelong commitment to another. Couples contemplating marriage and even those already married sometimes overlook this sacramental meaning.

Romantically, marriage can simply be thought of as a time of fulfillment. For some, marriage is a way to escape current problems. Still others see marriage as a means of having children to continue the family name.

So, then, what is marriage? Why is marriage important? How can marriage be, in fact, a sacrament or sign of God's love? What is the best way for couples to plan and prepare for marriage? These are some of the questions that you will consider in this chapter.

209

Resources

Resource 11A from the Teacher's Resource Book is a sacrament review. Accept all reasonable answers.

A Special Relationship

Lesson Overview

All of the joys and sufferings of married life are an essential part of Jesus' work of salvation. The witnessing of love by a married couple to the world is a powerful example. Have the students reflect on the values involved in a loving marriage relationship. How are these values different from the values often accepted by society?

Teaching Approaches

- Say: "Jesus wants to be an active participant in the lives of a married couple." Then, assign the reading.
- **Reteach**—Ask: "How is Jesus a part of your present relationships? How would you want Jesus to be present in your marriage?"
- **Extend the Lesson**—Assign **Application** Project 1. Allow time for follow-up sharing and discussion.

Modeled in Marriage

Teaching Approaches

- Ask the students to suggest examples from the Gospels of how Jesus' relationship with His disciples is modeled in intimacy, commitment, and love.
- Read the first paragraph, including the text from the Letter to the Ephesians. Allow time for the students to share comments or reflections on any specific passage, or the entirety of the text.
- Summarize or read the story of the Wedding at Cana directly from Scripture *(John 2:1-12)*. Have the students form their own conclusions on its meaning. Then, share with them conclusions listed in the text.
- Explain that the Wedding at Cana story has been interpreted to mean that Jesus affirmed the sacredness of marriage. Jesus had a positive view of marriage and family life to which He later added special ideas of His own. These ideas would point to the importance of married life in bringing about the kingdom of God.

A Special Relationship

Marriage operates on many levels. In one sense, it is a series of special relationships. There is the social relationship between a man and woman who have freely agreed to be partners for life. But marriage can also go to the very heart of an individual's very being.

In marriage, a woman and man can find intimacy with God, the Creator, through their committed relationship. The Catholic Church teaches that the love shared by a couple in marriage is a sign or a manifestation of that intimacy. The couple enriches its relationship with Jesus Christ in the giving of themselves in love to each other. This love reflects Jesus' love for the Church. The sacrament of marriage is a reminder to everyone, married and single alike, of our desire to know and love God in a deep and personal way.

Jesus said, "As the Father loves Me, so I also love you. Remain in My love" *(John 15:9)*. Jesus' life was an expression of that love. Jesus shares not only our pain and suffering, but our joy as well. Jesus is an essential part of the relationship between a wife and husband in a Christian marriage. When the couple loves, Jesus is present!

In fact, Jesus is present whenever there is love in any vocation. The Gospel shows how Jesus lovingly accepted everyone: "Come, follow Me" was His constant invitation. In the same way, God's love is made real through our loving relationships.

Modeled in Marriage

The Church itself has been described as a kind of sacrament. We, the people of the Church, are sacrament; we are a visible sign of God's presence to the world. Jesus' relationship with us is reflected through the intimate, committed love of marriage.

We find in the *Letter to the Ephesians,* a message that married Christians are invited to share a strong mutual love for one another. Saint Paul compares Jesus' love for the Church to the love of a wife and husband. The Church finds the following text to be of immense importance for understanding the sacramental nature of marriage:

The intimacy a couple experiences in marriage is also an expression of God's love.

Background

Jesus promises His disciples that He will remain with them *(John 15:9)*. In the relationship between a man and woman in Christian marriage, Jesus' presence in the union is even more intimate.

Journal Assignment

"Choose one passage from the text of Paul's Letter to the Ephesians and write your own reflection of its meaning and how it relates to Christian marriage."

"Husbands, love your wives, even as Christ loved the Church and handed Himself over for her to sanctify her, cleansing her by the bath of water with the Word, that He might present to Himself the Church in splendor, without spot or wrinkle or any such thing, that she might be holy without blemish. So husbands should love their wives as their own bodies. He who loves his wife loves himself. For no one hates his own flesh but rather nourishes it and cherishes it, even as Christ does the Church, because we are members of His body...This is a great mystery, but I speak in reference to Christ and the Church. In any case, each one of you should love his wife as himself, and the wife should respect her husband."

(Ephesians 5:25-30,32-33)

John's Gospel account suggests Jesus' willingness to be an active participant in a couple's married life in the story of the Wedding at Cana *(John 2:1-12)*.

You are probably familiar with the story. The planning for the wedding feast seems to have been a little short-sighted. Before the feast was to end, they ran out of wine, a sorry state of affairs sure to cause the family public embarrassment. This situation would perhaps cast a shadow of doubt over this new marriage. What future disasters will this couple experience, if this is any indication of their readiness for marriage?

Mary, Jesus' mother, realizes the couple's dilemma.

"They have no wine," she says to Jesus. In her own way, Mary is telling Jesus that this marriage could be in deep trouble without His help.

"Woman, how does your concern affect Me?" Jesus answers.

Mary accepts Jesus' comment and tells the servers, "Do whatever He tells you."

So six large jars are filled with water. When the headwaiter tastes what is poured from the jars, he is surprised. "You have kept the good wine until now!" he says.

The Wedding at Cana has been read by the Church as being particularly symbolic for the celebration of marriage. While there are many ways of reading the story, it can apply to marriage in at least these ways:

1. Jesus revealed His power at a wedding to help a couple in need and offered hope to all couples. It also supports the belief that Jesus blesses marriages by His presence and power.

2. Mary turned to Jesus on the couple's behalf. Catholic weddings traditionally pay special tribute to Mary and ask her to remember the couple's needs to Jesus, as she did at Cana.

3. Jesus' response should be read as the question it is. Imagine Jesus answering, "What can I do to help?" Jesus is waiting and ready to assist all marriages, but He waits for us to ask for His help.

In Focus
A Wedding Feast

Cana was a village about eight miles north of Nazareth, or about a three-hour journey for people traveling on foot. When guests attended a wedding, they would stay for awhile. The celebration might last for a week, with much dancing (the first led by the bride and groom), singing, eating, and drinking.

Perhaps Mary had a friend or relative in Cana, but no one knows the identity of the wedding couple.

The six stone jars that Jesus ordered filled with water were probably the common water jars used for the Jewish rites of purification. Jews used these containers to wash themselves upon entering a host's home. Each container held anywhere from 20 to 30 gallons of water.

Background

Saint Cyprian once described the Church as a "sacrament of unity." Paul's exhortation to the Ephesians is for strong mutual love. Paul sees Christian marriage as taking on a meaning symbolic of the union between Christ and the Church.

Teaching Approaches

- Share the definition of sacrament as "mystery" with the students. Have them focus on the adventurous aspects of mystery as they read the descriptions of married life presented in this section.
- Discuss the scenarios presented. What do they say about the mystery of marriage?
- **Reteach**—Explain that sacraments are also visible signs of Christ present in the world. How can marriages make the mystery of Christ understandable to others?
- **Extend the Lesson**—Ask each student to write on a slip of paper one sentence describing a possible, future married life scenario. For example, "Your spouse will be in the military; you will live all over the world." Collect all the slips. Randomly pass one to each person. Then, call on students to expand on the scenario they received and tell what married life would be like for them.

☽ Well-Being

Teaching Approaches

- Have the students rank the list of factors from most to least important. Compare rankings and discuss the differences in opinion. Have the students give reasons for ranking one higher than another.
- Discuss the statement: "If these signs of success are not witnessed before marriage, they probably won't appear after the wedding." (Why do students agree or disagree with this statement?)

Amar and Sasha find many ways to convey their love to each other.

4. Marriage is a celebration of the richness of God's kingdom. In John's account, the first sign of the presence of the kingdom happens at this wedding. What conclusions might you draw about the importance of marriage from this fact?

Great Mystery

A sacrament is "a visible sign of God's presence," from the Latin *sacramentum* meaning "mystery." A sacrament reflects the mystery of how God is fully present in life. Nowhere is this more apparent than in the sacrament of Marriage. Consider the following:

◊ Amar and Sasha had been high school sweethearts. Sasha imagined that her marriage to Amar would be a romantic adventure: foreign travel, exquisite dinners, and Sunday picnics in the park. Rather, Amar works close to 60 hours a week at the local Rural Electric plant. Sasha works the swing shift as a nurse's assistant. They spend about eight waking hours all week together. Although married life is not what they had intended, their marriage grows. The time they do have together is well-spent renewing their love. Amar leaves Sasha affectionate notes around the house, shops and cooks special dinners. Sasha hides treats in Amar's briefcase so that he will find them during the day and think of her. True, marriage isn't what they expected, but somehow it works for them.

◊ Suzanne grew up near the beach. All her boyfriends were surfers with sun-bleached hair. She always imagined herself marrying a guy like that. In college, she went to a Halloween party and was attracted to a tall, skinny guy dressed like the Jolly Green Giant. He proved to be quite different than her previous boyfriends. Jeff was more a bookworm than a surfer, more into serious discussions than parties. Suzanne fell in love with Jeff. After they married, Jeff convinced Suzanne to study for her real estate license. They moved to a small town in the mountains, miles from the ocean, and opened a business. Suzanne describes her marriage as "different, but fun."

◊ Larry had always been a sports fan, but he never thought that he would marry a basketball coach. That was before he met

---

Resources

Resource 11B outlines other customs and practices of weddings in biblical times.

Jackie, a high school mathematics teacher who also coached the girls' varsity team. Sitting right behind the team's bench for all of the games, Larry still chuckles every time his wife yells at a referee or when one of her students walks by him and whispers, "He's Mrs. Miller's husband." When Jackie's team won a state playoff game last season, Larry was the most excited fan. Married life had certainly brought many new surprises!

The mystery of married life includes the surprises couples experience and how God continues to be revealed through the events. These surprises can be harmful if the couple is unprepared for or unwilling to deal with the unexpected. In happy marriages, there is a willingness to include God in the relationships and to move in directions that only God can imagine. Being flexible is an important virtue in marriage! Marriage is unpredictable, but it is also guaranteed to be full of adventures, to people open to God's will.

Talk It Over

1. How is the Wedding at Cana an example for Christian marriage? What does it suggest about Jesus' concern for marriage?

2. What are some expectations that you have for married life? Would you want to be married if those expectations were not met?

Marriage as Sacrament

During the first thousand years of Christianity, marriage was acknowledged as an acceptable way of life for Christians, but it was not celebrated as a sacrament. Couples were married in civil ceremonies. The marriages were frequently blest by the Church, but this was not a requirement. Weddings were usually not performed in a Church or witnessed by a priest.

The Church did not take a more active role in marriage for civil and philosophical reasons.

- Civilly, marriage was regulated by the state. Remember, Christianity was persecuted by the state for roughly the first 400 years of its existence.
- Philosophically, the widespread acceptance of a philosophy called *Manichaeism* challenged the sacredness of marriage.

Manichaeism taught that the body was evil and that the spiritual, or soul alone, was good. In this philosophy, people who controlled their carnal appetites were considered closest to God. Marriage was only tolerated because of its close association with childbearing. Unfortunately, some early Christian writers were influenced by this philosophy and often incorporated this belief into their theology.

Well Being
Getting Along

Successful marriages usually grow out of relationships where the early stages of married life are happy. According to researchers, the first years of marriage are most likely to be happy when the husband and wife:

1. Agree on critical issues in their relationship.
2. Share common interests and activities.
3. Demonstrate affection and share confidences, even publicly.
4. Have few complaints about the marriage.
5. Do not generally feel lonely or irritable.
6. Treat each other with respect.

If these signs of success are not witnessed before marriage, they probably won't appear after the wedding.

Background

Every valid marriage between two baptized persons (even two non-Catholic persons) is sacramental. The union of two Christians also provides a community of faith where Christ is present.

Resources

Resource 11C provides more information on manichaeism.

Talk It Over

Use Question 1 as a review. Check to see that the students can summarize the conclusions to the story raised in the text. For Question 2, you may wish to have the students break down their answers to "needs" and "wants." What are some things they must have in a marriage? What are some things they would like to have?

Marriage as Sacrament

Lesson Overview

Without the "little churches" of Christian families, there would be no "big" Church. Thus, the Church has always recognized the importance of Christian marriage. This lesson traces the development of the sacrament, and of its sharing of God's love among husband and wife, parents and children, and couple and the Christian community.

New Words

Manichaeism was a form of "gnosticism," the belief that one must have special knowledge to be saved. Manichaeism held a deeply pessimistic view of the world, which was seen as being dominated by evil powers. Part of the teaching included the idea that all "matter" was bad, and that there was a tension between body and soul. This led to a practice of purging the body to rid it of impurities. Abstinence and self-denial were two of the purges used to purify the body.

Teaching Approaches

- Read or summarize the text section.
- Ask: "What reasons do people give for wanting or not wanting to be married in the Church?"
- **Reteach**—Recall with the students that Saint Dominic's outreach was the beginning of his ministry. From this came the idea of an order of preachers, the Dominicans.
- **Extend the Lesson**—Discuss the importance of celebrating one's marriage as a member of a faith community, not just "getting married in church."

The Marriage Covenant

New Words

A *covenant* is an agreement between two people, between a person and his or her superior, or between two groups. In a religious sense, a covenant is made between God and humanity. The basic covenant of the Hebrew Scriptures was the "testament" that God would always and forever remain faithful to the Hebrew people. Faithfulness from both parties is important in a covenant relationship.

Teaching Approaches

- Highlight the origins of both the unitive and procreative dimensions of marriage from Hebrew Scripture. The creational and relational aspects of marriage are ways to model the very life of God.

- Read or summarize the section. Refer to the Scripture text directly when necessary.

- **Reteach**—Ask: "How do Adam and Eve represent all people? What can we learn from their relationship with one another and with God?"

- **Extend the Lesson**—Examine the two creation stories in Genesis. How do they differ? How are they similar? Can these stories be used to prove the superiority of men or the inferiority of women? (They differ in that the first story has man and woman created together after all of creation—they are the completion of creation, while the second story has woman made from and as a companion to man. The stories are similar in that they both show the creative power of God and that man and woman together are responsible for caring for all of creation. These stories are stories of faith, not science, and so cannot be used to prove or disprove anything scientific. Consult a Scripture commentary for more information about these stories.)

Prior to the Middle Ages, Christians were married according to the local customs of their homeland. The Christian community then recognized the couple's union as binding.

During the Middle Ages, the following changes occurred:
- The Church began to require priests as the official Church witnesses at weddings.
- The Council of Florence (1438-45) declared that marriage was one of the seven sacraments.
- A century later, the Council of Trent (1545-1563) confirmed the seven sacraments and stated that if a marriage was to be valid, it must take place in the presence of an ordained Catholic priest. Any exceptions required special permission from the Church.

The spirit of the Church's positive acceptance of marriage is captured in the wedding or nuptial Mass liturgy. After the Lord's Prayer, the priest extends his hands over the couple and using these or similar words says:

My dear friends, let us turn to the Lord and pray that He will bless with His grace this woman now married in Christ to this man and that, through the sacrament of the Body and Blood of Christ, He will unite in love the couple He has joined in this holy bond... Father, You have made the union of man and wife so holy a mystery that it symbolizes the marriage of Christ and His Church.

The Marriage Covenant

In marriage, a woman and man make a lifelong agreement with each other. This agreement is known as a *covenant,* and is similar in many ways to the relationship that God has with the Hebrew people and with the Church.

Marriage is a binding agreement of love; that is, each partner has freely and irrevocably chosen to love the other just as God has promised to be with the Hebrew people since the time of Abraham. Just as God has remained faithful to the covenant promise, each person promises to remain faithful

In marriage, the couple makes a binding commitment to love one another.

Journal Assignment

Have the students write several conclusions to this metaphor: "A marriage built on faithfulness is like . . ."

Resources

Resource 11D is an activity that helps the students to differentiate between a contract and a covenant.

Covenant or Contract

The Fathers of the Second Vatican Council voted by a margin of 20 to 1 to use the word "covenant" rather than "contract" to describe the relationship of marriage because, in their words, "God is the author of matrimony." The Fathers continued:

> Thus a man and a woman, who by the marriage covenant of conjugal love 'are no longer two, but one flesh' *(Matthew 19:6),* render mutual help and service to each other through an intimate union of their persons and of their actions. Through this union they experience the meaning of their oneness and attain to it with growing perfection day by day. As a mutual gift of two persons, this intimate union, as well as the good of the children, imposes total fidelity on the spouses and argues for an unbreakable oneness between them.

(The Church Today, #48)

to his or her spouse. The origins of this relationship are recognized in the Creation stories found in the Book of Genesis.

In the first account of Creation *(Genesis 1:1-31),* man and woman are created in the image and likeness of God. This likeness is everlasting; each person has a share in God's image. According to the biblical author, man and woman are essential participants in Creation: "Be fertile and multiply; fill the earth and subdue it" *(Genesis 1:28).* Procreation is recognized as an important part of the marriage covenant.

The second account of Creation *(Genesis 2:4-25)* recognizes the human need for companionship. God said: "It is not good for man to be alone. I will make a suitable partner for him" *(Genesis 2:18).* With that, God created a wife for Adam, whom the man called Eve.

The Hebrew people recognized in these and similar stories God's involvement in human relationships. They understood that God blessed the intimacy of marriage and established its importance in the role of human affairs. God is shown as being directly involved with marriage from the outset.

The authors of the Genesis story were also keenly aware that the relationship between humanity and God became fractured. They show the broken relationship through story; Adam and Eve exclude God by their sin.

Sin continues to affect relationships between people as it affected the relationship between humanity and God. All of life is affected by sin. Married life does not escape the tension between the grace of knowing and living with God and the evil that comes from the false independence of sin.

Remember that the Creation stories of Genesis present an interpreted history of the relationship between God and creation. When the Book of Genesis was written, its stories were meant to describe the Divine-human relationship. In that sense, Adam and Eve were typical examples of humanity: they started out in God's favor through grace, yet selfishly turned away from God and lost their privileged position. Even in the Book of Genesis, however, there is the recognition of the need for forgiveness.

The major theme of the Hebrew Scriptures is God's faithfulness to the covenant made with the Chosen People. Marriage is built on the same type of promise. The faithfulness of a married couple to each other is related to God's faithfulness to them.

Covenant or Contract?

Teaching Approaches
- Ask: How is Christian marriage more like a covenant than contract?
- Have students identify the key statements from this quotation and list their answers on the board. Discuss what makes these statements so important.

Background

The Second Vatican Council wrote, "The well-being of the individual person and of human and Christian society is intimately linked with the healthy condition of the community produced by marriage and family" *(The Church Today, #47).*

New Covenant Images

Teaching Approaches

- From what they know about how Jesus treated others, have the students write a paragraph on how Jesus viewed marriage.
- Read or summarize the text. Support the suggestion that Jesus would have viewed marriage as a union of love between a man and a woman.
- **Reteach**—Explain that (1) Jesus taught that the marriage relationship is violated when one's heart—one's basic feelings about one's marriage partner—is compromised, as in adultery. Adultery twists one's heart toward another, who is not one's partner. (2) Jesus also taught that marriage is a deeply personal relationship which influences a couple like no other possible relationship. (3) We can learn much about how Jesus felt about marriage from what He did not say. For example, He did not subscribe to the dominant cultural patterns of His time concerning male superiority. From the evidence of the many encounters Jesus had with women, he clearly treated women with dignity and respect.
- **Extend the Lesson**—Have the students research and report on Jesus' attitude toward women as suggested in Matthew 9:18-26, 15:21-28, 26:6-13, 28:1-10, and John 8:1-11.

Talk It Over

Both questions can be discussed in a small group. Prior to the discussion, you may wish to have the students jot down notes for Question 2, either on a piece of scratch paper or in their journals. This will allow them time to reflect on this example.

Married couples face the challenges of life together. Decisions affecting the relationships and those requiring personal sacrifice are shared.

New Covenant Images

Although Jesus did not directly say much about marriage, His teaching on life in the kingdom influenced how marriage would be understood thereafter. From the positive way Jesus treated women, it would be hard to imagine Him supporting marriages where the woman was treated as if she were property. Male dominance that considered the woman subservient would also be unacceptable to Jesus.

While we know little about Jesus' views on marriage, we do know that He treated women with respect for their dignity and humanity. In Jesus' day, men did not usually associate with women in social settings, yet Jesus had female friends. Several of these women distinguished themselves by staying with Him during His suffering and death while the male disciples fled for their lives.

Couples embark on a risky journey into unfamiliar territory when they marry. Yet, those who take the risk emerge enriched by the experience. A married couple is called to explore life together, to live and share with each other, even at the cost of personal change and sacrifice. God desires to be a part of this whirlwind of change and excitement. The couple is asked to be open to God's providence and to perceive the mystery of God's love unfolding in the new directions resulting from their love.

Talk It Over

1. Which do you consider the more important aspect of marriage: procreation or companionship? Explain your answer.
2. What do you think would be the most difficult part about being married? the most exciting part?

Background

Jesus, without question, taught through his preaching, that man and woman were joined together through the design of the creator. Christ's death and resurrection is a continuing source of grace for all Christian marriages to help them fulfill God's plan. See *Catechism of the Catholic Church,* 1614-15.

II. APPROACHING MARRIAGE

Just as each marriage is unique, so, too, is the *engagement* process that leads to the wedding day. Some people who have known each other and dated for years, might focus mostly on practical issues: arranging for a new place to live, buying life insurance, or reserving a place for the wedding reception. Another couple might spend most of their engagement continuing their discussions about past experiences, present values and beliefs, and their goals for the future. They continue to explore their decision to marry, making sure that it is the right one. There is much to be done during the time of engagement.

Getting Engaged

The engagement process will be filled with many kinds of experiences. The man and woman have the chance to examine life as a couple and to evaluate the relationship on many levels. Engagement is also an opportunity to analyze their serious decision to marry.

To "engage" means to "bring together." That is what occurs in the period before marriage. Two people (and often their families) are brought together. Wedding ideas are discussed, as are the many expectations about marriage itself.

Annulments

Because of the sacramental nature of marriage, the Catholic Church insists that couples thoroughly prepare before the wedding. Sacramental marriages are for "as long as we both shall live." When marriages end in divorce, the Roman Catholic Church will not recognize a later marriage by either spouse as a Christian covenant or sacrament unless the other spouse has died.

There are cases when the Church will rule that a previous marriage was never a sacramental union of the couple, called an *annulment*. An annulment declares that from the beginning of the marriage the couple was unable to make a free commitment of love and fidelity.

No sacramental marriage has taken place if one or both people are not free to give their consent to marry because of:

- Duress or pressure.
- Serious psychological problems.
- The refusal or inability to consummate the marriage.
- The refusal to have children.

An annulment can also be granted if the wedding itself lacked certain requirements. For example, if the wedding was not performed in the presence of a priest or deacon. If an annulment is granted, a second marriage can be recognized by the Church.

A declaration that a marriage is annulled does not affect the legality of the marriage or the status of the children from that marriage.

Background

Technically, what is often referred to as an "annulment" is really a "declaration of nullity." That is, a Church marriage tribunal has found that there was something lacking at the time of the wedding which is considered an essential part of Christian marriage, so that no sacramental marriage actually occurred. The basis of nullity may exist because of psychological immaturity, emotional distress, or some type of abuse present in the relationship.

II. APPROACHING MARRIAGE

Aims

1. To examine the preparations that take place in the engagement process.
2. To help students become familiar with the Church's requirements for marriage preparation.

Begin the Section

1. Ask the students to play word association with the term "engaged." List some of their responses on the board.
2. Define the word "engagement" as a "promise of marriage." Ask: "What do you think is the most important function of the engagement process?"
3. Read the opener to the section. Explain that some of the issues already raised will be covered in this section.

Annulments

Teaching Approaches

- Read or summarize this feature as an accompaniment to the "Getting Engaged" text. State the Church's teaching on annulments, but be sensitive to the fact that many of your students may have experienced divorce in their own families.
- Assign individual students or small groups of students to work on **Application** Project 8.

Getting Engaged

Lesson Overview

The engagement process is all about preparation. If done well, a couple can be reasonably assured of entering marriage with an understanding of each other's expectations. Preparing for marriage involves more than simply readying for a wedding; it concerns preparations for sharing life with another person on a deep and demanding level. Engagement is a crucial process, if the marriage is to get off to a good start. As a beginning, you may refer the students to **Application** Project 6. If possible, arrange for a married couple to be present to respond to the students' questions.

Getting Engaged

Teaching Approaches (continued)

- Discuss the importance of preparation.
- Ask: "What are some things for which you spend time preparing? How has your preparation helped you to have success and reach your goals?"
- Read or have the students read the text section. Ask: "What are some specific issues that must be discussed (a) when two families come together? (b) concerning wedding ideas? and (c) about the expectations of the man and woman?"
- **Reteach**—Assign **Application** Project 4. (See **Resource 11E**.)
- **Extend the Lesson**—Mention some of the ways that the Church helps to prepare a couple for marriage during the engagement process (Pre-Cana, discussions with pastor, support couples, counseling).

Sharing Dreams

New Words

Marriage banns are the public proclamation of an intended marriage. If the marriage does not take place before the expiration of six months, the banns must be repeated. An *impediment* to marriage is either an external fact or a circumstance that prevents a marriage, sacramental or legal, from actually taking place and makes it invalid or unlawful. Couples that go through the wedding ceremony with an impediment are *not* married.

Teaching Approaches

- Read or summarize the text section.
- **Reteach**—Ask the students to share stories about what happens during an engagement. Press them for details.
- **Extend the Lesson**—Ask: "Does your family have any engagement customs? What are they?" Refer the students to **Application** Project 7.

The engagement process is filled with many types of experiences.

In the process of joining together, the couple may discover differences that seem to pull them apart. They may begin to think that they might not want to marry each other at all.

The Church provides help for couples who are engaged. Through interviews, counseling sessions, marriage workshops, and retreats, the Church assists in both the interpersonal and practical aspects of an engaged couple's preparation for marriage.

Sharing Dreams

The engagement process has evolved from many customs and practices. Today, in Western cultures, engagements begin with a decision by a couple to marry. That decision is only then announced to the parents. It is customary in some communities for the man to ask the woman's parents (especially the father) for permission to marry their (his) daughter. This is a far cry from the days when the parents would arrange the marriages of their children.

The traditional symbol of engagement is a ring, traditionally given by the man to the woman, but the woman will also give the man an engagement gift. With these visible signs of the engagement, the couple formally announces their engagement to family members and friends.

Sharing Secrets

When Sharon turned 25 she felt ready to marry her longtime sweetheart, James, 27. They had dated seriously for several years and Sharon felt she knew James well. She was still surprised by all she learned during their engagement. As Sharon tells the story:

"James asked me to marry him while we were in line waiting to see a movie. Although I had been ready to marry him for some time, his request still caught me off-guard. It was freezing outside that theater, but suddenly I felt warm all over. We gave each other a long, long, hug. The other people in line must have thought we were crazy!

"I told James that he had to ask my Dad's permission for our marriage, as my sisters' husbands had done. James was so nervous! The poor guy sat through an entire TV movie that I know he hated before he even opened his mouth. When he finally did, I heard him tell my Dad how much he loved me. I felt that I would burst from my happiness.

Resources

Resource 11E can be used to help introduce the "Approaching Marriage" section.

Background

The Church requires a definite period of preparation and instruction for marriage (usually six months to one year). During that time, couples work to learn more about themselves.

"Our lives seemed to change overnight. It was like planning a military campaign: Where would we live? Who would we invite to the wedding? How would we pay the bills? What did we have to do to be married in Church? Neither of us had given much thought to all of those issues before our engagement. Everyone seemed so busy. I was afraid that our engagement would be lost in the rush.

"One night, my perception of 'being engaged' changed. James and I hadn't seen each other for three days when we went out for dinner. After we ate, he took me across town. We stopped at the end of a street. James pointed to a wood-framed house with one light on in the window. 'That's where we used to live,' he said quietly. 'My father had his heart attack right in that driveway.'"

"James began to cry. He sobbed with his head on my shoulder. I knew James's father had died when he was a child, but I had never heard the whole story. I had never seen James cry before, either. I just held him. At that moment, I knew that our engagement meant more than rings and dishes and what kind of music to have at the wedding. Our relationship was changing. Our trust was growing stronger. We would love each other even more."

Weddings involve making many basic decisions that will take much of a couple's time prior to marriage. While practical plans and preparations must certainly be handled during an engagement, the most important thing a couple can do is concentrate on building the foundation for their life together by getting to know each other even better.

Engagement is the beginning of a more advanced stage of commitment and honesty. The couple can speak their minds and open their hearts with a new courage because they feel confident that their thoughts and feelings will be heard, understood, and accepted. It is also a time when a new awareness of personal values can surface; you will learn more about your own and those of the person you intend to marry.

✳ Media Watch
Marriage Banns

In the movie, *Three Men and a Little Lady*, the climactic scene involves a mad rush to the church. One of the heroes attempts to reach the service with evidence that will prevent the wedding from occurring. The minister stalls for time by constantly repeating, "Speak now, or forever hold your peace."

The phrase, "Speak now, or forever hold your peace" is included in some wedding services to prevent a wedding when there is just cause for it not to occur. For example, a person still married or formally engaged is not free to marry someone else. The intent of the phrase is to prevent fraud and deception.

The "speak now" phrase is no longer part of the Catholic marriage ritual, nor is it needed. Since the Lateran Council of 1215, engagements have officially been announced through the publication of *marriage banns*. For three successive Sundays, the names of the couple to be married are published in the church bulletin or announced at the liturgy.

Banns insure that the public is aware of those who intend to marry. People who know of a reason why the marriage should not occur can come forward and present it before the service, thus preventing scandal or public embarrassment.

Marriage banns are no longer published in every parish or diocese. Each local bishop is responsible for the practice in his diocese.

During the engagement, the man and woman need to learn whether there are any *impediments* that would interfere with their ability to marry. Last minute rescues only happen in the movies.

Talk It Over

Have the students discuss both questions with a partner. To extend, have the students illustrate or write about a romantic dream about being engaged.

✠ To Your Health

Teaching Approaches

- Assign the panel for reading.
- Ask the students to list some of the medical history issues they feel should be revealed to a marriage partner. Which issues do they think would be the most difficult to share? the least difficult?

Sacrament Preparation

Lesson Overview

Many people still believe that preparing for a marriage means simply reserving dates and places on a calendar, sending out invitations, and buying the right apparel. In this lesson, the students will be made aware of the formal and informal preparation procedures offered and required by the Church. They will see how a "church" wedding is different from a *Church* wedding.

Teaching Approaches

- Say: "True or false? The only requirement for marriage in a Catholic Church is to reserve a time for the wedding six months in advance." Call on any students who answer "false" to explain more of the preparation process.
- Choose two or three students to read the section aloud.
- Ask: "What are some things that could keep a person from making his or her vows freely? How can a preparation period help to make sure that the marriage vows are made freely?"
- Equally divide the class into three to five groups of students. Each group has the task of planning their idea of the "perfect" wedding. Have each group present their project to the class for critique and comment, you may have each group role-play its wedding service to see what can go wrong! Combine this activity with the feature, "Sharpening Your Skills" and "The Wedding Checklist" on page 223.

In many ways, marriage is an adventure into the unknown.

Talk It Over

1. What do you expect to happen during the engagement period?
2. What would be the benefits of a relationship built on complete trust?

Sacrament Preparation

"That's the third crazy call I've had this week," Dorrie, the parish secretary, exclaimed. "The couple is not Catholic, but are looking for a church with a long aisle for the bride to walk down. They want to know what it would cost to get married in a Catholic church. I tell them we do not rent the church out, period. If they want a Catholic wedding, they will just have to become Catholic."

When many people think of marriage they imagine a big church wedding: maid of honor and bridesmaids dressed in matching gowns, best man and groomsmen in fancy tuxedos, bride in flowing white and the groom in waistcoat and tails. A young niece or sister will be the flower bearer, scattering rose petals to cushion the bride's walk up the aisle while the organ plays the familiar wedding march: "tum, tum, te tum." The set is

✠ To Your Health
Medical History

Your personal and family's medical history is part of who you are. Your potential spouse has a right to know whether you are likely to go bald (inherited from maternal grandfather), have twins (it runs in families but often skips a generation), or run the risk of dying young, just as you have the right to know his or her family history.

At times, couples seem to simply ignore these personal and family medical histories rather than avoid or try to hide problems. However, any critical medical information is required if a person is to make a truly free choice to enter into a marriage. Why do you think it would be important to know whether your future spouse's mother had cancer, or father died of a heart attack at forty-two?

Today, because a person may be infected with HIV and not test positive immediately, people have the obligation to inform their future spouses if they have had sexual intercourse even once prior to marriage, shared drug needles, or engaged in any other high risk activities.

Background

The Revised Code of Canon Law places great emphasis on the couple's need for adequate marriage preparation. Canon 1063 says that the "family of God" is indispensable for the transmission of the human and Christian values of marriage and family, which are needed if a couple is to freely give their consent. See also the *Catechism of the Catholic Church,* 1632.

Sacrament Preparation

Teaching Approaches (continued)

- **Reteach**—Assign **Application** Project 3 as for extra credit.
- **Extend the Lesson**—Have the students research the wedding requirements in their parish or diocese.

> ⚊ **Sharpening Your Skills**
>
> **Teaching Approaches**
>
> - Assign small groups to research the cost of particular items. Then, pool all the information together to find out an estimated cost for a wedding in your community.
> - Have the class debate the issue presented in **Application** Project 5.

The priest usually asks the couple: "Why do you want to be married in the church?"

completed by a young boy bearing the rings on a velvet pillow. The religious significance of the ceremony is often lost in the rather exotic festivities.

While weddings in the Catholic Church are formal enough to fulfill even the most romantic fantasies, every effort should be made to preserve their religious significance.

Some people may think that marriage preparation means finding the most beautiful church, making a reservation, and showing up on the day of the wedding. Couples preparing for a Catholic wedding find that the Church requires a much greater commitment from them than a reservation and a deposit for the hall!

Most dioceses in the United States want a couple to announce to the parish priest their intent to marry at least six months prior to the wedding. The six months notice allows for a period of formal preparation, and is not done simply to reserve the parish church. (People who desire a particular wedding date and time, especially during May and June—the traditional wedding months—may have to announce their engagement more than a year in advance if they hope to reserve the church or hall.)

Thirty years ago, marriage preparation meant little more than setting a date and meeting with the priest a day or so before the wedding for rehearsal. The preparation process is now more involved and is designed to help couples ready themselves for the challenges they will face during the first years of marriage. The Church believes that through preparation, couples can learn the skills they need to better adjust to married life. This period of preparation, then, should be understood as a blessing, not a hurdle to be jumped.

In the sacrament of Marriage, the man and woman are the actual ministers of the sacrament. The priest and the rest of the gathered community function as witnesses to the couple's expressed promises which form the marriage covenant. The

> ⚊ **Sharpening Your Skills**
> **A Fancy Party**
>
> What do you think it costs to host a fancy wedding and reception? The average wedding and reception in 1992 cost $12,000!
>
> How much do you think your own wedding and reception will cost? To get a better idea, research the costs for flowers, tuxedos, dresses, a hall or restaurant, caterers, photographers, and musicians in your area. What can you do to make this event reflect your beliefs, values, and pocketbook?

Journal Assignment

An added wedding expense is the cost of celebrating the wedding in the church building. This expense varies by diocese and local custom. Some parishes ask for a donation from the wedding party, often "suggesting" a $250 minimum. Other parishes operate strictly on the philosophy of donations; whatever the couple chooses to give. In still other parishes, couples are aked to donate to the Church an amount equal to 10% of the total cost of the wedding and reception.

Preparing for Marriage

Teaching Approaches

- Ask: "What do you think about the situation where a priest, when he does not perceive that a couple is willing to live the Christian faith, will refuse their request for a Catholic wedding?"

- Read the opening paragraph of the section. Explain that the inventories and marriage preparation sessions will often help to inform the couple on specific issues that need to be explored before they marry.

- Read or summarize the rest of the section. Have the students write down the main steps of the marriage preparation process and formulate any questions they have about each step. Allow time for the students to ask the questions.

- **Reteach**—If not already completed, assign students to find out the specific requirements for marrying in their parish.

- **Extend the Lesson**—Invite an engaged or newly-married couple to visit the class and explain the marriage preparation program they experienced. If a local parish uses a couple-to-couple approach to marriage preparation, invite a teaching couple from there to discuss what they do and how the process works.

marriage vows are given as personal gifts from one partner to the other. During the six-month or longer preparation period, the Church wishes to make sure that couples understand the full significance of their vows and that they are able to make their promises freely.

Preparing for Marriage

When an engaged couple calls and makes an appointment with the parish priest to announce their engagement, the priest will ask if they are practicing Catholics and members of the parish. If the answer to either of these questions is no, the priest, in consultation with the couple, may decide to delay the marriage, even if both people are baptized, although exceptions are made.

During the initial interview, the priest will usually ask the couple why they want to be married in the Catholic Church. He wants to find out if they have a basic understanding of the sacramental nature of marriage. It is at this meeting that the couple may schedule a date and time for their wedding, establish appointments for further interviews with the priest, and find out about any other steps they must take in order to be married in the Church. Depending on the parish, these steps may include:

- Pre-Cana Conferences.
- Engaged Encounter Weekends.
- Natural Family Planning sessions.
- Adult sacramental preparation meetings.
- Couple-to-couple marriage preparation sessions.

After the initial interview, the couple may be asked to complete an inventory that examines their preferences and temperaments, and analyzes their understanding of each other. Taking these inventories does not determine whether a person will be permitted to marry. They simply raise issues and questions to promote mutual discussion during the engagement period.

The couple will also likely be asked to participate in a marriage preparation course. The time and format of the course will vary by parish or diocese, but generally the courses cover such issues as:

- Sexuality.
- Parenting.
- Communication skills.

Couples are asked by the Church to attend various meetings prior to their marriage.

Background

Many parishes have gone away from large classes for marriage preparation to the more intimate experience of couple-to-couple sessions. The focus of these sessions is not to convey information, but to engage the to-be-married couple in a dialogue that benefits from the wisdom and experience of the teaching couple.

The Wedding Checklist

Imagine that you are getting married in a year. Draw up an action plan to accomplish all of the following steps. Be as thorough as possible. For example, decide where you would celebrate the wedding and reception, who would be in the wedding party, who would accomplish each of these tasks, and how the expenses would be paid. You may also include other preparation tasks not presented in the list.

Six to Twelve Months in Advance
√ Determine a budget and style for the wedding (informal, formal).
√ Decide where to hold the wedding.
√ Visit with a priest in the parish where the wedding is to be held.
√ Plan the reception.
√ Choose the wedding party (best man, maid of honor, ushers, bridesmaids, ring bearer, flower girl).
√ Make a guest list.
√ Select a wedding dress and bridesmaids' dresses. Consult a formal wear specialist if desired.
√ Make arrangements with the photographer and florist.
√ Plan the wedding, including readings, prayers, vows, and music.
√ Begin attending marriage preparation sessions.

Three Months in Advance
√ Order invitations, personal stationery, and notepaper.
√ Plan the honeymoon.

Two Months in Advance
√ Address and mail invitations.
√ Choose gifts for attendants and ushers.
√ Buy wedding rings.
√ Plan to get marriage license according to state law. Have a blood test, if required.
√ Plan recording and display of gifts.

One Month in Advance
√ Have hair styled the way it will be worn at the wedding.
√ Have final fitting of gowns and suits.
√ If necessary, plan the rehearsal dinner.
√ Plan accommodations for out-of-town guests.

Two Weeks in Advance
√ Write thank-you notes as gifts are received and recorded.
√ Send wedding announcement to newspaper.
√ If bride's and/or groom's name will change, arrange to do so on social security card, driver's license, credit cards, bank accounts, school or employment records, medical records, insurance.

One Week in Advance
√ Finalize plans with caterer, florist, photographer, and musicians.
√ Confirm rehearsal plans with the priest and the attendants.
√ Arrange to have traveling guests picked up at the airport.
√ Arrange where bride will get dressed for the wedding.
√ Arrange for the collection and registration of gifts at the reception.
√ Arrange for transportation to the church and the reception.
√ Arrange for all bills to be paid.

223

High Risk Marriages

Teaching Approaches

- Have the students debate this statement: "The negative aspects of teen marriages far outweigh whatever positive benefits that might come from them."

- Read or summarize the text section. Discuss the issues that classify a marriage as being at high risk of ending in divorce.

- **Reteach**—Ask: "Why is the Church hesitant about witnessing marriages that fall into high-risk categories?"

- **Extend the Lesson**—"What other issues would make for a 'high-risk' marriage?" "What should be done for the people who are in these 'high-risk' relationships?"

♣ Prayer in Action

Teaching Approaches

- You may wish to use this prayer as a conclusion to a lesson or as a blessing for any married couples who participate in the lessons.

- Have the students use an art medium of their choice to make this prayer a gift to a married couple that they know.

- Have students develop their own personal prayer for newlywed couples. Prayers may be in any form the students prefer, including song or poem.

- The sacramental aspects of marriage.
- Conflict resolution.
- Financial planning.

The courses may be held over a weekend in a retreat format, or as part of a weekly meeting at the home of an experienced married couple who serve as leaders.

Just prior to the wedding, the couple will meet again with the priest. At this meeting, it will be determined whether or not the couple's decision to marry is being made freely without outside pressure, and if they truly understand the meaning of their marriage vows.

High-Risk Marriages

For some couples who wish to marry in the Catholic Church, the preparation process is even more demanding. Couples who fall into a high risk category generally receive more specialized attention.

Who are the people considered high risk? This group is made up of couples where one or both of the people are teenagers, when the woman is pregnant (especially if she is a teen), or when one or both have had a previous marriage. In these cases special effort is made to help the couple prepare for the wedding.

These couples are considered as high-risk for a number of reasons:

1. When pregnancy is involved there is often great pressure placed on the couple to marry before the baby is born. The Church wants to be assured that the couple is truly marrying of their own free will and are not being coerced by the pregnancy.

2. When one or both members of the couple have been previously married and divorced, the Church requires that the previous marriages be declared *null* or nonexistent. This process is commonly referred to as an annulment. No dates can be set for the wedding until the annulment is received from the diocesan Marriage Tribunal. Also, if the priest has concern about the couple's readiness to

---

♣ Prayer in Action
Send-Off

Before the final prayer and dismissal at a Catholic wedding, the priest blesses the bride and groom and prays:

May almighty God, with His Word of blessing, unite your hearts in the never-ending bond of pure love.

May your children bring you happiness, and may your generous love for them be returned to you, many times over.

May the peace of Christ live always in your hearts and in your home.

May you have true friends to stand by you, both in joy or sorrow.

May you be ready and willing to help and comfort all who come to you in need.

And may blessings promised to the compassionate be yours in abundance.

Amen.

Pray these words for a married couple that you know.

---

marry, he may ask them to spend more time in preparation.

High-risk marriages are much more likely to end in divorce than other marriages. The numbers are staggering:

- More than 70 percent of second marriages end in divorce.
- More than 75 percent of teen marriages end in divorce.
- More than 95 percent of teen marriages that involve pregnancy end in divorce.

These numbers paint a disturbing picture. Whatever can be done to help these marriages survive needs to be done, but even with special help they usually fail. Often it would be better if most high-risk marriages never took place.

Journal Assignment

Assign the following: "You are a member of a parish marriage preparation team. Couples preparing for marriage meet with you to fill out the paperwork and answer some basic question about their intentions to marry. It is your task to determine if a couple falls into a "high-risk" category. What questions would you ask and what answers would you look for to make your decision?"

Celebration!

After reviewing Pete and Lisa's wedding liturgy with them, Father Bernie looked disappointed.

"What's the matter, Father?" Pete wanted to know.

"It's just that I was hoping that you and Lisa might wish to share a brief, personal statement of your love for each other as part of your wedding," Father Bernie said.

"Do we have to?" wondered Lisa.

"No," said Father Bernie, "but, anything we can do to make the statement of your love and the witness of the sacrament of Marriage clearer to your friends and family, the better."

"Why, you want to use us Father!" Pete laughed.

"Yes, I guess I do," Father Bernie admitted.

Father Bernie was right. Love, honor, and commitment are rare and strong statements in a time when many couples look at the wedding ceremony as an unnecessary bother. "Why marry?" some men and women wonder. "Our love is strong as it is. We don't need a ceremony to validate our feelings for one another."

While it's true that the love between a couple is very personal, and that the vows and promises they make need only to be made to each other, the real benefit of proclaiming them publicly is that they provide a great source of strength to the community. Marriage is part of a web of many relationships involving families and friends. Marriage is part of the "ecology" of life. As the couple strengthens the community, friends and family who witness the beginning of this public commitment of love, will offer their support to the couple in the coming years.

The wedding ceremony is a celebration that is most at home within the celebration of the Eucharist, where the community normally gathers to worship.

The sacrament of marriage is a statement of commitment to the entire faith community.

Journal Assignment

Ask the students to complete the following assignment: "How are the wedding vows related to the Gospel counsels of poverty, chastity, and obedience?"

Background

The Church teaches that the practice of living together in sexual union before marriage is sinful. This practice diminishes the meaning of sexual intercourse, using it for a lesser purpose than was intended by God.

Celebration

Teaching Approaches

- Have the students read the text section individually or in small groups.
- Ask: "What is the real benefit of proclaiming vows publicly? Why do couples live together prior to marriage?"
- Explain that: (1) Cohabitation is not a practical preparation for marriage. Statistically, marriages where the couple cohabited prior to the wedding are more likely to end in divorce than in those marriages where the couple did not live together. (2) Preparation for marriage which includes self-sacrifice with honest communication, and time spent planning a future together, is a much more effective way for a couple to gain insight into each other's character and allows them to develop a special trust.
- Reread each of the wedding vows. Ask: "With which of these vows would you have the most difficulty? Why?"
- **Reteach**—Recall with the students the definition of vow—a solemn promise or pledge. Vows were associated with the Gospel counsels of poverty, chastity, and obedience. Ask the students to notice the types of promises married couples make during a wedding.
- **Extend the Lesson**—Have the students write their own wedding vows and explain why they include in the vows what they have written. Explain that while most dioceses require couples to use only the approved wedding vows, writing your own vows is an effective way to realize what you truly believe about your marriage and feel about your partner.

▲ Family Living

Teaching Approaches

- Ask students who have practiced these listed skills in their dating relationships to share the results.
- Brainstorm other ideas for developing a good relationship between the family of a future spouse.
- Choose students to role play conversations between a spouse and in-laws that reflect the skills presented in the feature.

▲ Family Living
The Other Family

A popular saying points out that "You do not marry an individual, you marry the whole family." The engagement period, then, is a time to become familiar with the other person's family.

Many comedians have made a living telling mother-in-law jokes. To hear the jokes, one would think that mothers-in-law were demons from hell rather than the mother of the person you love so much. The jokes most surely were developed from people who have not formed a good relationship with their spouse's mother.

How long has it taken you to really know your own parents? Remember that your parents will be your spouse's in-laws, and his or her parents yours. Also remember that your spouse's family knew him or her before you did and their influence is quite deep.

It takes time to be accepted into a new family. You will want to establish a reasonable bond with your future spouse's parents from the beginning of your relationship. Knowing as much as possible about them will make the transition into married life that much easier.

What can you do now to prepare yourself to one day have a harmonious relationship with your spouse's parents? The following skills can be practiced during your dating years:

1. Project an honest image of yourself.
2. Be reliable and trustworthy.
3. Share something about your interests, skills, and goals.

If you practice these skills now, meeting your in-laws for the first time will be made much more enjoyable.

The rite of Marriage occurs after the Liturgy of the Word. The priest or deacon questions the couple about their freedom of choice, their pledge of faithfulness to each other, and their acceptance of and rearing of children. The couple then is asked to express their vows.

> "Pete and Lisa, have you come here freely and without reservation to give yourselves to each other in marriage?" said Father Bernie. "I do," Pete and Lisa answered enthusiastically.
>
> "Will you love and honor each other as man and wife for the rest of your lives?"
>
> "We will."
>
> "Will you accept children lovingly from God, and bring them up according to the law of Christ and His Church?"

Pete and Lisa answered "I will" one last time. Then, Father Bernie asked them to join hands and declare their consent to wed. They each stated loudly:

> "I promise to be true to you in good times and in bad, in sickness and in health. I will love you and honor you all the days of my life."

Father Bernie then winked at the couple, who each brought forth a crumpled piece of paper. They took turns reading into the microphone:

> "Dear God, We thank You for bringing us to this day. We will never forget the love we have experienced through our family and friends. We will always love You. We thank You for bringing us together. We pray that Your grace will be with us in all that we

---

Background

The exchange of marriage vows is a sign that each person consents to the marriage. This act of consent is a "human action in which spouses give themselves to each other and accept each other"*Revised Code of Canon Law,* 1057. According to the *Catechism of the Catholic Church,* this consent must be a free act of the will and cannot be taken under any fear of coercion or other outside forces in order for the marriage to be valid, in accord with Canons 1057 and 1103.

do, all that we are, as husband and wife. We ask Your blessing on those gathered here today. We make this prayer in the name of Jesus, Your Son, and our Lord. Amen."

Father Bernie clapped his hands on their shoulders as if to say, well done!

The wedding vows a couple makes binds the two together as one. How do these vows also join the couple to the faith community?

Talk It Over

1. How long an engagement does your diocese require before you can marry in a Catholic Church?
2. What could you tell a couple about the Church's preparation process for marriage that would convince them of its importance?
3. In what ways does marriage witness to Christian values?
4. What is the importance of a personal witness statement at a wedding? What would you write in your statement?

Chapter Summary

- Jesus' presence at the Wedding at Cana is a sign of His presence in all Christian marriages.
- A married couple's intimate and loving relationship is aptly imaged in Jesus' intimate and loving relationship with the Church.
- Part of the mystery of marriage involves accepting God's design and influence in your life.
- Marriage is a special way of life based on a covenant promise.
- The most important thing a couple can do during the engagement process is to concentrate on building a foundation for the rest of their life together.
- In the sacrament of Marriage, the man and woman minister the sacrament to each other. The priest, family members, and other invited guests serve as special witnesses of the couple's love.
- Preparation for marriage in the Catholic Church involves preparation interviews, counseling sessions, marriage workshops, and retreats.

Talk It Over

For Question 1, help the students find out your diocesan requirements for marriage. For Question 2, have the class brainstorm a list of practical answers. Encourage the students to share specific stories to illustrate their answers to Question 3. For Question 4, allow students who wrote on this subject in their journals to share what they wrote if they wish. The other students can add to the summation of their personal statements.

Chapter Summary

- This section lists the main points of summary of this chapter. To use as a review, you might have the students list examples from the text to illustrate each point, rewrite each point in their own words, or find creative ways to teach each point.
- Have the students share their review techniques with partners.

If free and full consent is lacking, there is and can be no marriage! See the *Catechism of the Catholic Church*, 1626-1630.

Chapter 11 Review

What Have You Learned?

Listed below are suggested answers. For many of the questions, the answers will vary.

1. The sacramental significance of the Cana story is that Jesus affirmed the beauty and sacredness of marriage by His presence and participation in the wedding feast.

2. Saint Paul compared husbands' love for their wives with Christ's love for the Church.

3. The Book of Genesis shows marriage to be both procreative and unitive.

4. In marriage there is a surrender between man and wife, as Jesus surrendered His life for us. A marriage begins with a sense of committed love, and a sense of where that love will take the couple. Its possibilities are limitless.

5. Answers will vary.

6. Traditional engagement practices used today include a man giving the woman a ring, or asking her father's permission to marry.

7. The Church asks a couple to: interview with a priest, attend counseling sessions, attend marriage preparation workshops, complete compatability inventories, and participate in retreats, all as part of the preparation process.

8. Eucharist is the place where the community gathers to celebrate and give thanks for God's goodness, and therefore, the most appropriate place for a wedding.

9. The couple administers the sacrament to one another. The priest, family and friends are witnesses to the sacrament. They are signs to the newlywed couple that the faith community recognizes their love and celebrates in it.

10. Marriage banns are public announcements made by a parish that a couple intends to marry. Banns give other people the opportunity to bring up evidence as to why the marriage should not take place.

REVIEW

What Have You Learned?

1. What is the sacramental significance of the Wedding at Cana story?
2. How did Saint Paul compare the relationship between a husband and wife with that of Jesus and the Church?
3. What are the two purposes of marriage as shown in the Creation stories from the Book of Genesis?
4. How does the love of a married couple for each other reflect Jesus' love for the Church?
5. What are some of the ways couples may profitably spend their engagement period?
6. What are some traditional engagement customs that are still practiced today?
7. Describe the preparation the Church asks of an engaged couple before marriage.
8. Why is the celebration of the Eucharist the most appropriate setting for a Catholic Wedding?
9. What is the married couple's role in the sacrament of Marriage? What is the role of the priest, family, and friends?
10. What are "marriage banns" and why are they used?

Application

1. Write personal witness statements for a wedding between two Christians. In the statements, have each partner express his or her love and respect for the other, and acknowledge the intimacy and trust present in their relationship.
2. Research various wedding traditions concerning the ceremony and reception.
3. Gather materials explaining all or part of the Church's preparation program for marriage. Interview someone connected with the programs. Arrange for a spokesperson of a marriage preparation program to speak directly to your classmates.
4. Make two lists. On one, write all the practical things you would need to do to prepare for a marriage. On the other, write some of the issues you would need to bring up with your partner before the wedding. Which list was easier to make? Why?
5. Arrange for a panel debate of the following issue: "Christian weddings and receptions should be simple and meaningful."
6. Ask a married couple to explain the reasons why they chose to get married. Then ask, "How important are those reasons to you today?"
7. Other than a ring, what would be an appropriate symbol for the engagement period? for marriage?
8. Prepare a report on the annulment process in your diocese. Information for this report can be obtained from your local parish or from the diocesan Marriage Tribunal. Interview a person who has participated in the annulment process. Explore what the experience was like for this person.

Background

The Church does not allow couples to write their own marriage vows because a wedding is considered a formal liturgical act of the Church and thus should follow standard liturgical form using the vows provided in the Rite of Marriage.

REVIEW

Chapter Vocabulary

- banns
- companionship
- covenant
- engagement
- intimacy
- Manichaeism
- marriage preparation
- mystery
- procreation
- sacrament of Marriage
- wedding

We shall not cease from exploration
And the end of all our exploring
Will be to arrive where we started
And know the place for the first time.

T.S. Eliot, "Gerontion"

Putting Vocabulary to Use

Answer the following questions about the vocabulary words.

1. What is "sacramental" about the sacrament of Marriage?
2. How can a couple find intimacy in their relationship with God?
3. Why can marriage be described as a mystery?
4. What is the definition of "covenant" as it relates to God's relationship with the Chosen People from Creation?
5. What does the first Creation story in the Book of Genesis say about the importance of procreation in marriage?
6. How does the second Creation story highlight the need for companionship in marriage?
7. What preparation should take place during the engagement process?
8. How do the Church's current requirements for marriage preparation differ from those of thirty years ago?
9. Why is a church the most appropriate place for a Catholic wedding?
10. How did Manichaeism affect the understanding of marriage as a sacrament?
11. Are marriage banns still used in your diocese? If so, bring to class an example of a bann. If not, find out why.

Application

Read the directions and descriptions of each project to the students. Allow the students to choose their own project. Suggest the following steps: (a) formulate a plan; (b) complete the tasks; (c) share the initial project with a partner for comments; (d) revise and finalize the project.

Putting Vocabulary to Use

Suggested answers:

1. Sacrament means "mystery." Marriage reflects how the mystery of God is present in married life.
2. Couples can find intimacy in their relationship with God in many ways, including through a committed sexual relationship.
3. Mystery leads to many new possibilities and directions. Marriage is about a couple responding to that mystery in faith.
4. God's promise is a covenant to be faithful to the Chosen People.
5. The first creation story says the purpose of marriage is to "be fertile and multiply; fill the earth and subdue it" *(Genesis 1:28)*.
6. The second creation story highlights companionship by stating: "It is not good for man to be alone" *(Genesis 2:18)*.
7. Answers will vary.
8. The Church's requirements for preparation today are more detailed; thirty years ago a couple might have met only once with a priest before the wedding.
9. The Church is where the community gathers. The community is able to support the new couples; the couples in turn strengthen the community.
10. The belief of Manichaeism, that the body was evil and the soul alone was good, was incorrectly incorporated into Catholic theology.
11. Answers will vary.

Final Thought

Background

Thomas Stearns Eliot (1888-1965) was a British poet and critic. This quotation is taken from the work, *Gerontion.*

Focus on: Chapter 12

The first years of married life can be especially difficult; it's important to be aware of the challenges from the start. Married couples face many complex issues. Jobs and finances, competition, conflict, changing family relationships, and adjusting to sexual intimacy are among the many challenges. In marriage, as in any friendship, communication is a key to success. Good communication skills are constructive tools needed to build solid marriages.

How does a couple learn to cope with the reality of parenthood? Rearing a family is probably one of the most difficult roles one can have. Unfortunately, very little is done to prepare parents for this difficult challenge.

Chapter 12 covers some of the adjustment issues that are most apparent during the first years of marriage. The use of effective communication skills is encouraged. The dual dimensions of sexual expression—procreative and unitive—are presented and some parenting issues are examined.

Plan Ahead

- Incorporate formal and/or spontaneous prayer in each lesson. A participatory prayer service that is suitable for use on retreat is provided in the Teacher's Resource Book.
- Note **Resources** which can be applied to, or extend, the lessons of this chapter.
- Preview the **Application** projects in the Chapter Review. Refer to **Teaching Approaches** for suggestions on when to assign the projects. Or, the projects may be used as part of lesson, section, or chapter reviews.
- Decide on a method for grouping students for projects and discussion.
- In advance, invite guest speakers to participate in selected lessons.

The First Years of Married Life

Which of you would hand his son a stone when he asks for a loaf of bread, or a snake when he asks for a fish?

Matthew 7:9

This chapter will help you to:

- Practice the skills needed for effective communication in marriage.
- Explore the unitive and procreative dimensions of sexual expression.
- Understand the sacred responsibilities of being a parent.
- Examine the reasons couples give for having children and the Church's teaching on birth planning and responsible parenthood.

Media Suggestions (Optional)

- *Joys in Parenting* (Franciscan Communications) Four 30-minute segments focus on the major concerns parents have about child rearing: self-image, discipline, siblings, and spiritual values.

- *Husbands and Wives* (Direct Video Services) 43 minutes. Dr. Clayton Barbeau examines issues surrounding the intimacies between wives and husbands.

Aims

1. To look at some common issues confronting newly married couples.
2. To examine the issues of competition, social growth, sexual expression, and parenting, and how these issues affect marital adjustment.

Begin the Section

1. Divide the class into small groups. Read or have the students read the first paragraph of the text. Assign each group to come up with answers to the in-text questions. Have each group summarize its answers and share them with the large group. Record the answers on the board.
2. Repeat the process with the second paragraph of the text. Ask the students to focus especially on the third question: "In what ways can the 'we' relationship of a husband and wife develop without a complete loss of the personal 'I'?"
3. Read the third paragraph. Ask the students to connect how the slogan relates to the beginning of married life. Introduce the aims of the section.

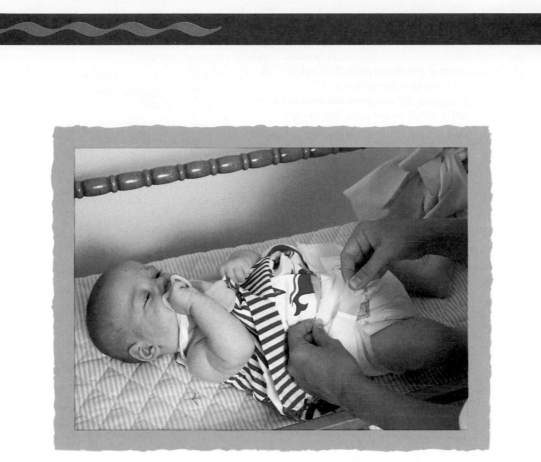

1. ADJUSTING TO MARRIED LIFE

"I would like to be the first to introduce you to Mr. and Mrs. ..."

the priest happily announces to the congregation. The couple, after sharing a kiss, retreats hurriedly down the aisle amidst cheers and applause. Following the reception, the couple goes off on their honeymoon to begin their married life. Awaiting them are the many joys and challenges that accompany marriage. The practical question is this: how do they adjust to being married after years of living as single people?

There are many adjustments which surface at the beginning of a marriage. For example, as working adults, either or both may experience career changes. How will new schedules affect their marital relationship? How will they each maintain their sense of autonomy yet mature in their relationship as a couple?

Journal Assignment

Have students consider the struggle for autonomy that is part of every marriage. Ask: "How would you balance your needs as an individual with a marriage's needs for shared living?

Being Prepared?

Lesson Overview

The issues of (1) competition between spouses (or competing against the imaginary "ideal" spouse); (2) the letting go of old friendships after marriage; and (3) sexual (mis)communication are introduced. Lead the students to recognize the main points of each issue. Choose the most comfortable format for having the students express their reactions to each scenario.

Teaching Approaches

- Present each scenario to the entire class. You may wish to use one of the following formats: (1) Choose students to read each scenario aloud to the entire class. Pause for discussion. (2) Divide the class into four small groups. Assign each group a scenario and have them report on it or present it to the large group as a skit. (3) Have each student read the scenarios individually. Then, working with a partner, have them discuss the main issues and share their reactions.

- Allow time for comments, questions, and summary in a large group follow-up.

- Read or summarize the final two paragraphs of the section. Ask: "If you were married, what would you find to be the hardest part of replacing the vision of 'I' with the vision of 'we'?"

- Explain that there are certain kinds of changes that are healthy in a relationship. For example, change can occur in marriage as a response to a very specific situation. Suppose a couple shares household chores, but the outdoor work is always done by the husband. He might feel that this should be shared as well. An open discussion may bring about needed changes in attitude.

Both partners bring different interests, friends, and family into a marriage. In what ways can the "we" relationship of a husband and wife develop without a complete loss of the personal "I"?

While the wedding day is a great celebration of love, the old slogan, "Today is the first day of the rest of your life," is more apt here than, perhaps, any other time. A couple's wedding is just the beginning of an exciting and always challenging shared adventure.

Being Prepared?

Marriage creates a new lifestyle that require people to live and think in new ways. Many couples experience a great deal of difficulty trying to make this transition to a new lifestyle. Consider the following stories of newly married couples.

Corrina was anxious to go to the game with her old friend, Bridget.

What help does each of these couples need to build a successful marriage?

◊ Married just one month, Frank bounded into the apartment with big news: "Theresa, we're going to Indiana!"

Considering that the couple lived in Arizona, Theresa wondered what he could mean.

"Honey, I've been promoted. A better job in the company and more money. We'll be able to afford our own house," he said.

Theresa had many questions. What about her own career? True, nurses usually can find employment anywhere, but she liked the hospital where she worked now. And, what about Indiana? It was so far from their families and friends. She wasn't sure if she could ever live that far from her mother.

- What problems must Frank and Theresa face?
- If you were Theresa, how would you react to this situation?

◊ Corrina was heading home after work when her car phone rang. "Hey, fancy lady, it's me, Bridget," the voice on the other end said. Bridget was Corrina's friend from childhood, her maid of honor. Bridget said, "I've got baseball tickets. Bottom deck. Call Kevin and tell him these tickets are too good to pass up. Get over to my house right now and we can stop and get dinner before the ball game."

Corrina thought it over. Kevin knew that she was a big baseball fan, and he really didn't like baseball that much. She called and told him about the tickets.

"Go ahead and have a good time," Kevin said. He put the lasagna and wine into

---

Journal Assignment

Answer this question: If you were married, whose career would come first, yours or your spouse's? Explain why you answered as you did.

Well Being
Accepting

"I will not be able to intentionally change my spouse after we are married."

When newlyweds keep this statement in mind, married life is made much easier. People do not suddenly give up smoking, become neater, or start going to church just because they get married.

Of course, individuals do change. A person may stop smoking or begin to attend church.

But these changes are always self-motivated. Any influence a spouse has is probably more through example and support than through commands.

Remember: If you can't accept a person's behavior or values before marriage, you will probably have trouble accepting them after the wedding as well.

---

the refrigerator, and cleared the good china off the table. Their special dinner would have to be another night.

- What problems must Corrina and Kevin face?
- If you were Kevin, how would you respond to this situation?

◊ "I'm bushed. Stop by the grocery and do the shopping on your way home from work," Elva had said. It was definitely more of an order than a request, which Julio didn't like at all. He, too, had worked all day and was tired. The grocery store was definitely not on his way home.

Though she was sorry for what she had said last night, Elva refused to apologize. Besides, she thought, the argument was no big deal.

Julio and Elva didn't speak much all evening, and went to bed without saying anything more about the situation. Elva knew that Julio was in a bad mood and hoped that sexually stimulating her husband would solve the problem. She snuggled closer to Julio, but he seemed cold and unresponsive. "No, Elva," Julio whispered. "We need to talk."

- What problems must Elva and Julio face?
- How would you resolve their conflict?

◊ Anne knew she was pregnant. She had rarely missed a period. Besides, she could just tell that something, someone was growing inside her body. Still, Steve insisted that she take one of the home pregnancy tests. Sure enough it revealed what Anne already knew.

"I can't believe it!" an excited Steve said. The couple had decided to wait a few years before having children, but Steve was delighted with the news. "Let's call everyone and tell them," he said to Anne.

At that point, he noticed that her expression was still rather glum. "What's the matter?" he wanted to know.

"Are we ready to have children?" she asked.

- What problems must Anne and Steve face?
- What advice would you offer them to resolve their concerns?

As the previous examples indicate, no matter how well a couple prepares for marriage, they cannot imagine all of the changes they will experience after marriage. Couples who are well-prepared for marriage will be better equipped to respond to the challenges of married life than will couples who are ill-prepared. Growth in the married relationship takes no small measure of skill, patience, support,

---

Background

Whenever something bothers a person in a marriage, he or she must evaluate its importance. Important issues must be com municated. Note that open communication is different than whining, complaining, nit-picking, or simply being difficult.

- **Reteach**—Review the six rules of effective communication from Chapter 4, page 73. Look for ways that these skills can be used to enhance a couple's marital relationship.
- **Extend the Lesson**—With students, develop additional scenarios and role play them as part of a class. The scenarios can be made up or may reflect problems/issues in relationships of which students are aware. Students should present the problems in the relationships and suggest what can be done to improve the marriages.

Well-Being

Teaching Approaches
- This topic has been raised on numerous occasions. Review with students why they cannot expect a person to change after marriage.
- Discuss why a person's behavior might worsen after marriage.

Talk It Over

Have the students remain with the same partner or small group. For Question 1, first have the students write three goals they have as a single person. Then, have them revise the goals to fit with married life. After the students have discussed Question 2, call on volunteers to share some of their ideas of "most difficult adjustments" with the entire class.

Adjusting to Marriage

Lesson Overview

This lesson examines in more detail the issues presented in the scenarios of the preceding lesson. The overriding point to communicate to the students is that marriage is a lesson in reality; the dreamlike aura surrounding the courting period is replaced by the reality of living with someone on a day-to-day basis. It is the reality of forming a "we" out of two "I's."

Teaching Approaches

- Ask the students to recall times they have gone camping or travelled with a friend, or simply spent the night at a friend's house. Ask: "In spending so much time together, do you ever get on each other's nerves? How so?" (Have small groups role play scenes of tension between friends.)

- Read or summarize the section. Have the students imagine some of the other "things that could go wrong" between a husband and wife in the first days of a marriage. Don't be afraid to discuss how newlyweds often struggle with sexual intimacy.

- **Reteach**—What does it mean to say that "after the wedding, the race, in a sense, has been won"?

- **Extend the Lesson**—Assign **Application** Project 1. Allow time for the students to present their skits before the entire class.

love, and prayer. Couples who share a common vision and skills concerning the realities of marriage are blessed!

Couples develop a common vision primarily through everyday conversations. They express their beliefs and opinions honestly and freely, without fear of being forced or contradicted. Each person believes that his or her spouse will listen and try to understand divergent points of view. When couples find areas where they disagree, they express their individual concerns without consciously intending to change their spouses' minds.

In marriage, one of the most difficult things for couples to understand is that all decisions affect both people, not just one. For a new husband or wife, it can be very difficult to put the needs of their relationship above private needs. In some ways, it means replacing the vision of "me" with the vision of "we." This is a skill that is often difficult to learn.

Talk It Over

1. Why might adjusting from being single to being married be difficult for some people?
2. What would be some of the most difficult problems an individual might have in adjusting to married life?

Adjusting to Marriage

You're finally married. Congratulations! After several years of courting, you've finally made this permanent commitment. Of course, you were a little nervous when you stood in front of your family and friends (and your spouse's family and friends) and promised to love, honor, and cherish each other until death. You knew this person better than you knew anyone else in the world; what could possibly go wrong?

As it turns out, almost anything can go wrong.
- You like to watch TV while you eat, a habit which your spouse abhors.

- Your spouse wakes in the morning very slowly, and can't seem to function without at least two cups of coffee, the smell of which makes you ill.

- Whatever happened to the person you dated; the person who was always ready to go, whenever you decided?

- You thought you had reached agreement on whose career came first, but now your spouse is angry because you spend too much time on the job.

Marriage is so different from the days when a couple courted or were engaged. In many ways, courting and engagement can lead to unreal expectations. When people are courting they usually try extra hard to please each other, going so far as to do things that they don't particularly enjoy doing in order to promote a loving response from their boyfriend or girlfriend.

In Focus
More Factors

Here are several critical factors associated with adjusting successfully to married life. Couples tend to make the adjustment easier if:
- They have similar family backgrounds.
- Their parents' marriages were happy.
- There is a lack of conflict with parents and in-laws.
- Both spouses have reached similar educational levels.
- They have friends of both sexes.
- They belong to various organizations.
- They knew each other for several years prior to marriage.
- They have secure and stable occupations (more important than income).
- They agree on children.

The more of these factors couples agree to, the better chance they have of adjusting to marriage.

Background

Studies indicate that these factors found in the feature, "In Focus," are not nearly as significant in isolation as they are when combined. That is, the more factors involved, the better the chance of marital adjustment. Note that most marriages meet some of these criteria, but that only the best marriages meet most of them.

In marriage, some sign of affection or concern needs to be shown regularly.

The phrase "win her hand in marriage" comes from the situation when the woman agreed to marry one person over another. The men in this situation would do everything in their power to please the woman in order to be the one chosen. Although the phrase is less valid today than it was in the past, men and women may still act out the assumed role of "the perfect person" to insure that they are accepted.

After the wedding, the finish line (in a sense) has been crossed; the race is won. Both the man and the woman have what they wanted: marriage. The extra effort that preceded the marriage is no longer given. Both spouses may begin to take each other for granted.

In reality, it takes as much or more effort for a relationship to grow during marriage as it did for the relationship to arrive at marriage in the first place. A marriage where the couple fails to treat each other as special people is threatened. Every night does not have to be a romantic date, with candlelight dinner, flowers, and dancing. But every night does call for expressions of affection and concern. If spouses treat each other in ways that suggest lack of concern, the relationship will decay and weaken. However, if spouses treat each other with love and dignity, the marriage will flourish.

Competition in Marriage

Whether or not you are aware of it, a certain amount of competition will exist in every marriage. Sometimes, the competition is with each other. One spouse may have a more prestigious or better paying job than the other. This may become a source of annoyance. Other times, the competition may be with an unnamed foe—the image of the perfect wife, for example. A newly married woman may be mentally comparing herself to TV characters or to her husband's "perfect" mother. When she can't meet these unrealistic standards, the woman may feel like a failure.

Competition in Marriage

Teaching Approaches (continued)

- **Extend the Lesson**—Have the students make a list of women's issues that are currently being discussed. Discuss how an understanding of these issues can be used to strengthen a Christian marriage. Use **Resource 12A** from the Teacher's Resource Book which lists important women's issues.

Family Living

Teaching Approaches

- Read or summarize this panel to accompany the lesson, "Competition in Marriage."
- Have the students make a list of all the ways they rely on their families now. Then, ask: "How would a marriage change the focus of your lists?"

Family Living
Changing Family Ties

Most men and women in Western culture today have lived apart from their parents at some time prior to marriage. Still, many people find the separation from their parents especially difficult once they marry.

The relationship between a single person and his or her parents may have changed little. The single person may continue to rely on parents for loans, laundry, or free meals on the weekend. While the parents may rightfully continue to be a source of emotional support for their son or daughter, the child must eventually learn to become independent from them.

What are some of the problems people might experience when their parents are no longer their primary focus in life?

When marriage partners compete, either with each other or with themselves, the marriage becomes like an athletic contest or even a war.

Frank, from the opening stories, felt intimidated by Theresa's position as head surgical nurse at the local hospital. Once, Theresa's mother had said to him, "When you get a better job, she won't have to work as many hours." This competition between his career and the expectations of his mother-in-law led him to accept a job in Indiana without telling his wife. What damage was caused to Frank and Theresa's marriage because of this?

Competition should be reserved for games and athletic contests. In marriage, it can be deadly. Couples in flourishing marriages work together and direct their energies toward common goals. Couples in these marriages tell each other honestly how they feel and what they think. They keep each other informed about any developing ideas, opportunities, and goals. They work at continually listening to the other spouse's concerns as well.

Removing sexual stereotypes and affirming the equality of men and women has had a profound

Competition in marriage should be reserved for games and sporting events.

Background

Many people try to overcome loneliness with material things. The use of drugs and alcohol, although widespread, are negative ways of coping with loneliness. There is only one real solution to loneliness: establishing interpersonal relationships.

effect on marriage and family life. Equality of the sexes is essential today because the deep friendship and personal commitment demanded by marriage is impossible without it. If one person feels superior to the other, the couple's love may degenerate into pity or abusive power. If a person feels inferior to his or her spouse, the couple's love can reach either the extreme of subservience or of hero worship. Neither pity nor homage is a solid foundation for developing mutual and respectful love.

However, equality does not mean that the sexes are identical. You were created male or female by God. Both your personality and your interpersonal relationships are influenced by your sexual identity. If we properly interpret the Genesis Creation stories, the equality of the sexes is affirmed. The two are not described as identical—they are different. In noticing that difference in their first naked encounter, Adam and Eve were amazed, not ashamed. Shame came only after they sinned.

New Social Habits

A husband and wife have a new priority after the wedding: each other. If a married person's most intimate relationship is not with his or her spouse, the marriage will experience difficulties.

This requirement is often put to the test early in a marriage. A woman may have become accustomed to sharing the most intimate details of her life with her girlfriend, as Corrina and Bridget did. They had not only enjoyed attending sporting events together before Corrina married Kevin, but Bridget had also been with Corrina the night that she met Kevin at a work picnic. Corrina felt responsible for Bridget in some ways, now that she was married and Bridget was still single. In another way, Corrina was jealous of the single life Bridget still enjoyed.

In a healthy marriage there is time for both the spouse and other close friends. When a husband and wife trust each other there is no jealousy over moderate amounts of time spent with friends.

☀ Media Watch
Loneliness Doesn't Sell

Loneliness has a great power over people. It is sometimes tragically true that the desire to overcome loneliness is comparable to the desire to relieve hunger.

Everyone is lonely occasionally, but some people are lonely most of the time. For a single person, loneliness may present a more obvious problem. A single person may feel uncomfortable eating out in a restaurant, attending a party, or going to a concert alone.

Loneliness may also be a very discouraging part of a single person's everyday life. Opportunities to share personal successes, or simply discuss the events of the day with a trusted friend are sought, sometimes in vain.

Advertisers are quick to capitalize on the fear of loneliness. One of the techniques used in advertising is to show people in groups, obviously enjoying each other's company while using the sponsor's product. A group of friends enjoys a soda together after a hike in the wilderness. Attractive women and men flock to the owner of a fancy sports car. Advertisers realize the appeal of togetherness.

Take a random survey of ten ads and commercials. How many of them feature a couple or a group of people enjoying the benefits of the product? Would the same impressions of the product be given if only one consumer was featured in the ad?

Journal Assignment

Have the students write a poem or short reflection about a personal experience of loneliness.

Resources

Resource 12B offers more information on the issue of loneliness.

New Social Habits

Teaching Approaches

- Read or summarize the section.
- Discuss "Talk It Over," Question 2.
- Ask: "How would you tell your friend that you can no longer share with him or her the most intimate details of your life?"
- **Reteach**—Assign **Application** Project 3.
- **Extend the Lesson**—Often, children, careers, and individual social activities can get in the way of the exclusive relationship between husband and wife. Have the students list what they consider to be the five major obstacles to growth in married love. For each obstacle, they should provide at least one solution. Discuss their lists and solutions in class.

☀ Media Watch

Teaching Approaches

- Have the students work individually or in small groups to collect a portfolio of magazine ads that capitalize on the theme of togetherness rather than loneliness.
- Have students write their own conclusions from this exercise. What do they think advertisers are selling?

Sexual Expectations

Teaching Approaches

- Read or summarize the first two paragraphs.
- Ask the students to share a view on sex other than the Catholic view of sexuality discussed in this section. (See **Application** Project 4.) Then, ask: "What do you understand the Catholic philosophy of sexuality to be? What is the purpose of intercourse? What values and attitudes does a couple need in order to develop good sexual rapport?" Compare their views to the Catholic view.
- Read or summarize the rest of the section.
- **Reteach**—Ask: "What are some other ways for a married couple to share intimacy besides sexual intercourse?" The Catholic Church teaches that sexual intercourse is an act that connects the couple's whole life together. It is an essential part of the way a couple communicates their love to one another. Couples can also show their love by: (1) taking time to share with their spouses their experiences of the day—physically, emotionally, intellectually, and spiritually; (2) listening attentively and showing great interest; (3) writing an occasional love letter to one's spouse; (4) never using "the silent treatment" as a punishment, or to get back at one's spouse; (5) being imaginative in communicating love for the other person; (6) finishing arguments and not leaving differences unresolved; (7) not being afraid to disagree; (8) honestly facing differences and being willing to compromise when possible. Have students role play each of these examples.

Best friends share enjoyable experiences together.

Moderation means telephoning a friend once a week rather than once a day, or going to a ball game or movie with a friend three or four times a year rather than weekly. Moderation also means inviting your spouse to join you whenever possible.

In the case of Corrina and Kevin, the major problems are a lack of communication and sensitivity, not Bridget.

- Kevin was obviously hurt by Corrina's lack of sensitivity—she didn't ask if he had plans.
- Kevin did not tell Corrina of his special plans. If he had, she may have called Bridget back and cancelled out on the game.

Relationships thrive when intentions, desires, and plans are communicated well in advance of outside events. Married people depend less on friends and more on their spouses. The closeness once shared with a friend can be shared with a husband or wife. Some of the spontaneity of single life must be sacrificed for the many benefits of marriage.

Sexual Expectations

Sexual expression between a husband and wife is an important part of their total communication. Our present use of language, especially as used by the popular media and modern culture, tends to separate sexuality from a permanent relationship. Terms like "sexual needs" have replaced the words "loving commitment" in our vocabulary.

Sexual intercourse is a special form of communication that involves a person's whole body, mind, and spirit. Some couples enter marriage with the incomplete idea that intercourse is a means to satisfy sexual desires, a way of "taking pleasure" from another person. This self-centered attitude includes little attention to loving one's spouse.

The Catholic Church teaches that marital sexual intimacy involves the whole person, and is *holistic.* The Church places sexual intercourse in the context of the couple's total life together.

Resources

Resource 12C provides a format for the activity suggested in "Sexual Expectations."

Journal Assignment

Say: "Affection refers to the warm and tender feelings you have for another person. Write how important affection is in a relationship between a husband and a wife."

Chastity in Marriage

Sexuality is not simply a biological fact; it is a part of what it means to be human. The virtue of chastity helps a person use God's gift of sexuality as it was intended. Through the practice of chastity, people learn to use their sexuality appropriately, in accord with their vocation: people in single and religious vocations do not engage in genital sex; married couples engage in genital sex only with their partners.

In marriage, chastity helps the couple grow in love and trust. Chastity encourages a couple to experience God's fidelity in an exclusive sexual relationship.

The language of sexuality is communicated during the entire day, not just at bedtime. Sexuality speaks through the sharing of personal thoughts and insights, through expressions of tenderness, like hugs and kisses, and through moments of forgiveness.

Sexual intercourse is never a cure for problems. In fact, it can be a way of avoiding issues that need attention. Recall that sexual intercourse is an expression of the total love, the real love a couple has for each other. Because intercourse is so intimate, it involves a couple's deepest feelings. Intercourse communicates their love for each other exclusively and unconditionally.

Using sexuality selfishly to control one's spouse is very harmful to a marriage. Neither partner has an absolute right to intercourse. Sexual intimacy must be freely and mutually shared if it is to have a positive meaning. For Elva, it was a mistake to think that sexual intercourse could replace the need for reconciliation.

Couples in successful marriages learn to incorporate sexuality in their lives through honest communication. They say "no" when they mean no and "yes" when they mean yes. They don't play games with sexuality. They agree to respect the other's wishes and agree not to let hurt feelings prevail. These couples also learn that there are many more ways to express intimacy besides sexual intercourse.

Talk It Over

1. Identify an unhealthy competition you have had with a sibling, friend, or classmate.
2. How would being married change your relationship with your best friend?
3. What does the holistic vision of marital sex mean to you?

Marital sexual expression is holistic—it is part of a couple's total communication.

Sexual Expectations

Teaching Approaches (continued)

- **Extend the Lesson**—Explore student expectations concerning sexual intimacy in marriage. Ask students to anonymously respond to the following questions or statements: (1) Married couples, on average, engage in sexual intercourse how often each week? (Twice a week seems to be the average reported by sexual researchers.) (2) Sexual intercourse is available on demand in marriage. (Not true. In most marriages, according to researchers, sexual intimacy is a response to a close, loving relationship. This means that sexual intimacy must be built up to over the course of time, not just when one person is ready.) Allow students to also express their own expectations about sex in marriage.

Talk It Over

For Question 1, you may wish to have the students write a story describing "unhealthy competition." Then, call on volunteers to share their stories with the class. If you did not discuss Question 2 as suggested, do so now with the entire group. For Question 3, have the students give specific examples to support their ideas about the holistic vision of marital sex.

Background

One of the dysfunctions couples experience in marriage is trying to meet unexpressed sexual expectations. People's images of sexual intercourse are built, all too often, on the myth of popular fiction rather than on reality.

Teens need to learn that the real joy in sexual intercourse is not the plateau of physical pleasure reached but in the degree of bonding that couples achieve.

II. Open to Life

Aims

1. To help students view children as a great blessing to a marriage.
2. To help students understand the meaning of responsible parenthood from a Catholic perspective.

Begin the Section

1. Review the *unitive* meaning of sexual intercourse in marriage as discussed in the previous lessons.
2. Say: "Most people expect to be parents at some time in their lives. A second part of sexual intercourse in marriage is procreative. That is, the couple cooperates with God in the creation of new life."
3. Assign the students to interview someone who is a parent to find out how life changed when his or her first child was born.
4. Read or summarize the opening text section. Ask the students what they think is the meaning of the heading, "Open to Life."

II. Open to Life

According to Church teaching, the intimate sharing of sexual intercourse in marriage has two inseparable meanings:

1. *Unitive.*
2. *Procreative.*

This chapter has been describing sexual intercourse in its unitive meaning: the expression of love by which the couple is united intimately and faithfully. Marital intercourse is also for *procreation;* the couple cooperates with God in the creation of new life.

For most married couples, news that they are expecting a child is a cause for celebration, even though they might also experience some normal anxiety as well, especially if they are newlyweds. A baby brings many exciting and dramatic changes to a relationship. The dynamics between a husband and wife are never completely the same again after childbirth. Their relationship has to be redeveloped with another person involved.

Like any contact with the sacred—which new life certainly is—humans seem to have two responses: excitement and fear. These same reactions occur in marriage when a couple first learns of their "blessed event."

Married couples are called by God to be open to new life. According to the Second Vatican Council:

> "By their very nature, the institution of matrimony itself and conjugal love are ordained for the procreation and education of children, and find in them the ultimate crown. Children are really the supreme gift of marriage and contribute very substantially to the welfare of their parents" (*Pastoral Constitution on the Church in the Modern World*, #48-49).

Infants discover new things by the minute. Having a child teaches a couple many new things as well.

Journal Assignment

Say, "The Second Vatican Council said that marriage and lovemaking are 'ordained for the procreation and education of children.' Explain why you agree or disagree with this statement."

Background

For more information on this issue see *Humanae Vitae* and the *Catechism of the Catholic Church,* 1652-1654.

Married couples cooperate with God in the creation of new life.

Parenthood

Although concerned about her readiness to have a child, Anne's enthusiasm for a baby eventually caught up with Steve's.

"But, where will the baby sleep?" she wondered. "We only have a one-bedroom apartment."

"Honey, we have been gifted by God with this pregnancy," Steve said. "Believe me, your gift to this baby as a mother will be many times more important than a room. We will be just the parents this baby needs!"

Anne smiled and reached for the phone. "I want to call my mom with the good news!" she said happily.

Having children is often the greatest adjustment married couples face in their married lives. Children are a tremendous responsibility. An infant requires around-the-clock care. As a child grows, the constant responsibilities of a parent change, but they do not diminish.

Nevertheless, children are among the greatest of blessings for any married couple. They are tangible signs of the couple's love for one another. They are an eternal statement of a couple's involvement in the Family of God.

A child embodies the parents' hope for the future. Parents become like archers, with their child as the arrow being sent further on. Christian parents live in hope that the child's direction is towards God's kingdom. By welcoming children as a blessing to their marriage, a couple makes a public statement that human life is good, and that the goodness of life will survive to the end and beyond.

Why Have Children?

People give various reasons for having children: to express their love; to offer hope for the world; to educate and nurture new life; to continue the family name; to work in the family business; or even as an insurance policy for their older years.

Resources

Resource 12D lists other important tasks involved with raising an infant.

Resource 12E lists some reasons that couples have given for having children.

Why Have Children? (continued)

Teaching Approaches

- Have the students write down each of the listed joys and benefits of childbearing. Below each, ask them to write one sentence explaining why it is a good reason for having children.

- Read or summarize the section.

- **Reteach**—Review the list of positive and negative reasons for having children. Then, have the students read the first two paragraphs of the text section. Ask: "What could be the results of having children for the wrong reasons?"

- **Extend the Lesson**—Invite a couple with an adopted child or children to speak to the class about their reason for wanting a child. Discuss what it is like to want a child and to not physically be able to have one.

Responsibility

Teaching Approaches

- Have the students make a chart entitled "Responsibilities and Joys of Parenting." In the first column, they should list five typical parental responsibilities. Next to each item, they should write their feelings about the demands of parenthood. In the second column, they should list five joys of parenting. Next to each of those items, ask them to write why they perceive those experiences as being joyful. Call on volunteers to share one example of a responsibility and one example of a joy of parenting.

- Read or summarize the text section.

- Ask: "Do you think a child who does not know the love of a parent can relate to the experience of God's love? How much does our experience of human love determine our experience of God's love?"

While there are many reasons for a couple to have children, there are also reasons why couples should not have children. For example, people who imagine that a child will bring stability to an already shaky marriage often learn that the pressures of having a child weakens their relationship. People sometimes have children in order to make up for their own unhappy childhoods. They may desire to live vicariously through the lives of their children. The problems are not with the children, of course, but with the motives of the parents.

The United States Catholic bishops list several joys and benefits of childbearing:

- The conception and birth of every child are something of a miracle.

- Couples possess a remarkable opportunity for cooperating with God in the creation of new human life.

- The one conceived flows out of, manifests, and deepens the spouses' self-giving love for one another.

- The infant is a unique reflection of the singular and special bond between husband and wife, for no other combination of persons could have produced this particular child.

- Parents have the awesome, but challenging, possibility and duty of handing down to their offspring the very Christian faith and positive values given to them by their parents, relatives, community, and Church.

- A child offers the potential for repeated unique moments of tender intimacy and profound satisfaction for many years. These feelings cannot be experienced in any other way (*Faithful to Each Other*, p. 38).

The Catholic Church considers every child a *blessing,* "a gift of divine favor." The very act of creation itself is a gift—unexpected and filled with mystery. We have been given life as a part of God's creation.

Responsibility

The responsibilities of parenthood are magnificently challenging. It is quite a change in lifestyle for a couple accustomed to coming and going as they please to alter their activities because of a baby. Babies have a way of establishing their own personal schedules.

To a newborn infant, there is little distinction between day and night. Caring for a baby 24 hours a day can leave the parents tired and frustrated because the task never seems to end.

Caring for an infant can also be rewarding. Absorbed in the beauty and wonder of their child, parents watch this new person as he or she discovers the world. Many parents keep written journals, photo albums, or collections of video tapes to record special moments in their child's life. They wonder in amazement at the growth in their

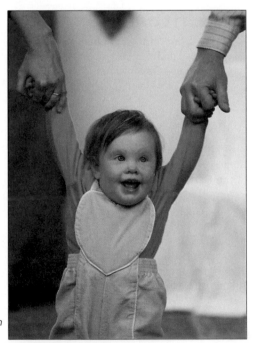

Inspite of the work involved, raising children is a great blessing to any married couple.

Resources

Resource 12F provides a format for completing the activity suggested in "Responsibilities and Joys of Parenting."

Listening for Feelings

Did you know that when you speak with other people you are communicating on both the thinking and feeling level? When you announce that you passed your driving test, you are telling a fact and also expressing emotions. The fact is that you passed the test and so now have a driver's license. The emotions contained in the same words, however, communicate quite another message: "I'm proud of myself," "Are you proud of me?" "I'm good!" and many more.

How well do you understand the feelings expressed by other people in conversations? Dr. Thomas Gordon felt that parent and child relationships would improve if parents developed their ability to understand the feelings expressed by their children.

Imagine that you are a parent of an eight-year-old child. Use this inventory adapted from the Parent Effectiveness Training manual developed by Dr. Gordon to evaluate your abililty to hear feelings behind your child's words.

Child Says:

I don't know what is wrong. I can't figure it out. Maybe I should just quit trying.

Child is Feeling:

(a) Stumped.
(b) Discouraged.
(c) Tempted to give up.

Directions: Write a word or words that express the feeling in each statement.

1. Oh boy, only ten more days until school's out.
2. Look, I made an airplane with my new tools!
3. Gee, I'm not having any fun. I can't think of anything to do.
4. I'll never be good like Jim. I practice and practice and he's still better than me.
5. Jim's parents let him ride his bike to school, but I'm a better rider than Jim.
6. I want to wear my hair long—it's my hair, isn't it?
7. Do you think I'm doing this report right? Will it be good enough?
8. I can do it myself. You don't need to help me. I'm old enough to do it myself.
9. Go away; leave me alone. I don't want to talk to you or anybody else. You don't care what happens to me anyway.
10. I think I know what to do, but maybe it's not right. I always seem to do the wrong thing. What do you think I should do?

Score your results using this key.

Scoring:

Give yourself a 4 on those items where you feel your choices closely match those on the Scoring Key. Score yourself a 2 on items where your choices only partially match or where you missed a particular feeling. Give yourself a 0 if you missed altogether.

Scoring Key:

1. (a) Glad. (b) Relieved.
2. (a) Proud. (b) Pleased.
3. (a) Bored. (b) Stumped.
4. (a) Feels inadequate. (b) Discouraged.
5. (a) Feels parents are being unfair. (b) Feels competent.
6. (a) Resents interference.
7. (a) Feels some doubt. (b) Not sure.
8. (a) Feels competent. (b) Doesn't want help.
9. (a) Feels hurt. (b) Feels angry. (c) Feels unloved.
10. (a) Uncertain, unsure.

HOW YOU RATE:

31-40 Superior recognition of feelings.
21-30 Above average recognition of feelings.
11-20 Below average recognition of feelings.
0-10 Poor recognition of feelings.

243

Listening for Feelings

Teaching Approaches

- Deciphering the feelings behind spoken messages is the main focus of this activity. Read the first two paragraphs. Ask the students to suggest other examples.
- Explain the directions for the activity. Go over the example with the students. Say: "Write the feelings behind the eight-year-old child's words."
- Have the students work individually, but allow time for them to share what they have written with a partner or in a small group.

Background

   Dr. Thomas Gordon developed the *Parenting Effectiveness Training* program to help men and women learn how to be better in their roles as parents. According to Gordon, parents need to learn to communicate better with both themselves and their children.

Responsibility

Teaching Approaches (continued)

- **Reteach**—Explain that according to the Second Vatican Council: "The family is therefore the principal school of the social virtues which are necessary to every society. It is, therefore, above all in the Christian family, inspired by the grace and the responsibility of the sacrament of matrimony, that children should be taught to know and worship God and to love their neighbor, in accordance with the faith which they have received in earliest infancy in the sacrament of Baptism. In it, also, they will have their first experience of a well-balanced human society and of the Church. Finally it is through the family that they are gradually initiated into association with their fellowmen in civil life and as members of the People of God. Parents should, therefore, appreciate how important a role the truly Christian family plays in the life and progress of the whole People of God" (*Declaration on Christian Education,* #3).

- **Extend the Lesson**—In discussing the "domestic Church," recall Jesus' words: "For where two or three are gathered in My name, there am I in the midst of them" *(Matthew 18:20).* Recall these words as the scriptural origins of the domestic Church.

⬞ Sharpening Your Skills

Teaching Approaches

- Introduce this panel as part of the lesson, "Models for Parenting."
- You may wish to have the students share their answers to the questions with a partner, and then write a title and description of their own "unique parenting style."

---

child knowing that this living being is the product of their love, a gift from God sent to enrich their marriage and the world.

⬞ Sharpening Your Skills
Choosing a Model

Look at the seven common approaches to parenting. Which approach most closely models your relationship with your parents? Which model or which combination of models would you likely emulate as a parent? Use these models to develop your own unique parenting style.

The role of a parent includes being a guide, guard, provider, mentor, and particularly a teacher. Parents teach their children physically, intellectually, socially, emotionally, and spiritually. Professional educators recognize that a child's parents are truly his or her primary educators. The Church teaches that children come to know God most directly through their parents.

Helping a child toward a life of growing confidence and independence is a monumental task. Few parents are fully prepared for their roles. Unlike a schoolteacher working from a lesson plan, parents must work from life itself. Children learn primarily from following their parents' examples.

Real life education happens every day in small, almost imperceptible ways: children learn to communicate with people from the ways their parents talk to them; learn to value things the way their parents value them; to react to situations the way their parents react; and to think and act toward God and other people the way their parents do.

The religious influence of parents is also great. The parent will reflect God to the child more than any other person or thing. When a child thinks of greatness, power, knowledge, or love, he or she will naturally think of those qualities in his or her parents. Children learn an image of God from their parents. And it is the parents' actions and attitudes, far more than their words,

that influence the child's attitudes about God and the world.

A child's perceptions of the world are influenced by his or her understanding of the relationship between his or her mom and dad. Further, the child is guided to perceive that he or she is loved and accepted through the parents. As the child grows to understand the meaning of parental love, the Good News of Jesus can be communicated more effectively.

In assisting the child's understanding of God, the parents themselves are deepened in their faith. Seeing the world through the eyes of a child can restore some of its wonder and novelty back to the parents. Children take the time to smell flowers and watch clouds. They remind their parents of the everyday pleasures of life and the abundant blessings they have received from God.

The Catholic Church calls the family the "domestic Church," or the "Church of the home." The family is where the Christian community, in its smallest and most basic form, shares Jesus' life of faith, hope, and love.

Models for Parenting

Each relationship between a parent and child is unique, but usually each one will fall into one of the patterns below.

1. **"I'd do anything for my child."** The parent is overly generous, making any personal sacrifice cheerfully. The happiness and well-being of the child is the parent's major concern. The parent literally lives for the child. (This pattern can be unhealthy.)

2. **"Let's be pals."** The parent wants to be the child's friend. Spending time together in enjoyable activities is greatly valued. The child is encouraged to make his or her own decisions which the parent supports. The parent feels hurt when affection is not returned. (This behavior can be unhealthy when taken to an extreme.)

3. **"Do it the way I tell you."** The parent views the child in much the same way that a Marine

---

Journal Assignment

Ask: "How is the Christian family the 'principle school of social virtue?' How can the family teach children to 'know God and love their neighbors' as suggested by the Second Vatican Council?"

drill sergeant views recruits. The parent has all the correct answers and right ways to do everything. Parenting is a process by which views and behaviors of the parent are poured into the child. The authority of the parent is ultimate. Failure to follow the parent's way is met with punishment. (This pattern can be unhealthy when taken to an extreme.)

4. **"I'll show you how."** The parent acts as a teacher. The various skills needed for survival are shared with the child. Explanations are based on the child's capacity to understand. The parent stands beside the child in the learning process. The parent is particularly proud of the child's achievements. (This pattern is generally healthy.)

5. **"You can do better."** The child is pressured to improve in his or her performance by the parent. The parent cheers loudly for the run scored or the race won. Often, the parent will see the accomplishments of the child as his or her own. This parent never rests from parenting for fear the child will become slack in achieving the parent's goals. (This pattern can be unhealthy when taken to an extreme.)

6. **"Live your own life."** This is the laissez-faire parent. Whatever happens is okay. Both success and failure are met with the same level of parental response: indifference. The parent is concerned about her own or his own affairs. The child is given what is needed for survival, but not much else. The parent and child spend little time together. The parent doesn't tell the child anything about his or her life and doesn't ask the child for personal information either. (This pattern is usually unhealthy.)

7. **"I'll be there if you need me."** The parent wants the child to feel supported, but with a wide range of personal freedom. There are times when the child may want more parental

Parents lead their children to a life of growing confidence and independence. The method of parenting they use, however, is very important.

Talk It Over

Use Questions 1 and 2 for review. Have the students write their answers and share them with a partner. Discuss Questions 3 and 4 in the large group. Call on volunteers to share their experiences.

Having Children

Lesson Overview

According to a law of the Church: "Any marriage where the procreation of children is perpetually and intentionally excluded in principle will not be a valid marriage" *(Canons 1013, 1086, 1092)*. The Church does not request blind adherence to its teaching, nor does the teaching imply that a family should have as many children as possible. In this lesson, the issues of responsibility related to child-bearing are addressed.

Teaching Approaches

- Point out that discussions about "responsible parenting" often focus on birth control. Point out that responsible parenting means more than just limiting or avoiding pregnancies.

- Read the opener to the section. Leave the questions open-ended, telling the students that the answers will be explored in the rest of the lesson.

- **Reteach**—Explore how students would define "responsible parenting."

- **Extend the Lesson**—Debate: "A married couple's decision to have or not have children is their decision alone."

Responsible Parenthood

Teaching Approaches

- Read the first paragraph. Make sure the students clearly understand the Church's position that the "conjugal act cannot be separated from its procreative dimension within marriage." Ask: "What practical implications does this statement have for a married couple?"

- Read or summarize the rest of the section. Ask: "What are some factors a couple must consider before having children? Who, ultimately, decides if and when a couple will have children? How is this decision reached?"

presence, but knows that if the parent is really needed, the parent will come quickly. Basically, the parent gives the child a sense of family independence; the bond between the parent and child is relaxed but trustworthy. (This pattern is usually healthy.)

Talk It Over

1. Explain in your own words how marriage is both unitive and procreative.
2. Discuss people's motives for having children. What motives would you consider "right"? Which would you consider unacceptable? Be prepared to explain your answers.
3. Tell about any experiences you have had caring for an infant. What are the responsibilities for caring for such a young child?
4. How has a parent or older family member been a model of God for you?
5. Describe the "ideal parent."

Newborns are totally dependent on their parents for everything. How would having a baby affect a couple's life?

Having Children

As part of their wedding, a couple is asked if they are willing "to accept children lovingly from God." Every couple who marries in the Catholic Church makes this promise, although many couples do not plan to have children until they have established homes and careers. What does it mean to accept children lovingly from God? Can couples intentionally postpone the birth of children and yet honestly make this marriage promise?

Responsible Parenthood

Marriage is the rightful place where a couple can give themselves totally to one another—physically, psychologically, socially, and spiritually. The Church's teaching on sexual intercourse is clear; the relational meaning cannot be separated from its procreative dimension. This statement also implies the couple's right to determine when they will have children, how many children they will have, or, in some specific cases, if they will have children at all.

In affirming the great gift that children are to a marriage, the bishops at the Second Vatican Council praised couples willing to have and raise children. They wrote:

> Whenever Christian spouses, in a spirit of sacrifice and trust in divine providence, carry out their duties of procreation with generous human and Christian responsibility, they glorify the Creator and perfect themselves in Christ *(Pastoral Constitution on the Church in the Modern World,* #50).

The Catholic Church affirms responsibility for married couples, while also being aware of the pressures of population, housing, income, illness,

---

Background

According to the Second Vatican Council, "Everyone should be aware that human life, and the task of transmitting that life, cannot be restricted to this world or measured and understood by its standards, but must always be seen in terms of our eternal destiny" *(Gaudium et Spes,* 51). (See also the *Catechism of the Catholic Church,* 2366-2378.)

and other family concerns that couples face. The stress on parents because of the many demands of parenthood, are known and acknowledged. The Second Vatican Council qualified the idea of parenting with the adjective "responsible." On whom does the responsibility fall? Again, the message is clear:

> The parents themselves should ultimately make this judgment, in the sight of God. But in their manner of acting, spouses should be aware that they cannot proceed arbitrarily. They must always be governed according to conscience dutifully conformed to the divine law itself, and should be submissive toward the Church's teaching office, which authentically interprets that law in the light of the Gospel. That divine law reveals and protects the integral meaning of conjugal love, and impels it toward a truly human fulfillment (*"Pastoral Constitution on the Church in the Modern World,"* #50).

Birth Planning

Any time there is a discussion of "responsible parenting," the emphasis is usually placed on birth control, or, more to the point, choosing not to have children. Responsible parenting means much more than that. It means that the couple accepts children lovingly if pregnancy should occur. Responsible parents put the needs of children ahead of career goals or material possessions. Responsible parents nurture and care for the children they are given.

If a couple wishes to regulate when they have children, this is perfectly acceptable, as long as they remain genuinely open to accepting God's unexpected blessings. The methods a couple uses to regulate having children is guided by Church teaching.

Responsible parents accept children willingly, lovingly from God.

Artificial Contraception

The Church's *Magisterium*, or teaching office, says that no artificial means should be used to prevent conception. If conception has taken place, nothing should be done to prevent the implantation of the fertilized egg in the lining of the uterus.

Church teaching, particularly in the document *Humanae Vitae*, prohibits Catholics from using the various contraceptive devices and chemicals available today. These methods either prevent the sperm from reaching the ovum (condom, diaphragm), prevent implantation (IUD), or prevent ovulation (the contraceptive pill). Catholics are also prohibited from choosing sterilization for contraceptive purposes (tubal ligation or vasectomy). Finally, abortion is never an option.

There are health reasons as well for avoiding artificial contraceptives. The birth control pill interferes with the body's metabolism particularly in the processing of vitamins B12, B6, and C; it can also interfere with the absorption of trace minerals by the body, including copper, zinc and magnesium.

Responsible Parenthood

Teaching Approaches (continued)

- **Reteach**—Recall with the students the unitive dimensions of sexual intercourse in marriage. In presenting the material in this lesson, help the students to see how the unitive and procreative dimensions are both a part of sexual expression.
- **Extend the Lesson**—Assign **Application** Project 6.

Birth Planning

Teaching Approaches

- Read or have a student read the section aloud.
- **Reteach**—Explain that the Church is sensitive to the need married couples have to space the birth of their children responsibly: "If, then, there are serious motives to space out births, which derive from the physical or psychological conditions of husband and wife, or from external conditions, the Church teaches that it is then licit to take into account the natural rhythms immanent in the generative functions, for the use of marriage in the infertile periods only, and in this way to regulate birth without offending the moral principles which have been recalled earlier" (*Humanae Vitae,* #16).
- **Extend the Lesson**—Ask: "What does it mean to put the needs of children ahead of career goals or material possessions?"

Artificial Contraception

New Words

The Latin words, *"Humanae Vitae"* are the title of Pope Paul VI's encyclical issued on July 29, 1968 and mean "of Human Life." The document focuses on marriage and the issues related to marriage. Among the most noted issues is the Church's reaffirmation of its teaching against the use of artificial contraception and the promotion of a comprehensive meaning of marital sexuality.

Artificial Contraception (continued)

Teaching Approaches

- Read or summarize the text section. Emphasize some of the health risks associated with the artificial birth control methods mentioned.
- Ask: "Why do you think some people choose to ignore Church teaching on artificial birth control? How would you respond to their reasons?"
- **Reteach**—Assign **Application** Project 7.
- **Extend the Lesson**—Have the students interview someone knowledgeable about the public reaction to *Humanae Vitae*. What kind of press did it get? How did Catholics around the world respond to it? Have the students ask the people they interview if they remember if the local bishop spoke or sent a letter to parishes on the topic. Then, have the students go to a library that has old newspapers from 1968 on microfilm, and make copies of any article they can find on *Humanae Vitae*. Back issues of religious publications are another source of information. Have the students report to the class on their findings. Also have several students read and report on the document *Humanae Vitae* itself.

Natural Family Planning

New Words

When the *Sympto-thermic Method* and the *Ovulation Method* are used together, NFP is even more effective.

Teaching Approaches

- Introduce the lesson by explaining that Natural Family Planning is the only method of family planning approved by the Catholic Church.
- Read or summarize the section. Point out that the Sympto-thermic Method and Ovulation Method can both be used simultaneously.
- Explain that Natural Family Planning is as effective in preventing pregnancy as the birth control pill and higher than the IUD, without any of the problems or physical side effects of either artificial method. Natural Family Planning also has the added benefit of helping couples trying to have children conceive.

To Your Health
Signs of Pregnancy

A woman begins to change internally almost from the moment of conception, and, soon after, obvious signs of a pregnancy occur. The most immediate sign is that the woman's uterus retains its lining, and she misses her menstrual period. Most women also experience some nausea in the first weeks of pregnancy.

A blood or urine test can determine a pregnancy one to two weeks after a missed period. Urine tests are available in kit form and may be purchased at drug stores or supermarkets. However, home tests are unreliable if improperly administered. A blood test must be given by a doctor and analyzed in a lab.

By the sixth to eighth week of pregnancy, physical changes are visible to a doctor. The cervix will be softened and bluish or purplish. The uterus will also be enlarged.

Women who are pregnant are encouraged to seek prenatal care, to get plenty of rest, and to eat well-balanced meals. Since cigarette smoke, drugs, and alcohol can seriously harm the fetus, women who even think they might be pregnant are encouraged not to smoke, to take any drugs (even prescribed medicine), or to drink any alcohol.

About 75 known diseases are tied to the use of the pill. Women who use oral contraceptives are strongly advised to see their doctors regularly to monitor the effect on their circulation: the use of the pill may increase the risk of blood clotting. Note also that most recent birth control pills contain both estrogen (which inhibits ovulation) and progesterone (which makes the uterus hostile to potential implantation), which work as abortifacients (drugs which cause abortions).

Natural Family Planning

The Church is sensitive, however, to the needs married couples have for delaying the start of a family, spacing the births of their children, and in some cases—for example, if the mother's health would be in danger or there is a possibility of genetic deformity in the fetus—to avoid pregnancy altogether. It is Church teaching that couples do such planning by natural means only.

There are several ways that a couple can regulate the birth of a child, all of which involve responsibility on the part of the husband and wife. Each of these methods require *abstinence* to various degrees. Abstinence means that a couple refrains from sexual intercourse for a period of time. Most of these methods also take note of the biological ebb and flow of the woman's fertility cycle.

In recent years, techniques of *Natural Family Planning* (NFP) have become very accurate in predicting a woman's fertile periods. While men are almost always potent, women are capable of conceiving for only a few days a month. The goal of couples who practice Natural Family Planning techniques is to monitor the woman's fertility cycle and predict the days that she is able to conceive. By avoiding sexual intercourse during the woman's fertile period, the couple is able to prevent pregnancy. Likewise, couples who hope to have a child can have sexual intercourse during the times in the woman's cycle when she is most likely to become pregnant.

Natural Family Planning methods are medically safe, inexpensive to use, and have no injurious side effects. Couples who use these methods point to the values in being more familiar and comfortable with one's body because its natural processes are known and respected. Although

Background

How effective is Natural Family Planning? A five-nation study in the 1970s found that ninety-seven percent of women could correctly identify fertile mucus after only three cycles of observation. NFP has been proven effective ninety-eight percent of the time when couples know what they are doing and don't try to cheat on the rules.

there are times in the month when abstinence is practiced, there are still many opportunities to share sexual intercourse. During the times of abstinence, the couple can express their love for each other in other ways—sometimes that simply means they will fall asleep in each other's arms.

The two most common and effective NFP methods are the *Sympto-thermic Method* and the *Ovulation Method*.

The Sympto-thermic Method is based on the fact that a woman's morning temperature rises from its basal (or normal) level soon after ovulation. The infertile phase of the cycle begins on the third day after this temperature shift. This method requires a careful daily accounting of the woman's temperature. Other signs that indicate fertility are a change in cervical mucus discharge, mid-cycle ovulatory pain, and changes in the texture and shape of the cervix.

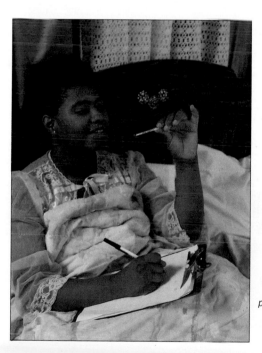

Natural Family Planning techniques help a couple plan when or when not to have a child.

The Ovulation Method (sometimes called the Billing's Method) is based on identifying the mid-cycle vaginal discharge that indicates the fertile phase of the cycle. While every woman's fertility cycle differs to some degree, the following signs are usually present:

- Following menstruation, most women experience a dryness or absence of vaginal mucus which denotes an infertile period.
- The dry days are followed by the development of mucus that is originally sticky, cloudy, and tacky, but soon becomes clear, slippery, and stretchy.
- The last day of clear mucus is called the peak day. Ovulation ordinarily occurs one day after the peak day.
- The fertile period lasts from the beginning of the mucus discharge until about three full days past the peak day.
- From about the fourth day past the peak until the beginning of the next cycle the woman is infertile.
- A couple hoping to have a child could use the clear mucus as a sign of when intercourse would most likely lead to conception.
- Couples hoping to space their children would avoid intercourse during the fertility phase.

NFP is more complicated than taking a pill or using a device to prevent conception. For NFP to be effective, the fertility cycle needs to be understood, the husband and wife needs to communicate openly, and they need to agree to cooperate with the process.

Natural Family Planning is a nonintrusive method of birth planning. People using NFP do not introduce substances into their bodies, and therefore do not alter the body's processes or chemical balance.

Resources

Resource 12G provides a diagram of a woman's reproductive organs and more information on the menstrual cycle.

Background

See the *Catechism of the Catholic Church,* 2368-2370.

Natural Family Planning

Teaching Approaches (continued)

- Share with students this statement by Pope John Paul II: "The Church does not claim that responsible parenthood is easy, but the grace of the sacrament of Marriage gives Christian couples a readiness and a capacity to live out their commitments with fidelity and joy. At the same time, the use of natural methods gives a couple an openness to life, which is truly a splendid gift of God's goodness. It also helps them deepen their conjugal communication and grow closer to one another."

- Discuss "Talk It Over," Question 2. Ask: "What do you think would be the greatest disadvantage of NFP for you? Explain your answer."

- **Reteach**—Recall the definition of abstinence ("the practice of living without something"). Ask: "How do you think abstinence plays a part in responsible parenting in a marital relationship?"

- **Extend the Lesson**—If possible, arrange for a Natural Family Planning instructor or a couple who practice NFP to give a detailed presentation about the method.

✚ To Your Health

Teaching Approaches

- Read the feature to the students. Remind them that a physician administered test is the only sure way to test for pregnancy.

- Explain that some of the early signs of pregnancy are a missed menstrual period, unusual tiredness, swelling and tenderness of the breasts, frequent urination, and nausea or "morning sickness." All of these signs may occur for reasons other than pregnancy. Even if a woman has all of the symptoms of pregnancy, that does not mean that she is pregnant. Stress can cause a woman to experience many of the signs related to pregnancy even if she has never had sexual intercourse, a necessary precursor to being pregnant.

Support for Couples

Teaching Approaches

- Read or have the students read the text section.
- Discuss the statement from Pope John Paul II.
- Ask: "What are ways the Catholic community can support those who are trying to follow the model of responsible parenting?"
- **Reteach**—Have the students write a speech that persuades their audience of the value of NFP. Have them use the information presented in this chapter and from other sources. Ask them to address the issues of health, self-knowledge, self-discipline, and communication.
- **Extend the Lesson**—Debate the merits of NFP and artificial contraceptives. How will students make a wise choice for using either as part of marriage?

The use of NFP encourages honest communication and creativity within the marriage. These practices can be a wonderful "side effect" to the couple practicing NFP. Couples planning marriage are encouraged to learn about NFP prior to the wedding so that they can begin to practice it from the beginning of their married life.

Should a couple want to practice NFP, they should attend a program given by trainers qualified in the practical use of the methods. Many of these programs are sponsored by local dioceses or hospitals.

Support for Couples

Issues of family planning are among the most difficult issues faced by married couples today. The couple that supports, respects, and nurtures each other is able to address this issue responsibly.

They will discuss their feelings and beliefs about these important matters, research what the Church teaches, and seek guidance (and grace) from God through prayer. The couple can also seek the support of their Catholic community, which remains with them to share in the difficulties and joys of married and family life.

Pope John Paul II refers to Christian marriage as a treasure worth defending:

> The Church and humanity entrust to you the great reality of that love which is the basis of marriage, the family and the future. The Church and humanity firmly believe that you will bring about its rebirth; they firmly believe that you will make it beautiful: beautiful in a human and Christian way. In a human and Christian way great, mature, and responsible *(To the Youth of the World).*

The joys of married and family life are worth defending.

Journal Assignment

Use this activity as part of "Support for Couples, Extend the Lesson." Ask students to answer the questions: "How will you make a wise decision in shoosing to use NFP or artificial contraception in your marriage? What say will your spouse have in this decision?"

Prayer in Action
Family Intentions

The following prayer is used as an opening prayer at Masses devoted to family intentions. Offer this prayer as your personal hope for your family of the present and your family of the future:

"Father, we look to Your loving guidance and order as the pattern of all family life. By following the example of the Holy Family of Your son in mutual love and respect, may we come to the joy of our home in heaven.

We ask this through our Lord Jesus Christ, Your Son, who lives and reigns with You and the Holy Spirit, one God, for ever and ever.

Amen."

Talk It Over

1. What is your response to the Church's position on responsible parenting?
2. What do you consider the advantages of Natural Family Planning? the disadvantages?
3. Tell why you believe marriage is a "treasure worth defending."

It is through the family that hope in the future is best revealed.

Chapter Summary

- Marriage requires many adjustments, both for the individual and the couple.
- A shared vision helps a couple survive the first years of marriage.
- Sexual intercourse is a special form of communication for married couples that involves mind, body, and spirit.
- Sexual intercourse both unites the couple and leads to children.
- Responsible parenting means couples make parenthood decisions with God's help.
- The Church teaches that birth planning is acceptable if it uses the woman's natural fertility cycle.

Prayer in Action

Teaching Approaches

- You may use this as a concluding prayer to the lesson or chapter. Have the students recite the prayer together.
- Form small groups. Each group is to compose its own prayer for family life. Each prayer should contain the students' personal intentions for their families.

Talk It Over

Have the students share their opinions on Questions 1 and 3 with a partner. If you have not already had the students discuss Question 2, allow them to brainstorm advantages (and disadvantages) of NFP and write their ideas on the board.

Chapter Summary

- This section lists the main points of summary of this chapter. To use as a review, you might have the students list examples from the text to illustrate each point, rewrite each point in their own words, or find creative ways to teach each point.
- Have the students share their review techniques with a partner.

Background

The issue of artificial birth control, according to the studies of Fr. Andrew Greeley, has caused more people to leave the Church in the past 25 years than any other issue. This text attempts to challenge students to faithfully follow Church teaching in regards to Natural Family Planning.

Chapter 12 Review

What Have You Learned?

Listed below are suggested answers. For many of the questions, the answers will vary.

1. Honest communication can help couples avoid competition, develop new social habits, and communicate better through sexuality and thus better adjust to married life.
2. Competition can pull couples apart and lead them toward separate goals instead of working toward a common goal.
3. Depending less on friends for support means increasing the amount of support needed from one's spouse. This support is crucial in a marriage because it strengthens the marriage commitment.
4. The language of sexuality can be communicated through the sharing of special thoughts and insights with one another, or through expressions of tenderness like hugs and kisses.
5. Sexual intercourse in marriage is unitive and procreative.
6. There are many good reasons for having children, including having a great love for them.
7. The parent is a child's primary guide, guard, provider, mentor, and particularly teacher.
8. Responsible parenting means that a couple will accept children lovingly, put the needs of their children before their own career goals or material possessions, and nurture and care for the children that they have.
9. The Church approves the use of Natural Family Planning as a means to regulate birth. It is based on understanding the woman's fertility cycle.
10. A married couple can turn to the Catholic community for support.

Application

Read the directions and descriptions of each project to the students. Allow the students to choose their own project. Suggest the following steps: (1) formulate a plan; (2) complete the tasks; (3) share the initial project with a partner for comments; (4) revise and finalize the project.

REVIEW

What Have You Learned?

1. Why is effective communication so important in the adjustment to married life?
2. What are some ways that competition can damage a marriage?
3. Why is it important for the marital relationship to be closer than relationships with other friends?
4. How can the language of sexuality be communicated between husband and wife through the course of an entire day?
5. What two meanings does sexual intercourse have in marriage?
6. What are some good reasons for having a child?
7. How is the parent the primary teacher of life
8. What is the meaning of "responsible parenting"?
9. Of which method of birth planning does the Church approve? How does it work?
10. Besides each other, who can a married couple turn to for support?

Application

1. Develop a skit illustrating one couple who practices effective communication, and another couple that does not. Share your skits with the class.
2. In small groups, devise a plan of action that will help you overcome the kind of competition that can be destructive to a marriage. Make your plan concrete. Devise a master plan with other groups.
3. Interview someone you know who is married. Ask the person what effect relationships with friends have had on his or her marriage.
4. List two popular views about sexual intercourse other than the Catholic view. For each view, write what you understand its philosophy to be, the purpose of intercourse, what is and isn't acceptable, and the values and attitudes a couple needs to develop good sexual rapport. After describing these views, compare one of them to Catholic teaching.
5. Make a list of reasons why a married couple should have a child. Compare them with reasons given by other students. Develop a list of "ten reasons for having a child."
6. Write a paper that expresses your opinion on why marriages and society benefit when parents choose to have children and raise them in an environment of love and trust. Include economic considerations and how parents adjust their careers to more adequately care for a child.
7. Research various kinds of birth control. Develop a list of positive and negative reasons for each. Write a paper that examines the birth control issue. If you offer your own conclusions, support them with evidence.

Journal Assignment

Ask: "How is the Church affected when many of its members choose to ignore Church teaching and use artificial contraception? Should people who make this decision be considered sinful or outside of the Church?"

REVIEW

Chapter Vocabulary

- effective communication
- shared vision
- competition
- holistic
- unitive
- procreative
- blessing
- responsible parenting
- domestic church
- natural family planning

Like a human parent, God will help us when we ask for help, but in a way that will make us more mature, more real, not in a way that will diminish us.

Madeleine L'Engle

Putting Vocabulary to Use

Supply the missing words for each sentence from the vocabulary list.

1. The Catholic view of marital sex is _____ because it places the discussion of sex into the total context of the couple.
2. _____ means that the couple is always most qualified to make decisions regarding childbearing and childrearing.
3. Many of the difficult adjustments of married life can be lessened by _____ between husband and wife.
4. A child should always be thought of as a _____ or a gift of divine favor.
5. The _____ dimension of sexual intercourse in marriage means that the couple is brought closer together through their intimacy and fidelity.
6. The family may be called the _____ or the Church of the home.
7. Openness to new life is associated with the _____ dimension of sexual intercourse in marriage.
8. A level of _____ may exist between a husband and wife in marriage; most often it is harmful.
9. _____ is the birth regulating technique used by couples that is based on the woman's fertility cycle.
10. Developing a _____ in marriage often means that a husband and wife will have to alter the ways they thought of themselves before marriage.

Putting Vocabulary to Use

1. holistic
2. responsible parenting
3. effective communication
4. blessing
5. unitive
6. domestic Church
7. procreative
8. competition
9. Natural Family Planning
10. shared vision.

Final Thought

Journal Assignment

Ask for comments on the passage. Ask: "What does it mean to say that God will help us, but not in a way that will diminish us?"

Unit 3 Review

Aim

To reinforce the main concepts of Unit 3, especially that the call to Christian vocation requires commitment and dedication.

Looking Back

Listed below are suggested answers. For many questions, the answers will vary.

1. Poverty, chastity, and obedience are the vows traditionally taken by people entering religious life.

2. The phrase "live simply so that others may simply live" reflects the call all Christians have to express the vow of poverty in their lives.

3. Couples refrain from sexual intercourse at certain times in their marriage for important reasons. Couples promise to remain chaste with people other than their spouses out of loving fidelity.

4. The "laity" refers to all the baptized with the exception of the ordained clergy.

5. Teachers, nurses, missionaries, and college presidents are just some of the ministries performed by men and women religious.

6. A diocesan priest is ordained to serve in a diocese and promises celibacy and obedience to the bishop. A religious priest usually lives in a religious community. His obedience is promised to the superior of his order.

7. Generally, the requirements are: (1) intellectual; (2) physical; (3) religious; (4) psychological; (5) moral; and (6) motivational.

8. Today people have a great deal more freedom in selecting their marriage partners, usually through the process of dating and courtship. In the past, many marriages were arranged.

9. Couples who share common interests will feel more comfortable sharing important information about themselves than if they have to search for something to discuss.

10. Falling in love usually involves sexual attraction and is not permanent.

11. The testing stage of love involves finding out as much about the other person as possible.

For a Lifetime

Looking Back

1. What are the vows traditionally taken by those who enter religious life?
2. What is the meaning of the phrase "live simply so that others may simply live"?
3. How is the vow of chastity a part of marriage?
4. Who are the laity?
5. What are some of the various ministries performed by men and women religious?
6. What is the difference between a diocesan priest and a priest who is a member of a religious community?
7. What are the six general requirements for priesthood or the religious life?
8. How does the way marriage partners are chosen today differ from the way they were chosen in the past?
9. Why is it usually advantageous for a married couple to have a great deal in common?
10. What are two factors to consider about the term "in love"?
11. How is the third stage of love like a two-part test?
12. What are the three important issues a couple must raise when considering marriage?
13. How is true love more than an expression of a feeling?
14. How does the Wedding at Cana express Jesus' attitude toward marriage?
15. What images does Saint Paul use in the Letter to the Ephesians to describe the love that married couples should have for one another?
16. How is mystery a part of married life?
17. List two characteristics of the engagement period.
18. What are the steps a couple goes through in order to be married in a Catholic Church?
19. Why is a shared vision between husband and wife especially important in the first months and years of marriage?
20. How can competition affect married life?
21. How is marital sex holistic?
22. What are the two inseparable meanings of sexual intercourse according to the Church?
23. Why might "teacher" be the best job title for a parent?
24. What does the Church teach about birth regulation?

12. Issues include: (1) supporting each other's interests; (2) roles in marriage; (3) religious beliefs; (4) personal autonomy; (5) the motivation; and (6) feelings about children.

13. True love is a commitment to persevere even when it is threatened.

14. The Wedding at Cana story shows that Jesus approved of marriages, He supports couples, and His willingness to help, and give us an idea of the richness of God's kingdom.

Making It Real

1. What can you learn about marriage from people who live that vocation? Look through magazines and newspapers for quotations made *about* marriage *by* married couples. Cut out the quotations and include them in a class scrapbook on marriage tips.

2. Work on one or more of these projects on your own, with a small group, or with the entire class:

● Research contemporary statistics on marriage. Gather information on issues such as the size of families, the divorce rate, two-income marriages, and the like. Add any other issues recommended by the group.

● Describe a parent who knows that children are not personal property, but are gifts entrusted to the parent by God for love and guidance.

● Review the values that the Church hopes to protect with its stand on birth control, and the values of people who take a stand opposing the Church. Write a paper examining both sides of the birth control issue. Offer your own conclusions and opinions, too.

● Write a speech to persuade your audience of the values of Natural Family Planning. Address the issues of health, self-knowledge, self-discipline, cooperation, and communication.

A Time of Prayer

Use this prayer exercise with your classmates. Before beginning, write a "Letter to Me" describing your personal visions for the future.

Leader: We are called to prepare. Our lives are at the crossroads. There are many roads open to us. Help us, God, to always do Your will no matter which vocational path we choose. We make this prayer in the name of Your Son, Jesus Christ.

All: Amen.

Reader: A Reading from the Gospel of Luke 14:27-33.

All: Praise to You, Lord Jesus Christ.

(Pause for shared reflection. After everyone who wants to has had a chance to speak, play a reflective piece of music that the class has chosen.)

Leader: What will we be like in the future? Who are we to become? Let us take some time to share.

(Previously selected volunteers take turns sharing their "Letters to Me.")

Leader: Let us pray to do God's will in the words that Jesus taught us.

All: Our Father who art in heaven…

Leader: Let us go in peace to always love and serve the Lord.

All: Thanks be to God.

255

Resources

Resource U3 from the Teacher's Resource Book provides suggestions to help plan a class Mass or other liturgical service suitable for use during a retreat or mini-workshop.

15. The love between husbands and wives reflects Jesus' love for the Church.

16. The Latin meaning of sacrament is "mystery." Mystery is a part of married life found in the many unexpected directions in which the couple is led by God.

17. During the engagement process, the man and woman have the chance to examine what life will be like for them as a couple and to seriously analyze their decision to marry.

18. Interviews, counseling workshops, inventories, and retreats.

19. The husband and wife develop an understanding of "we."

20. When couples are in competition, their energy is directed away from a common goal.

21. In marriage, sexual intercourse involves the whole person and is viewed in the context of the couple's total life.

22. Sexual intercourse is always to be unitive and procreative.

23. Parents teach their children physically, intellectually, socially, emotionally, and spiritually. They are their children's primary educators.

24. The Church teaches that no artificial means should be used to prevent conception.

Making It Real

Teaching Approaches

● Read the directions and descriptions of each project to the students.

● **Reteach**—Evaluate the projects as they are being developed. Have students report on their progress.

● **Extend the Lesson**—Have finished projects presented in class.

A Time of Prayer

Teaching Approaches

● The students may write the "Letter to Me" in their journals. It may include personal, community, and global visions for the future.

● **Reteach**—Choose a leader and Scripture reader and practice parts beforehand. If possible, have the students select the reflective music that is to be used.

● **Extend the Lesson**—Use the prayer to conclude a class meeting.

The Church's restored catechumenate for adult converts to the faith lends itself well to the personal conversion needs of people. It adjusts to the catechumen's journey from the initial inquiry through a more thorough catechesis and deeper searchings to the reception of the sacraments of initiation at the Easter Vigil. The journey does not end with Baptism, however. The newly baptized continue for many years to learn what it means to be part of the Body of Christ as represented through the Church. The catechumen's journey is really a model of the journey that is taken by all Christians.

Everyone changes, even people who have made vocation choices publicly. While their promises don't change, people must learn to implement them in new ways.

In Unit 4, students will:

- Examine the continuing journey of life—careers, relationships, and vocations.
- Recognize the major transition stages of life and the ways people move from one stage to the next.
- Look at why people change jobs and careers and consider ways to adapt new styles of ministry into previously chosen vocations.
- Consider the next steps on their journeys. What must they do to make their dreams come true?

Like the catechumen's journey of faith, the journey of life never stops. It continues to move forward toward the destination of God's kingdom.

Unit 4 Overview

Chapter 13 Responding to Life's Challenges

Life is a series of transitions, taking a person from one stage to the next.

Chapter 14 Preparation for Life

We can begin planning for the future right now.

Teaching Objectives

- To prepare the students to deal with the inevitable changes of life.
- To help the students develop strategies for planning their futures.

Unit 4

Always Evolving

We believe that Christianity gives us a foundation on which to live and helps us in everything we do. We have built our home, our family, our marriage, and our lives on this foundation.

After thirty years together, with three children and two grandchildren, we are continually learning that Christian marriage is for us. We feel that it is the only way for us to live our vocations and be faithful to ourselves, each other, our family, and the glorious community of God's creation.

While we love each other dearly, our marriage has not always been easy, and it has not always been fun. There have been moments when we wondered if our relationship could endure. Each time, however, God has given us the strength to pull ourselves together and resolve our differences. And each time our marriage survives another crisis, it grows stronger.

Background

Evelyn and Wilmer Hatch live in Chicago, Illinois where they have belonged to the same parish for twenty-four years. Besides his vocation to married life, Wilmer Hatch is a permanent deacon. It took the family over a year to decide whether or not he should take this major step. Then, for three years, Mr. and Mrs. Hatch attended formation sessions in preparation for ordination. Evelyn Hatch said, "The deacon classes were very helpful for us. They brought us closer together as a

NAME: *Evelyn and Wilmer Hatch*
CAREER: *Homemaker, Insurance Manager*
VOCATION: *Married Life*

"We progress through life in a series of transitional changes, leaving part of ourselves behind as we move forward.

'Living in His spirit, therefore, Christians are to deny themselves, take up the cross each day, and follow in His steps'(cf.*Luke 9:23ff*). Christ's atoning sacrifice is 'the vital principle in which the Christian lives, and without which Christianity is not.' As brothers and sisters of Jesus who are also His followers and members of His body, Christians must accept suffering and death as He did, and in so accepting them, share His life. 'If we have been united with Him through likeness to His death,' so also 'through a like resurrection' we shall be raised from the dead by the glory of the Father *(Romans 6:4ff)*. By union with Christ, one has already begun to share the risen life here on earth (cf. *2 Peter 1:4*)" (*National Catechetical Directory*, #99).

Begin the Unit

1. Ask the students to speculate on the relationship between the unit title and the titles of Chapters 13 and 14.

2. Read the unit objectives.

3. If you wish, ask the students to write down any questions that have persisted through the course of study. Make time to refer to the questions at some point during one of the lessons of this unit.

4. Read the unit opener feature on married life.

5. Ask: "What would you imagine would be some of the difficulties couples experience in marriages? What difficulties would men and women experience as priests, brothers, or sisters?"

6. Have the students present this statement to a married couple that they know for comment: "Each time our marriage survives another crisis, it grows stronger."

couple, and proved to be very helpful as we raised our children." Commenting on Mr. Hatch, she added, "He's not perfect, but he's a really good man. Through his ministry I have a deeper understanding of who I married. Any time this man has wanted to give to others, it has made our life richer. The more he gave to others, the more he had to give to us. His commitment to ministry has made my faith stronger and has helped me in my own ministry."

Focus on: Chapter 13

Changing relationships with oneself, others, and God is a part of each stage of life. Studies have tracked the patterns of physical, social, and intellectual change from conception until death. Change takes place in every area of life: in vocations like marriage or religious life, and in chosen jobs or careers. Ultimately, life is a journey, a series of beginnings and endings, deaths and resurrections. For a Christian, the goal of life's journey is a significant relationship with Jesus Christ, a relationship that leads to salvation.

In this chapter, the students will examine the various transitions in life and they will come to an understanding of their continuing need for spiritual development as disciples of Jesus Christ.

Plan Ahead

- Incorporate formal and/or spontaneous prayer in each lesson. A participatory prayer service that is suitable for use in a retreat setting is provided in the Teacher's Resource Book.
- Note the **Resources** suggestions which can be applied to, or used to extend, the lessons of this chapter.
- Preview the **Application** projects in the Chapter Review. Refer to **Teaching Approaches** for suggestions on when to assign the projects. Or, the projects may be used as part of lesson, section, or chapter reviews.
- Decide on a method for grouping students for projects and discussion.
- Invite guest speakers who will participate in selected lessons well in advance.

Responding to Life's Challenges

You have no idea what your life will be like tomorrow.

James 3:14

This chapter will help you to:

- Recognize transitional stages in life and learn ways to move from one stage to the next.
- Understand that social relationships change with time.
- Discover the importance of the transitional stages in marriage.
- Examine job and career satisfaction.
- Consider the need for ongoing spiritual development.

258

Media Suggestions (Optional)

- *Everybody Rides the Carousel* (Pyramid Films) Three 24-minute vignettes. This is an animated view of Erik Erikson's eight stages of life. The excerpt on "Adolescence" is especially recommended.

Aims

1. To help students understand some of the characteristics of human development.
2. To examine attitudes about work, job, and career satisfaction.

Begin the Section

1. Arrange for a retired adult—married, single, or religious—to recall with the class the dreams that he or she had as a high school student. Ask: "How were your dreams realized? What experiences made you alter your dreams? What have been some of the major transitions in your life? How would the high school graduate of many years ago recognize the person you are today?" Allow the students to ask questions and to participate in the discussion. (In lieu of this activity, have the students complete **Application** Project 1.)
2. Read or summarize the text opener. Ask the students to suggest other important times of transition. (Recall the "timeline" the students began in Chapter 1 and allow time for them to update it with any new ideas.)

I. TRANSITIONS

Lining up for graduation rehearsal, everyone is in a festive mood. You've been measured for your cap and gown, and soon you will actually step to the podium. Your mom will wipe away a tear as you receive the diploma. Of course, Uncle Don will record the evening on video tape for posterity. What a time you'll have! High school graduation—an occasion that once seemed so distant—now evokes many new thoughts and feelings.

There are always plenty of laughs, and some tears, on graduation day; the normal reactions to the joy of completion and the sorrow of leaving friends and familiar places behind. Graduation is a signal that one part of your life is over, and that another is commencing. Graduations are often refered to as commencement ceremonies.

Sadly, some people never grow beyond the person they are on graduation day. They go through life trying to relive their lives as high

- *Princess* (Paulist Productions) 25 minutes. Laurie is an above average student, popular, and athletic; she also has a boyfriend. Her parents' divorce shatters her security and sends her into a deep depression. She learns to accept the reality of the situation and that her parents still love her.

Tracking Changes

Lesson Overview

There are several models that attempt to explain the stages of human development. Ask: "What is the value of understanding how people develop?" Point out that from these models it is often possible to predict the type and rate of growth to be expected at each stage of life.

Teaching Approaches

- Read or summarize the text section. Introduce the types of human development to be presented.
- Ask the students to comment on how "a bit of the past is left behind as the person adapts to a new environment."
- **Reteach**—Explain that any treatment of human development must include a discussion of spiritual development, including moral and religious issues. Oftentimes, morality is seen as the development of socially acceptable attitudes and values without providing a definition of what is right and wrong. There is little mention of how religious training, or the lack of it, affects development. All the issues of development—physical, social, emotional, and spiritual—must be viewed as part of the overall picture.
- **Extend the Lesson**—Assign **Application** Project 2. (See **Resource 13A**).

In Focus

Teaching Approaches

- Read this panel as part of the lesson, "Tracking Changes."
- Ask the students to write their own definitions of adulthood and share them with a partner.

Physical Changes

New Words

Anorexia means "without appetite."
Anorexia nervosa is a behavior that involves the irrational fear of becoming overweight and leads to severe weight loss through intentional starvation.

school athletes or Homecoming Queen candidates. Or they carry with them the stigma of being the loner who never had a date, or the slow learner with bad grades. They are unprepared to respond to the challenges life offers them.

High school graduation is just one of life's many transitions. The person you will be five, ten, twenty, and fifty years from now will be different from who you are now. You will have new friends, new interests, and new responsibilities. Learning to cope with life's ever-evolving, ever-changing situations is a sign of maturity. Changes also occur in lifetime commitments, like marriage or the religious life, and in your understanding of God.

In this chapter, you will look at how life's transitions will affect your relationships, careers, and spirituality. In each transition, you will find that while something is ending, something new is beginning. The old passes away while the new dawns.

In Focus
When Does Adulthood Begin?

There is no definitive answer as to when adolescence ends and adulthood begins. While 18-year-olds can vote or marry, they cannot legally drink alcohol or gamble. To serve as a United States senator a person must be at least thirty; the minimum age for the President of the United States is thirty-five.

Adulthood is often equated with financial independence from one's parents'—having a job and being self-supporting—or beginning with marriage.

Many people argue that adulthood is determined by a person's maturity and behavior. Wisdom, integrity, and stability are words that are used to describe a mature person.

What criteria would you use to determine when a person becomes an adult?

Tracking Changes

People grow and develop at different rates. While physical development is best understood, social, emotional, and spiritual development are harder to pinpoint. Behavioral scientists of human development have described life as a series of stages to be navigated successfully if a person is to reach maturity. The step-by-step transition through the stages is necessary if a person is to become a mature adult. At each stage, a bit of the past is left behind as the person adapts to the new environment.

Physical Changes

Other than the first year of life, puberty is the period of fastest physical growth. Growth during puberty, however, is uneven. One part of a person's body may have matured while another has not. This can sometimes create a feeling of awkwardness. Living with a changing body brings happiness for some, pain for others.

Physically, your body will continue to change throughout life, only not as drastically as it did during puberty. People who are now the "perfect" weight may fight a losing "battle of the bulge" after the age of thirty. Women who bear children find that they must exercise regularly to regain the figure they once had. By their mid-twenties, men will notice whether they are destined to baldness, grey hair, or both.

As you age, you will be measured physically by how well different parts of your body function. People with 20/20 vision as teens may be farsighted at forty; easily reading traffic signs two blocks away, but not having arms long enough to read the newspaper. Chronic or serious illness can also have a dramatic effect on a person's life, affecting not only the body, but one's whole life as well.

If you ask an adult how old he or she feels, you might receive an answer that would surprise you. Many adults wonder aloud where the time has gone: when did this wrinkled old man in the mirror replace the handsome dancer from college?

Resouces

Resource 13A from the Teacher's Resource Book can be used with the "Extend the Lesson" exercise from "Tracking Changes."

Background

Adulthood is often defined by the stages of (1) young adulthood (from twenty-one to the mid-thirties, usually marked by marriage, family, and career); (2) middle adulthood (thirties, forties, and fifties, career

Many adults say they still feel like they are young, except when they see themselves in mirrors.

Realistically, however, physical changes after puberty mean little, except for the cases involving traumatic injury or illness. While your appearance may affect how you feel, physical changes will probably not change your life very much.

Social Changes

During his sister's wedding reception, Scott wondered who the man and woman were in the corner, laughing and swapping stories with his father.

"Who are those people anyway?" Scott asked when he finally caught up with his father in the food line.

"That's Victor. He was the best man in my wedding. His wife is Sheila. I took her to the senior prom in high school. Let me introduce you to them."

As he walked over to meet Victor and Sheila, Scott thought it strange that once-strong friendships would take years to renew. It had taken Scott's sister's wedding to bring these old friends together again.

As individuals change, relationships change, too. Your present friendships will not be the same when you are older. As an adult, you are likely to meet and interact with a great number of new acquaintances through work, the neighborhood, and church. While you may be friendly with these people, you are less likely to form as many friendships as when you were younger.

New career and vocation responsibilities will limit the time available for establishing new friendships and maintaining old ones. A working mother with two young children has much less time (and energy) for regular contact with old friends. A newly-ordained priest meets many new people at the parish, but lacks the time to form deep friendships with but only a few of them.

To Your Health
Eating More Is Okay

Teenagers may need to eat 500 more calories a day than adults to assure proper nutrition. An average thirteen-year-old girl needs 2,600 calories a day; an average sixteen-year-old boy needs 3,600 calories a day.

The reason for the increase is obvious: growing bodies need fuel. Adolescents may gain 20 pounds in one year without becoming overweight. Unfortunately, some adolescents worry about being overweight. Rather than eating properly, they don't eat at all. This can lead to very serious health problems. The medical term for one form of this self-abuse is *anorexia nervosa.*

Remember: it's okay to eat more. Your body needs it!

advances and raising children); and (3) older adulthood (mid-sixties and beyond, traditional retirement years when people are able to look back on their lives and view the contributions that they have made).

Resources

Resource 13B from the Teacher's Resource Book helps the students understand a variety of definitions of adulthood.

Resource 13C provides suggestions for maintenance of good nutrition.

Social Changes

Teaching Approaches (continued)

- Ask: "Who is one of your parent's oldest childhood friends? How often do they get together now? What caused their relationship to change?" If students don't know the answers to these questions, have them ask their parents.

- Read or summarize the rest of the text section.

- **Reteach**—Have the students debate this statement: "Forming new relationships and maintaining old ones is an essential part of human development."

- **Extend the Lesson**—Have the students role play a future reunion between two friends. Choose volunteers to share their role plays.

▲ Family Living

Teaching Approaches

- Have the students use the facts presented in the feature to support their side in the "relationship debate" suggested in the "Social Changes" lesson.

- Ask: "Who has the most friends, you or your parents? Who has the closest friends, you or your parents?" Discuss student answers.

Emotional Changes

Teaching Approaches

- Have the students describe a person represented by the phrase "He (she) will never grow up."

- Read or have the students read the section. Allow time for shared comments and questions.

- **Reteach**—Recall that before people make lifelong commitments they should: know themselves and accept their own strengths and weaknesses; know what is and is not important; set goals and have plans for reaching those goals; understand someone else's needs and feelings; be able to put other people's needs ahead of their own.

Behavior often changes with age, as does taste in music, movies, television, reading, and other forms of entertainment. The fact that a favorite high school team lost in overtime at the state championships might be a crushing blow to a high school student right now, but in ten years he or she probably won't even notice the current year's score. People establish new criteria for what they consider important and essential.

Emotional Changes

"When I was a child, I used to talk as a child, think as a child, reason as a child; when I became a man, I put aside childish things" *(1 Corinthians 13:11)*. Saint Paul's comments capture succinctly the changes that come with emotional maturity. Behavior and attitudes that were appropriate for you at eighteen will be left behind by the time you are twenty-five.

Emotional growth can be quite challenging. Some people enjoy their childhoods so much that they appear to remain stuck at that level forever. They refuse to accept full responsibility for their actions and put off decisions. While physically mature, their behavior and attitudes are no different than those of a child.

Research conducted during the last half-century by developmental psychologists also shows that we grow through stages toward greater moral maturity. There are many theories as to how this growth occurs, and these theories often reach widely different conclusions. What they all have in common, is the recognition that personal maturity doesn't end when a person reaches the age of sixteen, twenty-one, or fifty. Maturing is a lifelong process.

Spiritual Changes

James Fowler, building on moral development research, has identified stages in the development of religious faith. According to Fowler, people start with a faith borrowed from their parents and grow into a faith that is more personal. People eventually believe and practice their faith because they want to, not because someone else wants them to believe and practice it.

If Fowler's theory is correct, most people will spend much of their young adulthood struggling to come to a personal acceptance of faith. The difficulties that people face during this time seem necessary if they are to grow, and are to be expected.

Many young adults investigate other religious traditions and churches in an attempt to find a spiritual home. After years of searching, many return to the faith of their youth, but with a new, mature level of appreciation and understanding.

Talk It Over

1. What changes do you expect in your life during the next few years? How well prepared do you feel in addressing these changes?

▲▲▲ Family Living
Longterm Friendships

A recent study reports that while young adults have more friends than do people in their mid-forties and older, few of the young adult's friendships last six years or longer. For people older than forty, their friendships seem to last much longer than six years.

The study also found that as people grow older they rely more on their friends than on their families for emotional support. This is especially true after children leave home, or if a husband or wife are widowed or divorced.

The most complex friendships are formed in a person's later years. Older people tend to choose friends who are different than themselves and appreciate their uniqueness more than do younger adults. Young adults tend to choose friends with similar interests.

Journal Assignment

Finish this sentence: "One thing that is not as important to me now as it was ten years ago is . . ."

Background

According to psychologist, Abraham Maslow, we are motivated by needs which are met in a hierarchical order of priority. The most basic needs are physical—hunger, thirst, sleep. Unless these needs are met, a person

---

Media Watch
Radical Dude

Long before the era of TV and movies the phrase, "Life imitates art; art imitates life," was coined. Today this phrase means that what we see in the media influences how we live, just as how we live is captured on the screen. The clothes worn by rebellious youth in the 1950 films *The Blackboard Jungle* and *Rebel without a Cause* soon became the

style of dress for teenagers around the world. The line, "I am as mad as hell and I am not going to take it anymore," from the 1970 movie, *Network* has become a popular rallying cry for adults.

What influences how you dress or wear your hair? What phrases that you use regularly come from the popular media?

2. How have physical changes in your body affected your hopes for the future?
3. How have you changed emotionally and socially during the past year? How have you adjusted to these changes?
4. In what ways is your religious faith similar to or different from the faith of your parents?

After years of searching, many people return to the faith of their youth.

Career Changes

Today, few people work at the same job or for the same company for their entire working lives. In fact, it is increasingly common for a person to change careers every ten years or so. On average, statistics show that today's typical worker changes careers three times during the course of his or her adult life.

What do people look for in a career? Why do some people look at work as an opportunity to excel while others see it as a painful chore? Let's find out.

Job Satisfaction

There are two perspectives about the world of work:
1. Work is a painful experience that must be done to survive.
2. Work is our participation with God to create the world and so can be both a joy and a pleasure.

Both attitudes find support in sacred Scripture, and both can be true at times. The perspective that you adopt may influence the type of employment you choose and the degree of satisfaction you experience in your work.

• **Extend the Lesson**—Have students name five common problems faced by adolescents today. List these problems on the board. Next, ask: "How do adolescents solve these problems?" List the solutions on the board. Discuss which of these solutions reflect the greatest maturity.

Spiritual Changes

Teaching Approaches

• Read or summarize the section. Ask: "What would you say about the premise that 'people grow from a faith modeled after one's parents to one that is personal'?"
• **Reteach**—Discuss how an adolescent's religious practice often changes prior to adulthood. Note that during adolescence, a young person's image of God is more likely to develop from the literal to the abstract.
• **Extend the Lesson**—Discuss the concerns students have with the practice of their faith. How has their practice changed during the past year?

Talk It Over

For Question 1, have the students focus their responses to the categories discussed in this lesson: physical, social, emotional, and spiritual changes. Allow the students the choice to share their answers to Questions 2 and 3 with a partner, or write it as part of a personal reflection. Allow them time to discuss their answers to Question 4 with a partner or in a small group.

Media Watch

Teaching Approaches

• Read or summarize the panel. Discuss the in-text questions.
• Have the students brainstorm a list of television programs, movies, or advertisers most "out of touch" with today's adolescents.
• Survey advertising aimed at young children. What values are being communicated by the products being promoted?

has little awareness of the other needs. Emotional needs (for example, the need to love and be loved) come next. We all need to achieve—to have others recognize that we are competent.

Resources
Resource 13D is an exercise involving Maslow's "hierarchy of needs."

Career Changes

Lesson Overview

Have the students recall some of the factors that influence a person's career choice; for example, combining personal talents and skills with the needs of society. Ask: "What are some factors that would lead a person to change careers?"

Teaching Approaches

- Read the lesson opener.
- Ask: "What do you find satisfying about something you do now? What would be a source of satisfaction for a job or career that you might have in the future?"
- **Reteach**—Review the career activities conducted in earlier lessons. How have students' understanding of their personal career goals changed?
- **Extend the Lesson**—Assign **Application** Project 4.

Job Satisfaction

Teaching Approaches

- List on the board the two attitudes about work. Refer to them as you go through the lesson.
- Assign the students to read and comment on both attitudes about work.
- **Reteach**—Discuss Question 2 from "Talk It Over."
- **Extend the Lesson**—Ask: "Which would you prefer: a high-paying job with little job satisfaction, or a low-paying job with high job satisfaction? Why?"

The Catholic View of Work

Teaching Approaches

- Read or summarize the section.
- Ask the students to comment on Pope John Paul's words, "Work in a specific way forms us, and in a certain sense creates us."
- **Reteach**—Ask: "How are you defined by the work that you do?"
- **Extend the Lesson**—Assign students to read and report on the papal encyclical, "On Human Work."

Work is a painful experience. Genesis 3: 17-18 explains that humankind must work hard to survive because of sin.

"Cursed be the ground because of you!

In toil shall you eat its yield all the days of your life. Thorns and thistles shall it bring forth to you,

as you eat of the plants of the field.

By the sweat of your face

shall you get bread to eat,

Until you return to the ground,

from which you were taken;

For you are dirt,

and to dirt you shall return."

People who hold this attitude believe that work is a punishment for sin and is part of life's difficulties. From this perspective it makes no difference the job you do or how well you do it. Job satisfaction is unimportant.

Any work that allows us to grow in our talents and gifts, can be our honest participation in God's creation.

Work is our participation in God's creation. People who have this second attitude work to support human life and fulfill their role as co-Creator with God. People who cooperate with the gifts that God has bestowed on them in a way that benefits the world are always the most satisfied in their jobs.

The Catholic View of Work

While the Catholic Church certainly recognizes the consequences of sin, it would strongly support the second attitude. The Catholic belief recognizes work as a normal human condition, not the effects of sin. As Pope John Paul II says:

"Work—all work—is linked to effort and this experience of hard work is shared by each person from his or her earliest years. At the same time, however, work in a specific way forms us, and in a certain sense creates us. So it is always a question of effort which is creative."

Work is one of the ways that we can grow closer to God. Work is then chosen, not simply for the money it provides, but for the challenges it offers us to use our God-given gifts and talents more fully. Work is an expression of ourselves, and allows us to offer God, without shame, the work of our hands.

This is not a modern idea. The great cathedrals of the world were crafted with devotion and care. The workers who built these works of art showed their love for God in their labor. Painters and musicians offered their prayers through their marvelous works; God's presence can still be felt in the work of those who preceded us.

There is no reason why work that people do today should be any different.

Background

Said Pope John Paul, "Jesus looks with love on our work, on its various forms, seeing in each one of them a reflection of man's likeness to God the Creator. Work is willed and blessed by God: it no longer carries with itself the weight of condemnation, but the nobility of a mission, that of making a protagonist with God in the building of human society and of the dynamism that reflects the mystery of the Almighty" (*Address to the Bishops of Italy*, March 12, 1982).

Paying Bills

The car bumper sticker evokes a chuckle: "I owe, I owe, so off to work I go." The car's owner was advertising that he or she has credit problems. Many people borrow money and then have a difficult time paying back the loan. They often have to work two jobs to catch up; jobs chosen not because of career or likes, but for their availability and how much they pay.

What do you know about credit? How can you use credit wisely to avoid being squeezed by your bills?

Credit is a method of buying on trust; you promise to pay for what you buy over a certain period of time. People use credit to make major purchases such as houses or cars when they don't have the cash to pay the entire bill. People also use credit cards for convenience.

There is a cost to credit. When you buy a car, for example, you promise to pay the lender back a certain percentage of the money you borrowed each month along with interest. Credit cards work the same way. You borrow money and agree to pay it back. Let's look at an example:

The music center she wanted was on sale for $475, instead of $550. Monique had just enough money in her account to buy it and she was thrilled. Because she was 18 and was working part-time, the sales clerk offered to sell her the music center on credit. Each month for a year she would pay $44.33. This way she could take the sound system home with her and still have money in her savings. Monique decided that buying on credit was a good idea.

Later, at home while listening to music, Monique thought about how she would pay the $44.33 a month. Then she realized that credit wasn't free. Instead of paying $475, she would end up paying $532—$44.33 x 12 months. Maybe buying on credit wasn't such a good deal after all.

What do you think? Was Monique misled by the sales clerk or did she get an honest deal? How would you judge?

Consider the following activities to learn more about the use of credit.

1. You are going to buy your first car. You've found the perfect one for only $2500. You've worked hard and saved your money. You have almost $2200 in the bank. You can use all of your savings and borrow the rest from your dad or you can spend $500 and borrow the rest from the bank. What do you think would be the best decision for you to make? Give reasons for your decision. (**TIP**—Check with a bank for the current interest rates on savings and used car loans in your community before making your decision.)

2. A good credit rating is important if you wish to borrow money. Compile a *Young Adult's Credit Guide*. How can you qualify for a department store or gasoline card? a major credit card? a bank loan? Once you have credit, how do you keep the credit record clean?

3. Some people have problems with buying on credit. They don't realize that they have to pay back what they borrow with interest. What can you do to avoid credit problems? Develop credit rules that will keep you from getting too deeply in debt. (**TIP**—many communities have debt crisis assistance programs to help people who misuse their credit pay back what they owe. Contact your local agency to help you develop your credit rules.)

265

Recurring Dilemmas

Teaching Approaches

- Review some of the reasons the students listed for changing careers from the beginning of the lesson. If anyone mentioned a particular moral dilemma as a reason for a job change, focus on this reason as a way to introduce the lesson.

- Read or have the students read the text section. Make sure the students are able to recognize the main issues involved in Karl's dilemma.

- **Reteach**—Review the function of conscience and the discernment process from Chapter 3. How is Karl's decision an act of conscience and the result of discernment?

- **Extend the Lesson**—Have the students work individually, or with a partner, to develop other career-related moral dilemmas. Ask them to leave the solutions to their dilemmas open-ended. Choose some of the dilemmas to be shared with the class. Discuss possible solutions.

◊ Jonathan operates his own towing business. He makes a living hauling cars that break down on the highway. He also gets great satisfaction out of helping people in need. When he rescued a stranded woman and her two young children on a deserted highway late one night, he was paid in more ways than just financially. The look of relief on the woman's face at his arrival told Jonathan the value of his labor.

Job satisfaction is related to how well we follow God's plans for our lives. One thing is certain: everyone needs to know that they and their efforts are appreciated. The most fulfilling praise for a job well done often comes from within, from knowing that you are doing God's work.

◊ As a young girl, Annette wanted to be a dentist so she could help others in need. Now that she is one, Annette is unfulfilled by her work. The practice she joined does not accept patients who cannot pay. She can't change her office's policy, but Annette has decided she can do something on her own. This summer she will provide dental care at an orphanage in Mexico as a volunteer. She will give up her vacation and stay at the orphanage for ten days to fulfill her original goal of helping others.

Recurring Dilemmas

Why would people who have devoted years of their lives studying for a profession suddenly decide to change careers?

There are no simple answers to this question. There are, however, explanations that people offer for changing careers. Some, like Annette, enter a career for one reason only to find that the business structure in which they work operates with different values. Some people's skills are rendered obsolete by technology, while others chose their careers based on unrealistic expectations or due to outside influences or pressures. Others change their careers because they are concerned with serious ethical and faith-related dilemmas at work.

Job satisfaction is related closely to how we follow God's plan for our life.

Journal Assignment

Share a true story about someone you know who loves the work that he or she does. Explain why this person is so happy with his or her work.

Well Being
Zero to One

What options would a person have after working twenty years in one career, only to learn that this work was no longer possible? If the decisions are so difficult, how can people make them without being overcome by the risks?

Erik Erikson, a psychologist, said that most middle-aged people need to feel that their work is productive, that it will make the world a better place in which to live, and that it has some lasting value. If, by middle age, a person does not feel that his or her career is meaningful, a change is often attempted. The financial values given away in one change are not as important as knowing that one has acquired something of greater value.

◊ Karl was an aerospace engineer by training. During the 1960s he worked on the manned space projects that put astronauts on the moon. When the project ended, Karl continued to design rocket engines. He loved his work and felt that his efforts were leading to progress.

Karl began to question his work when he realized his engines were being used on rockets that would carry nuclear weapons. While his work had not changed, the purpose of it had. The engines he designed were attached to a weapon that could destroy millions of humans within seconds. This thought made Karl uneasy about his chosen career.

For a while, Karl continued to justify his work, saying that it was beneficial and that the responsibility for evil lay at the feet of others. As time went on, however, Karl could no longer live with that answer.

After much prayer and guidance from Scripture and Church teachings, he eventually quit his job and went back to college for a teaching degree in physics. Although the pay would be less, Karl felt that as a teacher he could help people learn to use their knowledge to create a better world. He traded one kind of work, and the security it provided, for the peace of mind gained from doing what he judged to be God's will.

Many other types of work can cause similar dilemmas.
- A nurse who believes the Church's teaching on the sanctity of life may work at a hospital that performs abortions.
- A construction foreman may be employed by a contractor who builds shoddy houses.

If you were in one of these dilemmas, what do you think you would do? How would your decision differ if you had two young children to feed, with a third on the way?

Solutions to dilemmas invite serious prayer and reflection. Those who choose to follow their consciences may be led to heroic decisions. They definitely need the support of friends, family members, and the Church community in making their decisions.

Talk It Over

1. What career do you actually think about pursuing? What are your reasons for choosing this career? What does this choice say about your values?
2. Develop and share a situation where a moral dilemma might cause you to reconsider your career.

Well-Being

Teaching Approaches
- Read the panel. Have students comment on the implications of Erikson's findings.
- View the movie, *Everybody Rides the Carousel.* How realistic do students find these stages?

Talk It Over
The students can share ideas related to Question 1 with a partner. To extend, make a class banner listing all the careers people are considering. Hang it in the classroom. If you did not do Question 2 earlier, discuss it now with the large group.

Background
Society has changed greatly during the twentieth century. During the first half of the century, workers expected to have the same job all of their lives and to be taken care of by the company to which they dedicated their lives. Today, workers change careers on average of two to five times in a lifetime, with little expectation of loyalty from a company.

Aims

1. To examine some of the transitional stages of married life.
2. To help students understand that Catholic Christians are called to daily conversion.

Begin the Section

1. Recall with the students the timelines that they began in Chapter 1. Ask: "What are some examples of painful experiences at various stages of life?"
2. Read the section opening. Relate being "more Christ-like" to ways of handling the painful experiences.
3. Introduce the topics and aims of the section.

Facing Changes

Lesson Overview

Point out the lesson heading, "Facing Changes." Have the students speculate on some of the times of transition in the life of a married couple, a single person, and a religious sister, brother, or priest.

Teaching Approaches

- Assign the section for reading.
- Have the students work with partners or small groups to outline some of the ways a vocation might change over the years. Have the students compare these ideas with those suggested in the opening brainstorm.
- **Reteach**—Review with students the importance of self-esteem. Discuss how a person's self-concept might affect how he or she responds to transitions.
- **Extend the Lesson**—Invite a guest speaker to discuss how his or her vocation has changed since adolescence.

II. ALWAYS IN TRANSITION

What keeps people going through the many transitions they experience? For Christians, it is living the Good News of Jesus that gives them the strength and hope they need to continue on the journey. Religious faith is not something that is taken off like a coat when one arrives at work only to be put back on upon leaving. If we are grounded in faith, then we can draw strength from Jesus during the most trying times.

Facing Changes

What types of transitions would you expect to find in married life: birth (and sometimes tragically, the death) of children? career changes—finding a new position, being promoted, being transferred across the country, being fired or laid off, failing at business?—children grow up and leave home? retirement? caring for aged or infirm parents?

How would you expect a religious vocation to change over the years? What would a priest or religious experience that might cause them hardship or troubles?

Transitions in Religious Life

Men and women who have taken the religious vows of poverty, chastity, and obedience do not live in "happily ever after" worlds any more than do married couples or the storybook characters. They, too, face a life of continual changes and experiences.

Priests will sometimes speak of times when they regretted not having wives or children, or discuss their struggles to live faithfully to their vows. Priests also know the pressures of career advancement and job satisfaction.

Living the vow of obedience is not always easy. A young associate from the suburbs, assigned to a parish in the inner city or rural area, may experience culture shock. Here is something completely different from anything he has ever experienced before. Adjusting to this assignment can be difficult.

Priests who have been teachers or administrators for thirty years may suddenly be assigned as pastors of parishes. Suddenly they are expected to have all of the skills of a pastor without having any experience in parish ministry. They may have replaced pastors who were much loved by the parishioners, and who are not ready yet to make room in their hearts for the replacements. Or the parishes face financial problems that force the new pastors to implement tight budgets. The experiences can be as challenging as any faced by married couples.

Sister Therese (shown in the cab of the tractor) has found great satisfaction as a pastoral administrator of a new parish she is building.

Journal Assignment

Say: "Would you find the variety of ministry assignments in religious life an advantage or disadvantage?"

Background

Some of the difficulties religious men and women have in making transitions today are caused by the laity's expectations of religious. With traditional roles under scrutiny, the pain of change often becomes more pronounced.

Men and women who live in religious communities experience many of the same struggles as do ordained ministers. Women religious talk about the biological urge to bear children that they experience in their late thirties and early forties.

Men and women religious may also experience difficulty with job and career satisfaction as well. Claretian Brother Modesto Leon taught school for years, then decided that he could do more for inner city kids outside the classroom than in. He accomplished his dream when he left teaching and established a gang prevention program. Theresa Harpin, a Sister of St. Joseph of Carondolet, spent years as a campus minister only to find her real satisfaction as a pastoral coordinator of a priestless parish.

Brothers, sisters, and priests sometimes leave the religious communities to which they belonged. After a few years outside of religious life, some return to their old orders or join a new religious community, while others are dispensed from their vows and marry. Adapting to life's challenges can be difficult in any vocation.

Marital Transitions

All marriages experience some transition. The relationship between a couple changes repeatedly over the years, starting soon after the wedding. Have you ever heard the phrase, "the honeymoon is over," applied to a newly married couple? What do you think it means? For certain, the phrase recognizes that the marriage has entered a transition stage.

Changes in careers can cause major transitions. People with ambitious career goals often must work many hours to meet them. The extra time spent on a career is often stolen from marriage and family life. The other spouse and children may begin to feel like they are not important.

● When would you expect career pressures to be greatest? What choices would you have to consider if your career kept you from your family? if your spouse's career interfered with family life?

What transitions take place in a marriage as children grow up?

As discussed earlier, the birth of a child represents a major transition for most couples. Parenting can be an overwhelming experience. Many parents say that they feel like a taxi service: carting kids off to school, making seemingly endless trips to athletic practices, dance and music lessons, scouts, and religious instruction.

● How can parents find the time they need to keep their marriages strong and intimate?

How has your family changed since you've been in high school? Your parents may no longer chauffeur you (who wants to be seen in the same car with a parent?), but now they spend more time worrying about you. Parents often have difficulty adjusting to a child's new independence.

● How could teenagers affect the relationships of their parents?

The middle years of a marriage—usually after twenty or twenty-five years—are often stressful. This is often when children move from the family home and establish homes of their own. Possibly for the first time since their baby was born, the couple is

Background

"Let married people themselves, who are created in the image of the Living God and constituted in an authentic personal dignity, be united together in equal affection, agreement of mind, and mutual holiness" (*Pastoral Constitution on the Church in the Modern World,* #52).

Transitions in Religious Life

Teaching Approaches

● Read or have the students read the text section.

● Have students search through Catholic periodicals to find stories of priest and religious who have adapted to different ministries throughout their lives. Discuss their findings.

● **Reteach**—Discuss: "Would you expect priests or religious to respond to transitions any differently than any other person?"

● **Extend the Lesson**—Arrange for a priest or man or woman religious to share with the class some of the major transitional times of his or her vocation and how he or she coped with the transition.

Marital Transitions

Teaching Approaches

● Assign small groups one of these transitional times in married life: (1) change of career; (2) the birth of a child;(3) parenting teenagers; (4) middle years of married life (twenty to twenty-five years); (5) post-child rearing years; (6) returning adult children; (7) retirement.

● Have the groups make a list of the five major obstacles to growth in married love. (See **Application** Project 3.)

● The groups may work individually or together to outline the problems and stresses associated with their assigned stage. Correlate their surveys and conduct a large group follow-up.

● Write down the information the groups have researched on the board, then discuss possible ways to solve the problems and stresses of each transitional time.

● **Reteach**—Say: "A husband and wife have new best friends after their wedding—each other." Ask: "Why is this an important rule to follow?"

● **Extend the Lesson**—Have partners or small groups work on one of the following projects: (1) Make a "married couples" poster. Use magazine photos and write fictional captions to represent the different stages of married life. (2) Role play a conversation between a husband and a wife for each stages.

Ultimate Transitions

Teaching Approaches

- Introduce the effects of death or divorce on a spouse or close relative by having the students relate the grief process to the loss of a job opportunity or the breakup of a relationship. Ask volunteers to share something of the experience and how to get through it to a stage of acceptance. Be aware that some of your students will be from homes that have experienced death and divorce. Be considerate of these students' feelings. They may need your understanding and support. They can also be a valuable source of information and wisdom for their classmates.

- Point out to the students that divorced people are not excluded, or excommunicated from the Church in any way. However, a divorced person is not free to marry again in the Church without an annulment, since the marriage bond still exists.

- Choose one or two readers to read the text section through the story of Jorge and Olivia. Have the students identify emotions that Olivia might have felt. Comment on their suggestions.

- Read or summarize the rest of the section. Recall the student's suggestions, from the beginning of the section, for dealing with painful experiences in a Christ-like way.

alone together. During the early years of parenthood, many couples neglect their own relationship to take care of the children. Now that the children are gone, these couples experience a feeling of emptiness. The man and woman have to rediscover what life as a couple alone together requires.

- How would marriage be different for a wife and husband during the post-child rearing years than when the children were at home?

Many couples experience a different phenomenon in the middle years of their marriage. Their children leave home but may be replaced by an aged or infirm parent or other relative.

- What problems would you expect for a couple who has finished rearing one family only to become responsible for soneone else.

Many mid-life couples also experience children leaving for marriage or their own apartments only to have them return a few years later because of divorce or lack of finances.

- What stresses would be placed on a marriage by these situations?

The later years of marriage offer new transitions as well. After being part of a family headed by the older generation, they are now the elders. By their early or mid-sixties, one or both partners may have retired from work. After being apart from one another during the day for all the years of their marriage, how will the couple react to spending all of their time together? Many couples find this a difficult transition to make. Whether or not they adjust to this depends on the couple's ability to develop new common interests. As one wife said, "I married him for better or worse, but not for lunch!"

Ultimate Transitions

Few of life's transitions are as difficult to accept as divorce or death. The fact that divorce has become socially acceptable doesn't help a person face the feelings of failure and regret that come with the legal ending of his or her marriage. The death or illness of a spouse, a child, or other family member is always extremely painful and difficult to accept. Knowing that everyone eventually dies offers little comfort to a parent watching a comatose child struggling to survive after a traffic accident.

What are some of the transitions a couple must face during the later stages of marriage?

Resources

Resource 13F is a reference sheet listing psychiatrist Elizabeth Kubler-Ross's five stages in the acceptance of death.

Background

1 Corinthians 15:54-55 is in answer to a question raised by Paul earlier in his letter: "How are the dead raised? With what kind of

Divorce. Divorce is a final stage of transition in marriage for many people. Divorce occurs much more frequently today than it did forty years ago, with nearly half of all marriages ending this way. You are sure to know of at least one family in your community which has experienced a divorce.

People choose divorce when they are unwilling or unable to overcome the problems in their marriage. Divorce is usually a destructive process, that is painful for everyone involved. Adjusting to the transitions caused by divorce can take a person many years to accomplish, and is never easy.

While divorce ends a marriage relationship, it does not affect a person's relationship with the Church or with God. People who have received a divorce are encouraged to participate in the sacraments and in parish functions. Many parishes sponsor support groups for people suffering from the pain of divorce.

Death. When a child dies, parents often blame themselves. They might feel that there was something they could have done to protect their loved one. Even couples who have developed strong marriages find that their relationship is threatened by the illness or loss of a child. Many marriages fail because they cannot cope with this added stress.

Couples marry, promising to be faithful to each other until death. What happens to the surviving spouse after losing a husband or wife? Let's look at one example.

◊ When Jorge died, Olivia felt abandoned. The companion who she thought would be with her throughout life was suddenly gone.

What was she to do now? She had worked for the last twelve years, but her salary was nowhere near what she and her husband had earned jointly. The life insurance would pay the funeral costs and cover the mortgage, but there would be nothing left for savings. She would get by on her salary, but what would she do when major repairs were needed on the house or car?

With the recent weddings of their two sons, she and Jorge had looked forward to life alone together. They had even talked about taking the honeymoon cruise that they had postponed twenty-nine years ago. Now, the house felt so empty.

In the days after the funeral, she had taken to sleeping on the couch in front of the television. She wasn't quite so lonely there. She hated sleeping in their bed; the pain was too great when she reached out to touch him in the middle of the night only to realize that he was gone forever. On the couch, her sorrow was at least bearable.

Death is such a painful mystery. Eventually, most people learn how to respond to their grief,

---

Sharpening Your Skills

Support

Sometimes it's hard to know what to do or say to someone who is terminally ill and near death. Here are some suggestions:

- Visit often. Sometimes people only visit a sick person in the first days after the illness is diagnosed. It's important to maintain contact.
- Recall happy memories. Share good news stories about events going on in the world today.
- Help the person feel useful by asking for assistance.
- Simply enjoy each other's company. You don't have to talk. Quiet, too, can be appropriate.
- Be aware of your own feelings: joy, anger, sadness. Turn to trusted friends with whom you can share these feelings.

---

body will they come back?" *(1 Corinthians 15:35)*. Paul's answer is that God alone has the power to transform, and God alone will exercise it.

Journal Assignment

Finish this sentence: "The way I am learning to handle death is . . ." Or, have them write about what they imagine heaven to be like.

Ultimate Transitions

Teaching Approaches (continued)

- **Reteach**—Assign the students to work with groups, or on their own, to research the grieving process. Allow time for them to share their information with the class. If possible, arrange for the students to talk with a grief counselor or someone who has been a member of a grief support group.

- **Extend the Lesson**—Use **Resource 13F**. Explain that while these stages where developed to explain what happens to people at their death or the death of a loved one, these stages have also been used to understand what happens to people in divorce. Divide the class into five groups. Give each group a stage. They are to identify behaviors one might see in someone at this stage, and ways one might be supportive of a friend in this stage.

Sharpening Your Skills

Teaching Approaches

- Read and discuss the suggestions offered.
- Have the students add other ideas to the list.

Talk It Over

Allow time for the students to formulate their answers to these questions. All four questions may be discussed with a partner or in small groups. Allow time for summary. Make sure to discuss the adjustments necessary for each transition that is mentioned.

Christian Development

Lesson Overview

You may wish to deal with any questions the students have about death prior to beginning the lesson. Or, have the students share their journal entry on death or heaven.

Teaching Approaches

• Read the first two paragraphs. Call on volunteers to share their answers to the in-text questions out loud. Point out that authentic discipleship means total commitment to Christ, and in turn, guarantees life.

• You may wish to read the text of 1 Corinthians 2:6-16 from the Bible. Say: "God's wisdom is seen in His plan for our salvation. It was a plan that was not completely revealed until the coming of Jesus Christ."

• Read or summarize the rest of the section.

• Explain that the words of the Letter of James clarify the connection between faith and good works. The implications of true faith is a life lived in loving and generous service of others.

• Ask: "Can you envision yourself putting your faith in action in any of these ways? Which one? What are other ways that you can put your faith in action?"

• Have the students write or share their responses to the in-text questions.

• Assign **Application** Project 5.

• **Reteach**—Remind the students' of Kay's plan to get to know Jesus (from Chapter 7): (1) prayerfully reviewing the events of the day; (2) reading Scripture; (3) participating in the sacraments, especially Eucharist.

• **Extend the Lesson**—Take the class on a silent walk. Consider walking near these places: the Blessed Sacrament, an activity involving children, or a beautiful natural setting. When you return, ask: "How was Jesus present on our walk?" Accept all answers.

and then begin to carve out a new life. Through our faith, we can imagine what awaits us after death, but we can never know for sure. Our best clue to what life after death will be like comes from Jesus. Jesus is the first fruit of the resurrection that is promised to each of us who believe.

Our belief is that the souls of the faithful join God in heaven after their deaths; their bodies are reunited with the soul after the Last Judgment. As Paul reassures us:

> Death is swallowed up in victory.
>
> Where, O death, is your victory?
>
> Where, O death, is your sting?
>
> *(1 Corinthians 15:54-55)*

Talk It Over

1. What do you think would be the most difficult transition for you to make within married life? Why?

2. Why would a married couple have difficulty adjusting to transitions? What other transitions would a couple face during marriage?

3. What other transitions would you expect priests or religious to experience in their ministries?

4. How is divorce a transition stage for many marriages?

Christian Development

In spiritual terms, high school graduation might be called a "little death"; you are ending one phase of your life, and opening to another. Life is filled with many such endings. Any time you move on to something new, you must say goodbye, even if you do so reluctantly, to the former way of life.

Jesus said, "For whoever wishes to save his life will lose it, but whoever loses his life for My sake and that of the Gospel will save it" *(Mark 8:35)*. What does this mean to you? What have you already learned by leaving things, people, and places behind?

Prayer in Action
"Whoever Has Ears to Hear"

Listen carefully to Jesus' words in the Parable of the Sower. What do they mean? How do they speak to you?

"Jesus spoke to them at length in parables, saying: 'A sower went out to sow. And as he sowed, some seed fell on the path, and birds came and ate it up. Some fell on rocky ground, where it had little soil. It sprang up at once because the soil was not deep, and when the sun rose it was scorched, and it withered for lack of roots. Some seed fell among thorns, and the thorns grew up and choked it. But some seed fell on rich soil, and produced fruit, a hundred or sixty or thirtyfold. Whoever has ears ought to hear'" *(Matthew 13:18-23)*.

These experiences of endings and new beginnings offer us a glimpse of the new life promised by Jesus' resurrection. They teach us that there is more to life than what we have experienced and give us glimpses of the world that "eye has not seen, and ear has not heard, and what has not entered the human heart, what God has prepared for those who love Him" *(1 Corinthians 2:9)*.

In the parable of the sower *(Matthew 13:1-9)*, Jesus speaks of the kinds of people who hear the word of God's kingdom. Only when a person hears the word, understands it, and makes it a part of his or her life does God's word take full effect. Knowing what to do is never enough. Acting on the truth is always necessary.

People who "put on Jesus Christ" are recognized through the service that they do for others. Their faith is visible through the good they do. According to Saint James:

> What good is it, if someone says he has faith but does not have works? Can that

Background

One of the promises of resurrection is that the bodies of the faithful will be raised and formed as heavenly bodies. We hope not only for the salvation of our soul, but of our whole body. In the kingdom of God, we are called to be fully alive in body and soul. (See *Catechism of the Catholic Church,* 1021-1060.)

How can your God-given talents be used to serve those in need?

Talk It Over

1. What is something you can do right now to make Jesus a part of your life? What are your good works?
2. How would you know that Jesus was truly active in your life? How would your life be different than it is now?

New Beginnings

You wearily make it back from the all-night graduation dance. The cap and gown are flung in the back seat of your dad's car. Your diploma is already hidden among the shuffle of dining room papers. High school is finally over.

You catch a couple hours of sleep until you're awakened by your mother, who drops a heavy envelope on your pillow. You tear it open to find this important news:

"Freshman Orientation, August 20-27. All new students are to meet in the University Relations Center for dormitory assignments."

Your heart beats a little faster; you hop out of bed and into the shower. You're ready to face the next challenge!

faith save him? If a brother or sister has nothing to wear and has no food for the day, and one of you says to them, "Go in peace, keep warm, and eat well," but you do not give them the necessities of the body, what good is it? So also faith of itself, if it does not have works, it is dead

(James 2:14-17).

You have spent some time visualizing how you will put your talents and gifts to use. Have you taken time to also consider how your God-given talents can be used to serve those in need? How can you incorporate your vocation, whether it is to the single, married, or religious life, with the call to service?

Chapter Summary
- Life is ever-evolving, ever-changing. You will experience many transitions in your life.
- A bit of the past is left behind with each new life stage.
- Married life includes many transitions.
- Job satisfaction comes from within. It is closely related to following God's plan.
- Faith-related dilemmas may cause Christians to change jobs or careers.
- Developing an intimate relationship with Jesus is a life task.
- A Christian's faith is visible through his or her good works.

Chapter 13 Review

What Have You Learned?

Listed below are suggested answers. For many of the questions, the answers will vary.

1. Answers will vary. A person who suffers severe physical injury may be forced to change career goals.
2. Friendships are more difficult to form as people get older because career and vocational responsibilities will limit the time available for establishing new friendships.
3. Some of the major transition times in marriage are: career changes, children growing up and leaving, retirement, caring for aged parents, or death.
4. An important factor in job satisfaction is that the worker participates in God's creation.
5. When people follow their consciences, faith-related dilemmas may arise. People have been known to give up jobs or careers because of such moral dilemmas.
6. "Little death" means the ending of one phase of life and the beginning of another.
7. One transition a priest or religious may experience is the beginning of a new ministry or assignment.
8. A Christian of mature faith may be recognized by his or her good works.
9. Often, the marriage is threatened or fails because of the stress following the death of a child. The death of a spouse also causes great anxiety.
10. Jesus' resurrection gives us a glimpse of the new life of God's eternal kingdom.

REVIEW

What Have You Learned?

1. How can physical changes affect the kind of person you become?
2. Why are friendships more difficult to form as one gets older?
3. Name the major transitional times in marriage.
4. What are the important factors in a person's job satisfaction?
5. How can faith-related dilemmas have an effect on a Christian's career?
6. What is the meaning of the phrase "little deaths"?
7. What transitions would a priest or religious experience in his or her vocation?
8. How can you recognize a Christian's mature faith?
9. How is death a transition stage for a marriage?
10. What does Jesus' resurrection teach Christians about eternal life?

Application

1. Write the names of three friends. Make predictions for each friend's future. What do you know about these friends that leads you to these observations? Exchange and share your predictions.
2. Research Erik Erikson's stages of life development. Present a report outlining the general characteristics of each age group.
3. List what you consider to be five major obstacles to growth in married love. For each obstacle you list, provide at least one solution.
4. Interview professional people. Ask them to tell about their career developments, including career changes and any moral dilemmas they may have faced on the job.
5. Ask three people of different ages the same question: "How have you experienced Jesus in your life?" Compare their answers.

REVIEW

Chapter Vocabulary

- transitions
- development
- "little death"
- death
- dilemma

Putting Vocabulary to Use

Supply the following information.

1. Develop a list of the major transitions that take place in a person's life. How do these transitions contribute to a person's overall development?
2. How can high school graduation be a "little death"?
3. Which do you fear most: your own death or the death of someone close to you? Why?
4. How can the Christian community help someone who is experiencing a career dilemma?

Do not be perturbed therefore by all that is going on. Give up crying for help to this person or that and chasing shadows—for such is all human endeavor. Rather should you incessantly invoke Jesus whom you adore, that He may but turn His face towards you. Then, in one decisive moment, all your trouble is ended.

Saint John Chrysostom

Application

Have the students read the directions for each project. You may assign a particular project, or allow the students to choose a project they prefer. Allow some time for the students to share their completed projects with others.

Putting Vocabulary to Use

Assign each student all the questions. You may wish to check the responses with the entire group, calling on volunteers to share what they have written.

Final Thought

Background

"Chrysostom" means "golden mouthed." Saint John Chrysostom lived from 344 to 407.

It was at Antioch that he delivered a series of sermons that made him famous throughout the East.

Focus on: Chapter 14

This chapter reviews the course and offers the students encouragement to live truthfully as they undertake the challenging process of pursuing their dreams.

After they have imagined several possibilities for their lives, Chapter 14 provides the students with a five-step process to help them plan their future. The students are given several practical suggestions for determining what they can do now to get started.

Chapter 14 also recalls the meaning of Christian discipleship. Whereas everyone is called to a personal vocation, the thread that joins each of these vocations together is discipleship in Jesus Christ. By doing well in what we have chosen to do, we are able to contribute our piece to the larger membership in the Body of Christ.

Plan Ahead

- Incorporate formal and/or spontaneous prayer in each lesson. A participatory prayer service that is suitable for use in retreat settings is provided in the Teacher's Resource Book.

- Note **Resource** suggestions which can be applied to, or extend, the lessons of this chapter.

- Preview the **Application** projects in the Chapter Review. Refer to **Teaching Approaches** for suggestions on when to assign the projects. Or, the projects may be used as part of lesson, section, or chapter reviews.

- Decide on a method for grouping students for projects and discussion.

- Invite guest speakers who will participate in selected lessons well in advance.

Preparation for Life

As for you, do not seek what you are to eat and what you are to drink, and do not worry anymore… Instead seek his kingdom, and these other things will be given you besides.

Luke 12:29-31

This chapter will help you to:

- Review what you have learned during this course.
- Consider your next steps toward your future.
- Examine other critical issues that lie ahead.
- Recognize what you can do now to make a difference.

Media Resources (Optional)

- *Realizing America's Hope* (South Carolina Educational Television) Two video kit. Offers suggestions on how adolescents can respond to the challenges they face in life.

- *Roses in December* (First Run Features) 55 min. A young woman, Jean Donovan, searches for meaning in her life working with the poor people of El Salvador. She was a lay Catholic Missionary martyred in 1980 for being committed to her faith.

Aim

To understand how God's Divine Providence gives people the freedom to shape the direction of their own lives.

Begin the Section

1. Recall the timeline that the students began in Chapter 1. Not only did they draw symbols for key events that had already taken place in their lives, but they also had some definite ideas about their own futures. Relate the exercise to the song lyrics. Ask: "In what ways can we imagine our own futures? In what ways is the future 'not ours to see'?"

2. Read or summarize the two interpretations of the song lyrics. Ask: "Which interpretation is closer to what you believe?"

3. Have the students write their responses to one of the in-text questions in the opening section. Then, read the questions aloud. Call on students to share what they wrote.

I. LIFE'S CHOICES

"Qué será, será.
Whatever will be, will be.
The future's not ours to see.
Qué será, será."

This 1950s song expresses an attitude toward life that in some ways might seem very inviting. A person might say, "If it does no good to worry about tomorrow, since I can't change it anyway, why plan (or study or work)? Better to live for today and let tomorrow take care of itself." That's one interpretation.

Another, more hopeful interpretation starts from a similar premise, but reaches a totally different conclusion. The person says, "I may not be able to change the future, but I can sure influence it. I'm going to do everything in my power to bring about the future that I want to build and let God take care of the rest."

277

Background

The young man in the picture is shown making a decision by flipping a coin. People will often put off the responsibility of making an important decision, choosing rather to rely on random chance, "luck," or "fate." Catholics believe that we must take an active role in our own future by implementing God's will.

Future Invention

Lesson Overview

The point of this lesson is to help students realize that what they do today will influence what their future will be. To illustrate this, invite one or two adults to speak to the class about their current careers or vocations. Ask them to tell at least three things they did as a high school student that prepared them for today. Or, have the students list three things they are doing now (classes, activities, jobs, relationships) that they think will directly be of benefit in the future.

Teaching Approaches

- Write this sentence on the board: "As people with free will, we help shape our own futures even though we cannot fully determine them."

- Ask volunteers to comment on the meaning and to give examples of how this statement is true.

- **Reteach**—Explain that freedom of will operates within God's Providence. Free will helps a person in the choice of a vocation. As Saint Paul wrote, "For you were called for freedom, brothers. But do not use this freedom as an opportunity for the flesh; rather, serve one another through love" *(Galatians 5:13)*.

- **Extend the Lesson**—Ask the students to imagine a long trail of ants going from one place to another. Imagine themselves putting an obstacle in the ants' way. Ask: "What freedom do the ants have in choosing how to reach their destination? How did you take on the role of God for the ants? How does this scene help you to understand your freedom and God's role in your life?"

♣ Prayer in Action

Teaching Approaches

- Explain that a canticle is a sacred prayer or song of praise or love directed to God.

- The students may illustrate all or part of the *Canticle of the Sun* through poetry, music, art, or any other creative medium.

- Recite this prayer together with the class.

Throughout this text you've learned about various vocations and some of the skills you will need in selecting a vocation and a career. Ultimately, you must make a choice concerning your life's journey. What can you do with your life now to make a difference in the future? How can your present actions help you become a mature adult? What more can you do to become a co-creator with God? The decisions are in your hands; how will you respond?

Future Invention

No one knows what the future holds in store except God, and God rarely reveals the ending of the story ahead of time. And, if you think about it, you'll recognize the wisdom of God's ways.

As Christians, we believe that God is active in our lives, but that God does not control them. God may know how we will live, but God is not going to force us to act. Our God is a God of surprises! As people with free will we help shape our own futures, even though we cannot fully determine them.

♣ Prayer in Action
Canticle of Life

Legend says that Saint Francis dictated the last verses of *The Canticle of the Sun* just prior to his death. The irony is that the canticle is a prayer of life, an expression of joy and love in celebration of the brotherhood and sisterhood of all God's Creation. Pray these words from *The Canticle of the Sun*, thanking and praising God for everything that is good.

Praise be to You, Creator God, in all Your creatures, especially in shining Brother Sun, who lights up the sky. Beautiful is he, and radiant with great splendor: of You, Most High God, he is a sign.

Praised be my Lord for Sister Moon and for the stars. In heaven You have formed them, clear and precious and fair.

Praised be my Lord for Brother Wind, and for the air and clouds and fair skies and every kind of weather, by which You give Your creatures nourishment.

Praised be the Lord for our Sister, Mother Earth, who sustains and keeps us, bringing forth rich fruits and grass and flowers bright.

And praised be my Lord for Sister Death. Blessed are those whom she finds doing Your most holy will, for the second death shall not harm them. Bless the Lord and give God thanks!

You shape your future in many different ways. For example, the classes you take in high school shape your future choices. By taking classes in chemistry and calculus, you prepare yourself for college and careers in the sciences. Taking automotive repair or bookkeeping classes prepares you to enter the job market directly from high school.

Can a person who excels in engine repair have a future in the sciences? Absolutely. Mechanical engineers often are wizards at repairing mechanical things. However, without a solid foundation in mathematics at the high school level, the potential mechanical engineer may not be admitted to college.

A Planning Process

You've learned many valuable skills that will help you choose a vocation and a career. While these skills are valuable, without a realistic process to plan for the future they are not enough. The following five-step process can help you begin to plan your future.

1. Imagine a number of different scenarios for your life ten years from now.

Resources

Resource 14A from the Teacher's Resource Book lists how high school courses relate to various professions.

Background

The Providence of God is the manifestation of God's will; nothing is allowed to fall outside of God's dominion. God permits the use of this power by other "secondary" causes.

What are some of the futures you can imagine for yourself?

2. Identify the futures that you would most like to have happen.
3. Pray for guidance, then choose the future you most desire.
4. Recognize what must happen over the next few years in order for you to accomplish this goal.
5. Determine what you can do now to prepare for the future.

Let's look at these steps in more detail.

Imagine Your Future. Gaze into your crystal ball, the one that appears when you close your eyes and you begin to daydream. What futures do you see?

At this stage in the process there is only one rule: your future must be humanly possible. Other than that, you are free to dream. Great wealth? living at a Catholic Worker house? organ transplant specialist? farmer? missionary? parent? President of the United States? priest? It's your dream, so imagine it the way you want. Let your imagination soar!

After each dream, write down what you like and don't like about that possibility. Maybe you don't care for the responsibility of healing sick animals, but love the idea of living in a foreign land. Use this information for another dream, such as a foreign correspondent on wildlife affairs. The more dreams you have at the beginning, the broader will be your list of possibilities.

Narrowing the Field. Once you have a long list of possible futures, you must then begin the process of narrowing your field of choices. Your goal is to limit your list to only a few possibilities. If you've dreamed broadly, narrowing the list should not be too difficult. For example, if you get sick at the sight of blood you may wish to eliminate the field of medicine (although not necessarily the field of medical research). If marrying and starting a family are high on your list, then choosing a career path that requires twelve years of additional schooling might be unrealistic.

Realism is the only rule that you must follow during this second step. Eliminate those futures that you don't like or can't see yourself accomplishing. But don't shortchange yourself. Be open to futures that might require effort as well as those that seem most obvious.

A Planning Process

Teaching Approaches

- Write the five steps of the planning process on the board. Check off each step as it is covered during the rest of the lesson.
- **Reteach**—Ask: "What are some skills that you have learned in this course that can help you choose a vocation and a career?"
- **Extend the Lesson**—Have students practice the five-step method using imaginary people before reading further.

Imagine the Future

Teaching Approaches

- Have the students work individually on this step of the process.
- Ask the students to write several personal dreams and develop broad lists. They are to write what they like and dislike about each possibility. Remind them to include both career and vocational ideas in their lists. **Resource 14B** provides a format for the suggested activity in "Imagine Your Future."
- **Reteach**— Assign **Application** Project 1.
- **Extend the Lesson**—Assign **Application** Project 2.

Narrowing the Field

Teaching Approaches

- Have the students rank their list of possibilities from most to least likely, or simply cross out unrealistic choices. Finish this sentence in regards to one of the possibilities on your list: "In the future, I can realistically see myself . . ."
- **Reteach**—Review student career paths discussed in Chapter 13.
- **Extend the Lesson**—Have students consider dreams totally opposite to their preferred careers. What will it take for students to honestly consider these other dreams?

Background

Saint Francis was torn between a life devoted exclusively to prayer and one of active preaching and service. Though he chose the latter, a series of serious illnesses near the end of his life led him to spend more and more time at prayer. Two years before his death, he received the stigmata—the wounds of Christ on his hands, feet and side. On his deathbed in 1226, Francis is reputed to have said the last words of his *Canticle*—"And praised be my Lord for Sister Death"—over and over.

Sharpening Your Skills

Teaching Approaches

- Have the students review the differences between long-term and short-term goals. Ask them to provide examples of each. For example, a short-term goal might be passing a difficult exam. A long-term goal might be learning to be more forgiving or planning for a vocation or a career.

- Practice writing examples of each type of goal.

God's Help

Teaching Approaches

- Read or have the students read the first paragraph. Allow them time to personally get in touch with the confidence they have in choosing the best possible futures for themselves.

- Read and discuss the rest of the section. Allow time for the students to reflect on the in-text questions. Review how God must be a part of any discernment process.

- Remind students that Jesus is the example of what it means to be a person of prayer. He prayed to the Father throughout His life.

- Remind students that prayer means to keep asking, keep seeking, and keep knocking. While God answers our prayers, we must often wait to see the full revelation of the answer.

- **Reteach**—Recall the definition of *discernment* as "the ability to distinguish between wants and needs, desires and wishes, and reality and dreams." Used in a religious context, discernment refers to a way of discovering God's will in one's personal experiences. Review the eight-step discernment process and how it relates to making career and vocational choices.

- **Extend the Lesson**—Have students plan a prayer service to be used as part of this "Future Invention" exercise.

Sharpening Your Skills
Goal-Setting

Goal-setting is a skill. It involves a process that gives you direction within which to work. You can use this process for everything from planning your whole life to arranging the next few hours of the day.

1. Decide one thing on which you want to work. Make your goal realistic, something you can attain.
2. List what you will do to reach your goal. Identify others who can help you and who will support your efforts.
3. Give yourself a definite period of time to reach your goal. Include several checkpoints to evaluate how well you are doing.
4. Reward yourself for achieving the goal.

God's Help. This is the step where people often have the greatest difficulty in realistically narrowing down their choices. Many people tend to rule out perfectly viable futures because they lack self-confidence:

"There's no way I can be a(n) _____. I'm (a) not smart enough, (b) not pretty (handsome) enough, (c) too poor, (d) too shy."

You may fill in the blank with any career and circle your favorite excuse or add one of your own.

Prayer puts you in touch with God. What you want to do here is hold up each of your possible futures to God and ask for guidance. Remember, God desires the best possible future for you, too. Ask yourself:

- Which of these tomorrows reflects my abilities and talents the best?
- Which will challenge me to grow as a person of faith?
- Which will allow me to help others most directly?
- Which will give me the most satisfaction and enjoyment?

Through God's guidance a particular choice may become clear.

Making Preparations. Often people who use this process find that their choices will be clustered in categories based upon their talents and self-concept. People with a love for literature and grammar might dream of Pulitzer Prizes for poetry, *The New York Times* best-seller list of nonfiction, and being an English teacher. These are not mutually exclusive dreams and could be combined into one larger dream. People who dream of service to others might well combine dreams of missionary work, religious life, and caring for the local homeless. Because we cannot exercise total control over the future, the specifics are not as essential as the common themes that are the foundation for our dreams.

Use the discernment process you learned back in chapter 3 at this point. The eight steps fit nicely into this process:

1. Define the problem.
2. Gather data.
3. Consider alternatives.
4. Consider the consequences.
5. Consider in light of your values.
6. Seek advice and pray.
7. Choose and act.
8. Re-evaluate.

After you've chosen a life path, congratulations are in order. You are now ready to begin making your action plan. Be as specific as possible and identify what you need to do now to accomplish your goal.

- What must you do now to prepare for a career as a dietician?
- How would you prepare to enter politics?
- How does marriage and family fit into your chosen dream?
- Can you accomplish your career choice best as a single person or through religious life?

Background

Pope Paul VI said, "Prayer is the first dialogue that man can desire to hold with God." When we pray, we can be assured that our prayers will be answered. "Ask and it will be given to you; seek and you will find; knock and the door will be opened to you" *(Matthew 7:7).*

Second thoughts are important. They help to clarify emotions and overcome any pressure we might experience.

There are a lot of questions waiting to be answered at this stage of the process, but it's crucial that those questions be answered. You may want to devote a good deal of time to researching the requirements of your chosen profession and work back from there. That is an easy way to establish a *career ladder.* If you break down the requirements into small steps, you will know what you must accomplish at each step.

When you look at your outlined steps, you may have second thoughts about this future. Are you willing to sacrifice the next ten years to become a physician? Music may be your life, but do you want to live on the road for years, hoping for your big break?

Second thoughts are important. They help to clarify emotions and overcome any pressure we might experience. Examining our dreams critically is never a wasted experience. In the process, we learn the importance of being honest with ourselves. Honesty now may prevent problems and disappointments in the future.

✚ To Your Health
My Talents

You can prepare your body for the future with regular exercise, proper rest and diet. Read and adapt these suggestions for a safe workout into your own life:

1. Begin and end each workout with loosening-up exercises.
2. Set realistic goals.
3. Listen to your body. Stop if an exercise is painful.
4. In warm weather, exercise less than your normal amount, giving your body time to adjust to the temperature change. Avoid exercising during the hottest part of the day.
5. Wear light-colored, loose-fitting clothing.
6. Drink plenty of fluids, particularly water.
7. On cold days, wear one layer of clothing less than you would normally wear outdoors if you were not exercising. Wear a hat in cold weather.
8. Wait two hours after eating a meal before strenuous exercise.
9. Exercise on soft surfaces, such as a track, grass, or dirt.
10. If you are moving during your exercise, try to land on your heels rather than your toes. This reduces the chance of injury to your feet and lower legs.
11. Use good equipment. Pay particular attention to the care of your feet.
12. If you walk, ride, or jog at night, wear light-colored clothing that can easily be detected by headlights.

Journal Assignment

Use this assignment with the feature, "To Your Health." Develop a personal exercise program for yourself. Evaluate your performance weekly.

Making Preparations

New Words

Career ladder refers to the defined intervals in one's chosen career from an entry level position to the top. In many careers, the intervals are not so well-defined; career ladder may also refer to reaching personal goals within a chosen field.

Teaching Approaches

- Read or summarize the text.
- Emphasize that the students should be as specific as possible when outlining the steps needed to make career goals come true.
- Help students decide on career steps that they can begin to work on immediately.
- **Reteach**—Assign **Application** Project 3.
- **Extend the Lesson**—Have each student work with a partner. Each should play the role of the "devil's advocate" for the other in regards to career and vocational choices, nicely challenging the honesty of the other's ambitions. After switching roles, have each person write about any second thoughts they have about their original dreams.

✚ To Your Health

Teaching Approaches

- Adapt this panel on an exercise program to the discussion on long- and short-term goals.
- Have students discuss the benefits of various types of exercise.

Teaching Approaches

- Discuss: "When have you failed at something because you did not start from the beginning?" Building a model, working a math problem, or making a friend are sample answers to this question.
- Read or summarize the first two paragraphs. Have the students take time to plan a first step in implementing their career or vocation choices.
- Read or summarize the final two paragraphs.
- **Reteach**— Highlight these two points: (1) You are responsible for putting your plan into action. (2) Start a plan at the beginning.
- **Extend the Lesson**—Distribute or display a college information bulletin and a list of majors and classes. Encourage the students to examine the many ways college can help them reach their final goal. For example, a person interested in law might major in English, history, or even business.

Remember, begin with the beginning of the process, not at the middle or the end.

Present Decisions. Once you've reached this stage, take time to identify your first step. Be wise enough to recognize that you must start at the beginning of a process, not at the middle or the end. Don't be like the young child who, after assuring everyone within hearing distance that he could swim, stepped off into the deep end of the pool and sank. He would have been better off if he had bothered to take a few lessons before leaping in feet first.

People implementing their plans often act like that young child. They think that marriage or running a business is easy, that they can simply jump in and start without first learning how to do it well. Unfortunately, "sinking" is not limited to children or to swimming. Marriages and small businesses fail with alarming regularity, and for similar reasons: people enter into the process unprepared for reality. To improve your chances of success, learn everything you can about the topic before you begin.

It's up to you to put your plan into action; no one else will do it for you. You might experience real concern as you take this first step, especially if it's the first real decisive act that you've ever made regarding your future. Until now you may have simply drifted along, doing what you've been told, learning what you've been told to learn. Motivated by your dreams and plans, you now are responsible for what happens in your life. That thought alone should make you stop and think before you act.

If you start at the beginning, you need not worry too much about this first step. Your choice is not irrevocable, nor will you be penalized too severely for failure. College students regularly change majors, fail courses, and drop out of school. That is not cause for alarm, however. Rather than being a reason for giving up, it is a reason for re-visioning one's dream and starting over again. Maturity is shown by how one rebounds from such setbacks.

Resources

Resource 14C provides additional helpful hints for college applicants.

Renting an Apartment

When they first leave home, ninety-two percent of all people live in rental housing. Choosing rental housing is a matter of taste, convenience, and finances. If you were planning to move away from home in the next few years, how would you make a decision concerning where to live? Imagine that you are apartment hunting. Working from the following guidelines and questions, locate an affordable apartment in your community with the features you desire.

1. Using your monthly budget, determine how much you can afford to spend on rent each month. A general rule-of-thumb is that housing costs should not be more than twenty-five percent to thirty percent of one's income.

2. Look at a map of the city or town where you want to live. Locate nearby shopping areas, churches, bus routes, and other necessities. Investigate several of the areas to determine which seems most appropriate to your needs.

3. Check the want ads of local newspapers. Try to find an apartment in an area where you'd like to live. Check with friends and co-workers who live in the area. Real estate agents or rental services will also help you find an apartment, for a fee.

4. When you choose to rent a unit, the owner may require you to make a security deposit equal to one month's rent before you can move in. A security deposit protects the owner against any damage you may cause to the rental unit. If you leave the unit clean and in good shape, the owner is required by law in most communities to return the deposit.

5. You may also be asked to pay in advance the first and last month's rent.

6. If you decide to rent the apartment, you may be asked to sign a lease. A lease spells out the conditions by which each party agrees to live. The lease may guarantee a rental unit for a certain length of time, and will also spell out who is to pay the water, utilities, and trash bills. A lease may restrict the number of people, children, or pets living in the apartment with you.

7. As a tenant, you are responsible for paying your rent on time (often rent is due on the first day of the month), keeping your apartment in good condition, and being a responsible neighbor. The owner is responsible for maintaining a safe and sanitary dwelling for your use.

Answer these questions:

- What would you expect to find in an apartment?
- How much money would you expect to pay to live in an apartment?
- How much money would you need up front in order to lease an apartment in your area?
- Explain why you would prefer to live alone or share an apartment with a roommate?

283

Bumps in the Road

New Words

Divine Providence is the order and care of all things shown by God. God exercises Divine Providence to bring everything—both natural and supernatural—to their prescribed end.

Teaching Approaches

- Read or have the students read the first two paragraphs. Ask volunteers to share any other examples of people responding to God's unexpected calling.

- Assign the rest of the section for reading.

- **Reteach**—Remind students that Jesus demands total commitment from His disciples: "Whoever wishes to come after me must deny himself and take up his cross, and follow Me. For whoever wishes to save his own life will lose it, but whoever loses his life for My sake and the Gospel will save it" *(Mark 8:34-35).* Remind the students that all career and vocation decisions must be made in light of their discipleship.

- **Extend the Lesson**—Ask the students to sit quietly and close their eyes. Ask them to envision with as much detail as possible a future dream coming true in relationship with their role as a disciple of Jesus.

Bumps in the Road

No process of inventing a future is foolproof. Dreaming that you are in the movies or the ballet will not give you the talent or determination you need to make that dream become a reality. People work hard to earn degrees, set up their own businesses, or learn a craft with various levels of success. Unfortunately, not everyone is successful in his or her chosen career or vocation.

Thomas Edison, the inventor of the incandescent electric light bulb and of the phonograph, is quoted as saying, "Genius is one percent inspiration and ninety-nine percent perspiration." Much the same thing can be said for success: the better prepared a person is to cope with life's challenges, the better chance one has of succeeding.

While much of life seems to happen by chance, working from a future plan will help prepare a person to take advantage of most opportunities. Even with detailed preparation, many things don't work out according to our schedule. For example:

◊ Brenda, a philosophy student working part-time in the college's admissions office to pay her tuition, was offered a full-time job before graduation because of her ability to treat people with respect. The job became available when the man who had the position moved to a new city because of his wife's promotion.

No matter how hard we work, practice, or plan, we cannot control everything that happens to us. We can, however, control our own behavior, and how we will respond to our opportunities.

Catholics believe in *Divine Providence,* not chance. Divine Providence means that God takes an active interest in each of our lives and puts

How is genius "ninety-nine percent perspiration?"

Background

"Imagining your future" is an important exercise in the process of achieving success. When All-American football player Chad Hennings attempted a comeback, his first step was to spend fifteen minutes each day visualizing himself playing football. He said, "You've got to have the dream before you can visualize it. You have to believe in yourself. I knew I was going to be All-American because I dreamed that dream. The magic is in the person."

Family Living
Giving and Receiving Care

The commandment "Honor your father and mother" takes on new and greater significance when one gets older: "Remember, of your parents you were born; what can you give them for all they gave you?" *(Sirach 7:26).*

For some adult children, caring for parents becomes a major, full-time responsibility. The strains of such full-time care can create tensions and problems for the caregiver. Here are some suggestions for any person involved in the care of an elderly, disabled, or sick family member:

- Get help. Share the responsibility of care with other family members. If family members are uncooperative, seek assistance from community agencies—senior centers or medical social workers, for example.
- Continue to develop personal interests. Make time to participate in activities that interest you.
- Talk over your care-giving role with others. If possible, join a support group with other care-givers.
- Look to the future. Explore alternative forms of long-term care (hospices, for example). Seek out medical, legal, and spiritual help when necessary.

Family Living

Teaching Approaches
- Ask the students to imagine their lives as senior citizens. Call on volunteers to share some ideas about what it would be like.
- Discuss student willingness to delay their own plans to care for a seriously ill or elderly friend or relative.

Talk It Over
For Question 1, have the students make a list on wallet-sized cards that they can keep with them as reminders and references. For Question 2, have the students discuss with a partner or in a small group. Point out that the difference between God's Providence and chance is that the motive behind God's Providence is always love. Have the students write their response to Question 3. Then call on volunteers to share with the whole group.

---

opportunities in our paths. God's love and concern for us is expressed through Providence. Providence is God's invitation to people to live life more fully. If a person happens to be in the right place at the right time when something unexpected happens, God has had a hand in shaping the event.

Imagining your future is an active exercise in taking responsibility for your life. If done honestly, this process can help you make workable plans. It cannot predict what your future holds, however. You must be prepared to respond to God's call as it is addressed to you, not as you'd like it addressed.

Your dreams and expectations may have little to do with what actually happens. You may need to re-imagine and revise your life regularly. Failing to fulfill your dream is not a tragedy as long as you are able to dream new dreams.

Every Christian is called to live as a disciple of Jesus. A future that leaves little room for discipleship is not a true Christian future. Remember that openness to discipleship is not the same as choosing a religious vocation. The thread that joins each of the different vocations together is that each is a special way of living as a disciple.

The choice is ultimately yours; no one can live your life for you. The decisions you make now will shape your opportunities tomorrow. Your willingness to respond to God's call will be tested throughout your life. How will you respond?

Talk It Over

1. Use the five steps for imagining your future. What must you do during the next year to implement your plan of action?
2. Discuss how Providence has played a role in your life thus far. What is the difference between Providence and chance?
3. Why are some people afraid to dream?

Background
Family relationships are a very important factor in helping a person successfully adjust to aging. Older people who do not have relatives living with or near them face the greatest difficulty in adjusting to old age. Also, elderly people who maintain friendships and contact with other people after retiring cope better with aging.

Aims

1. To help students discover ways to learn from mistakes and make better decisions at the next opportunity.
2. To help students understand the meaning of living truthfully.

Begin the Section

1. Review some of the predictions that the students made for each other's futures. If you have not done so already, randomly divide the class into pairs. Have the students write predictions for their partner's future and then exchange them. The predictions might be light-hearted or serious, or a combination of both.
2. Read or summarize the opening section. If possible, have the students suggest new, problematic endings to other famous stories or fairytales.
3. Have the students think of answers to the in-text question, "In face of everything that will happen, how will you live as a person of faith?" Answers should be given in light of the probable good and bad events that they will experience in life.

Living Truthfully

Lesson Overview

In December, 1983, and again in March, 1990, Cardinal Joseph Bernardin called for a consistent ethic of life. His statements refer to "the seamless garment" of human life that must be defended from conception to death. All of life's experiences must be viewed from the same perspective. This lesson calls the students to "see with God's eyes," to gain God's overall perspective through prayer and honest perception.

To live truthfully means to look honestly at ourselves and at those around us. Begin by asking the students what it means to see as God sees. Allow time for feedback.

II. WHEN YOU WISH UPON A STAR

In the musical, *Into the Woods*, Stephen Sondheim looks at fairy tales and asks, "What happens in the lives of the fairy-tale characters when the story is over?" Through the course of the play we meet Cinderella who has become disenchanted with her Prince Charming; Jack, who killed the giant and stole the goose that laid golden eggs; and many other people of legend who are unhappy with their "happily every after" lives.

Life is not a fairy tale, nor does it usually have a fairy-tale ending. Bad things do happen to good people. Our best-laid plans don't always work as they should. Dedication, preparation, and hard work do not guarantee success. In the face of all that can happen, how will you live as a person of faith?

Living Truthfully

Presented to Pontius Pilate as a criminal, Jesus announces that He has come into the world to testify to the truth. "Everyone who belongs to the truth listens to my voice," Jesus says. Dumbfounded, Pilate asks, "What is truth?" *(John 18:37-38).*

Is there an answer to Pilate's question? How many times do we find ourselves questioning what really is the truth? When two people witness the same event and yet reach different conclusions when asked to explain what happened, we question what truth really is.

The word "truth" connects with what is real. Truth is the way we recognize that something really

All life, from beginning to end, is connected as a seamless garment.

Journal Assignment

Have students write on one of the following subjects: (1) The meaning of "selective perception." (2) How to show our concern for life at all stages. (Tell students to use specific examples to support what they write.)

Media Watch
Dust in the Wind

Musical artists have always expressed their dreams, fears, and anxieties about the future in their music and lyrics. How do your favorite artists express their concern for the future?

A few years ago a rock group by the name of "Kansas" had a hit song entitled, "Dust in the Wind." One of the lines in the song went, "All we are is dust in the wind." How does being "dust in the wind" compare to our actual Christian destiny?

Evaluate the lyrics in a few current popular songs. How do they support or contradict Catholic teachings?

exists. When you live truthfully, you make an honest assessment of your talents and interests. You set your sights on dreams that can be reached. When you reach a roadblock, the truth can help you recognize it as a stopping point, not the end of the road.

When Jesus spoke of truth, He was referring to God. God can see the whole picture from beginning to end. While we are not capable of "seeing with God's eyes" in a perfect way, we can gain some of God's perspective through prayer and honest perception. You can see that all parts of life—from childhood to adulthood, happy times and sad times, good decisions and bad decisions—have value. Every part of life is important when you look at the whole.

A woman from Texas once wrote a letter to a newspaper advice columnist. In the letter she told of having a former neighbor whose son had just been executed by the state for the crime of murder. She wondered if and how she should go about consoling the parents of this man who had been put to death.

She wrote, "I never knew John as an adult, but I knew him as a boy. He came to our house to play with our children. He was a lovable child who sang with our daughter and made her laugh."

The columnist encouraged the woman to write and express her sympathy to the parents. But, what of the son?

Not a lot of sympathy is offered to those people who fail in life. Do you ever take time to look at others and wonder what has caused their hurt and pain? Do you ever look at someone who the world has labeled worthless or bad and wonder what he or she might have been like as an infant and young child?

This is part of what it means to look truthfully at the entire spectrum of human life. This is not always easy since we are often victims of "selective perception": we see only what we want to see. But not seeing what's there does not make it disappear.

Once looked at, we need to take the appropriate actions. The truth that we value is demonstrated by how we treat others. This broad, deep, pervasive sense of care has been described as "a seamless garment," connecting all of life together from beginning to end.

The Church has a special concern that human life be valued at all stages. We show this by the way we regard pregnancy and birth, the way we raise our children, by how we view older people in our families, and by the ways in which we support the life-enhancing efforts of others. It is not enough to protect only the lives of ourselves and our own family members. We must be committed to others as well.

You are invited to live life in its fullest measure. But all life is connected, a truth we have learned as life on our planet Earth has been threatened by pollution, global warming, and war. Valuing life in ourselves and in others is really part of the same process.

Resources
Resource 14F in the Teacher's Resource Book provides a checklist for the activity described in "Media Watch."

Teaching Approaches
- Introduce the section by reading the entire text of Jesus' trial before Pilate from *John 18:28-38*.
- Ask: "Why was Pilate puzzled by Jesus' use of the word truth?"
- Have the students offer one word synonyms for truth. Then, have the students read the next three paragraphs. Ask: "How did Jesus define truth? What does He mean?"
- Read the rest of the text section.
- **Reteach**—Ask the students to share incidents when people have been judged unfairly. Relate this back to what students learned previously about gossip.
- **Extend the Lesson**—Either **Application** Project 4 or Project 5 would work well with this lesson.

Media Watch

Teaching Approaches
- Assign each student to bring one or two favorite song lyrics to class.
- Choose a panel of students (or allow the whole class to serve as a panel) to offer their opinions on how the lyrics meet or do not meet Catholic standards.

New Wine, Old Wineskins

Teaching Approaches

- Read or summarize the section.
- Ask: "How did Jesus stand up for truth?"
- **Reteach**—Have the students find examples from the Gospel that show how Jesus stood up for the truth.
- **Extend the Lesson**—Have the students write a letter addressed to themselves that attempts to reconcile some of the hurt they continue to carry from the past. Have them seal the letter in an envelope. Say: "Do not open the envelope until you need to be reminded to leave the past behind and move forward."

☾ Well-Being

Teaching Approaches

- Read or have the students read the material.
- Ask: "What can we do to help people in need?"
- Arrange for your class to adopt or sponsor a local family in need.

New Wine, Old Wineskins

Jesus broke the laws of the Sabbath. He shared meals with tax collectors and sinners. He forgave the woman caught in adultery. These transgressions against the Jewish Law would lead to accusations of blasphemy, and ultimately to His death.

Jesus' answer to the problems that He created for Himself was, "No one pours new wine into old wineskins" *(Mark 2:22)*. As the Savior sent by God, Jesus superseded the old covenant of Moses. Jesus looked ahead and lived truthfully and honestly.

New wine as it ferments creates a lot of gases and is very much alive. An old wineskin is liable to burst during the fermentation process. When we choose to follow Jesus, we become like new wine, alive and active, bursting with energy. Like new wine, we cannot be bound by our old selves' fears, anxieties, and doubts. The result would be similar to new wine in old wineskins. We must first reconcile ourselves with the past which made us, before we can move forward toward the future which we will construct with God's help. In a sense, we must become a new person to hold the excitement of new life.

Hope

A major theme of both the Hebrew and Christian Scriptures is that of the passing from death to new life. In Exodus, the enemies of Israel were "frozen like stone, while Your People, O Lord, passed over" from a life of slavery to a new life of freedom.

Jesus brought about new life. He told his friends, Mary and Martha, upon the raising of their brother Lazarus: "I am the resurrection and the life; whoever believes in Me, even if he dies, will live, and everyone who lives and believes in Me will never die" *(John 11:25)*.

On a personal level, this insight into God's ways identifies for us the importance of the Christian virtue of hope. Hope provides us a reason for courage and an invitation to always move toward that which affirms life. Setbacks and defeats happen to everyone, but hope always has the

---

☾ Well Being
Adopt-A-Family

Recently, a diocese attempted to put a face on the needs of the poor. At Christmas, an "adopt-a-family" program was initiated. People who wished to help families in need could read a brief profile explaining a particular family's problems, and what could be done to help them in time for Christmas. This program led to a year-round sponsorship of one family by another—a way to extend in a real way the Church's support of the poor. Here are two stories of families in need:

- Two families share expenses for a small two-room apartment. There are four adults and eight children. They need blankets, sheets, and pillows. Special need: $150 for Christmas.
- Jose Luis is 16 years old. He is the sole provider for his sister, Maria, and his three young nieces. The family lives on $800 a month. Jose Luis would appreciate a donation of $100 so that he can get each of his nieces a holiday dress and a toy.

The local newspaper published these and several more stories before Christmas. People who were interested in helping a family did so. They could either designate which family they wanted to receive their gift, or they could contribute to a general fund that was established for all needy families in the area.

Background

Jesus reasoned, "No one sews a piece of unshrunken cloth on an old cloak. If he does, its fullness pulls away, the new from the old, and the tear gets worse" *(Mark 2:21)*.

What role does hope play in the life of a person who has done wrong or who faces a difficult decision?

◊ Josh's parents were recently divorced. To make matters worse, his father has lost his job. Josh's mom wants him to come and live with her and his grandmother in another state. As a junior, Josh had been an outstanding baseball player. Several college and professional scouts have watched him play. He feels that moving from this school would be absolutely the worst thing that he could do. He has been very depressed, but he can't think of a way out of his problem.

◊ Jodie's family has a decision to make about their eighty-five-year-old grandfather: Should they put him in a rest home or let him come and live with them? Even Grandpa admits that he needs help, although he has expressed no interest in leaving his home. For Jodie, it would mean sharing her private space and life with an old man.

With hope, bad choices can be corrected, problems can be worked out, and new and appealing directions can be attained. Through a deeper understanding of the way that God moves and acts in our lives, we understand that our life is always moving forward, and as long as we live as human beings, there is always time to seek God's ways.

Talk It Over

1. What does it mean to see through God's eyes? How can seeing this way help us understand the truth?
2. How is a Christian like new wine?
3. Why is the virtue of hope essential for your journey into the future?

last word. Hope calls us to look to the future and believe in the promises of life.

Consider the following examples. How can hope play a part in the restoration of these people's lives?

◊ Dawn cannot believe that she has been chosen a member of the varsity cheerleading squad. Although her dream has come true, Dawn can't seem to put her past behind her. When she was in the tenth grade, Dawn had an abortion. She has carried that painful secret with her, unable to share what she did with anyone, not even her mother. Her secret is driving her crazy. The offer to be a cheerleader sounds good, but Dawn doesn't feel worthy.

Hope

Teaching Approaches

- Read or have the students read the first three introductory paragraphs.
- Have the students share examples of how "struggles and suffering, setback and defeat" are not the last word in life.
- Read each of the scenarios. Have the students discuss or write how hope can play a part in restoring the lives mentioned in each scenario.
- Read the last paragraph. Ask: "Is there ever a point where a person runs out of time to seek God's ways?"
- **Reteach**—Refer the students to the parable of the workers in the vineyard (*Matthew 20:1-16*).
- **Extend the Lesson**—Have students act out the scenarios presented.

Talk It Over

Use the questions for review. Have the students discuss all three questions with a partner. Then, randomly call on volunteers to share their responses to the questions.

Background

Hope is one of the three theological virtues. It is the virtue that moves one's will to trust in the eternal rewards of heaven and in an all-good God. Hope gives Christians the assurance that the necessary graces to win eternal life will be ours.

Looking Back

Lesson Overview

The lesson recalls the opening story from Chapter 1 and the high school reunion between Charlie, Melissa, and Patty. It explores some of the choices they each made leading to their current states in life. Before reading the section, recall the original story and characters. Ask the students to speculate on how each person might have arrived at his or her own particular career or vocation.

Teaching Approaches

- Read or have the students read the section. Have them identify the roadblocks in Patty's and Melissa's lives (alcohol and a failed relationship).

- Ask: "What do you find hopeful about Patty's and Melissa's stories?"

- **Reteach**—Ask: "How do you see yourself in Patty's or Melissa's stories?"

- **Extend the Lesson**—Literature provides many examples of people who "wasted" parts of their lives only to change their lives when given the opportunity. Students should find examples of wasted time from literature, and present these examples to the class.

Looking Back

Remember Melissa, Patty, and Father Charlie from chapter 1? The occasion of their ten-year reunion from high school gave them a chance to step back and look at their lives. At the all-night coffee house, they remembered what they had done and how their actions had affected their lives.

Patty told of her "wasted" years. "I partied full-time for two years after high school," she said. "I lost interest in just about everything. I didn't have a job and I dropped out of college. All I wanted to do was hang out with the gang and stay high. We did a lot of drinking. Once, I even got arrested for public drunkenness at the park where I work today! I don't know why I started, but I'm glad I could stop. My friends stayed with me, although I was a complete jerk."

Charlie looked shaken. This didn't sound like the Patty he'd known in high school. What must have happened in her life to change her so much?

Melissa finally interrupted the silence. "My biggest mistake was Jim. After dating him for three years, I thought we would get married. One day he simply walked up and told me he was leaving for law school the next day. It was his way of telling me that it was over."

The conversation had become quickly depressing. Patty tried to shrug it off with a toast of her coffee cup. "Here's to all our mess-ups," she laughed. Melissa couldn't help giggling.

The girls looked at Charlie. He had tears in his eyes.

Charlie, Melissa, and Patty talked of how they had survived life's ups and downs.

Journal Assignment

Have students answer "Looking Back" questions as journal work.

In Focus
Discerning Life Choices

Mother Teresa described her vocation as belonging to Christ. She wrote:

"Our vocation is to belong to Jesus with the conviction that nothing can separate us from the love of Christ.

"Jesus has offered his lifelong, faithful, personal friendship in tenderness and love to each one of us. He has espoused us to Himself.

"So now by our presence we put that love, that undivided love for Christ in chastity into action. Our love in action is this service to the poorest of the poor.

"Jesus went about doing good. And we are trying to imitate Him now because I believe that God loves the world through us. Just as He sent Jesus to be His love, His presence in the world, so today He is sending us."

Building Blocks

"Did you ever imagine that I would be a priest?" he said softly. Both girls shook their heads slowly, looking for some clue to his tears.

"My father became ill during the summer after high school graduation. If you remember, he was a lawyer. He had just expanded his practice when they discovered the Leukemia. It was a horrible time.

It is the challenge faced by all priests and religious to put Mother Teresa's words into practice.

"My mother and father went out to lunch. It was a Wednesday and very hot. That's when he told her. Dad wanted to tell us himself, but when mom got home from that lunch she broke down. We tried to guess what was wrong and then mom told us how sick dad really was."

Melissa knew that what Charlie was telling them was the most important story of his life. Patty asked, "Did you decide to become a priest after your father died?"

Charlie let out a little smile. "I had thought a lot about being a priest, but hadn't done anything about it, except maybe dressing up in an old bathrobe and playing Mass as a boy." Charlie laughed, "I used candy wafers for hosts."

"My father's death had a lot to do with my final decision. The night before he died, he joked to make us all laugh. His faith inspired me. His strength gave me the courage to pursue my dream."

Melissa and Patty each took one of Charlie's hands and squeezed tightly. "One thing you can say about us," Patty broke in, "is that we haven't let life's ups and downs defeat us. But God sure works in strange ways."

Journal Assignment

"Write about a time when you discovered God's presence in a particularly difficult experience."

Building Blocks

Teaching Approaches

- Read or have the students read the section.
- Ask the students to share examples of people they know who have not let life's ups and downs defeat them.
- **Reteach**—Review how events outside of ourselves can affect what we do or who we become.
- **Extend the Lesson**—Have each student explain in writing the one event that has shaped his or her life the most to this point. Students are to discuss why this event has shaped them as it has and why they responded as they did, instead of responding in a different way. Students may share these events with the class if they wish to do so.

In Focus

Teaching Approaches

- Read the feature.
- Ask: "In what ways do Patty's, Melissa's, and Charlie's lives belong to Christ?"
- Ask the students to compare Mother Teresa's words with those of Saint Teresa of Avila: "Christ has no body on earth but yours, no hands but yours, no feet but yours . . . Yours are the feet with which He goes about doing good, and yours are the hands with which He is to bless us now."

Give Us Today

- Have the students read the section with partners or in small groups.
- Have them suggest practical things that Patty and Melissa did in order to make positive changes in their lives.
- **Reteach**—Examine the lives of Patty, Melissa, and Charlie. How could they have made different decisions that would have changed their lives?
- **Extend the Lesson**—In small groups, have the students develop, practice, and act out skits portraying a key event from either Patty, Melissa, or Charlie's life in the years between high school and their ten year reunion. The text material should provide a starting point for the role plays. Allow time for each group to share their role play in front of the entire class.

Give Us Today

In the Lord's Prayer, we ask for God's will to be done on "earth as it is in heaven." By the decisions that we make, we bring God's kingdom into our daily lives.

If you look back at your life, you can probably find decisions that you regret making. From time to time everyone makes poor choices. The wiser person, however, learns from his or her mistakes and makes a better decision at the next opportunity. Everything that you've studied in this course prepares you to make wise decisions.

Being Christian requires us to put our lives at risk for the sake of the kingdom. The cost of difficult decisions—overcoming peer pressure, refusing alcohol or drugs, abstaining from genital sexual activity before marriage, or choosing a religious vocation—might seem quite high. Going along with the crowd or giving in to desires can be much easier than being faithful to one's beliefs.

Strangely enough, life decisions don't get easier as you get older. Life becomes more complex with each passing year and the decisions become more complex as well. The rewards of learning from the past are the fact that, with practice, the decisions can become better.

Melissa remembered the heartbreak she experienced as Patty struggled with alcohol abuse. "Patty, you're a wonderful person, but you are so much easier to get along with since you've stopped drinking. I admire you so much for the changes you've made in your life," Melissa said.

Charlie asked Melissa, "Do you think you would have been happy married to Jim?"

"Well, that's a difficult question to answer. From where I am today, probably not," Melissa answered. "But at the time, I thought I would be very happy. Jim was fun to be with and he made me feel special. We had big fights, however, because he didn't want me to work. He would take

The cost of resisting peer pressure can be quite high. What strength do you need to stand up for what you believe?

Resources

Resource 14G in the Teacher's Resource Book provides a list of skills to help teenagers deal with peer and societal pressures.

care of me, he said. I cared for him a great deal, but decided that I needed the space to live my own life. I was so excited when I opened the seamstress shop. I think our relationship had died by that time, anyway. Two months after I opened the shop, he told me about law school.

"I often think what my life would be like if I had married him. I'm happy with my choice now, but I wonder what I'll think in a few years," she admitted. "Before I get too old, I do want to marry and have children, but not just yet!"

"Then, I guess things worked out," Charlie said.

"For you, too?" Patty wondered.

"Yes, for me, too," said Charlie.

Talk It Over

1. How were the lives of Patty, Melissa, and Charlie changed by events outside of their control? How did they handle these changes?
2. How might living as a Christian force a person to make some painful decisions?

Talk It Over

Both questions can be discussed in the large group. For Question 2, have the students cite specific examples.

Chapter Summary

- This section lists the main points of summary of Chapter 14. To use as a review, you might have the students list examples from the text to illustrate each point, rewrite each point in their own words, or find creative ways to teach each point.
- Have the students share their review techniques with a partner.

Although caring people can help you make wise vocational and career decisions, the final choice is yours alone. How will you choose?

Chapter Summary

- Planning one's future is an act of Christian hope.
- While it's possible to work toward a possible future, only God knows what the future actually holds in store.
- Christian disciples are open to God's will.
- Truth is an experience of God.
- Career requirements can be broken down into small, more easily attainable steps.

Journal Assignment

Have the students answer "Talk It Over" question 2 in their journals: "How might living as a Christian force a person to make some painful decisions?"

Chapter 14 Review

What Have You Learned?

Listed below are suggested answers. For many of the questions, the answers will vary.

1. Current decisions can affect the future in many ways. For example, courses taken in high school can prepare a person either for a career in medicine, welding, or banking.

2. These are five steps in the planning process: (1) imagine a number of different scenarios for your life ten years from now; (2) identify the futures that you would most like to have happen; (3) pray for guidance, then choose the future you most desire; (4) recognize what must happen over the next few years in order for you to accomplish this goal; (5) determine what you can do now to prepare for the future.

3. Realism is necessary because it helps us eliminate the futures we don't like or can't see ourselves accomplishing.

4. Divine Providence means that God takes an active interest in our lives and puts opportunities in our paths. Divine Providence can affect one's life by shaping events in new and previously unconsidered ways.

5. The first steps of the process are small, and therefore not irrevocable.

6. Everyone is called to discipleship; choosing a vocation is a personal, individual decision.

7. Only by looking at all of life as valuable, can we recognize the "truth" of God's goodness.

8. Discipleship is the "calling" for all Christians regardless of their personal vocations. If we are Christians, discipleship has to be part of our future.

9. Jesus' statement is appropriate because it recognizes that we must first reconcile ourselves with the past which made us before we can move forward toward the future which we will construct with God's help.

10. Hope is a necessary part of future plans because it provides a reason for courage and an invitation to always move toward that which affirms life.

REVIEW

What Have You Learned?

1. How can your current decisions affect your future?
2. Identify the five steps in the Future's Invention process.
3. Why is realism a necessary part of the planning process?
4. What is meant by "Divine Providence"? How does Divine Providence affect one's life?
5. Why are a person's first steps toward a future usually not irrevocable?
6. How is openness to discipleship different than choosing a religious vocation?
7. Why does the Church teach that life is to be valued at all stages in a continuum of care?
8. Why is a future that leaves little room for discipleship not acceptable for a Christian?
9. How is Jesus' statement, "No one pours new wine into old wineskins," appropriate to people planning their futures?
10. How is hope a necessary part of future plans?

Application

1. Make a "dream journal" for one week. Each night, write a detailed account of a vocation or career dream that you have. At the end of the week, consider each of your dreams using the five-step Future Invention's process. Which dreams seem most realistic for you now?
2. Start a collection of inspirational sayings. How can you use these sayings for personal motivation?
3. Develop a career ladder. Break your steps into short range (the next six months), medium range (one to two years), and long range (the next ten years). What will it take you to reach your goals?
4. Write a letter to a state or federal government official expressing your belief about the sacredness of life.
5. Design a "seamless garment." Include as many of the interrelated life issues on the garment as you can.

Background

Application, Project 5 has students designing a "seamless garment." This garment will contain the issues of abortion, health care, war and peace, welfare, capital punishment, care for the elderly, and any other issues that have implication for human life.

REVIEW

Chapter Vocabulary

- qué será, será
- career ladder
- Divine Providence
- truth
- seamless garment
- re-visioning

'Tis better to have loved and lost
Than never to have loved at all.

Lord Alfred Tennyson.

Putting Vocabulary to Use

Match the terms in Column A with the correct definitions below in Column B.

Column A:

1. Que sera sera
2. Truth
3. Seamless garment
4. Divine Providence
5. Career Ladder
6. Canticle of Sun

Column B:

A. continuum of care
B. process of breaking down career requirements into small steps.
C. "prayer for life"
D. Jesus' reference to God
E. can be both a positive and negative philosophy concerning planning for one's future
F. God's active interest in our lives.

Application

Read the directions and descriptions of each Project to the students. Allow the students to choose their own project. Suggest the following steps: (1) formulate a plan; (2) complete the tasks; (3) share the initial project with a partner for comments; (4) revise and finalize the project.

Putting Vocabulary to Use

1. E
2. D
3. A
4. F
5. B
6. C

Final Thought

Background

Have the students restate the quotation in their own words.

Unit 4 Review

Aim

To reinforce and evaluate the students' understanding of the information covered in Unit 4.

Looking Back

These questions review the main points covered in this unit. To use as a review, have the students individually write the answers to some or all of the questions, use the questions as a study guide for the unit material, or discuss and list points from the text.

Listed below are suggested answers. For many questions, the answers will vary.

1. The easiest area of human development to understand is the physical.

2. New career and vocational responsibilities limit the time people have available for establishing new friendships and maintaining old ones.

3. Erik Erickson says that middle-aged people need to know that they have accomplished something of value with their lives.

4. Built-in transitions include those associated with career changes, the birth of a child, the adolescent years of a child, the middle years of marriage, a child leaving home, and the later years of marriage including retirement.

5. Answers will vary.

6. Answers will vary.

7. Priests and religious experience the transitions and regrets associated with not having families, the pressures of career advancement and job satisfaction, or an unexpected change in ministry.

8. The Gospel stories about resurrection suggest that when we leave things, people, and places behind, we prepare for new life as promised by Jesus' resurrection.

9. A realistic plan for the future helps you to eliminate futures that you don't like or can't see yourself accomplishing.

10. By Divine Providence, we mean that God takes an active interest in each of our lives and puts appropriate opportunities in our paths.

11. Present decisions can be very important. For example, classes taken in high school can shape future career choices.

For a Lifetime

Always Evolving

1. Which is the easiest area of human development to understand—physical, social, emotional, or spiritual?
2. How can responsibilities to career and vocation hinder establishing new friendships and maintaining old ones?
3. What does Erickson say that middle-age people experience concerning their careers?
4. What are some of the built-in transitional stages of married life?
5. How would you define job satisfaction?
6. Describe a "little death" and "little resurrection" experience.
7. What are some of the transitions experienced by priest and religious?
8. What clues do the Gospel resurrection stories offer about life after death?
9. Why is it necessary to establish a realistic plan for your own future?
10. How is Divine Providence related to a person's dreams and expectations?
11. How are the present decisions you make important to your overall life plan?
12. How can hope play a vital part in your life journey?
13. Why must all life issues be looked at together, as if a part of a seamless garment?

Making It Real

Work on one or more of these projects on your own, with a small group, or with the entire class:

1. Interview an adult and ask them to describe a time when his or her faith was tested by something that happened at work. What did the person finally decide to do? What were the results of the decision? Write up the results of the interview. Then draw conclusions on job-related dilemmas based on these observations.
2. Plan a sober graduation party for the senior class. Make inquiries about potential places, food, entertainment, prizes, chaperons, and transportation. Present your final proposal to the school's student government or activity committee as your group's gift to your school's senior class.
3. Develop a poster to illustrate the Parable of the Sower *(Matthew 13:1-9)*. Capture the parable's message through some type of art.
4. Develop a career time-line. What do you hope to accomplish career wise between the ages of 20 to 30, 30 to 40, 40 to 50, 50 to 60, and 60 to 70 years?

12. Hope provides a reason for courage and an invitation to always move toward that which affirms life.

13. All life issues, from beginning to end, must be viewed together as if life were a seamless garment, because the death of an unborn baby is as tragic as the execution of a person on death row. Catholic teaching supports all life from womb to tomb.

A Time of Prayer

Arrange a life-chain or walk-a-thon in support of those who are threatened by destruction. Formulate a plan for the prayer event with your classmates. If possible, arrange for members of your school, parish, and community to sponsor your efforts. For example, a sponsor might contribute one dollar for every mile you walk. All the money raised could be contributed to a worthy life-supporting organization. Develop a title for the event. Include the traditional litany of the saints as part of the event. Here is an adapted version of the prayer:

Lord, have mercy.	Lord, have mercy.
Christ, have mercy.	Christ, have mercy.
Lord, have mercy.	Lord, have mercy.
Holy Mary, Mother of God,	pray for us.
Saint Michael,	pray for us.
Saint Joseph,	pray for us.
Saint Peter and Saint Paul,	pray for us.
Saint Mary Magdalene,	pray for us.
Saint Stephen,	pray for us.
Saint Ignatius of Antioch,	pray for us.
Saint Augustine,	pray for us.
Saint Benedict,	pray for us.
Saint Francis and Saint Dominic,	pray for us.
Saint Francis Xavier,	pray for us.
Saint John Vianney,	pray for us.
Saint Teresa of Avila,	pray for us.
All holy men and women,	pray for us.
Lord, be merciful.	Lord, save your people.
By your death and rising to new life,	Lord, save your people.
Jesus, son of the living God,	Lord, hear our prayer.
Christ, hear us,	Christ, hear us.
Lord Jesus, hear our prayer,	Lord Jesus, hear our prayer.

297

Making It Real

Teaching Approaches

- Read the descriptions and directions for each project to the students. Allow the students to choose one of the projects (other than Project 2), to work on individually, with a partner, or in a small group.
- **Reteach**—Have students present their projects to the class and explain how the projects reflect what has been studied.
- **Extend the Lesson**—Assign Project 2 as a class project.

A Time of Prayer

Teaching Approaches

- Have students organize a group activity that incorporates some form of common shared prayer, such as the litany of the saints.
- **Reteach**—Have the students work with a local parish peace and justice committee to arrange a prayer demonstration for life.
- **Extend the Lesson**—Use the litany of the saints as a regular opening or closing prayer to class sessions.

Resources

Resource U4A from the Teacher's Resource Book provides a schedule for recording sponsors' donations for the prayer-for-life event.

Resource U4B from the Teacher's Resource Book provides suggestions for planning a class Mass or other liturgical service suitable for a use during a retreat or mini-workshop.

Glossary

abbess: a superior of a religious order of women. (8)

abbot: a superior of a religious order of men. (8)

abortifacient: drugs, such as progesterone and estrogen, and physical objects (such as the IUD) that cause abortions. (12)

abortion: the termination of pregnancy before term. (6, 12, 14)

abstinence: refraining from sexual intercourse. (6, 12)

acquaintance: a person with whom you have some social contact, but with whom you are not particularly close. (4)

adulthood: a stage in growth associated with a person's maturity and behavior. (13, 14)

affirmation: a positive statement that can be used to build up a person's confidence. (1, 2, 3, 4, 9, 12)

agape: a Greek work for the most intimate kind of love. (6)

AIDS: acquired immunodeficiency syndrome. (6)

altruism: living for the sake of others. (6)

annulment: a declaration of nullity concerning a marriage. (11)

anorexia nervosa: a behavior that leads to severe weight loss through intentional starvation. (13)

artificial contraception: various chemical and physical devices designed to prevent the conception or the implantation of the fertilized egg in the lining of the uterus. (12)

autonomy: independence; being able to function without the control of others. (10, 12)

Baptism: an initiation sacrament. (1, 8)

Beatitudes: eight "blessings" proclaimed by Jesus at the Sermon on the Mount. (7)

betrothal: in former times, a fee paid by a man to the father of the bride. (10)

bigamy: a person who is still legally married and enters into another marriage. (10)

birth control pill: an artificial means of preventing pregnancy. (12)

bisexual: a person who feels sexual attraction to members of both sexes. (6)

bishop: along with the pope, bishops are granted fullness of authority from the Apostles. (8, 9)

blended family: families that are created when two single or divorced parents marry and bring their children together. (1)

blessing: a gift of divine favor from God or a dedication of something or someone to God. (12)

body language: a non-verbal means of communication. (4)

budget: a plan for spending and saving money. (8, 13, 14)

candidacy: a period when an aspirant to religious life lives with the community prior to vows. (9)

career: a job that expresses a person's talents and interest. (1, 2, 7, 12, 13, 14)

career ladder: the requirements of a career broken down into small steps. (14)

celibacy: a vow not to marry and to refrain from sexual intercourse. (6, 9)

chastity: appropriate sexual behaviour according to one's state in life. (6, 8, 9, 10, 12)

chlamydia: a STD that attacks the male and female reproductive organs. (6)

Christian values: values recognized from the life and teachings of Jesus Christ. (3)

Church tradition: a resource for uncovering God's presence in our lives. (7)

cohabitation: living together before marriage. (6)

commitment: a public pledge of trust or promise to another person. (1, 4, 5, 6, 8, 10, 11, 12, 13)

communication: the interaction between two or more people. (3, 4, 6, 10, 12)

companionship: fellowship; friendship. (11)

compatibility: a determination of how well two people agree on important issues. (10)

conception: the beginning of life. (6, 12)

condoms: a protective sheath for the penis. (6, 12)

Confirmation: a sacrament of initiation and commitment. (7)

conflict: a dynamic that may develop in relationships when one or both parties fails to show respect for the other. (2, 4)

conflict management: learned skills to help manage conflicts effectively and to reduce tension. (4, 11, 12)

conjugal chastity: sexual expression between a man and woman in marriage. (12)

consanguinity: the level of relationship between blood relatives. (10)

conscience: a person's sense of right and wrong, and the desire to make good choices. (3)

consecrated chastity: a promise a person makes to remain celibate for life. (8)

contemplative: traditionally, a person who lives a cloistered existence and practices prayer, self-mortification, and work. (9)

contraceptive: a device or agent used to prevent conception. (6)

contract marriage: a bound, formal agreement between a husband and wife, oftentimes arranged by families. (10)

convent: a place where women come together to live out the Gospel counsels. (8, 9)

conversion: a change from one way of life to another. (7)

courtship: a period of exclusive dating that leads to engagement. (6, 10, 12)

covenant: in a religious sense, an agreement between God and humanity. (11)

diaconate: a level of the sacrament of Holy Orders with an emphasis on Christian service. (8, 9)

diaphragm: a device inserted by a woman into her vagina to prevent sperm from reaching the ovum. (12)

dignity: the worth entitled each person. (4, 12)

diocesan priest: a priest who serves in a diocese and whose allegiance is to the local bishop. (9)

diocese: a district under a bishop's jurisdiction. (9)

discernment: the ability to distinguish between wants and needs, desires and wishes, and reality and dreams. (3, 7, 10, 14)

discipleship: a term meaning "to follow;" The disciple's goal is to learn and to follow the master. (7, 8, 9, 14)

dispensation: special permission of the bishop to remove the impediments of marriage. (10)

Divine Office: the public prayer of the Church; also called the Liturgy of the Hours. (9)

Divine Providence: God's active interest in our lives. (11, 12, 14)

divorce: a legal dissolution of a marriage. (1, 10, 11, 13, 14)

domestic Church: the Church community as lived out by individual families. (12)

dowry: a payment made by the family of the bride to the husband at the time of marriage. (10)

emotional maturity: an important factor in determining readiness for marriage. (10)

empathy: being aware and sensitive to the needs of others. (4)

Engaged Encounter Weekend: a marriage preparation retreat experience. (11)

engagement: promise of marriage. (11, 12)

episcopacy: from the Greek work, "episkopos," meaning bishop. (9)

estrogen: a chemical in a woman's body which inhibits ovulation. (12)

Eucharist: a sacrament of belonging. (2)

examination of conscience: reviewing thoughts and actions as a way to maintain a functioning and informed conscience. (3)

exclusive dating: a dating relationship when a man and woman date only each other. (5)

extended family: grown up children and other relatives living with a nuclear family in the same home. (1)

faith: an expression of hope in that which is unseen. (7, 8, 14)

fallopian tubes: a pair of tubes through which a mature egg may travel to the uterus. (6)

family values: the first source of values; children learn values from the way their families live. (3)

fertility cycle: a time from the beginning of one menstrual cycle to the next. (6)

fertilization: the act of impregnation. (6)

fetus: an unborn child. (12)

fidelity: promised faithfulness of a husband and wife to each other. (11)

filial love: the love suitable, or due, a son or daughter. (6)

finances: issues that deal with money and how to spend it are near the top of the list of those that are important in a marriage. (5, 10)

forgiveness: a gift offered by God and community in the sacrament of Reconciliation. (2, 4, 7)

Franciscans: a religious order founded by Saint Francis of Assisi. (9)

freedom: a gift that works in union with God's grace and with our own ability to choose. (3, 8, 9, 10, 14)

friendship: a relationship between people who like each other and share common interests. (4, 5, 7, 9, 10, 12, 13, 14)

gender: female or male behavior or attitudes. (6)

goals: an established intention one hopes to reach. (10, 14)

going steady: a term associated with exclusive dating. (5)

gonorrhea: an STD that is not always detectable and may have serious consequences if left untreated. (6)

Gospel counsels: a code of behavior referring to the vows of poverty, chastity, and obedience. (8)

gossip: a bad habit of talking about another person. (4)

grace-filled: touched by God. (7)

Great Commandment: love of God and neighbor have equal importance. (3)

group dating: a group of boys and girls who enjoy participating in social activities together. (5)

guilt: a feeling that warns you when you are doing wrong. (3)

heredity: the sum of qualities and genetic potentialities derived from one's ancestors. (1)

herpes simple x II: a virus that causes blister-like sores in the gential area. (6)

heterosexual: a person who feels sexual attraction to a person of the opposite sex. (6)

high risk marriage: marriages that run a high risk of divorce either because of age, pregnancy, or previous marriage failure. (11)

holiness: filled with the presence of God. (1, 9)

holistic: the Church's view on sex in marriage; sex is placed in the total context of the relationship. (12)

Holy Orders: a sacrament consecrating the ministries of bishop, priest, and deacon. (8, 9)

homosexual: a person who feels sexual attraction to someone of his or her own sex. (6)

honesty: an important basic value of fairness and straightforwardness. (3, 4, 5, 10, 11, 14)

hope: a virtue that provides a reason for courage and an invitation to always move toward that which affirms life. (14)

hormones: chemicals produced by the body that affect a person's emotional and social growth. (5)

HIV: Human immunodeficiency virus; the virus that causes AIDS. (6, 11)

Humanae Vitae: "Of Human Life;" a document by Pope Paul VI that focussed on marriage and and issues related to marriage. (12)

I-messages: speaking about what you know and feel. (4)

imagining: a process of dreaming great possibilities for your future. (14)

impediment: an external fact or circumstance that prevents a marriage, sacramental or legal, from taking place. (11)

infatuation: a feeling usually caused by strong physical or sexual attraction and based on impressions rather than the full turth. (6)

information interviews: a meeting with employers to determine job and career requirements. (7)

in-laws: the family members of a spouse. (11)

"in love": a feeling involving sexual attractions. (5, 10)

interest: the cost of borrowing money. (13)

internal messages: refers to communication between our unconscious and conscious minds. (2)

IUD: inter uterine device; prevents implantation of fertilized egg. (12)

intimacy: the close bond represented in a relationship between people. (5, 6, 10, 11)

job: a way to earn a living.(7, 13)

job satisfaction: related to how well we follow God's plan for our lives. (7, 13)

laborare est orare: "to work is to pray." (9)

laity: all the baptized; the "people of God." (8, 9)

life plan: a personal plan for life intimately tied to vocation. (1)

listening skills: important skills that help to improve communication. (4)

"little deaths": an experience of ending one phase of life for another. (13)

love: the greatest of all virtues, lasting into eternity. (2, 3, 5, 6, 10, 11, 12)

Magisterium: the teaching office of the Church. (12)

Manichaeism: a form of gnosticism, the belief that one must have special knowledge to be saved. (11)

marriage: a vocation based on the joint decision of a man and woman to form an intimate partnership. (1, 4, 5, 6, 8, 10, 11, 12, 14)

marriage banns: the public proclamation of an intended marriage. (11)

marriage covenant: the lasting, committed relationship between husband and wife, as between God and the Hebrew People, Jesus and the Church. (11)

martyr: a Greek word for witness. (8)

masturbation: stimulating one's own sexual organs to orgasm. (6)

mature love: a quality that develops from romantic attraction and allows a relationship to grow. (10)

maturity: a level of responsibility. (10, 13)

mendicants: religious orders who live the life of beggars. (9)

menstruation: the period each month when a woman discharges menses. (6, 12)

ministry: loving service to others, (7, 9)

mixed dating: dating that occurs between members of different races, religions, or cultures. (5)

modesty: a practice of discipline that helps a person manage his or her sexual feelings. (6)

monastery: a place where men come together to live out the Gospel counsels. (8, 9)

narcissism: an exaggerated love of oneself. (2, 6)

NFP: Natural Family Planning; the Church-approved method for planning the birth of children in a marriage. (6, 11, 12)

novitiate: a period of time marking a person's official entry into the religious community. (9)

nuclear family: a family with a mother, father, and children living under the same roof. (1)

obedience: a vow taken by a religious obliging him or her to listen to the will of God as expressed by a superior. (8, 9, 13)

offering: at Mass, literally Jesus Christ, the Lamb of God "who takes away the sins of the world." (9)

opinion: a statement of thought or feeling that may or may not have any basis in fact. (3)

opportunistic infection: a diseases that attacks the body of a person who is suffering from AIDS. (6)

ovulation: the process by which a mature ovum is released. (12)

ovulation method: a natural form of birth control based on a woman's menstrual cycle. (12)

parent: a mother or father charged with the responsibility of raising a child. (10)

pastoral ministry: the ministry of shepherding and caring for members of the Christian community. (9)

permanent deacons: often married men, they are ordained to serve the church. They remain deacons and do not go on for priesthood. (9, 10).

phile: a Greek word meaning love for a friend. (6)

polygamy: a marriage between a husband and two or more wives. (10)

pornography: sexually implicit material that encourages people to use others for their sexual pleasure. (6)

poverty: a vow religious take renouncing their right to own property. (8, 9)

prayer: a way of communicating—speaking and listening—to God. (3, 4, 7, 9, 12, 13, 14)

Pre Cana Conference: a marriage preparation program. (11)

pregnancy: the condition when a woman has an unborn child contained within her body. (1, 6, 12)

presbyterate: priests who are ordained to proclaim the Gospel. (9)

priesthood: a religious vocation of pastoral and sacramental leadership conferred in the sacrament of Holy Orders. (4, 8, 9, 13)

principal: the amount of money that is borrowed. (13)

procreation: a married couple's participation with God in the creation of new life through sexual intercourse and conception. (6, 11, 12)

progesterone: a chemical in the birth control pill which makes the uterus hostile to potential implantation. (12)

puberty: a time when adolescents change physically, emotionally, and mentally, and begin to relate to the opposite sex in a new way. (5, 6, 13)

Que sera sera: Spanish for, "whatever will be will be." (14)

rape: sexual intimacy through force or a threat of force. (5)

rate: the percentage changed by the lender to calculate interest. (13)

religious community: a supportive group of men and women who function as a family for priests, nuns, or brothers. (8, 9, 13)

religious life: a vocation associated with priests, brothers, and sisters who take vows of poverty, chastity, and obedience. (1, 4, 7, 8, 9, 14)

religious priest: a priest who is also a member of a religious community. (9)

rent: the monthly fee for living in an apartment. (14)

respect: valuing people. (1, 2, 4, 6, 9, 10)

responsibility: the quality, fact, or instance of being responsible. (5, 8, 10, 12, 13, 14)

responsible parenting: the married couple is always most qualified to make decisions regarding child-bearing and child-rearing. (12)

résumé: a short account of one's career and qualifications. (1)

RCIA: Rite of Christian Initiation of Adults; the adult catechumenate for entrance into the Catholic Church. (7)

romantic love: a love that grows from infatuation to the more intimate knowledge and experience one has of another person. (1, 6)

sacrament: a visible sign of God's presence. (11)

sacramental ministry: a primary ministry of the ordained as leaders of worship and sacrament. (8, 9)

saint: someone whose very life exemplifies the goodness of God on earth and in heaven. (9)

seamless garment: a continuum of care meaning that life should be respected at all stages. (14)

self-concept: the sum total of how a person views himself or herself. (2, 14)

self-esteem: the value one places on himself or herself. (2, 4, 5, 10)

self-image: the image one has of himself or herself; it is always evolving throughout life. (2)

self-love: acceptance of oneself as a creation of a loving God. (6)

self-worth: the overall value a person sees in himself or herself. (2)

service: the shared ministry of all the baptized to aid those in need. (7, 13)

sex: one's gender; often used to mean sexual intercourse, the physical expression of love that is reserved for married people as a way to show their love and to help God bring a new life into the world. (6)

sexual abuse: a crime that occurs when someone uses another for selfish sexual gratification. (6)

sexuality: the quality of having been created male or female. (6, 11, 12)

STDs: sexually transmitted diseases. (6)

sexual sterotypes: unrealistic ways of viewing males or females. (12)

shyness: a state of being self-conscious with other people; timid. (5, 10)

sin: a choice that separates one from God. (3, 11, 13)

single life: a vocation that is people-oriented and allows free response to God. (1, 8, 9, 12)

single parent family: families where children live with and are raised by one parent. (1)

skills: a developed aptitude or ability. (3, 14)

societal values: values learned from television, music, a movie, a book, or other people in society. (3)

spiritual changes: stages of development of religious faith. (13)

sterilization: a permanent form of birth control where one's reproductive organs are physically altered. (12)

stewardship: a responsibility to the life given you by God. (8)

sympto-thermic method: a natural form of birth control based on a woman's temperature. (12)

syphilis: one of the most dangerous STDs; left untreated it can destroy the vital organs. (6)

talents: a special gift or ability given to a person by God. (1, 2, 6, 7, 13 14)

transitional deacons: men who serve as deacons for a short time before being ordained to the priesthood. (8, 9)

trust: a placement of confidence. (4, 5, 10, 11, 12, 13)

truth: a reference to God and what is real. (3, 13, 14)

tubal ligation: a permanent form of birth control; female sterilization. (12)

unitive: the expression of love by which a married couple is united intimately and faithfully. (10, 12)

values: from the Latin word "valere;" to be worth, be strong. (3, 4, 6, 10, 13, 14)

vasectomy: a permanent form of birth control: male sterilization. (12)

violence: physical ridicule, and verbal abuse. (2, 6)

vocation: literally means "calling;" the call from God to live out our Christian commitment. (1, 2, 7, 8, 9, 11, 13, 14)

vows: a deliberate, voluntary promise made to God. (8, 9, 11, 13)

wedding: a ceremony celebrating the marriage of a man and a woman. (11, 12)

work: participation in God's creation. (1, 7, 9, 13)

Index

Photo Credits